BUSINESS AND GENERAL REFERENCE BOOK SERIES FROM IDG

# Opera For Dummies™

## Emergency Vocab Cheat Sheet

You're at the opera house. You open the program book, or you're listening to the opera snobs talk — foreign words are flying like bullets. Quick, what do they all mean?

**aria:** An emotion-expressing song in an opera; the big number.

**bel canto:** A style of sweet singing, taught to singers even today, that emphasizes breath control, a beautiful tone, and great flexibility in dynamics (going from loud to soft, for example).

**cadenza:** A moment near the end of an aria for the singer alone, with lots of fast, high, difficult notes, designed for showing off.

**coloratura:** A singer (usually soprano) with an extremely agile, light, pure-sounding voice, capable of easily singing fast, high notes.

**dynamics:** The loudness or softness of a musical composition, or the markings in the sheet music that indicate volume.

**Leitmotif** ("LIGHT-mo-teef"): A little melody that plays every time a certain character or object appears; invented by Richard Wagner.

**libretto:** The script of an opera.

**opera buffa:** Funny opera, especially from the 18th century.

**opera seria:** Formal, serious opera, especially from the 18th century.

**prima donna:** The singer who plays the heroine, the main female character in an opera; or anyone who believes that the world revolves around her.

**recitative** ("ress-it-uh-TEEV"): Speech-singing, in which the singer semi-chants the words, imitating the free rhythms of speech.

**Singspiel** ("SING-shpeel"): A German opera with spoken dialogue (instead of recitative) between arias.

**trouser role:** A man's part played by a woman.

**verismo:** A realistic, "documentary" style of opera that depicts the seamy underbelly of life.

## Timeline of the Great Operas

|  |  |
|---|---|
| 1780 | The Abduction from the Seraglio |
| | The Marriage of Figaro |
| | Don Giovanni |
| 1790 | Così fan tutte |
| | The Magic Flute |
| 1800 | |
| | Fidelio |
| 1810 | |
| | The Barber of Seville |
| | La Cenerentola |
| 1820 | |
| | Der Freischütz |
| 1830 | |
| | The Elixir of Love |
| | Lucia di Lammermoor |
| 1840 | |
| | Nabucco |
| | The Flying Dutchman, Tannhäuser |
| 1850 | |
| | Lohengrin, Rigoletto, La Traviata |
| | Il Trovatore |
| | Faust, A Masked Ball |
| 1860 | La Forza del Destino |
| | Tristan and Isolde |
| | Don Carlo, Die Meistersinger von Nürnberg |
| 1870 | Das Rheingold, Die Walküre |
| | Aïda, Boris Godunov, Die Fledermaus, Carmen |
| | Siegfried, Götterdämmerung |
| 1880 | Tales of Hoffmann |
| | Parsifal |
| | Otello, Romeo and Juliet |
| 1890 | Cavalleria Rusticana |
| | I Pagliacci, Werther, Falstaff |
| | La Bohème |
| 1900 | Tosca |
| | Madame Butterfly |
| | Salome |
| 1910 | Elektra |
| | The Girl of the Golden West |
| | Der Rosenkavalier, Ariadne auf Naxos |
| | Bluebeard's Castle, Gianni Schicchi |
| 1920 | Turandot |
| 1930 | |
| | Arabella |
| | Porgy and Bess |
| 1940 | |
| 1945 | Peter Grimes |
| 1950 | Dialogues of the Carmelites |

Copyright © 1997 IDG Books Worldwide, Inc. All rights reserved.

Cheat Sheet $2.95 value. Item 5010-1.

For more information about IDG Books, call 1-800-762-2974.

IDG BOOKS WORLDWIDE™

**...For Dummies: Bestselling Book Series for Beginners**

BUSINESS AND
GENERAL
REFERENCE
BOOK SERIES
FROM IDG

# Opera For Dummies™

Cheat Sheet

## Opera Voices and Where to Find Them

In opera, you can subdivide the human voice into dozens of finely differentiated categories, but here are the Big Six:

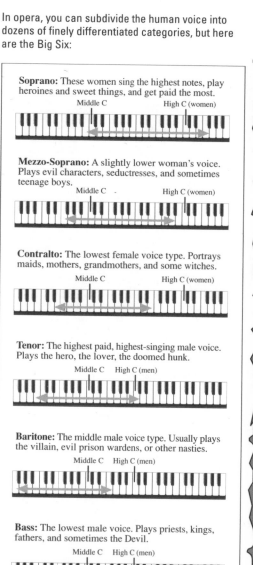

**Soprano:** These women sing the highest notes, play heroines and sweet things, and get paid the most.

Middle C — High C (women)

**Mezzo-Soprano:** A slightly lower woman's voice. Plays evil characters, seductresses, and sometimes teenage boys.

Middle C — High C (women)

**Contralto:** The lowest female voice type. Portrays maids, mothers, grandmothers, and some witches.

Middle C — High C (women)

**Tenor:** The highest paid, highest-singing male voice. Plays the hero, the lover, the doomed hunk.

Middle C — High C (men)

**Baritone:** The middle male voice type. Usually plays the villain, evil prison wardens, or other nasties.

Middle C — High C (men)

**Bass:** The lowest male voice. Plays priests, kings, fathers, and sometimes the Devil.

Middle C — High C (men)

## The Operagoer's Checklist

Going to a live opera performance isn't like going to a movie. For one thing, you're paying ten times as much for a ticket. For another, you'll be experiencing some pretty strange sights and sounds. Follow this pre-flight checklist for best results.

❏ **Choose the right opera.** Operas — their music and their stories — are 100 percent as varied as today's movies. Some are delightful romantic romps, such as *The Marriage of Figaro* and *The Elixir of Love*. The majority are heart-rending love tragedies, like *La Bohème* and *Aïda*. A few are nearly X-rated shockers featuring adolescent mother-killers *(Elektra)* or teenage necrophiliacs *(Salome)*. Don't walk into something you're not ready for — especially if you're on a hot date.

❏ **Get to know the opera in advance.** The opera's probably in a foreign language, it may be set in an exotic time and place, and it may have a complicated plot. By renting the video or listening to the CD (while following the words) beforehand, you'll be familiar with the story going into the gate. At the very least, check out the synopsis in Chapter 12 or 13 of this book. Your operagoing experience will be 50 times better.

❏ **Eat.** Going to an opera isn't like going to *Fiddler on the Roof* — it's probably much longer, especially if Richard Wagner wrote the show. Eat something light before you go, and then have a full dinner afterward. (Unless it's Wagner. Then take food *to* the show, which you can scarf down during the intermissions.)

❏ **Arrive early.** The people-watching alone is worth the ticket price. How many opera snobs can you find?

❏ **Check out the orchestra pit.** The instrumental musicians — half the opera's payroll — will be hidden from view all night. Before the show starts is the time to witness all the action down there, including all the strange warm-ups that the orchestra players go through.

❏ **Hit the restroom before the curtain goes up.** Your next opportunity may be the intermission, which may be hours away. Moreover, the 2,000 audience members will be trying to get into a restroom designed to hold 6. Ladies: This especially means you. Unless you want to stand in a line that could stretch to the moon and back seven times, go *before* the show.

*...For Dummies: Bestselling Book Series for Beginners*

# Praise For Opera For Dummies

"Having been a dummy about opera in my early days as an orchestral musician, and having discovered through experience how enjoyable it is, I hope and trust that legions of the operatically challenged will find their way to melodramatic enlightenment with the aid of this book. I hope those who read will, more importantly, listen." —Harvey Wolf, Cellist, The Cleveland Orchestra

"*Opera For Dummies* de-frocks the mystique of opera by artfully relating to, and weaving in, pop culture — TOTALLY ACCESSIBLE as originally intended!" —Barry Bowlus, opera enthusiast

"Reading *Opera For Dummies* has added a wonderful new dimension to my enjoyment of opera. I believe this book will help create a whole new generation of opera buffs." —Lotte Zinner, Lifelong opera enthusiast, St. Louis, Missouri

# Praise For EMI/Angel

"*Classics For Dummies* CD's, which are devoted to different genres and composers, allow listeners to isolate single instrumental lines within the thickest Wagnerian orchestral texture." —David Patrick Stearns, *USA Today*

"I'm head-over-heels for EMI's series of *Classics For Dummies* . . . the 'interactive stuff' is great fun." —Lloyd Schwartz, NPR's *Fresh Air*

" . . . a good basic introduction to classical composers for adults or children." —*The Wall Street Journal*

"We must applaud EMI, the MENC, and other groups and individuals who are dedicated to bringing the joys of music to a frightened, confused public." —*Scripps Howard News Service*

# Praise For David Pogue

"As a teacher, Pogue is not only competent and articulate . . . but also an enthusiastic cheerleader." —*The New York Times*

"Pogue is a wonderful teacher . . . he can teach anybody." —Gay Talese, Bestselling author of *Honor Thy Father*

"Enjoyed the humor. Loved the format. Absolutely well written. David Pogue is a marvel." —Virginia Kochanek, Plant City, Florida

"Thanks to Pogue, I now spend many hours a week with my Mac, accomplishing things I thought I never could." —Mike Nichols, Hollywood director

"Your *Macworld Macintosh Secrets* book is fabulous. Best I've read! Insightful, humorous, educational without being boring. Who else would tell me how Macintosh got its misspelled name, or where the model names came from?" —Bob Bender, Public Relations Director, Ohio

# Praise For Scott Speck

"Scott Speck is a great communicator of classical music, both as a conductor and as an eloquent spokesman. He exudes his passion for music in every gesture and every word. Concert audiences and readers alike can't help getting caught up in the joy of his subject." —David Styers, American Symphony Orchestra League

"Scott Speck's popularity with his audiences is phenomenal! His performances are fresh and exciting, eliciting a consistently enthusiastic response from his listeners." —Joseph McAlister, Director of Education, Honolulu Symphony Orchestra

"On the podium, Scott Speck achieves an outstanding rapport with the orchestra. Before an audience, Scott is an articulate and persuasive speaker about the power of music. What better person to write an introduction to classical music?" —Charles Calmer, Artistic Administrator, Jacksonville Symphony, former Education Director, The Cleveland Orchestra

# Praise For Classical Music For Dummies

"This book is the perfect way to go from dummy to expert in classical music!" —André Watts, Pianist

"*Classical Music For Dummies* should be the first book for anyone ages 5–105. Anyone from layperson to first-year conservatory music student should crack open this wonderfully diverse and enriching look into the world of classical music. I wish this book had been part of my beginning curriculum." —Tony Kniffen, Principal Tubist, Indianapolis Symphony Orchestra

"*Classical Music For Dummies* engages the reader with its flawless pacing, humor, and wit. It is a 'classic' in its own right." —Barry Bowlus, Classical music enthusiast

 ™

**BUSINESS AND GENERAL REFERENCE BOOK SERIES FROM IDG**

# References for the Rest of Us!™

Do you find that traditional reference books are overloaded with technical details and advice you'll never use? Do you postpone important life decisions because you just don't want to deal with them? Then our *...For Dummies*™ business and general reference book series is for you.

*...For Dummies* business and general reference books are written for those frustrated and hard-working souls who know they aren't dumb, but find that the myriad of personal and business issues and the accompanying horror stories make them feel helpless. *...For Dummies* books use a lighthearted approach, a down-to-earth style, and even cartoons and humorous icons to diffuse fears and build confidence. Lighthearted but not lightweight, these books are perfect survival guides to solve your everyday personal and business problems.

> **"More than a publishing phenomenon, 'Dummies' is a sign of the times."**
> — *The New York Times*

> **"...you won't go wrong buying them."**
> — *Walter Mossberg, Wall Street Journal, on IDG's ...For Dummies™ books*

> **"A world of detailed and authoritative information is packed into them..."**
> — *U.S. News and World Report*

Already, millions of satisfied readers agree. They have made *...For Dummies* the #1 introductory level computer book series and a best-selling business book series. They have written asking for more. So, if you're looking for the best and easiest way to learn about business and other general reference topics, look to *...For Dummies* to give you a helping hand.

# OPERA FOR DUMMIES™

by David Pogue
and Scott Speck

Foreword by Roger Pines

## IDG BOOKS WORLDWIDE

IDG Books Worldwide, Inc.
An International Data Group Company

Foster City, CA ♦ Chicago, IL ♦ Indianapolis, IN ♦ Southlake, TX

**Opera For Dummies**™

Published by
**IDG Books Worldwide, Inc.**
An International Data Group Company
919 E. Hillsdale Blvd.
Suite 400
Foster City, CA 94404
www.idgbooks.com (IDG Books Worldwide Web site)
www.dummies.com (Dummies Press Web site)

Copyright © 1997 IDG Books Worldwide, Inc. All rights reserved. No part of this book, including interior design, cover design, and icons, may be reproduced or transmitted in any form, by any means (electronic, photocopying, recording, or otherwise) without the prior written permission of the publisher.

Library of Congress Catalog Card No.: 97-80116

ISBN: 0-7645-5010-1

Printed in the United States of America

10 9 8 7 6 5 4 3 2 1

1DD/SR/QY/ZX/IN

Distributed in the United States by IDG Books Worldwide, Inc.

Distributed by Macmillan Canada for Canada; by Transworld Publishers Limited in the United Kingdom; by IDG Norge Books for Norway; by IDG Sweden Books for Sweden; by Woodslane Pty. Ltd. for Australia; by Woodslane Enterprises Ltd. for New Zealand; by Longman Singapore Publishers Ltd. for Singapore, Malaysia, Thailand, and Indonesia; by Simron Pty. Ltd. for South Africa; by Toppan Company Ltd. for Japan; by Distribuidora Cuspide for Argentina; by Livraria Cultura for Brazil; by Ediciencia S.A. for Ecuador; by Addison-Wesley Publishing Company for Korea; by Ediciones ZETA S.C.R. Ltda. for Peru; by WS Computer Publishing Corporation, Inc., for the Philippines; by Unalis Corporation for Taiwan; by Contemporanea de Ediciones for Venezuela; by Computer Book & Magazine Store for Puerto Rico; by Express Computer Distributors for the Caribbean and West Indies. Authorized Sales Agent: Anthony Rudkin Associates for the Middle East and North Africa.

For general information on IDG Books Worldwide's books in the U.S., please call our Consumer Customer Service department at 800-762-2974. For reseller information, including discounts and premium sales, please call our Reseller Customer Service department at 800-434-3422.

For information on where to purchase IDG Books Worldwide's books outside the U.S., please contact our International Sales department at 415-655-3200 or fax 415-655-3295.

For information on foreign language translations, please contact our Foreign & Subsidiary Rights department at 415-655-3021 or fax 415-655-3281.

For sales inquiries and special prices for bulk quantities, please contact our Sales department at 415-655-3200 or write to the address above.

For information on using IDG Books Worldwide's books in the classroom or for ordering examination copies, please contact our Educational Sales department at 800-434-2086 or fax 817-251-8174.

For press review copies, author interviews, or other publicity information, please contact our Public Relations department at 415-655-3000 or fax 415-655-3299.

For authorization to photocopy items for corporate, personal, or educational use, please contact Copyright Clearance Center, 222 Rosewood Drive, Danvers, MA 01923, or fax 508-750-4470.

**LIMIT OF LIABILITY/DISCLAIMER OF WARRANTY:** AUTHOR AND PUBLISHER HAVE USED THEIR BEST EFFORTS IN PREPARING THIS BOOK. IDG BOOKS WORLDWIDE, INC., AND AUTHOR MAKE NO REPRESENTATIONS OR WARRANTIES WITH RESPECT TO THE ACCURACY OR COMPLETENESS OF THE CONTENTS OF THIS BOOK AND SPECIFICALLY DISCLAIM ANY IMPLIED WARRANTIES OF MERCHANTABILITY OR FITNESS FOR A PARTICULAR PURPOSE. THERE ARE NO WARRANTIES WHICH EXTEND BEYOND THE DESCRIPTIONS CONTAINED IN THIS PARAGRAPH. NO WARRANTY MAY BE CREATED OR EXTENDED BY SALES REPRESENTATIVES OR WRITTEN SALES MATERIALS. THE ACCURACY AND COMPLETENESS OF THE INFORMATION PROVIDED HEREIN AND THE OPINIONS STATED HEREIN ARE NOT GUARANTEED OR WARRANTED TO PRODUCE ANY PARTICULAR RESULTS, AND THE ADVICE AND STRATEGIES CONTAINED HEREIN MAY NOT BE SUITABLE FOR EVERY INDIVIDUAL. NEITHER IDG BOOKS WORLDWIDE, INC., NOR AUTHOR SHALL BE LIABLE FOR ANY LOSS OF PROFIT OR ANY OTHER COMMERCIAL DAMAGES, INCLUDING BUT NOT LIMITED TO SPECIAL, INCIDENTAL, CONSEQUENTIAL, OR OTHER DAMAGES.

**Trademarks:** All brand names and product names used in this book are trade names, service marks, trademarks, or registered trademarks of their respective owners. IDG Books Worldwide is not associated with any product or vendor mentioned in this book.

is a trademark under exclusive license to IDG Books Worldwide, Inc., from International Data Group, Inc.

# About the Authors

After graduating from Yale in 1985, *summa cum laude,* Phi Beta Kappa, with Honors in Music, **David Pogue** spent two summers conducting operettas, and then moved to New York City. There he spent ten years on Broadway as a conductor, orchestrator, or synthesizer programmer for *Kiss of the Spider Woman, Welcome to the Club, Carrie,* Lincoln Center's *Anything Goes,* and other musicals. Over the years, he's worked as a music copyist, vocal arranger, or computer teacher for such musical-theater luminaries as Stephen Sondheim, Cy Coleman, Jule Styne, Jerry Bock, and John Kander.

In his other life, David Pogue is a Macintosh computer guru. He's the author of eight funny computer books (including the international bestseller *Macs For Dummies*), a novelist (having written *Hard Drive,* a *New York Times* "notable book of the year"), a monthly columnist for *Macworld* magazine, and a computer teacher to such clients as Mia Farrow, Carly Simon, Gary Oldman, and Harry Connick, Jr. He's been profiled on *48 Hours,* in the *New York Times,* in *USA Today,* and elsewhere.

In his spare time, David's a magician, composer, and lyricist, having written the music and lyrics for his theatrical wedding.

E-mail: pogue@aol.com; Web page: www.pogueman.com.

**Scott Speck has conducted many of the world's great musical masterpieces, including symphonies, concertos, operas, oratorios, and ballets, in hundreds of performances around the world. He has led the symphony orchestras of Baltimore, Oregon, Rochester, Honolulu, Louisville, and Jacksonville, among others. He is currently Associate Conductor of the Savannah Symphony Orchestra and Principal Guest Conductor of the China Film Philharmonic.**

**A graduate of Yale University (*summa cum laude,* Phi Beta Kappa, Honors in Music), Scott Speck received the Fellow's Prize for academic achievement and the Seymour Prize for outstanding contribution** to cultural life. He was awarded a Fulbright Scholarship to Berlin, Germany, where he founded an orchestra called Concerto Grosso Berlin. He's the recipient of the award for superior musicianship from Boston's Longy School of Music; a conducting fellowship at the Aspen School of Music; and a Master's Degree in Conducting from the University of Southern California, where he was honored as Outstanding Conductor and Outstanding Graduate Student.

Scott is on the faculty of the American Symphony Orchestra League's national conducting workshops. He's fluent in German, holds a diploma in Italian, speaks and reads French and Spanish, and has a reading knowledge of Russian.

E-mail: ScottSpeck@aol.com.

# ABOUT IDG BOOKS WORLDWIDE

Welcome to the world of IDG Books Worldwide.

IDG Books Worldwide, Inc., is a subsidiary of International Data Group, the world's largest publisher of computer-related information and the leading global provider of information services on information technology. IDG was founded more than 25 years ago and now employs more than 8,500 people worldwide. IDG publishes more than 275 computer publications in over 75 countries (see listing below). More than 60 million people read one or more IDG publications each month.

Launched in 1990, IDG Books Worldwide is today the #1 publisher of best-selling computer books in the United States. We are proud to have received eight awards from the Computer Press Association in recognition of editorial excellence and three from *Computer Currents'* First Annual Readers' Choice Awards. Our best-selling *...For Dummies®* series has more than 30 million copies in print with translations in 30 languages. IDG Books Worldwide, through a joint venture with IDG's Hi-Tech Beijing, became the first U.S. publisher to publish a computer book in the People's Republic of China. In record time, IDG Books Worldwide has become the first choice for millions of readers around the world who want to learn how to better manage their businesses.

Our mission is simple: Every one of our books is designed to bring extra value and skill-building instructions to the reader. Our books are written by experts who understand and care about our readers. The knowledge base of our editorial staff comes from years of experience in publishing, education, and journalism — experience we use to produce books for the '90s. In short, we care about books, so we attract the best people. We devote special attention to details such as audience, interior design, use of icons, and illustrations. And because we use an efficient process of authoring, editing, and desktop publishing our books electronically, we can spend more time ensuring superior content and spend less time on the technicalities of making books.

You can count on our commitment to deliver high-quality books at competitive prices on topics you want to read about. At IDG Books Worldwide, we continue in the IDG tradition of delivering quality for more than 25 years. You'll find no better book on a subject than one from IDG Books Worldwide.

John Kilcullen
CEO
IDG Books Worldwide, Inc.

Steven Berkowitz
President and Publisher
IDG Books Worldwide, Inc.

**Eighth Annual
Computer Press
Awards ≽1992**

**Ninth Annual
Computer Press
Awards ≽1993**

**Tenth Annual
Computer Press
Awards ≽1994**

**Eleventh Annual
Computer Press
Awards ≽1995**

IDG Books Worldwide, Inc., is a subsidiary of International Data Group, the world's largest publisher of computer-related information and the leading global provider of information services on information technology. International Data Group publishes over 275 computer publications in over 75 countries. Sixty million people read one or more International Data Group publications each month. International Data Group's publications include: **ARGENTINA:** Buyer's Guide, Computerworld Argentina, PC World Argentina; **AUSTRALIA:** Australian Macworld, Australian PC World, Australian Reseller News, Computerworld, IT Casebook, Network World, Publish, Webmaster; **AUSTRIA:** Computerwelt Osterreich, Networks Austria, PC Tip Austria; **BANGLADESH:** PC World Bangladesh; **BELARUS:** PC World Belarus; **BELGIUM:** Data News; **BRAZIL:** Annuário de Informática, Computerworld, Connections, Macworld, PC Player, PC World, Publish, Reseller News, Supergamepower; **BULGARIA:** Computerworld Bulgaria, Network World Bulgaria, PC & MacWorld Bulgaria; **CANADA:** CIO Canada, Client/Server World, ComputerWorld Canada, InfoWorld Canada, NetworkWorld Canada, WebWorld; **CHILE:** Computerworld Chile, PC World Chile; **COLOMBIA:** Computerworld Colombia, PC World Colombia; **COSTA RICA:** PC World Centro America; **THE CZECH AND SLOVAK REPUBLICS:** Computerworld Czechoslovakia, Macworld Czech Republic, PC World Czechoslovakia; **DENMARK:** Communications World Danmark, Computerworld Danmark, Macworld Danmark, PC World Danmark, Techworld Denmark; **DOMINICAN REPUBLIC:** PC World Republica Dominicana; **ECUADOR:** PC World Ecuador; **EGYPT:** Computerworld Middle East, PC World Middle East; **EL SALVADOR:** PC World Centro America; **FINLAND:** MikroPC, Tietoverkko, Tietoviikko; **FRANCE:** Distributique, Hebdo, Info PC, Le Monde Informatique, Macworld, Reseaux & Telecoms, WebMaster France; **GERMANY:** Computer Partner, Computerwoche, Computerwoche Extra, Computerwoche FOCUS, Global Online, Macwelt, PC Welt; **GREECE:** Amiga Computing, GamePro Greece, Multimedia World; **GUATEMALA:** PC World Centro America; **HONDURAS:** PC World Centro America; **HONG KONG:** Computerworld Hong Kong, PC World Hong Kong, Publish in Asia; **HUNGARY:** ABCD CD-ROM, Computerworld Szamitastechnika, Internetto online Magazine, PC World Hungary, PC-X Magazin Hungary; **ICELAND:** Tolvuheimur PC World Island; **INDIA:** Information Communications World, Information Systems Computerworld, PC World India, Publish in Asia; **INDONESIA:** InfoKomputer PC World, Komputek Computerworld, Publish in Asia; **IRELAND:** ComputerScope, PC Live!; **ISRAEL:** Macworld Israel, People & Computers/Computerworld; **ITALY:** Computerworld Italia, Macworld Italia, Networking Italia, PC World Italia; **JAPAN:** DTP World, Macworld Japan, Nikkei Personal Computing, OS/2 World Japan, SunWorld Japan, Windows NT World, Windows World Japan; **KENYA:** PC World East African; **KOREA:** Hi-Tech Information, Macworld Korea, PC World Korea; **MACEDONIA:** PC World Macedonia; **MALAYSIA:** Computerworld Malaysia, PC World Malaysia, Publish in Asia; **MALTA:** PC World Malta; **MEXICO:** Computerworld Mexico, PC World Mexico; **MYANMAR:** PC World Myanmar; **NETHERLANDS:** Computer! Totaal, LAN Internetworking Magazine, LAN World Buyers Guide, Macworld Netherlands, Net, WebWereld; **NEW ZEALAND:** Absolute Beginners Guide and Plain & Simple Series, Computer Buyer, Computer Industry Directory, Computerworld New Zealand, MTB, Network World, PC World New Zealand; **NICARAGUA:** PC World Centro America; **NORWAY:** Computerworld Norge, CW Rapport, Datamagasinet, Financial Rapport, Kursguide Norge, Macworld Norge, Multimediaworld Norge, PC World Ekspress Norge, PC World Nettverk, PC World Norge, PC World ProduktGuide Norge; **PAKISTAN:** Computerworld Pakistan; **PANAMA:** PC World Panama; **PEOPLE'S REPUBLIC OF CHINA:** China Computer Users, China Computerworld, China InfoWorld, China Telecom World Weekly, Computer & Communication, Electronic Design China, Electronics Today, Electronics Weekly, Game Software, PC World China, Popular Computer Week, Software Weekly, Software World, Telecom World; **PERU:** Computerworld Peru, PC World Profesional Peru, PC World SoHo Peru; **PHILIPPINES:** Click!, Computerworld Philippines, PC World Philippines, Publish in Asia; **POLAND:** Computerworld Poland, Computerworld Special Report Poland, Cyber, Macworld Poland, Networld Poland, PC World Komputer; **PORTUGAL:** Cerebro/PC World, Computerworld/Correio Informático, Dealer World Portugal, Mac*In/PC*In Portugal, Multimedia World; **PUERTO RICO:** PC World Puerto Rico; **ROMANIA:** Computerworld Romania, PC World Romania, Telecom Romania; **RUSSIA:** Computerworld Russia, Mir PK, Publish, Seti; **SINGAPORE:** Computerworld Singapore, PC World Singapore, Publish in Asia; **SLOVENIA:** Monitor; **SOUTH AFRICA:** Computing SA, Network World SA, Software World SA; **SPAIN:** Communicaciones World España, Computerworld España, Dealer World España, Macworld España, PC World España; **SRI LANKA:** Infolink PC World; **SWEDEN:** CAP&Design, Computer Sweden, Corporate Computing Sweden, Internetworld Sweden, it.branschen, Macworld Sweden, MaxiData Sweden, MikroDatorn, Natverk & Kommunikation, PC World Sweden, PCaktiv, Windows World Sweden; **SWITZERLAND:** Computerworld Schweiz, Macworld Schweiz, PCtip; **TAIWAN:** Computerworld Taiwan, Macworld Taiwan, NEW ViSiON/Publish, PC World Taiwan, Windows World Taiwan; **THAILAND:** Publish in Asia, Thai Computerworld; **TURKEY:** Computerworld Turkiye, Macworld Turkiye, Network World Turkiye, PC World Turkiye; **UKRAINE:** Computerworld Kiev, Multimedia World Ukraine, PC World Ukraine; **UNITED KINGDOM:** Acorn User UK, Amiga Action UK, Amiga Computing UK, Apple Talk UK, Computing, Macworld, Parents and Computers UK, PC Advisor, PC Home, PSX Pro, The WEB; **UNITED STATES:** Cable in the Classroom, CIO Magazine, Computerworld, DOS World, Federal Computer Week, GamePro Magazine, InfoWorld, I-Way, Macworld, Network World, PC Games, PC World, Publish, Video Event, THE WEB Magazine, and WebMaster; online webzines: JavaWorld, NetscapeWorld, and SunWorld Online; **URUGUAY:** InfoWorld Uruguay; **VENEZUELA:** Computerworld Venezuela, PC World Venezuela; and **VIETNAM:** PC World Vietnam.                    3/24/97

# Authors' Acknowledgments

This book was made possible by the efforts of our serene and supremely talented editor, Pam Mourouzis, and our hard-working copy editor, Diane Smith. Thanks are also due to the Chicago Lyric Opera's Roger Pines, whose unmatched knowledge of opera repeatedly kept us from tumbling over the brink of inaccuracy. And we truly appreciate the strenuous efforts of IDG Books' Mark Butler, Ann Miller, and Nickole Harris.

Our partners-in-writing crime included Steve Alper, who helped write the opera synopses in Chapters 12 and 13; Neal Goren, who authored the initial drafts of Chapters 2 and 4; Mary Lou Basaraba, who drafted Chapter 11; and Michael A. Lewanski, Jr., who wrote the initial drafts of our opera-history timeline and glossary. Thanks, too, to Michael Wartofsky for the gorgeous Finale-generated sheet-music examples in this book.

Moral support was graciously provided at no charge by our families, GQ, and the lovely Dr. Pogue.

# Publisher's Acknowledgments

We're proud of this book; please send us your comments about it by using the IDG Books Worldwide Registration Card at the back of the book or by e-mailing us at feedback/dummies@idgbooks.com. Some of the people who helped bring this book to market include the following:

### Acquisitions, Development, and Editorial

**Senior Project Editor:** Pamela Mourouzis

**Acquisitions Editor:** Mark Butler

**Copy Editor:** Susan Diane Smith

**General Reviewers:** Neal Goren, Roger Pines

**Editorial Manager:** Leah P. Cameron

**Editorial Coordinator:** Ann Miller

### Production

**Project Coordinator:** Regina Snyder

**Layout and Graphics:**
Lou Boudreau, Angela J. Bush-Sisson, Elizabeth Cardenas-Nelson, J. Tyler Connor, Pamela Emanoil, Angela F. Hunckler, Jane E. Martin, Heather N. Pearson, Brent Savage, Kate Snell, Michael A. Sullivan

**Proofreaders:** Nancy L. Reinhardt, Kelli Botta, Joel K. Draper, Rachel Garvey, Nancy C. Price, Robert Springer

**Indexer:** Lynnzee Elze Spense

### Special Help

Ethan Crimmins, EMI Classics; Elliot Hoffman, Highway One; Marc Mikulich, Vice President, Subsidiary Rights

---

### General and Administrative

**IDG Books Worldwide, Inc.:** John Kilcullen, CEO; Steven Berkowitz, President and Publisher

**IDG Books Technology Publishing:** Brenda McLaughlin, Senior Vice President and Group Publisher

**Dummies Technology Press and Dummies Editorial:** Diane Graves Steele, Vice President and Associate Publisher; Judith A. Taylor, Product Marketing Manager; Kristin A. Cocks, Editorial Director; Mary Bednarek, Acquisitions and Product Development Director

**Dummies Trade Press:** Kathleen A. Welton, Vice President and Publisher

**IDG Books Production for Dummies Press:** Beth Jenkins, Production Director; Cindy L. Phipps, Manager of Project Coordination, Production Proofreading, and Indexing; Kathie S. Schutte, Supervisor of Page Layout; Shelley Lea, Supervisor of Graphics and Design; Debbie J. Gates, Production Systems Specialist; Robert Springer, Supervisor of Proofreading; Debbie Stailey, Special Projects Coordinator; Tony Augsburger, Supervisor of Reprints and Bluelines; Leslie Popplewell, Media Archive Coordinator

**Dummies Packaging and Book Design:** Patti Sandez, Packaging Specialist; Lance Kayser, Packaging Assistant; Kavish + Kavish, Cover Design

◆

The publisher would like to give special thanks to Patrick J. McGovern and Walter Boyd, without whom this book would not have been possible.

◆

# Contents at a Glance

# Cartoons at a Glance

### By Rich Tennant

page 187

page 53

page 115

page 323

page 301

page 5

Fax: 508-546-7747 • E-mail: the5wave@tiac.net

# Table of Contents

# Foreword

pera!

There's nothing like it. Ladies and gentlemen, for thrills galore — music to leave you totally exhilarated, drama to make your hair stand on end, and spectacle to take your breath away — you've come to the right place.

Years ago, introductions to opera tended to be dull and stuffy, but no more: *Opera For Dummies* has arrived. David Pogue and Scott Speck bring to it all their impressive knowledge, but you'll never catch them becoming jaded or blasé — for them, opera's still the best entertainment imaginable. Their book takes in everything you'll need to join the ranks of happy opera buffs, whether it's plot synopses, information on singers and singing, explanations of who does what in an opera company, and a lot more. They've even included a CD to whet your appetite!

David and Scott encourage all of us to forget about stereotypes. It's time to admit that the barriers that may have interfered with our enjoying opera are gone forever. Opera singers are now, more often than not, as gorgeous to behold as anyone you'll find on *Friends* or *Melrose Place.* You think they just stand there and belt out the notes? No way — today's opera singers are also singing *actors,* and they act fabulously. If you were worried about inaccessibility because of the foreign languages being sung, we've left that barrier behind, too: Now there are *surtitles,* which help you follow the text just like subtitles in a foreign film. And opera isn't buried in another century, it's living *today;* exciting new operas are being introduced every year, and stage productions are keeping pace with our visually oriented age.

But still you wonder, "Why should I devote my hard-earned money and my limited leisure time to opera?"

Here's the very simple answer: Because when push comes to shove, an operatic experience is an experience in *beauty,* and beauty is what we have too little of in this world. When you hear a soprano float a soft high C, or a tenor singing a love song, or a full-throated chorus in the climax of a scene's dramatic finale, I guarantee that you'll get goosebumps you've never felt before. We're talking about the singing voice, the most human of all instruments — and the voice communicates emotions in a way that nothing else can match.

Scott and David constantly demonstrate that opera brings the most powerful emotions to life: the ecstasy of love, the pain of loss, the hunger for revenge. The plot synopses in this book prove that operas' stories can go way beyond A-loves-B-who-loves-C. They're often dealing with the most wrenching decisions anyone can make — matters of life and death, in other words. But, lest we forget, in opera you find terrific comedies as well — comedies that can have you laughing 'til the tears run down your cheeks.

When I was growing up, I knew no one else my age who loved opera. Until college, the only people I could talk to about opera were usually at least half a century older. I was pleased that they could share my excitement, but at the same time I wished that my peers could realize what they were missing and jump on the bandwagon.

If this book had been around, they would have changed their minds.

So to David Pogue and Scott Speck, I say "bravo" — sorry, "brav*i*" (see this book's section on applause) — for a job well done. And to *you,* the reader, I say open yourself up to a glorious new world. When it comes to entertainment, opera offers you everything you've ever wanted. Get ready to enjoy it!

— Roger Pines
  Program Editor, Lyric Opera of Chicago

# Introduction

● ● ● ● ● ● ● ● ● ● ● ● ● ● ● ● ● ● ● ● ● ● ● ● ● ● ● ● ● ● ● ● ● ● ● ● ● ● ● ● ● ● ● ● ● ●

*N*ow you've done it. You've taken the plunge into opera . . . that scary, mysterious, larger-than-life world of bearded men in togas and flying ladies with horns. Where strange mythical monsters prance about the stage. Where characters croon in weird, warbly voices, way up in the stratosphere, in words so foreign that you need *subtitles* to understand them.

In fact, plenty of opera snobs are perfectly *happy* that you don't understand. They'd love opera to be an exclusive club, an elite corps, a sacred order. They're *glad* that opera strikes many as the world's most obscure art form.

But don't be afraid — whether you know it or not, you've grown up with opera. Have you ever heard of the Three Tenors? Have you heard that "It ain't over 'til the fat lady sings?" More to the point, have you ever listened to a movie soundtrack, watched a TV commercial, or listened to the radio? If so, then you've experienced opera.

Be careful, though: For many people, opera becomes an addiction, a life-absorbing passion. There's something about taking a basic human emotion and singing it soaringly over three octaves, with a full orchestra of 105 instruments blazing at full force, that makes all other art forms seem lifeless and mundane.

This book is designed to unlock your capacity to experience one of the greatest highs in life: the indescribable, profound, cathartic joy of opera. It's a pleasure unlike any other.

## Who You Are

For starters, you're an intelligent person. We can sense it, and we're never wrong about these things. After all, you picked up this book, didn't you?

But in this vast, complex world, there are 1,006,932,408.7 subjects to know about. (The .7 is for line dancing, which is not *really* a complete subject, if you get our drift.) Opera just happens to be one of the topics you're not yet expert in. Fair enough.

In this state, you have nevertheless become aware of opera's power. You've seen it turn ordinary people into opera fanatics. You've observed its capability to arouse primal passions; to hearken to the loftiest reaches of the human spirit; and to inspire profound, exalted, emotional outpourings of unadulterated ecstasy. You've heard it mentioned on the Home Shopping Network.

And you'd like to know more.

# How to Read This Book

This book is organized in six different parts:

- ✔ Part I introduces you to the world of opera: the words, the music, and the people who sing them.
- ✔ Part II is a concise history of opera, including the lives of the great composers.
- ✔ Part III takes you into the opera house to experience this art for yourself, and then takes you on a backstage tour of the professional opera world.
- ✔ Part IV gives in-depth synopses of the world's most beloved operas.
- ✔ Parts V and VI take you even deeper into opera and help you get more out of it.

You may have noticed the free CD inside the back cover. This CD is your key to entering the world of opera — a painless introduction to the major composers, styles, and time periods. When we describe some of the great masterpieces, you can actually listen to them right away. That CD sets *Opera For Dummies* apart from all the other books on the shelf.

You can read from beginning to end if you want to, but that's not the point. We want you to explore anything that strikes your fancy. You don't have to finish one chapter before starting another. You can throw a dart at the index for a starting place, or start by listening to the CD, or, if you're in a romantic mood, cuddle up with a loved one and start at the beginning.

Now, a warning. Although we don't expect you to have any prior opera experience, we do presume a *certain* musical understanding on your part. For example, we may very well toss off such technical terms as these:

- ✔ singer
- ✔ song

Or, in the more advanced stages of the book, even these:

- ✔ singers
- ✔ songs

But never fear, Dear Reader, for we provide a glossary at the back of the book.

# Icons Used in This Book

Throughout the book, you'll find icons to clue you in about certain topics. They indicate material you may be especially interested in, or material you may be eager to skip. Let these icons be your guide.

This icon clues you in on a handy shortcut, technique, or suggestion that'll help you get more out of your operatic life.

So that we don't fry your brain by surprise attack, we place this icon next to advanced topics or special terminology.

Although we consider this book a great way to learn about opera, it can't hold a candle to *listening* to opera (or watching it). This icon marks a great selection worth checking out from the library.

The CD that comes with this book includes 13 excerpts from the greatest operas in the world. When we're discussing one of them, this icon lets you know.

Whenever we present a fact or discussion that's normally in the realm of the opera snobs, we warn you with this icon.

Let's face it: Opera's a classy art form, and knowing funny and interesting tidbits will get you attention and respect anywhere you go. This icon alerts you to great stories worth repeating.

Let's face something else: Opera's been around longer than some countries. This icon alerts you to the very beginnings of trends and rituals that are still with us today.

Every now and then, things get a little weird. Here's your clue that the world of opera is about to take a bizarre turn.

# Why Being an Opera Novice Helps You Enjoy Opera

We firmly believe that you have a great advantage over many opera fanatics worldwide. Unburdened as you are by vast musical preconditioning, you're in the best position to experience this art form. The composers of the great operas knew what they were doing — they created potent musical dramas aimed straight for the heart.

Many opera buffs forget that in opera, the intellect should take a back seat to emotion. More than many other arts, opera is meant to appeal directly to the senses. We're going to show you how to activate those senses.

So enjoy your present state of operatic innocence. Revel in it! To fully appreciate an opera, all you need are eyes, ears, and a soul.

# Part I
# Larger Than Life

The 5th Wave    By Rich Tennant

@RICHTENNANT

"Well, that's the last time we hire a high soprano to sing at the glass-blowers' convention."

## In this part . . .

One reason opera is so fascinating (and one reason it can be intimidating) is that everything about it is larger than life: the plots, the music, the singers' personalities — even the opera house itself.

This part explores the elements that make this art form so momentous. Here's your stress-free introduction to grand old opera.

# Chapter 1

# Curtain Up!

*W*e'll be the first to admit it: Opera's weird.

Everybody's wearing makeup. They're *singing* all the time. Even when they're singing in your language, which is rare, you still can't understand the words. Women play men, men play women, and 45-year-olds play teenagers. All the main characters seem to get killed off. And when somebody dies, he takes ten minutes to sing about it.

By golly, it's the greatest entertainment on earth.

Still, all that weirdness winds up intimidating plenty of people — including, when we were young, your present authors. As in skiing, dancing, or car buying, people tend to avoid whatever makes them insecure. Deep down, a little voice tells them that if they show up at an opera without any *clue* what's going on, the opera snobs will notice and laugh them out of the opera house.

But here's the great little secret about opera: *Nobody* knows what's going on without a little help — not even the snobs.

And help is here.

# Opera Defined

An opera's a theater piece, like a play. But instead of *speaking* their lines, the characters sing them. Even Broadway musicals in which the music never stops, such as *Les Misérables, Evita,* and *Tommy,* are actually operas.

Operas were invented to combine the best of all possible worlds — awesome singing, great-sounding orchestra, riveting drama, stunning dance, spectacular sets, lavish costumes, fancy lighting, and special effects. By uniting these arts, the founding fathers of opera managed to create an art form more powerful than any other.

Over the centuries, in fact, opera has become more fun than it ever was, because

- ✔ We now know all about the shocking, amazing lives of the great composers (see Part II).
- ✔ The act of going to an opera has become a modern-day eye-opener (see Chapter 10).
- ✔ The baffling mystique of the opera star has become entertainment in itself (see Chapter 4).
- ✔ The world has accumulated so many *more* operas! (See Chapters 12 and 13.)

# The Popular-versus-Classical Myth

Apart from their insecurity, some people avoid opera because they think it's an old, musty, highbrow art form reserved for people who wear tuxedos and long dresses and talk about the cotillion dance and borrow Grey Poupon in their limousines. Most people would rather go to a movie.

The funny thing is, until very recently (at least in geological terms), going to an opera *was* like going to a movie. People went to an opera as you might go to a rock concert: to have fun! They went to see their favorite stars and hear their favorite tunes. They wore casual clothes; they brought along food and drinks; they even cheered (or booed, or threw flowers or tomatoes) during the show if the spirit moved them. Classical music *was* pop music.

In fact, when Verdi wrote his opera *Otello,* the crowd went crazy, calling him back to the stage over and over again with standing ovations, finally carrying him all the way home on their shoulders, and then serenading him under his window. Even ♀ doesn't get that kind of treatment today.

Opera is just as entertaining as it ever was. But these days, it has become much less *familiar*. That's all. After you become familiar with this art form, you'll be amazed at how entertaining it becomes.

# You Know More Than You Think You Do

You'd be astounded at how much opera you know *already*. The commercial with the soprano singing at the top of her lungs, inside the luxury car, is opera. The other car commercial, in which the hero loses his keys on the way to the opera, is opera. Even the Bugs Bunny classic, "The Rabbit of Seville," with Elmer Fudd singing "Kill the wabbit, kill the wabbit" to the tune of the Ride of the Valkyries, is opera. In all these TV tidbits, the tunes are 100 percent pure opera music.

So the world's most beloved opera melodies are already hopping around inside your brain. Now, to become comfortable with this universe of weirdness, you need to explore a few more things: some history, some conventions, and a few of the best operas out there. That's what this book is for.

In the immortal words of Mr. Spock: Captain, there is no cause for alarm. And the immortal words of *Dr.* Spock: You know more than you think you do.

# How Do I Know If I Like It?

Not every opera will turn you on right away. And that's perfectly okay.

Some operas are, as we euphemistically say in the classical-music biz, more "accessible" than others. That is, some have beautiful melodies that you can hum instantly, whereas others, on first listening, sound more like a cat in a Cuisinart.

Furthermore, just as you have favorite popular composers, you're bound to have favorite opera composers. Perhaps one style will seem to speak to you more at first than all the others.

 See what you like best at this moment. Take out the accompanying CD at the back of this book and play the first minute of each track. Each one is an operatic masterpiece, and each is in a different musical style. The CD includes excerpts from Italian, French, German-Austrian, and American operas, by different composers, from different time periods. There are no right or wrong answers; opera is supposed to be fun to listen to.

Does one selection appeal to you more than all the others? If so, begin your exploration of opera by delving into other works in that style or by that composer.

Or if you love them all, fantastic! Our job just got a whole lot easier.

# The Seven Habits of Highly Effective Operas

Despite this incredible variety of styles within the world of music, certain consistent qualities make an opera great. Of the 25,000 operas listed in the Library of Congress, fewer than 100 are regularly performed today; here are the seven reasons why they made the cut.

## They come from the composer's heart

In the best operas, the composers themselves were deeply moved by their material. They chose subject matter that they felt strongly about.

Beethoven's *Fidelio* is about an individual struggling to break free of the bonds of tyranny and oppression — just as he struggled against the burden of his own deafness. *Die Fledermaus* is Johann "Blue Danube" Strauss's most popular operetta, and that's no surprise; the opera's full of sparkling waltzes and polkas, the very qualities that made Strauss a superstar. Giacomo Puccini had spent years as a starving young composer, and he poured his life experience into *La Bohème,* his biggest hit.

Giuseppe Verdi, one of opera's greatest composers, considered himself an ordinary guy. Sure enough, he had an affinity for stories about common people in uncommon situations. Other composers had read and rejected the libretto for *Nabucco,* for example; but Verdi was captivated by this story of Hebrew slaves yearning for freedom, and the opera became his first huge success. (Listen to Track 6 on your free CD for a sample.)

In every case, the composer was able to set a story to music because he understood it well. The result is completely convincing.

## They're driven by primal human emotions

All good operas — and all great movies and Broadway musicals, too, for that matter — express deep-seated human emotions (except *Cats,* which expresses deep-seated *feline* emotions).

We're not talking about your everyday, run-of-the-mill emotions like the frustration of America Online busy signals or the grossness of finding a bug on your pizza. No, we're talking about *enormous* emotions, such as love, anger, pride, lust, greed, and envy. In the best operas, these emotions become the engine that drives the plot.

The reason is simple: These emotions are universal. No matter what the story, no matter what strange times and places are depicted, the emotions remain constant.

And *that's* why people *sing* in operas. Putting emotion to music somehow immortalizes it, making it larger than life and casting it in stone.

And speaking of casting in stone: When the doomed lovers sing *"Oh terra, addio"* at the end of *Aïda,* you cry, not because two ancient characters are getting walled up in an Egyptian tomb, but because two good people have to suffer so greatly for their love. *Primal,* man, *primal.*

## *They're rattling good yarns*

Good operas have good stories. You may as well find out this little secret right now: Most opera plots involve a lot of sex and violence.

But nonstop sex and violence can be boring, as we can tell you from experience. *[Yeah, sure. — Editors.]* Effective opera composers (and the *librettists,* who write the words) know how to use *variety* to keep you listening. If the librettist includes some funny scenes for comic relief, the shocking conclusion will be all the more shocking. Similarly, if the composer uses a variety of musical ideas, or dynamics (loudness and softness), or melodies, or harmonies, he's much more likely to keep your interest.

In an opera, as in a movie, a climactic moment of violence can be thrilling if it's approached with a suspenseful buildup. Effective composers know how to use dramatic *pacing.* Their music builds up suspense as it approaches the climax. Great composers take care that no scene is aimless, that no aria is too long, and that the action, like this sentence, always progresses toward its inevitable heart-pounding, pulse-racing, brow-sweating, nail-biting, earth-shattering, toe-tapping conclusion!

*[We apologize for the preceding excess. The authors have been hosed down. — Editors.]*

## They feature exotic sets, costumes, and special effects

Since the early days, nearly all operas have transported the audience to a different place and time. Even during the Renaissance, which you'd think would have been early enough, the operas were about even *earlier* times — ancient Greece and Rome.

Gluck's *Orfeo* takes place both on earth and in the Underworld. The action of Berlioz's *Les Troyens* transpires in ancient Troy. And Wagner's *Ring* cycle takes place underwater, in the depths of a primeval forest, and up in the heavens, among other places.

The key word is *exotic*. The more exotic the locale, the greater the possibilities for interesting sets, costumes, and special effects. Verdi's *Aïda* is one of the most popular operas of all time. Sure, sure, it has great music and a wonderful plot; those are prerequisites. But besides all that, *Aïda* is set in Egypt and has elephants. You can't say *that* about *My Fair Lady*.

## They're creative and original in style

You hear again and again that some of the greatest composers were misunderstood in their own day — their music was considered too "modern." Not everyone could relate to the operas of Handel, Beethoven, Tchaikovsky, or even Puccini when they were first performed. And yet today, these operas are considered easy listening.

The reason for this original lack of acceptance is *unfamiliarity*. Each composer's unique musical language was completely new. And yet, this is one of the things that makes these operas so great. Effective opera composers have their own ideas.

Did you see the movie *Amadeus?* The composer Salieri is the "host" of this movie; he's depicted as one of the most famous non-great composers — he lived at the time of Mozart, wrote operas at the same time Mozart did, and was completely overshadowed by him. Now, Salieri was not a bad composer; in fact, he was a very good one. But he wasn't one of the world's *great* composers because his work wasn't *original*. What he wrote sounded just like what everyone else was composing at the time.

## They have catchy tunes

In the modern pop-music world, the word *hook* refers to the catchy, re-peated element in a piece of music. Beatles songs are catchy because nearly every one of them has a hook. Think of "Help!" or "A Hard Day's Night" or "She Loves You" ("Yeah, Yeah, Yeah!"). Catchiness is not a scientifically measurable quality; still, you know a hook when you hear it.

In opera, the same concept applies. A hook helps you remember, and identify with, a particular aria, duet, or chorus. The operas of Mozart, Rossini, Verdi, Puccini, and Johann Strauss have hooks galore. The music of the most effective composers is full of elements that stick in your mind.

Of all the composers we just mentioned, Verdi and Puccini take the cake; your average non-opera person can hum several of their melodies without even trying (and without even knowing that these famous tunes came from operas). Is it any wonder, then, that these are the two most popular opera composers of all time?

## They allow the singers to show their stuff

But what's a good tune if nobody can sing it? The next habit of highly effective operas is to accommodate the great talents of the opera world.

For at least 300 years, opera composers have known that a superstar singer in the title role can mean success for an opera. And what better way to highlight that superstar than to give her a great vehicle in which to shine?

Most opera composers, from Handel to the present day, have written with particular singers in mind. If a particular opera has lots of high Cs, for example, you can bet that the composer knew who would be singing them. And if another opera seems to avoid them altogether — well, the composer probably had a good reason there, too.

# Combining All the Habits

An opera doesn't *have* to have all seven habits listed here to make it into the Hall of Greats. For example, the operas in Part IV of this book generally manage to have at least five or six of them. A special few, though — Mozart's *Don Giovanni,* for example, or Verdi's *Rigoletto* — combine all seven. *Wow,* are those good operas!

# Chapter 2

# The Libretto's the Thing

*B*efore plunging headfirst into the untamed crocodile swamp of opera, we'd like to take you on a little boat tour of the opera-creation process.

Like a stage play or a movie, an opera starts with words — *thousands* of words. In a stage play, the words are called the *script;* in a movie they're called the *screenplay;* and in an opera they're called the *libretto.*

Libretto means "little book" in Italian, and that's precisely what it is; your average libretto is scarcely thicker than a *TV Guide.* But because *singing* a sentence takes about three times longer than *saying* it, a "little book," when set to music, becomes a full evening in the theater. (And if you've ever experienced a Wagner opera, you know that his little books are a little less little than others.)

# A Libretto Is Born

In pop music, the writer of the lyrics is often forgotten. (Quick, who wrote the *words* to "Hound Dog?") In fact, we often don't even know the *composer's* name — we still talk about the *singer* as though he wrote the songs, as in "Barry Manilow's 'I Write the Songs.'" (He didn't write *that* one.)

In opera, the *librettist* (the libretto writer) likewise gets ignored far too often; we still say "Mozart wrote *The Magic Flute,*" when actually he wrote only the *music.* Granted, Mozart could probably set the IRS Tax Form 1040EZ to music and create a masterpiece, but he's the exception. Opera composers usually need something more substantial to kindle their imagination, and providing that kindling is the librettist's responsibility.

The plots of most librettos — like most movies and plays — feature *larger-than-life* characters and situations. Everyone loves a good, juicy story, regardless of its plausibility (see *E.T.* or *The Terminator,* for example). It's fun (or cathartic, or moving) to empathize with the nightmarish plight of an operatic protagonist for an evening.

An opera's libretto has a huge impact on its music. The words influence the rhythm and melody of a musical phrase; the emotion in the drama affects the mood of the music; and the plot determines the overall structure of the opera.

## Where librettos come from

Say that you're an opera composer looking for a libretto. Where will you find one? Well, you might see a play and think, "Holy smokes, I could *do* something with that!" You might get approached by a librettist who says, "I think that we could make music together." Or if you're very lucky, you might even receive a commission from a patron who has a librettist in mind and money to burn.

But regardless of how you and the librettist discover one another, your relationship is a collaboration, often a very intimate one. Like a marriage, this relationship could be tempestuous — after all, we're talking about gigantic colliding egos here! It's not unusual for a composer to dismiss a librettist, find another for a time, and then return to the original librettist later on. (Was Elizabeth Taylor an opera composer in another life?)

## Opera's most famous librettists

Opera history includes three truly legendary librettists: Lorenzo da Ponte (who collaborated with Mozart), Arrigo Boito (who wrote two scripts for Verdi), and Hugo von Hofmannsthal (Richard Strauss's greatest collaborator).

Of these three, the most *interesting* was Lorenzo da Ponte (1749–1838), partly because he provided Mozart with the inspiration for *Don Giovanni, The Marriage of Figaro,* and *Così fan tutte,* and partly because of his colorful life. It's a long story, but for now, suffice it to say that da Ponte was a Venetian priest who fathered a child with a married woman, was run out of town, moved to Vienna, forged a letter of introduction, passed himself off as a librettist, worked with Mozart, had several affairs with leading divas, moved to London, got heavily into debt, and fled to New York, where he started a grocery store and the Italian department at Columbia University. It's safe to say that Lorenzo da Ponte is the greatest librettist ever to be buried in Queens.

Arrigo Boito (1842–1918) was a composer in his own right (he had used his own libretto for his opera *Mefistofele*). But his collaboration with Giuseppe Verdi, who was at the height of his powers and the end of his brilliant career, produced two of the finest Italian operas ever: *Otello* and *Falstaff.*

But when it comes to emotionally fraught, therapy-ready relationships, it would be hard to beat that of Richard Strauss and his librettist Hugo von Hofmannsthal. Though they worked together for 23 years, and often lived just an hour apart, they rarely met. Through nearly three decades of correspondence, Strauss and Hofmannsthal never called each other by their first names.

Both men were brilliant but touchy; time and again, one or the other would threaten to pull out of the project, and the other would have to bully or mollify in response. Their correspondence is full of nasty quotes, couched in traditional niceties: "This strikes me, forgive my honesty, as odious." "It is you alone who must take the blame." "Your ideas are rubbish . . . utter nonsense . . . truly horrible. Hope you are well."

For all their bickering, their collaboration gave birth to some incredible operas — including *Elektra, Der Rosenkavalier,* and *Ariadne auf Naxos.* (See Chapters 12 and 13 for complete summaries.)

On the other hand, Richard Wagner, the greatest musical control freak of all time, never had to fight with his librettist — because he *was* his librettist. (This arrangement made it tough for him to redirect the blame when the going got rough, however.)

# How Come Operas Aren't in English?

Now, we, your authors, are nice guys, but we're also honest. We'd be the first to tell you if you had a piece of spinach between your teeth. Therefore, we must make one confession regarding opera's modern-day reputation, in some circles, for being boring:

If you can't understand what's going on, operas *are* boring.

Of course, that stems from one inconvenient fact: Most of the time, operas are in a *foreign language.* And for many years, this fact posed a real problem for would-be opera lovers worldwide.

Opera snobs, of course, had no sympathy for this predicament. "If the audience doesn't understand," they sniffed, "that's their problem." Others, only somewhat more understanding, said, "Well, as long as you know the general plot outlines, you can catch the gist by watching the action. it doesn't matter if you catch every word."

We understand that point of view, but we have to disagree. It's all well and good to know, by looking at the stage, that one character is really, *really* upset with another; but it adds a whole new dimension when you know he's saying, "I'm going to throttle you because you used the last of the mayonnaise, which I was saving for a *very* special occasion."

## Lost in the translation

So why didn't people just translate those operas into English? Well, sometimes they did. But unfortunately, when translated, great European operas can turn into a mess. If you've ever studied a foreign language, you know that a literal translation can never communicate the subtle emotional overtones of the original language.

To make matters worse, every syllable of text in an opera is matched up with a note of music — so when translating a foreign opera into English, you must not only maintain the same number of syllables in a sentence, but also make sure that the accented syllables land on accented musical notes. Furthermore, many arias have words that rhyme, and you can seldom translate a rhyme without completely destroying its meaning.

In Weber's *Der Freischütz,* for example, Agathe sings: *"Leise, leise, fromme Weise, schwig' dich auf zum Sternenkreise!"* (which actually means "Soft, soft, devout melody: vibrate up to the circle of stars!"). Now, to match the music, the translator has to retain the same number of syllables as the original. But there's also a rhyming pattern! About the best anyone has come up with is, "Holy, holy, meek and lowly, Rise, my soul, where stars swing slowly!", which changes the subject of the sentence from "melody" to "soul" — and, of course, adds that nonsense about the stars *swinging.*

When the meaning of every phrase of an opera is subtly altered like this, the audience is in for a pretty confusing evening.

So for nearly two centuries, operagoers have had a lousy couple of choices: either hear operas performed in a language that they didn't understand, or have them mangled into English. Wasn't there *any* solution?

## It's a bird, it's a plane . . . it's supertitles!

Modern technology to the rescue! When operas started appearing on TV in their original language, someone came up with the idea of superimposing simultaneous translations at the bottom of the screen, just as in foreign movies. Now that the audience knew what Tosca said after she plunged the knife into Scarpia's belly (*"Here's* Tosca's kiss!"), more and more people started tuning in.

It was just a matter of time before someone had the idea to use this technology in the opera house itself — and *surtitles* (also called *supertitles*) were born. Surtitles are actually film slides — usually somewhat more complicated than the slides you used in your old carousel projector. They work exactly like the subtitles in foreign movies and TV operas, except that they're projected on the wall *above* the stage.

Since their debut in the 1980s, surtitles have found their way into most of the world's opera houses. Opera sales, attendance, and performances have been climbing ever since, growing 35 percent in the last five years alone. (See Chapter 10 for more on surtitles.)

# How to Use a Libretto

As great as surtitles are for understanding opera, they can't take the place of a libretto. Luckily, when you buy an opera CD or tape, a libretto almost always comes along as standard equipment. Armed with this little booklet, you can sink back in your chair, let the music play, and visualize exactly what's going on onstage. Here are our tips for getting the most out of your libretto.

## Read the synopsis before you begin

No matter what form your opera encounter is about to take, read the synopsis (in Chapter 12 or 13 of this book, for example) before you begin. Then you'll pretty much know what's going on onstage even if you get temporarily lost in the script.

Yes, this suggestion rules out the possibility of being surprised by the ending; but remember, this is *opera*. We've got news for you: Most of these stories *don't* end happily — so much for surprise.

## Follow the translation

A libretto usually features the original language on the left side of the page and a translation on the right. If you glance back and forth as you listen, you'll do more than follow the story: You'll also discover all kinds of interesting tidbits about how foreign languages work. Read on.

## Scan for look-alike words

Even if you're looking at the words they're singing on the CD, you may not *recognize* them because the same words are pronounced differently in different languages. Take the word *Albert,* for example; a French person sings it "ahl-BEAR." Tricky.

Therefore, savvy CD listeners scan for words that mean the same thing in both languages, and *look* it. In this example from *La Bohème,* you can see how certain words in Italian are pretty recognizable:

| | |
|---|---|
| *Chi son? Sono un **poeta**.* | Who am I? I'm a **poet**. |
| *Che cosa faccio? **Scrivo**.* | What do I do? I **write**. |
| *E come vivo? **Vivo**.* | And how do I live? I **live**. |
| *In **povertà** mia lieta scialo da **gran signore** rime ed inni d'**amore**.* | In my carefree **poverty**, I squander rhymes and **love**-songs like a **rich lord**. |

Words such as *poeta, povertà,* and *amore* should be pretty easy to figure out. You may even recognize *vivo* from the English word *vivacious,* and *scrivo* from the words *scribe* and *inscribe.* Hooks like these make it much easier to follow librettos in Italian, French, German, and other languages that share some roots with English.

## Watch for CD-booklet track numbers

Even if you have the libretto in front of you as you listen to an opera, it's sometimes easy to get lost when a bunch of people are singing different things *simultaneously* — or, especially in Mozart's operas, when they're singing fast, overlapping sentences.

If you're listening to an opera on CD, a great little high-tech feature helps you stay with the libretto even after a patch of musical chaos: Use the track numbers as a reference. They generally appear in the left margin of your booklet, like this: 8. If you're temporarily lost, just glance at your CD player; when the number changes, you'll regain your bearings.

## Sopranos are high; basses are low; choruses have more than one voice

Here's another trick for figuring out where you are in a libretto as you listen: Use the printed character names to figure out who's singing what. If your libretto contains a long solo by Rodolfo, and then a solo by Mimì, you can just wait until you hear a woman singing on your CD, and you'll have found your place.

But what if two characters are singing, and they're both women? How do you tell them apart? In that case, you can use *voice parts* (soprano, mezzo-soprano, contralto, tenor, baritone, and bass) as a point of reference. A high-singing woman is a soprano, a low-singing woman is a contralto, and so on — details in Chapter 4. At the beginning of every libretto, you can find a list of all the characters and their voice parts. When you hear a particular type of voice singing, scan your libretto for the corresponding character. And if you hear a big chorus singing, well, by golly, scan your libretto for a "Chorus of sailors" or "Chorus of nuns" or "Chorus of happy villagers."

# The Opera For Dummies Guide to Pronouncing Opera Lyrics

All our cheerful advice about following along in an opera libretto is well and good — if you *can* follow along. Easier said than done, however: Each foreign language features lots of sounds you aren't used to.

It takes years to master the pronunciation of a foreign language — but we can get you started. Here is a quick, grossly oversimplified cheat sheet to pronouncing the most common opera languages: Italian, German, and French.

## Italian

Italian is pronouncer-friendly: Its vowels only have one pronunciation each, and nothing is silent; when two appear together, you just pronounce one after the other:

| These Letters | Sound Like | As in |
|---|---|---|
| a | ah | gran ("GRAHN") |
| e | ay | crudele ("croo-DAY-lay") |
| i | ee | destino ("day-STEE-no") |
| o | oh | non (rhymes with *moan*) |
| u | oo | una ("OO-na") |
| aiu | ah-ee-oo | aiuta ("ah-ee-OO-tah") |

And these simple vowel sounds — called "pure vowels" by singers and linguistic types — are a breeze to sing, allowing a singer to bring out the beauties of her voice without strain. *No wonder* singers love Italian!

## *German*

German's much trickier to pronounce and to sing, especially because of the consonants that don't sound the same as ours, and because of the little dots that appear over certain vowels. And Germans often like to run little words together into one giant word — like *Feuerversicherungsgesellschaftspräsident* ("fire insurance company president") or *Götterdämmerung* ("twilight of the gods").

| These Letters | Sound Like | As in |
|---|---|---|
| a | ah<br>or sometimes uh | Das ("DAHSS")<br>Dass ("DUSS") |
| ä | eh | Männer ("MEN-ner") |
| au | ow | Frau ("FRAU") |
| äu | oy | Mäuser ("MOY-zer") |
| e | short e<br>or sometimes ay | wenn ("VENN")<br>leben ("LAY-ben") |
| i | short i | will ("VILL") |
| ie | ee | die ("DEE") |
| o | oh | wo ("VOH") |
| ö | euh | schön ("SHEUHN") |
| u | oo | Busen ("BOO-zen") |
| ch | kh | machen ("MAKH-en") |
| j | y | ja ("YAH") |
| st | sht | still ("SHTILL") |
| v | f | von ("FOHN") |
| w | v | wenn (VENN) |

By the way: When you read German for the first time, you'll probably think that Germany is positively overrun with names, because *every single sentence* contains several capitalized words! Actually, there's a simple explanation: Every *noun* is capitalized in German.

## French

In French, the most common vowel seems to be the toughest one to pronounce: It's that *awwwwwnnngggh* sound you can get by talking like a donkey through your nose: "EEE-yawww!" In the following table, an asterisk (*) refers to that very sound, or a close approximation of it.

| These Letters | Sound Like | As in |
|---|---|---|
| a, -as, -at | ah | face ("FAHSS") |
| an, ans, ant | * | dans ("D*") |
| au | oh | pauvre ("POE-vr") |
| e | eh *or* euh | belle ("BELL") *or* de ("DEUH") |
| é, ai | ay | flambé ("flahm-BAY") |
| en, ens, ends, ent | * | attends ("ah-T*") |
| i | ee | ami ("ah-MEE") |
| o, -os | oh | vos ("VOE") |
| ou | oo | tout ("TOO") |
| un | u(n)h | chacun ("shah-KUNH") |
| g | zh | gentil ("zh*-TEE") |
| j | zh | je ("ZHEU") |

In general, you don't pronounce final S's or T's in French. Interestingly, you don't say final E's either, *except* (sometimes) when singing! *Fille* gets one syllable when speaking ("FEE"), but two notes when singing ("FEE-yeuh").

# Sex, Betrayal, Murder, and Other Operatic Techniques

Once you know how to navigate an opera libretto, you'll discover something shocking: The vices portrayed in opera make TV's offerings look positively sugar-coated.

From the beginning, opera producers realized what the people wanted, which is just what they want today: sex, violence, and murder without too many commercials. Of course, the problems encountered in opera are far more dramatic than those in your everyday life; after all, how often have you been impregnated by a god? (Note to Mrs. Theresa L. Bucocks of Eagar, Arizona: Don't answer that.)

So forget the *National Enquirer;* forget *Hard Copy;* when it comes to tales of vice, there's nothing like opera.

## Renaissance vice

One of the earliest opera composers, Claudio Monteverdi (1567–1643) chose a deliciously raunchy subject for his final opera, *The Coronation of Poppea.*

As the story begins, the valiant warrior Ottone returns from battle to discover that his girlfriend, Poppea, has been shacking up with Emperor Nero. Gold-digger that she is, Poppea makes Nero swear that he'll give up his wife for her (did we mention that Nero is married?) and crown her empress. Ottone pleads with Poppea to leave Nero and return to him, but she refuses. At that moment, Ottone realizes that, as much as he loves Poppea, he is simply going to have to kill her. The attempted murder is unsuccessful, however, and Poppea gets to become empress after all. We're talking about one of the first operas *ever,* and already we've got — in *one plot* — adultery, infidelity, murder, and an Anna Nicole Smith prototype.

## Vice work if you can get it

Mozart's opera music is awesome, uplifting, and sublime. But unless you know Italian, you'd never guess that they're singing about the scandalous sexual doings and undoings of one Don Giovanni (Italian for *Don Juan*), the impetuous, insatiable sex maniac. Just look at the litany of vices perpetrated by a single character within a couple of days:

- **Attempted rape:** At the very beginning of the opera — offstage, thank goodness — Don Giovanni tries to force himself on Donna Anna; as the action of the opera begins, she chases him out of the house.

- **Murder:** When Donna Anna's father comes to rescue her, Don Giovanni kills him.

- **Abandoning a woman at the altar:** Still feeling a bit rambunctious, Don G. spies a veiled, grieving woman and goes to her aid, sensing a likely date prospect. But the woman turns out to be Donna Elvira, with whom our hero is already well acquainted. In fact, she's crying because she was supposed to *marry* Don Giovanni, but he deserted her.

> ✔ **Seducing a woman on her wedding day:** Next, Don Giovanni spies a beautiful country girl, Zerlina, at a rustic celebration and concocts a plan to be alone with her. Only one minor snag: The celebration is a wedding feast, and it's Zerlina's wedding. This complication doesn't even remotely deter our hero. While momentarily diverting the unhappy groom, he manages to sweet-talk Zerlina into running away with him.

Mozart and his librettist, Lorenzo da Ponte, got away with a story like this, even in their highly moralistic time, because of two mitigating circumstances. First, Don Giovanni goes to Hell at the end (as you can hear on Track 3 of your CD). Second, everyone comes onstage afterward to say, "Look what happens when you act like that!"

This moralizing wasn't the purpose of the opera — only the excuse for it. In Mozart's time, the moralizing was a requirement so that the audience could feel really *good* about the vices it just witnessed. Sound familiar? Sure it does — it's the formula for every American adventure movie ever made. The villain gets killed in the end; that's a given. But the fun part is, you get to see him do a lot of really wicked stuff first.

But not all operas pretend to take the kind of moral stand that *Don Giovanni* does. Let's look at some that don't.

## Valhalla vice

You can't discuss opera without encountering Wagner's enormous four-opera *Ring* cycle (also known as *Der Ring der Nibelungen*). This 18-hour mini-series deserves a Mature Audience Only rating: Not only is there incredible violence in this plot, but there's surprisingly little remorse or moralizing about it.

You can read the complete stories of these operas in Chapter 12. For the purposes of our Vice Squad, though, just check this out: In *Das Rheingold* (*The Rhine Gold* — opera number one), the action of the *Ring* cycle is launched by greed. An ugly, greedy dwarf steals Rhine-river gold from the Rhine maidens and makes a ring out of it that has magical powers. Greedy Wotan, Chief of the Gods, steals the ring from the gnome. He then gives the ring to two greedy giants as ransom for a goddess they've got the hots for. The giants quarrel over the ring, and one kills the other.

*Die Walküre (The Valkyrie)*, opera number two, is about incest and murder. Separated at a young age, Wotan's twin kids, Siegmund and Sieglinde, meet again years later. Unaware that they're siblings, they fall in love. Then they *find out* that they're siblings — and have a passionate affair. Unfortunately, Sieglinde is already married. Her husband kills Siegmund in revenge. Naturally, the twins' father (Wotan, King of the Gods) kills the husband. (Now you know where the term *Godfather* came from.)

Opera number three, *Siegfried,* is about the illegitimate child of the afore-mentioned incestuous lovers, Siegmund and Sieglinde. (Wagner could have helped us keep these characters straight by at least giving their names different first syllables — but *noooooo.*) Siegfried, after growing up and learning of his messy heritage, begins by killing a giant. Then, in the true spirit of equal-opportunity slaying, he kills a dwarf.

The fourth and final episode of the *Ring* cycle is called *Götterdämmerung (Twilight of the Gods).* If you thought Siegfried was asking for it by going on a murder spree in the last opera, you're right — he promptly gets murdered himself by Hagen, *son* of the ugly dwarf who got this whole thing started by stealing that gold. The Rhine maidens kill Hagen. And Siegfried's wife immolates herself. At the very end, the gods' home of Valhalla (including Wotan and just about everyone else left alive) is consumed by fire, and a new age of humanity begins.

But you probably already guessed the ending.

And the moral? For the purposes of this chapter, the moral is that, in the *Ring* cycle, one vice leads to another, and another, and another. Morality is hardly at the center of *this* play.

## Vice-a-Roni

Some of the juiciest vices can be found in the great Romantic Italian operas, especially those of the great masters Giuseppe Verdi and Giacomo Puccini.

In Verdi's masterpiece *La Forza del Destino (The Force of Destiny),* a blood-feud keeps the bodies dropping. Alvaro starts things off by killing his girlfriend's father (not on purpose, mind you — his pistol just goes off). Later, he also kills her brother in a duel; the brother finds one last burst of energy with which to kill his sister. Practically nobody is left alive to sell the story rights to Hollywood.

Puccini delivers his share of gore in most of his operas — but especially *Tosca.* The title heroine's boyfriend is tortured in the second act at the hands of Scarpia, the villain. Scarpia then tries to force himself on Tosca, but she stabs him to death. (So much for the theory that a woman saying "no" really means "yes.")

## *The Vice-Meisters*

We've only begun to name the outrageous acts depicted on the opera stage in the pursuit of high entertainment. Oh, sure, we could talk about *Oedipus Rex,* brought to life by Russian composer Igor Stravinsky, in which the king unwittingly kills his father and marries his mother. Or Dmitri Shostakovich's *Lady Macbeth of Mtensk,* in which Katerina kills her father-in-law by lacing mushrooms with rat poison. Or one of the most popular operas of all time, Georges Bizet's *Carmen,* in which José stabs his ex-girlfriend Carmen for breaking up with him. Or even *Hansel and Gretel,* by Engelbert Humperdinck. *Hansel and Gretel* — violent? Darned right: The witch plans to eat these fine youngsters, so they bake her to death.

# *What am I, Sliced Salome?*

When it comes to vice, you just can't beat the German and Austrian operas of the early 20th century, in which some of the most graphic depictions of violence made it onto the opera stage. For a great example, check out Alban Berg's wildly dissonant, psychologically twisted opera, *Lulu.* In this virtuosic display of horror, some character gets bumped off in nearly every scene. As an added bonus, Lulu herself is ultimately killed by none other than Jack the Ripper. Hope we didn't spoil the ending for you.

But the mother-of-all-vice stories is the 1905 opera, *Salome* ("ZAHL-oh-may"), by Richard Strauss. This opera is so graphically violent, horrible, and disgusting that it was banned at the venerable Metropolitan Opera in New York for decades.

It's one of our favorites. (See Figure 2-1.)

Salome is the teenage stepdaughter of King Herod. Stepdaughter? Right, because Salome's mother killed her husband to marry King Herod. Now that Salome is becoming a woman, King Herod desires her and will do anything to get her. Salome's not interested, of course — because she has the hots for John the Baptist. Nice family, huh?

Fortunately, Salome knows how to wrap her stepfather around her little finger. When he asks her to a dance for him, she agrees on one condition: that he grant any wish she might have when she's done. Herod, who's not exactly thinking with his brain, agrees.

**Figure 2-1:**
*Salome:* Catherine Malfitano in the title role. Bryn Terfel as John the Baptist (Jochanaan), Lyric Opera of Chicago, 1996-1997 (photo: Dan Rest).

Salome proceeds to do the "Dance of the Seven Veils," the most suggestive and lascivious striptease in the history of opera. She's wearing seven veils, strategically located over various parts of her body. At certain well-defined points in the dance, she removes a veil, becoming progressively less clothed.

How far does this striptease go? Well, it depends on the singer. Very few sopranos in the world will strip totally naked in front of a live audience. (Demi Moore would probably do it, but she's an alto.) As a result, many opera productions feature instead the dance of the *eight or nine* veils, leaving a veil or two here or there on the soprano.

But we digress. What comes next outdoes even the "Dance of the Seven Veils." At the end of the dance, Herod asks Salome for her wish. And Salome replies: "Bring me the head of John the Baptist on a silver platter." When the head is brought to her, Salome begins *kissing* it; Herod immediately orders her crushed to death, to the great relief of everybody in attendance.

So there's opera for you: incest, nudity, decapitation, and murder. We've tried, but we just can't top that one.

# The Book of Virtue

Every once in a while, someone writes to the local newspaper saying, "Why don't you ever publish any *good* news? If you didn't just print the bad things, then people might not have such a negative view of society." If you recognize yourself as the author of such a letter, this sidebar is for you! Because although mortal sins drive the plots of *most* operas, Truth and Goodness drive *some*.

For example, Mozart's *The Magic Flute* is a rather confused fable about the search for Goodness and Truth, not to mention Honesty, the redemptive powers of Love, and lots of other Nouns with Capital Letters.

Beethoven spent years searching for a suitable subject for his only opera, *Fidelio.* Its plot deals with humans' inhumanity and the power of Love — all this through the most sublime music ever written. No rapes, no murders — just pure overarching Love that saves the day.

Even Richard Wagner, though holding a hallowed place in our Hall of Vice, occasionally held his own in the realm of Virtue. For example, his opera *Tannhäuser* eventually involves lessons in Love, Forgiveness, and even meeting the Pope. (It also opens with a full-blown orgy, but that's a minor detail.) And then there's *Parsifal,* about Goodness, Redemption, and the Holy Grail — an opera so sacred that Wagner called it a "Consecrational Festival Drama."

But except for these and a small handful of others, the byword of opera seems to be "No good deed goes unpunished." What can we say? Sin sells.

# Chapter 3

# The Score's the Other Thing

▶ A crash course in reading sheet music

▶ How an opera's music is put together

*W*hat's especially impressive about opera singers is the fact that, for three hours, they're not only up there acting and singing and belting out enough sound to top as many as 105 orchestra players, but they're doing all this *from memory*. That's a feat impressive enough to forgive the occasional opera-singer eccentricity (see Chapter 4).

Not only must opera singers memorize a tall stack of sheet music for each part they play, but they also must translate all its information into actual performance characteristics. They must memorize where to breathe, when to get louder, how to pronounce the words in several different languages, and much more. This chapter gives you a glimpse at the opera *score* — the book containing all the sheet music — and how it affects the opera singers and conductors who use it as their road map.

## Duets, Trios, and Other Assortments

The first thing you notice when you open up an opera score is that it's divided into sections. Most operas consist of between two and five *acts*. Furthermore, each act is usually divided into *scenes*.

But even these scenes consist of smaller sections — individual musical chunks that are labeled with the following names in the sheet music:

✔ **Recitative:** As you can read in Chapter 5, *recitative* ("ress-it-uh-TEEV") was invented by early Italian composers to advance the action in a scene. It's a talky kind of singing in which the words usually don't rhyme, and there's no real beat to the music. (Nobody walks out of an opera humming the recitative.) Recitative, on paper, looks like Figure 3-1.

**Figure 3-1:**
The talky singing called recitative.

So what's the point? Well, in a Broadway show, musical numbers alternate with dialogue (talking) scenes; in most operas, there *aren't* any talking scenes, so the big musical numbers alternate with *recitative.* These sections achieve the same purpose as dialogue: They let characters converse casually and give the audience a break between the major songs.

✓ **Aria:** Means "air," or "song." An aria is a big number — a song you'll walk around humming after the show — that enables the singer to simultaneously reveal her feelings and show off her voice. Little or no plot action takes place during an aria; the music simply expresses the emotional content of a single instant.

✓ **Arietta:** A little aria, generally short and relatively lighthearted.

✓ **Cavatina** and **cabaletta:** In *bel canto* operas (see Chapter 5), an aria is sometimes divided into two parts. The *cavatina* is slow, expressive, and melodic, allowing the singer to show off her beautiful tone. The *cabaletta* that follows is usually much faster, enabling her to display her vocal pyrotechnics. The cabaletta section usually has a high note just before the end, which the singer sustains for a long time, driving the audience into fits of screaming ecstasy.

✓ **Arioso:** This kind of song falls halfway between aria and recitative. It has more of a melody than recitative does, but it advances the action of the plot.

✓ **Duet** (or *duo* or *duetto*): An aria built for two. Two characters express their feelings, either to each other, or to the audience, or both.

✓ **Trio** (or *terzetto* or *Terzett*): An aria built for three. These characters don't necessarily have to sing to *each other,* by the way. For example, two of them may profess their love for each other while a third, peeking through the keyhole, sulks.

✓ **Quartet** (*quartetto, Quartett, or quattuor*), **Quintet** (*quintetto, Quintett, or quintette*), **Sextet** (*sestetto, Sextett, or sextuor*): Arias for four, five, or six.

✓ **Chorus** (*coro, Chor, or choeur*): A big number during which the opera chorus gets to sing, playing a happy band of villagers, for example, or a horde of victorious warriors.

## Cadenzas and other opera furniture

Near the end of some arias is the opera singer's favorite moment: the cadenza. A *cadenza* (not to be confused with *credenza,* Italian for "piece of dining room furniture") is a wild vocal fireworks display — an extended moment when the conductor stands still, the orchestra shuts up, the audience sits forward in hushed anticipation, the plot stops dead in its tracks, and the diva sings a staggeringly difficult bunch of notes, often in one long breath.

A cadenza in the sheet music appears below.

Three things scream "Cadenza!" to anyone who's looking at the score:

✔ A cadenza is usually written in little notes. The reduced size is meant to imply: "This is one suggestion," a throwback to the days when musicians were meant to *improvise* the cadenza — to make up their own notes on the spot. But in opera cadenzas, singers almost always stick to exactly what the composer wrote.

✔ If you examine the score, you can see that the orchestra isn't playing. This moment is for the singer alone.

✔ If you happen to know how to read sheet music, you'll notice that there are *way* too many beats in the cadenza measure. That's okay; it just means that the music is "out of time," that the usual law of regularly spaced foot-taps in each measure has been temporarily suspended on this special occasion.

If she does it well, an opera singer can actually create suspense and anticipation, just like a sneezer who goes, "Ah...*ah*...AH..." and makes you wait for the *"choo!"* Then, after the soloist finishes, the orchestra finally comes back in with a satisfying boom. It's great.

✔ **Finale:** The last number of the act, often involving a large group of singers.

✔ **Finale ultimo:** The *final* finale of the show, often involving a *really* large group of singers.

# *How to Read a Score*

For a crash course in understanding sheet music (the *score*), we modestly recommend this book's companion, *Classical Music For Dummies*. It walks you through the basics of music, from the simplest notes and rhythms to the structures of symphonies and sonatas — with lots of amazing tidbits and anecdotes along the way.

For now, though, here are the basics: Music is written on a timeline, called a *staff,* that you read from left to right. If several instruments are playing at once (the voice counts as one instrument), you see *several* staff timelines, running parallel across the page from left to right. All the instruments whose notes line up from top to bottom are being played simultaneously (see Figure 3-2).

**Figure 3-2:** A musical score, showing several staff timelines running simultaneously.

## *Fast and loud*

All the little markings and words written *around* the notes (see Figure 3-3) specify how loud, how fast, and *how* the notes should be played or sung.

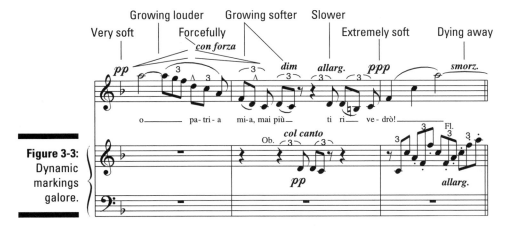

Figure 3-3: Dynamic markings galore.

Figure 3-4 shows the range of possible *dynamic* (volume level) markings you may see in the sheet music, from barely audible to deafening.

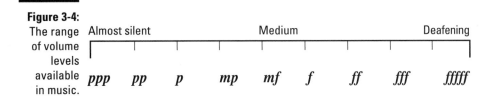

Figure 3-4: The range of volume levels available in music.

The sheet music also contains markings telling the conductor and the singer how *fast* to go. Some of the most common *tempo markings,* as they're called, are the fun-to-say Italian words shown in Figure 3-5.

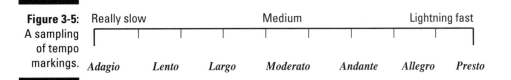

Figure 3-5: A sampling of tempo markings.

The beauty of live musical performance, of course, is that the music doesn't always snap sharply from one dynamic level to another. More often, it smoothly ebbs and flows, as emotion and energy carry the players along. Watch the VU-meter — the little volume-ometer gauge — sliding around on your stereo while an opera is playing sometime, and you'll see what we mean.

A composer can't do anything about specifying emotion and energy, but he *can* inform the players that he'd like a gradual change from soft to loud. To do so, he just writes in a long, sideways V shape between the two markings involved, like this:

That symbol, which means to get gradually louder as you play, is called a *crescendo* ("creh-SHEN-doe"). This musical term, like others you meet in this book, also has been co-opted by jealous wannabes from other art forms. In a sports article, you may read about "a crescendo of energy." In cooking magazines, you may encounter "a crescendo of flavor." We'd even wager that at least one hotel-industry newsletter out there has used the phrase "a crescendo of toiletries."

The opposite symbol, meaning "get gradually softer," is called a *decrescendo* ("day-creh-SHEN-doe") or a *diminuendo* ("dee-mee-noo-END-oe"). (We bet you can figure out where those words came from without our help.) That symbol looks like this:

Italian words meaning *gradually speeding up* and *gradually slowing down* are other popular opera-score components, by the way. The composer writes *rallentando* or *ritardando* (abbreviated *rall.* or *rit.*) for slowing down, and *accelerando* (abbreviated *accel.*) for speeding up.

Like so many music students before you, you may well ask, "What's the deal with these pretentious Italian words? Why don't people just write 'soft' or 'fast' into the score *in English?*"

Well, you've got a point. The funny thing is, that's exactly what the Italians *thought* they were doing when they dreamed up these symbols to begin with! It isn't the Italians' fault that the rest of the world picked up on their system and has used it ever since.

# How to sing the notes

The score is filled with notations that tell the singer and conductor *how* the notes are to be sung. Figure 3-6 shows some of most common markings in this category as they may appear in an opera score.

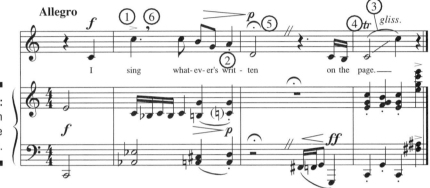

**Figure 3-6:** Common score markings.

① This little > symbol is an *accent mark*. It means that the singer should emphasize this note. You can hear Samuel Ramey sing some strong accents on Track 2 of your free CD, at 1:05.

② A *staccato* ("stah-KAHT-toe") mark means to make the note very short, to bounce right off of it. Our friend Samuel Ramey sings plenty of staccato notes through the first half of his aria on Track 2 of the CD.

③ A *slur* (the long, curved line above the notes), on the other hand, tells the singer to run the notes together, gliding smoothly from one to the next — the opposite of staccato notes, if you think about it. Listen to Maria Callas sing a dazzlingly fast passage of slurred notes on Track 4 of the CD, at 0:13.

④ The letters *tr.* tell the singer to *trill* this note — to rapidly alternate between this note and the one above it.

⑤ The birds-eye marking, called a *fermata* ("fair-MAH-ta"), means to stop the music and stay on the note you're on. The conductor stops conducting, the singer holds the note, and the orchestra waits — usually until the singer is good and ready to proceed. (One of our favorite music-geek T-shirts says, "I'm a fermata. Hold me.") Maria Callas and Tito Gobbi sing a hair-raising fermata together at 4:52 on Track 4 of the CD. Nicolai Gedda sings one of his own on Track 7, at 3:35. And Damon Evans has a veritable fermata-fest on Track 13, at 1:49 — he sings *three* fermatas in a row!

⑥ If you see a big, black comma floating in the sheet music, you may think, at first, that the typesetting machine was on the fritz. Actually, though, this comma is called a *breath mark,* and it's the composer's friendly suggestion that the singer breathe at that moment — for effect, perhaps, or to make the words clearer, or because a difficult section is coming up and otherwise she's gonna pass out.

And you thought all she had to do was open her mouth!

# Chapter 4

# Opera Singers and Their Equipment

. . . . . . . . . . . . . . . . . . . . . . . . . . . . . . . . . . . . . . . . . . . . . . . . . . . . . .

## In This Chapter

▶ The opera singer's appetite (for food and otherwise)

▶ The range of opera voices

▶ The effort to train "the voice"

▶ The good, the bad, and the ugly: opera's inside story

. . . . . . . . . . . . . . . . . . . . . . . . . . . . . . . . . . . . . . . . . . . . . . . . . . . . . .

*W*hen Hollywood moguls cast their latest extravaganza, they rely on certain casting conventions: The good guys have a particular look that's recognizably different from that of the bad guys. Although they *might* cast John Malkovich as the boy next door, he's probably not their first choice.

Opera has its own typecasting conventions — as you may have guessed if you've ever attended an opera in which a 50-year-old, 180-pound woman portrays the waiflike teenage heroine. But whereas movies generally rely on *physical* types, operas rely on *vocal* types. In opera, the important thing is that the good guys *sound* different from the bad guys. Although, in an ideal world, a Brad Pitt could sound like a Pavarotti, with a few rare exceptions, this isn't the case.

But if a singer's voice sends you into fits of ecstasy, why complain? Considering how rarely beauty and brains are allied in any one individual, it's no surprise that someone who sings like a god rarely looks like one. Orpheus or Adonis — take your pick.

## But Do They Have to Be So Big?

Well, yes and no. Operatic roles are written for big voices capable of being heard, without microphones, over a full orchestra; and big voices often come in big packages. A German shepherd's bark is bigger than a Chihuahua's, and a human bark works the same way.

But get one thing straight: *Big* doesn't necessarily mean *fat.* Some great Wagnerian sopranos we can name, such as Birgit Nilsson, were built like tanks, but that body size came from other factors: big bones, toned muscles, and an absolutely enormous chest cavity — all the better for producing a prodigious sound.

Still, we must admit that a fair number of opera singers *are* fat. Why? Well, a professional opera voice often requires special care and feeding. People drawn to the singing profession tend to possess great appetites, both gustatory and otherwise.

On the subject of *otherwise:* The opera world is rife with stories of singers' immense sexual appetites, including one famous soprano who was said to require servicing between acts to sing her best. (This clause wasn't exactly in her contract, but opera houses of her day spared no expense in ensuring the best possible performances.) You can read some juicy stories in "Diva Tales" at the end of this chapter.

We can only guess why singers possess larger-than-usual, er, appetites; maybe it's because they spend their lives playing larger-than-life characters.

# Sopranos, Tenors, and Other Freaks of Nature

In the opera world, human voices come in six basic varieties, from highest to lowest: *soprano, mezzo-soprano, contralto, tenor, baritone,* and *bass.* Women and children are sopranos, mezzo-sopranos, and contraltos; most men are tenors, baritones, and basses.

Opera aficionados show off by using the German word *Fach* (pronounced "FAHkh," meaning compartment or pigeon-hole) to refer to these four voice types. If you want to look knowledgeable about opera, try to get a handle on the *Fach* concept. Don't worry, though — you're granted a wide margin of error. Opera fans' favorite topic of discussion seems to be whether Soprano X is really a soprano at all, or whether she's actually a mezzo trying to gain higher fees. Throw these terms around, and you'll see how quickly opera fans respect you.

All voices, regardless of their *Fach,* are further defined by their *color.* Opera voices come in two colors: *lyric* and *dramatic.* Lyric voices sound sweet and tend to be easier on the ears than their dramatic counterparts. Dramatic voices, however, have a steely edge that helps them cut through a large orchestra more easily than their sweet-voiced counterparts. You wouldn't hear an opera singer described as a "sweet-voiced dramatic tenor" or a "steely-toned lyric soprano" any more than you'd hear about a thin sumo wrestler; they don't exist.

Opera composers use these two voice colors to their full advantage. When depicting a villain, a composer generally writes for a *dramatic* voice, saving the *lyric* voices for characters who are pure of spirit. The composer may not actually specify "lyric voice" or "dramatic voice" in the sheet music, but he doesn't have to; if the singer has to compete with a full orchestra, it's understood that the composer wants to hear a dramatic voice in the role. Any singer with a lyric voice who tries to tackle a dramatic voice role is tempting both vocal strain and audience disapproval, two things that any singer with a bank account hopes to avoid.

# Just the Fachs, Ma'am

We hate to break this to you, but there are many more voice types than the six we just mentioned. Each category contains a bunch of *sub*categories. This section describes the most common ones, from highest voice to lowest.

## Sopranos

Sopranos are the highest-paid female singers. Why? First, they get the most sympathetic roles. But second, and more important, they sing the highest notes — and those are the notes that audiences pay to hear.

- *Coloratura sopranos* are the tweety-birds of the musical aviary. Their voices sound like flutes: light, pure, and capable of great agility way up high. (In fact, coloratura *arias,* or songs, are often written as duets with a flute, where one imitates the other.) The most famous coloratura roles are Lucia di Lammermoor (in Donizetti's opera of the same name) and the Queen of the Night (from Mozart's *The Magic Flute*). The most famous coloratura singers in recent decades were Lily Pons, Joan Sutherland, and Beverly Sills.

- *Lyric sopranos* are the white bread of sopranos; the majority of sopranos around the world, by far, fit into this category. Whenever a composer wants to write for a sweet goody-two-shoes — a virginal, pretty, young thing — she's likely to have a lyric soprano voice: not so high as to be grating, not so low as to be growly. Many of the best-loved operatic roles have been written for lyric sopranos, including Mimì (in *La Bohème*), Violetta (in *La Traviata*), and Marguerite (in Gounod's *Faust*), plus most of Mozart's leading ladies.

    In past decades, the most famous lyric sopranos included Eleanor Steber and Mirella Freni. One of the greatest lyric sopranos today is young and American: Renée Fleming. Catch her performances where you can.

✔ *Soubrettes* are either cutie-pies or streetwise servant girls. Mozart lavished great love on the latter characters in the roles of Susanna (*The Marriage of Figaro*), Despina (*Così fan tutte*), and Zerlina (*Don Giovanni*). Some current famous soubrettes are Dawn Upshaw and Kathleen Battle.

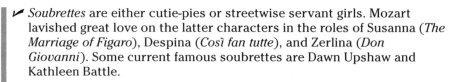

✔ *Spinto sopranos* are named after the Italian word *spingere,* meaning "to push." These voices aren't really pushed, but they do naturally possess more power than lyric sopranos. Spinto characters are generally long-suffering, victimized women in opera — the grand roles, the meat of the operatic repertoire, the province of the divas. The most famous spinto parts are Puccini's Madame Butterfly, Manon Lescaut, and Tosca (featured in Track 8 on the free CD that comes with this book); Verdi's Aïda; and the two Leonoras (from *Il Trovatore* and *La Forza del Destino*).

Among the legendary spinto sopranos of this century: Rosa Ponselle, Renata Tebaldi, and Leontyne Price. Ponselle, Callas, and Price were all U.S. born — must be something in the water.

✔ *German dramatic sopranos* are the horns-and-helmet ladies, the real heavy-hitters of the opera world. A German dramatic soprano doesn't actually have to *be* German, but she specializes in singing German *roles,* specifically those by Wagner and the title roles in Richard Strauss's two operas about female nut cases, *Elektra* and *Salome.* Her voice must be able to cut through a huge orchestra; therefore, it must be both warm and metallic in color and immensely powerful. Many a singer has ruined her voice trying to tackle roles like these.

Surprisingly, the women who actually sing these roles are usually the most gentle of all the sopranos in real life, maybe because they know that nobody's going to mess with them. The two great German dramatic sopranos of recent decades are Kirsten Flagstad and Birgit Nilsson — neither one of them was German, by the way.

## Mezzo-sopranos

The word *mezzo* ("MET-soe") means "half" in Italian. Mezzo-sopranos are so named because they earn about half as much money as sopranos do. (Either that, or because their vocal range falls about halfway between soprano and contralto.) They earn less because they can't sing high notes as effortlessly — so much for political correctness. But mezzos get their revenge by playing some of the spiciest, juiciest roles ever dreamed up for the stage.

Mezzos come in two varieties: dramatic and lyric. These women's opera roles can be summarized as tramps, vamps, witches, and britches (the last of these referring to the odd opera practice of assigning the roles of adolescent boys to the voices of obviously post-adolescent women).

- *Dramatic* mezzos play the vamps and tramps (such as Delilah in Saint-Saëns' *Samson and Delilah,* and perhaps the greatest mezzo role of all, Bizet's *Carmen*), witches (such as Azucena from Verdi's *Il Trovatore,* who's really a withered old Gypsy rather than a bona-fide witch, but let's not quibble), and other wicked female roles (like Eboli in Verdi's *Don Carlo* and Amneris in *Aïda*). Most dramatic mezzo roles are the foils for the ever-pure sopranos — the evil characters that cause the sopranos all the suffering. These characters are often supposed to look like hags, fortunately for a few of the mezzos who play them (ahem).

Interestingly, composers often ask a dramatic mezzo to sing just as high as a soprano does. But whereas these notes are effortless for the sweet, well-bred soprano, they cause the evil mezzo character to strain at the upper edges of her range — thereby sounding appropriately wild and out of control.

In the 1950s, Ebe Stignani led the mezzo field, followed later by Giulietta Simionato, Fiorenza Cossoto, Grace Bumby, and in our time, Delorah Zajic.

- *Lyric* mezzo soprano singers, on the other hand, often tend to obsess about their waistlines, because they're supposed to play adolescent boys! In opera, these parts are known as *trouser roles,* and the two foremost examples are Cherubino in Mozart's *The Marriage of Figaro* and Octavian in Richard Strauss's *Der Rosenkavalier.*

Then there are the *female* lyric mezzo roles — and some of them are gorgeous. Rossini wrote two of his greatest roles, full of fast notes, for lyric mezzo: Rosina in *The Barber of Seville* and Angelina in *La Cenerentola* (Italian for *Cinderella,* "chen-e-REN-toe-la"). An American, Frederica von Stade, has been one of the world's leading lyric mezzo-sopranos since the early 1970s, and she shows no signs of slowing down.

## Contraltos and assorted combos

*Contraltos* are the lowest (and by far the rarest) female voice category; on their lowest notes, they sound almost like guys. Although usually assigned to play maids, mothers, and grandmothers, contraltos occasionally get deliciously juicy roles: Ulrica in Verdi's *Un ballo in maschera* (another witch), the Goddess Erda in Wagner's *Ring* cycle, and the ever-faithful wife Lucretia in Britten's *The Rape of Lucretia.*

In addition, contraltos are often assigned the roles originally written for *castrati* — castrated boys (described in Chapter 5) — when they're not claimed by the countertenors (see the next section). The greatest contraltos of this century have included Ernestine Schumann-Heink, Marian Anderson, and Kathleen Ferrier.

Quite a few singers defy categorization, by the way, and are therefore *Fach*less (though not feckless). Christa Ludwig, Régine Crespin, and Victoria de los Angeles (whom you can hear on Track 12 of your CD) are just a few great singers who performed both soprano and mezzo roles with great success in recent decades. Marilyn Horne has been equally successful in both mezzo and contralto roles. And in our own time, Jessye Norman wraps her glorious voice around whatever repertoire she deems appropriate.

But for breaking the rules and moving freely from one vocal category to another, no one compares with the late Maria Callas. Coloraturo soprano, dramatic, lyric, even mezzo-soprano (in her late years) — she sang 'em all. Many critics thought that she'd damage her voice by stretching it this way, and they were right. Although her emotional ups and downs, as well as her considerable and rapid weight loss, seem to have contributed to her long vocal decline (her prime lasted barely ten years), it's clear that her wish to take on roles for virtually every voice part also created major difficulties. At the end — in her ill-advised 1973 comeback — it was tragic to hear that she couldn't comfortably manage any of the music in which she'd once reigned supreme.

## *Tenors*

*Tenors* compete with sopranos when it comes to fees and decibels. Nothing matches the visceral thrill of a tenor's full-throated high B-flat — and he knows it. That's what the audience shells out the big bucks for!

Tenors, too, come in different flavors:

- ✔ *Lyric tenors* sing some Mozart roles, as well as some choice picks from the French repertoire (such as the title characters in Gounod's *Faust* and Massenet's *Werther*) and many standard Italian opera roles (including Edgardo in *Lucia di Lammermoor,* Alfredo in *La Traviata,* and Rodolfo in *La Bohème,* featured on Track 7 of this book's CD). These characters are generally likable, vulnerable men who love too much; if they didn't have an opera to sing in, they'd be showing up on the Sally Jessy Raphael show.

  Luciano Pavarotti is truly — how shall we put this? — the biggest lyric tenor around. (His glorious voice has made him the most famous opera singer of *any* kind.) Others include John McCormack, Beniamino Gigli, and Fritz Wunderlich.

- ✔ *Spinto tenors* sing the big, juicy roles (Manrico in *Il Trovatore,* Radames in *Aïda,* Cavaradossi in *Tosca,* Canio in Leoncavallo's *I Pagliacci,* and Don José in *Carmen*), plus some parts written for lyric tenors. A spinto tenor's characters tend to be more heroic than those of a lyric tenor, while retaining their lack of moderation in the love department. Some legendary spinto tenors of this century are Enrico Caruso, Franco Corelli, Richard Tucker, Carlo Bergonzi, and Plácido Domingo (see Figure 4-1). Their voices could make a stone weep.

**Figure 4-1:** *Carmen:* Plácido Domingo as Don José, Alicia Nafé in the title role, Lyric Opera of Chicago, 1984. (Photo: Tony Romano)

✔ The Germans have their own dramatic type. The *Heldentenor* ( pronounced "HELL-den tay-NOR") is the male counterpart to the German dramatic soprano, singing primarily Wagnerian roles. This is the guy who has to woo the helmet-and-horns soprano; no mean feat, you'll admit. Lauritz Melchior and Jon Vickers dominated their eras in the Heldentenor department, and at this writing we're still waiting for a successor to show up.

✔ Hovering above all the rest are the *countertenors,* a different category altogether. Countertenors are men who train their *falsetto* voices rather than their lower range. If you're a guy, you know what falsetto is: It's when you sing way up high, above the point where your voice cracks, in that light, kind-of-girlish voice. The Monty Python comedians used their falsetto voice when they played women. But American David Daniels proves that countertenor voices can sound macho with the best of them!

Countertenors specialize in parts originally written for *castrati* (see Chapter 5 for more on *that* fascinating topic) — when they can yank such parts away from the contraltos.

## Baritones

*Baritones* are men with voices in the medium range. If you sang in high school choir and had neither high nor low notes, you were probably called a baritone (among other things).

The CD that comes with this book has some marvelous examples of the baritone voice. Listen especially to the beautiful voice of Tito Gobbi in Rossini's *The Barber of Seville* (Track 4) and Verdi's *A Masked Ball* (Track 5).

The baritone voice has its own subcategories, too:

- The baritone has its own subcategories. One of these is the sweet-voiced *lyric baritone.* Lyric baritones tend to play the all-around fun-guy roles: the ringleader (Marcello in *La Bohème*), the guy who sticks his tongue out at the world (Mercutio in *Roméo et Juliette*), the wise-guy schemer (Malatesta in *Don Pasquale,* Figaro in *The Barber of Seville,* and Dandini in *La Cenerentola*), or the comic relief (Guglielmo in *Così fan tutte* and Papageno in *The Magic Flute*).

- *Italian dramatic baritones* are harder to find, and greatly prized by opera producers. Also known as *Verdi baritones,* they sing such great villainous Verdi parts as Di Luna in *Il Trovatore* and the title role in *Rigoletto,* as well as Tonio in Leoncavallo's *I Pagliacci* and Scarpia in Puccini's *Tosca,* one of the greatest villains of all time. In the world of Italian dramatic baritones, the standard set by Titta Ruffo has never been surpassed.

  German dramatic baritones, sometimes called *Heldenbaritones,* are something else altogether. The defining role for this Fach is Wotan, King of the Gods, in Wagner's *Ring* cycle. Germany's Hans Hotter and, more recently, James Morris lead the field in godliness.

- *Bass-baritones* are the he-men of the opera world, combining the ringing quality of the baritone with the depth of the bass. Bass-baritone roles avoid the extremes of range, singing in the most beautiful central part of the voice. Mozart composed two of his most sublime creations for the bass-baritone: the guy with the greatest excess of testosterone known to man, Don Giovanni (in the opera named for him), and the guy you'd most like to have around the house, Figaro (in *The Marriage of Figaro*). A Welshman, Bryn Terfel, is the bass-baritone of choice today.

## Basses

*Basses* are the lowest of them all. By definition, they sing the lowest notes that the human voice can reach. Their strong, booming voices seem to resonate from the depths of some enormous cavern.

Basses often play priests or fathers, but they occasionally get star turns as the Devil (in Boito's *Mefistofele* and Gounod's *Faust*) or reigning potentates (King Philip in Verdi's *Don Carlo* and the title role in *Boris Godunov*). The great Russian bass Fyodor Chaliapin set the standard at the turn of the century, followed by Boris Christoff, Alexander Kipnis, and Nicolai Ghiaurov. There's also the Italian *basso profondo* (deep bass), as well as the *basso cantante* ("singing bass," suited for Verdi roles and bel canto operas), and what Germans call *schwarzer baß* ("black bass," for portraying old men and sometimes villains, singing in German or Russian).

If you've read and understood this entire section (or if you're a good faker), you should be able to wow 'em at your next cocktail party. It must feel pretty good to know that you've got your *Fachs* straight.

# Getting at "the Voice"

Suppose that you're just crazy enough to consider becoming an opera singer. How do you acquire a big voice in the first place?

Much of it comes from genes. It really helps if you're born with great pipes. Most of today's vocal superstars have great natural ability — Luciano Pavarotti more than most.

But potential isn't enough; to develop your voice, you have to *get at it* somehow. And that's where the real challenge lies. After all, a voice is the only musical instrument that can't be seen or touched. Maybe that's why some singers and voice teachers never speak of "my voice" or "your voice." It's always "*the* voice," as if it were an alien creature lurking within the body. "It's an unruly voice," a singer might say. "Untamed and wild." Or: "It's a mischievous voice. Just yesterday it stole my lip gloss and wouldn't give it back."

Because there's nothing to see or touch, singers need to be creative and resourceful in order to train their voices — and this is where teachers come in. Effective voice teachers know how to engage their students' imagination. To that end, they are always giving their students different concepts to think of. "Imagine that you're placing the voice in the mask," they might say. "Sing behind the teeth. Now float the voice up to the top of your range." Of course, these same words conjure up different images for different people (and freak others out completely), so voice teachers need to be able to explain the same thing in plenty of different ways.

One concept that all singers understand, however, is *breath control*. This is the technique — some may say the art — of using your breath efficiently as you sing a long melodic line (and not wasting it all at the beginning of the phrase) so that you don't run out of wind before the high E-flat.

For an example of breath control, try saying the whole last sentence in one breath. Now try *singing* it, at the top of your lungs, to the tune of "The Girl from Ipanema."

See what we mean? No wonder some singers say that breath control is 90 percent of singing technique.

## Your two secret voices

Anyone who's ever taken voice lessons knows another important pair of opera-singer terms: *chest voice* and *head voice.* Want to hear the difference?

We know that you sing in the shower. (We've heard it, and frankly, it could use a little work.) Next time you head off to the shower, try this little experiment:

Open your mouth wide and get ready to yell "Hey!" Make sure that you don't get a mouthful of water. Now start to holler, like this:

He - e - e -

    e - e - e - e-

       e - e - e - e-

          e - e - e - e-

             -eyyyy!

As you do, put your hand over your chest. You'll feel it vibrating. You're now using your chest voice. Do the same thing staying on one pitch (or note), like this — "He-e-e-e-e-e-e-e-e-e-e-eyyy!!!!" — and you're *singing* with *chest voice,* which most people consider their normal voice. Pop and rock singers use chest voice all the time; they're basically shouting on pitch.

Broadway star Ethel Merman was one of the prime exponents of chest voice. When she belted out "There's No Business Like Show Business," she used 100 percent chest voice. Opera singers learn how to modulate the sound so that it's not quite so raucous, but the principle is the same.

Now to find your *head voice.* Back into the shower with you.

Put your hand over your chest and get ready to holler "Hey!" again. Now go ahead and yell; but this time, make your voice go up and up and up, like this:

             eyyyy!

          e - e - e - e-

       e - e - e - e-

    e - e - e - e-

He - e - e -

At a certain point, you'll probably feel or hear a "break" in your voice — a point where the quality changes, usually becoming lighter-sounding. Around the same time, the vibration in your chest disappears. Now you're using your *head voice.*

If your head voice sounds weaker than your chest voice, you're not alone. But opera singers are capable of incredible projection with their head voice. They use the bones and cavities of the head and face (really!) as speakers, giving great carrying power to the sound. As a result, an opera singer can send her high notes to the back of a 4,000-seat hall.

Because chest voice and head voice sound so different, moving smoothly between them is a singer's greatest challenge. Great singers can do it effortlessly — you don't even hear the shift. In fact, this ability is a requirement for all trained opera singers.

# It's Not Easy Being a Prima Donna

With few exceptions, great singers don't simply roll out of bed and sing like angels. They adhere to a strict training regimen that gets their voices (if not their bodies) in top form.

On important rehearsal or performance days, a singer focuses all her activities on her performance — arranging everything in order to peak for those few hours. She gets plenty of sleep, avoids certain foods (generally dairy and all acidic foods), and dodges drafts and temperature changes (keeping in mind that a *sick* singer is an *unemployed* singer).

Unlike a gymnast, who peaks in her early teens, a singer peaks much later (from the late 20s for smaller voices to the late 40s for larger voices) and has to keep up this obsessive behavior day in, day out, year after year. No wonder they're all nuts.

# Diva Tales

Opera singers are the stuff that legends are made of. They epitomize the phrase "larger than life." Their fans expect no less.

As a result, opera companies deal with some interesting predicaments that don't come up in other professional situations. At rehearsals for a major U.S. opera house, we watched the prima donna refuse to stand where the director asked her to. Instead of questioning his judgment, the diva — an American — affected the most artificial British accent, shrieked "I *cahn't!* I *CAHN'T!*", burst into sobs, and collapsed into a crumpled heap on the floor. (Imagine if your secretary did that every time you asked for the Wite-Out.)

To some extent, this outrageous behavior is the result of the super-strict regimen described in the preceding section. To another extent, it's a natural outgrowth of the operatic art, full of high drama and overblown emotions. But *sometimes,* it's a shameless, calculated demand for attention.

It's always been that way. In centuries past, singers knew that they had to do something outrageous in order to become legends. They'd do anything for publicity — make any demands — if they thought that it would guarantee them an enduring place in the operatic pantheon.

One of the earliest examples was Francesca Cuzzoni, the notorious soprano who refused to sing an aria from Handel's *Ottone* — even though her accompanist and conductor was Handel himself. Unfortunately for Cuzzoni, Handel was an even bigger prima donna than she was — and his reaction was to hang her out the window until she agreed. (If a composer tried that today, he'd be sued for every dollar he's worth — all 50 of them.)

Musicians sometimes tell the story of the famous tenor, on tour in Mexico, who was kidnapped by bandits. They turned out to be opera lovers, though, and they promised to let him go if he could *prove* that he was an opera singer. They asked him to sing for them. "What?" he scoffed. "Sing in a slovenly place like this? Before swine like you? With no costumes, makeup, or lighting? No exalted audience, no critics, *no money?* Absolutely not!" The kidnappers let him go. He was an opera singer, all right.

## Nellie Melba

If you hang around the opera world long enough, it won't be long before you hear the name Nellie Melba. This lady, shown in Figure 4-2, had one of the most beautiful voices of the golden age of opera, around the turn of the century. But along with her voice came the personality of a pit bull.

**Figure 4-2:**
Nellie
Melba, one
of history's
notorious
opera
singers.

Melba (as opera fans call her — for some reason we can't fathom, they never use first names) was born Helen Porter Mitchell, and she adopted the name of her native Melbourne, Australia, for her stage name. She became an absolute sensation, as famous in her day as Madonna is in ours. Peach melba and melba toast are named after her — that's how famous she was.

Melba, however, could have no rivals. Onstage, she was known to butt in on other sopranos' arias, interrupting their high notes and grabbing the spotlight for herself. In at least one case, she caused the other singer to run screaming from the stage (forcing the cancellation of the opera) and offered her own song recital in its place.

Tenor John McCormack had the misfortune to make his London debut in a production in which Melba was singing. At curtain-call time, he started to go onstage with her to take a bow — but she violently thrust him back. "In this opera house," she said, "nobody takes a bow with Nellie Melba."

# Callas and Tebaldi: dueling sopranos

But if you remember the names of only two divas, we'd like to suggest Maria Callas and Renata Tebaldi. They are the names you're most likely to hear at cocktail parties and opera gatherings worldwide.

Actually, you usually hear these singers mentioned by last name only: Callas and Tebaldi. The names are legendary, spoken in awed, hushed tones.

Opera fans at the middle of this century fell neatly into two camps: pro-Callas and anti-Callas. Both camps were rabid. Her supporters praised her natural acting ability, incredible sense of high drama, vivid characterizations, and headlong, spontaneous portrayal of opera's most tragic characters. Maria Callas sang at a time when singers were not expected to act well, but simply to sound nice. Her mission was to change all that. She focused on expression, both in her acting and in her voice. And indeed, when you listen to her voice (on Track 4 of the accompanying CD) you can hear a warm, vibrant, passionate, red-blooded human being behind it.

Callas's detractors couldn't fault her acting — but they hated her vocal quality. Instead, they worshipped the cool, gorgeous tone of Renata Tebaldi, her greatest rival. According to Callas fans, of course, Tebaldi acted like a lump. To this day, the Callas-Tebaldi feud is carried out by their fans and their fans' fans.

# Blood feuds

We can guess that feuds like this one, and the comparisons that spark them, are the reason for much of the outrageous behavior of many opera singers of the past.

Adelina Patti, known in her time as the Queen of Song, was known to sabotage her rivals on the stage. Once she stared at another soprano in mock horror during a performance. "What's wrong?" whispered the other. "Your right false eyebrow has come off!" Patti cried. The other soprano turned her back to the audience and ripped off her false left eyebrow, to match. But there had been nothing wrong with the *right* eyebrow, and she went through the performance with a lopsided face.

We know of many cases when a singer stipulated no specific fee — as long as it was higher than what the *other* singers were getting. In fact, there's a great story of a particular tenor who, upon signing a contract with one of the world's finest opera houses, demanded a fee of $1 more than the soprano got. After the opera, he received a check for $1. The soprano had agreed to donate her services.

Francesca Cuzzoni, whom we already mentioned, was less subtle. She physically attacked her rival onstage, trying to beat her up. Nobody said that opera was going to be pretty.

## Nice guys do sing opera

Not all opera stars are mean people; the opera world has its share of wonderful, sweet singers who also happen to be amazingly talented. Some get to be legends.

One was Enrico Caruso (shown in Figure 4-3), blessed with the most beautiful tenor voice anyone could hope to hear. It was smooth and lush, but capable of resounding power. When Puccini first heard him sing *La Bohème*, he remarked, "Who sent you to me? God?"

**Figure 4-3:** Enrico Caruso: masterful tenor, king of the Metropolitan Opera, and all-around nice guy.

On top of all that, Caruso was a nice guy, modest and self-effacing. Once he met John McCormack, the tenor whom Nellie Melba had thrust off the stage. "How's the world's greatest tenor doing?" McCormack asked him. Caruso's response: "Since when have you become a baritone?"

Caruso even went so far as to lend his voice to a colleague in a moment of need. The other singer, a bass, had lost his voice at the end of *La Bohème,* just before his big moment. Seeing the panic in the bass's eyes, Caruso grabbed him as if to hug him, turned so that they both faced away from the audience, and sang the part for him. Nobody except the conductor figured it out.

If there's anything we can say about *all* opera singers, however, it's that they must be prepared for the spotlight. By the nature of their profession, they wind up being the center of attention, onstage and off.

So we can forgive them if they sometimes behave badly. After all, they're just showing their stuff — and making opera all the more entertaining for people like us.

# Part II
# The Story of Opera

The 5th Wave    By Rich Tennant

"Swashbuckling heroism, doomed obsessive love, and the bitter wages of sin. My word, Harold — it's the story of your life!"

## In this part . . .

**W**e know what you're thinking: "Gadzooks, I used to think that *opera* was boring — opera *history* must be boring times ten."

Turns out, however, that the annals of opera aren't dull in the least; in fact, they're nearly as full of sex, scandal, and sensation as operas themselves. Taking a ride through the last few centuries will help you understand opera rituals that survive to this day; introduce you to the weird and wonderful guys who composed the great operas; and make you glad that you live in the age of CD players.

# Chapter 5

# A Little Greece, a Little Italy

. . . . . . . . . . . . . . . . . . . . . . . . . . . . . . . . . . . . . . . . . . . . . . .

### In This Chapter

▶ It all began with the Greeks

▶ Medieval Bible stories

▶ Meet Rossini, Donizetti, Bellini, Verdi, Puccini, and friends

. . . . . . . . . . . . . . . . . . . . . . . . . . . . . . . . . . . . . . . . . . . . . . .

*O*f the world's many countries and cultures, only a handful made an impression on the world opera market: Italy, France, Germany, Austria, and Russia, with occasional help from other countries. Most of the world's operas (and operatic techniques), by far, came from Europe — and of those, the vast majority came from Italy, the honest-to-gosh birthplace of classical operas.

But if you *really* want to find the beginnings of opera, you have to dig farther back into the attic-boxes of time — all the way back to ancient Greece.

## The Grecian Formula

If you ask the man on the street to name the three greatest contributions of ancient Greece to humankind, he'll probably say democracy, philosophy, and feta cheese. He'd probably be completely unaware that the Greeks also dreamed up the precursor to opera, thousands of years ago.

Let us take you back to one of these earliest musical theater performances. Close your eyes and picture yourself in an ancient Greek amphitheater.

Why are you still reading? Oh, r-i-i-i-ight: You're too *sophisticated* to actually close your eyes, is that it?

# Pre-History: the Ancient Greeks

Anyway, you're sitting in an outdoor amphitheater watching a live performance of one of your favorite religious stories (today, we call them myths; but at the time, they were gospel). The actors are depicting some hideous tale of Zeus's retribution on one hero or another. Along the way, a choir occasionally chimes in with a song or two, in which the words comment on the story in progress. "Oh, foolish man!" they're singing. "You should never have ticked off the Almighty God of All Universes! Now you're gonna go through the rest of your life mooing!"

You applaud. You throw money. You go home. Two thousand years pass.

# The Battle between Good and Medieval

Okay, now you're in Europe during the 10th century. You're a monk — a monk with a mission. Your job is to spread the message of Christianity, the hot new religion sweeping the land. You have a brainstorm: "Hey, didn't the ancient Greeks use some kind of musical plays in their religious services? Why, we could do that, too!"

And that's just what happened. To break up the monotony of long ceremonies, these clever Europeans started writing little *Bible* opera-ettes, complete with costumes, sets, and, of course, singing. These medieval church shows were a spectacular hit.

# The Renaissance Men

Musicals had become a standard part of the Italian entertainment scene, although shows were kept short and snappy. *Straight plays* (that is, plays without music) often featured some musical entertainment during the intermissions. For example, in 1539, when Duke Cosimo de Medici married Eleonora of Toledo, he commissioned a straight play to entertain their guests. To fill the gaps between acts, he had a buddy named Francesco Corteccia compose some madrigals. They were sung, complete with an orchestra, to the presumable delight of his Italian guests eating their Italian ices.

These tiny between-act shows were cleverly called *interludes* (or *intermedi* in Italian). They had gags, clowning, and lotsa laughs — and they were the first musical shows that you'd recognize as the ancestors of today's opera.

As the art form developed, the composers of these musicalettes drove themselves crazy trying to imagine what those famous Greek musicals were *like* — and they had precious little to go on. About all they knew was that these early entertainments involved music, dancing, and a Greek chorus standing around and singing to explain the plot.

## Recitative and the instant Camerata

To try to re-create the glories of the lost Greek art, a particular clump of composer friends, in 1590, started meeting at the house of a wealthy Florence patron, Count Bardi. They called themselves the Florentine Camerata, and they were determined to hammer out how musical dramas should be performed.

One aspect of the existing musical practice especially bugged them: the *madrigal* ("MAD-drig-gull"), the most popular musical form of that day. In a madrigal, at least three different voices sing together in elaborate *counterpoint,* usually without accompaniment. In those days, families or groups of friends gathered together to perform these madrigals, each person taking a different vocal line and elbowing each other when they hit wrong notes.

But with all these different lines — each containing different words — being sung simultaneously in interwoven melodies, it was tough for the audience to catch the lyrics.

To solve the problem, the Florentine Camerata Club came up with a brilliant solution. "Hey, I've got it," someone said in Italian. "Instead of everyone singing counterpoint melodies, which we all agree are distracting" — and here there were murmurs of assent — "why don't we have the important parts of the plot sung as *recitative*?" Murmurs of excitement. Raised eyebrows. Then a timid voice from the back said, "What's that?"

"It's pronounced 'ress-it-uh-TEEV.' In recitative, just a few instruments of the orchestra play a simple chord and *hold* it. Meanwhile, *one* singer, alone, *chants* the words of the poem, in any rhythm he wants, with a very simple melodic line. That way, there's no *way* the audience will miss these important words!"

Euphoria. Cheers. The other Camerata Club members agreed that *singing* the important lines of the poem or lyrics was even better than *speaking* them, because the music seemed to heighten the emotion and drama of the moment. Thus was born an incredibly important opera technique that's with us to this day. You'll hear a lot of recitative — and a lot about it.

# *Claudio to the rescue*

Despite the clever experiments of the Camerata Club, the world waited for somebody to turn their theories into glorious, living, onstage reality. Enter Claudio Monteverdi (1567–1643), the Great-Granddaddy of Opera.

By the time his composing career was in full swing (in the early 1600s), what musical theater *wasn't* lacking was spectacle. If you thought that the flying chandelier in Broadway's *Phantom of the Opera* was a big deal, you should have seen the sets on the Italian stage: Plays and musicals of the day had movable scenery pieces, smoke machines, and even roof-mounted harness rigs that made actors fly around the stage. The sets were amazingly painted, too, by such masters as Brunelleschi, a brilliant artist (not to be confused with *Bruschetta,* a brilliant hors d'oeuvre).

But dazzling sets don't make dazzling operas. That was Claudio's job. By the time he was 39, he was making a solid name for himself as the man who could tell great stories with great songs, incorporating the old Camerata Club's theories and making them work. One of his most impressive, and still remembered, shows is *Orfeo.*

Now, composing an opera based on the Greek myth of *Orpheus* was nothing new. In fact, almost *all* Renaissance plays and operas used Greek myths as their plots, and *Orpheus* was the most popular of them all. Practically every composer alive wrote an opera about *Orpheus,* sometimes more than once.

Here's an *Orpheus* synopsis for the mythology impaired: Boy meets girl. Girl dies. Boy wants to go down to Hades, Land of the Dead, to get her back. Gods cut boy a break, and approve his highly irregular plan, on one condition: that he, Orpheus, *not look back* as he leads his true love back up to earth. But halfway home, like an idiot, he turns back to look at her — just in time to watch her fall all the way back to Hades, shrieking. Boy loses girl.

Anyway, Claudio Monteverdi's version of *Orpheus* (called *Orfeo* in Italian) became instantly famous for numerous reasons. First, he had a huge orchestra on hand. Second, he used that orchestra's various sounds in powerful and new ways, skillfully evoking various moods and places. Third, the dance music was great. And fourth, the songs themselves were emotionally satisfying, evoking especially well Orpheus's grief when his wife dies.

Then, in 1628, the son of the Grand Duke of Parma got married. Sure, sure, there was cake, and dancing, and probably a videographer, but the *main* event was the new Monteverdi opera, *Mercury and Mars.* Whoa, what a spectacle: This little skit featured, among other stunners, a ballet performed *on horseback* and a grand finale in which the stage itself was flooded so that sea monsters could romp and frolic — as Zeus himself, aka Jupiter (or, rather, an actor portraying him) flew in from the sky to bless the newlyweds.

Monteverdi's brand of storytelling was a huge hit with Italian audiences, and his opera spread rapidly to other cities and even beyond Italy. Suddenly, Greek-myth musicals and *pastorals* — countryside tales of shepherds, goat-men, and nymphs — were all the Renaissance rage. In Venice alone, hundreds of operas were produced in the second half of the 17th century, performed in 16 new opera houses built just for that purpose. Operamania ran wild.

# The Way They Were

The Italian audiences' appetite for big fancy sets, in fact, was just beginning. (Can you guess where the term *grand opera* comes from?) For example, the very first opera performed for the *public* in Venice (the year was 1637), called *Andromeda,* featured a whole swarm of gods zooming around the stage, suspended on flying rigs.

This plot device — having some god or another swoop down to save the day at the last moment — was used so often in these early operas that it's part of our lives even today. In two ways, really: First, the Latin term for "a god flown in by a machine" (the flying rigs the actors wore) is *deus ex machina* ("DAY-oose ex MAHKY-na"), which people still use occasionally in everyday speech. ("The fire in the kitchen was your *deus ex machina,* young lady, because I was about to spank you.") Second, practically every movie Hollywood cranks out features a *deus ex machina* — a last-minute, usually contrived development that provides a happy ending, such as the hero's partner — who you'd assumed was dead after getting shot to a bloody pulp — rising from a crumpled heap and rescuing the just-about-to-get-beheaded hero. Next time that happens in your neighborhood, remember: That's *opera,* man.

In the beginning, the next most important element of the show was the script — the story itself. But as Monteverdi and his followers (such as his student Pier Francesco Cavalli, 1602–1676) perfected the art of telling stories through songs, the music became more important. Gradually, as the music increased in importance relative to the words, the singers moved from singing, "I lost a melon on the way home" to "I, I lost! I lost a me-hel-hel-hel-lon, on the way, on the way, on the way, ho-o-o-o-ome!" Italy was witnessing the birth of the *air* — the big number, the intoxicating melody that lifted the words aloft and buoyed them along.

The Italian word for "air" is *aria* — and, by the 1700s, this kind of emotion-expressing musical number had become the most important ingredient in the opera cookbook. It's been the main attraction ever since.

## You've got to be seria

Two kinds of operas were taking shape as humankind hurtled through the 18th century: the formal, serious operas (which the Italians called *opera seria*) and the comical ones (which you'd think would be called *opera funnia*, but they're not, as we'll explain later).

The serious operas were stately, formal, and hopelessly dignified, befitting the majesty of the royalty that attended and sponsored them. Indeed, for much of the audience, the royalty in the audience often *were* the show. People went to the opera, in part, to see who else showed up, where they sat, and what their outfits looked like — pretty much as people do at operas today.

To you, the rigid formality of the action onstage in an *opera seria* would look bizarre. The main characters were extremely stylized in their delivery. When singing an aria, the singer assumed the position — ballet's third position, that is, with bent, bowlegged knees and heels nearly together, with one ankle slightly in front of the other — and remained in that exact, unnatural position for the *entire* song.

But trust us on this: If you think that the onstage behavior was peculiar, you'd *really* flip to see what went on in the *audience.* For operagoers of the 18th century, opera wasn't to be listened to on CD, watched on PBS, or peered at through little binoculars; instead, it was more like Muzak for a theater-wide cocktail party. It never dawned on theatergoers to come and stay for the whole show. The custom was to show up for a while, enjoy some entertainment, catch up with friends, and move on to the next event of the evening. ("Hey, wanna go opera-hopping tonight?") Nor was anyone particularly concerned about hearing the words; the audience chatted away throughout the performance.

Furthermore, because many opera composers knew that they were writing primarily for the pleasure of the Prince of Whatever, political correctness was the order of the day. If you could write an opera whose triumphing main character bore a strong resemblance to the Earl of Whoever-Signs-Your-Paycheck, you were strongly advised to do so.

If the opera *wasn't* written for the benefit of the sponsoring royalty, on the other hand, all bets were off; any topic was open for musicalizing. In 1642, our old friend Claudio Monteverdi composed the first Italian opera based on a real historical figure, called *The Coronation of Poppea.* (Greek myths and legends had always been the plots before.) But because this opera's audience was to be the general public, with no nabobs to annoy with unflattering references, the show was a jet-propelled sleigh ride through sex, violence, and scandal.

As you can find out in Chapter 13, the story concerns Poppea, a vicious, conniving man-eater who sleeps her way to the top (but who's probably a very nice person, once you get to know her). With this show, Monteverdi broke all kinds of time-honored rules that were traditionally in force at royal opera houses, such as:

- ✔ Operas have happy endings.
- ✔ Serious operas don't have funny bits.
- ✔ Sex and violence belong at home.

The Venetians ate it up.

## *Eunuchs For Dummies*

If you woke up tomorrow in the middle of a 17th-century Italian opera performance, two strange things would strike you: peoples' feet, as they trod over your suddenly materialized body, and the fact that men played the female roles as well as the male ones.

In Italy in those days, women were not allowed to sing onstage — not even in a chorus. This rule was hard and fast, and accepted by the public, musicians included.

Of course, this brings up a delicate question: You can dress a guy up as a woman and shave off his beard, but he's not going to *sound* like a woman without taking quick gasps from a helium balloon all night long.

Some bright young surgeon soon came up with an extremely effective solution to this little dilemma: Simply lop off, er, two of the three things that make a man a man, if you get our drift. Without the necessary hormones, these denatured preteens never had to shave, never had to worry about accidentally fathering children, and — more to the point — never had to face that awkward voice-changing phase. These former tenors- and basses-to-be remained sopranos and altos.

But don't think that forever sacrificing their fatherhood option bothered all these young men; it didn't. An amazing thing happened to many of these *castrati,* as they were called in Italy: Because their lungs and chest matured normally, their voices took on an incredible combination of male power and female beauty. Few singers volunteer for the surgery these days, so you'll probably never get to hear a real Italian eunuch's voice. But history tells us that they sounded *amazing,* combining the power of a trumpet with the clarity and beauty of a flute.

As a result, these equipment-free guys were idolized by the opera-going public, treated like superstars, and showered with riches and glory. More and more operas were written with major parts for castrati. And not just the "female" roles, either; castrati played male characters as well. The title role in Monteverdi's *Orfeo* was composed for a castrato, and so was the main character in Handel's *Julius Caesar*.

The most famous eunuch of all time was Farinelli. (His real name was Carlo Broschi. We call him Farinelli because *most* castrati went by one name, just like Cher or Madonna.) Farinelli became immensely rich, despite a reputation for being greedy, self-centered, and vain (plus he threw like a girl).

Because the ranks of the International Eunuchs Union have dwindled away to nothing, all those parts written for castrati present modern-day opera companies with something of a dilemma. Sure, the female roles can be played by women. But what about the male castrato roles? Well, of course, a woman could sing them, reversing centuries of discrimination. Usually, however, the solution is to have a male singer tackle a part, singing it at a lower pitch. And in some cases, regular, fully functional guys with really high voices, called *countertenors,* sing the castrato parts in their original vocal range.

## *Seria numbers*

Most of the plot setup in an *opera seria* was communicated through recitative. The harpsichord played a chord, accompanied by a low string instrument like a cello, and the singer chanted his line in a free rhythm. The lyrics for sections like these were proselike free-verse poetry.

The script for the recitative in an *opera seria* version of the movie *Speed* would look like this:

*(The harpsichord plays a chord and holds, as Dennis Hopper sings.)*

**Dennis Hopper:**    I'm an incredibly evil bomber with a particularly nasty little plan!

*(Another chord.)*

**Dennis Hopper:**    I've put a bomb on your bus! A bomb! And it's going to go off and kill you all if the bus's speed drops below 50 miles per hour!

*(Two chords.)*

At particularly intense emotional moments, other instruments joined in to enhance the mood — and when, occasionally, the words became actual rhymed poetry, the composer could write an *aria* (what we think of today as the main musical number, the one you can tap your toe to and hum along with):

**Sandra Bullock:**  What'll we do? Oh, what'll we do?
A bomb is on the bus!
You're gonna die, and I'm gonna, too
Yes, every one of us!

Come on Keanu, give me a kiss!
Bridge out? Oh, what a pain!
Anyway, I can promise you this:
Next time, I'll take the train.

Onstage, the main characters in *opera seria* were accompanied, as always, by a retinue of nonsinging (read: cheap) actors who played their servants, train-bearers, and so on. And rather than madmen with a thing about public transportation, *opera seria* plots generally concerned a love triangle — or a love quadrangle, quintangle, or hexagon. Key plot points inevitably turned on mistaken identity — "What, you're the king? And you've been a poor slave all your life!" (Two hundred years later, Gilbert and Sullivan had a field day making fun of this kind of plot twist.)

# In the buffa

In addition to serious opera, plenty of composers were tackling the tougher task of writing a *funny* opera, called (in Italian) *opera buffa* ("BOOF-ah") — meaning "buffoon opera."

For a composer, then as now, writing music for funny songs wasn't easy. For one thing, in comedy, the performance isn't funny unless the audience catches all the words — and *sung* words are more difficult to understand than spoken words. Comedy depends on timing and on voice inflections, too; singing the funny words in rhythm that's dictated by the *composer* can kill the joke. Finally, comedy is *fast,* especially when the material is back-and-forth dialogue between two characters. The composer can't exactly write slow, lyrical, hauntingly beautiful melodies if the words are like this:

**Orpheus:**  My dog has no nose.

**Eurydice:**  How does it smell?

**Orpheus:**  Terrible!

Try singing *that* to the tune of "Feelings," and you'll get our point.

Bu Italian composers discovered that, if done right, music could make the dialogue *funnier.* Their operas featured short musical phrases, with quick, disjointed snippets of melody, perfectly suitable for comic exchanges. They made a hysterical servant seem even more so, for example, by writing his melody so that it jumps high, then low, and then back again.

Most of the hundreds of funny operas of the 1700s and early 1800s are lost forever. But the comic techniques developed during this time are with us today — such as sight gags, quick verbal exchanges, and of course that delicious specialty, a final party scene that keeps building, getting funnier and more chaotic as more characters arrive. Sort of like the classic stateroom scene in the Marx Brothers' *A Night at the Opera.*

All right then: you know the setup. Now come and meet the guys.

# Gioachino Rossini

As you can discover in this book's companion, *Classical Music For Dummies,* it was a pretty firm unofficial rule, in the days of the great classical composers, that you had to die before you were appreciated.

Gioachino Rossini (1792–1868), however, was one of the lucky ones. Rossini ("ross-EE-nee"), shown in Figure 5-1, wrote both funny and serious shows, with great catchy tunes, and these operas turned Europe into one gigantic fan club. (Listen to Track 4 on the CD that comes with this book, and you'll hear a great example of Rossini's wonderful music.) Real, human, and immensely likable as a person, Rossini was adored by the public, and was easily the number one Italian opera composer in his own lifetime.

Rossini was a prodigy. At the age of 15 he had already developed such a superhuman musical mind that he could go to the opera and then write down entire arias from memory — and not just the vocal line either, but the orchestral accompaniment as well.

Rossini's talent and seemly inexhaustible reservoir of melodies served him well in the opera realm. He wrote his most enduring favorite, *The Barber of Seville,* in just 13 days. (In fact, he wrote the whole thing in his bathrobe, and he didn't shave the whole time.) Besides *The Barber,* Rossini wrote some of the best-known operas of his time, including *Cinderella, Semiramide,* and *The Italian Girl in Algiers.*

When several of Rossini's adoring friends and fans took up a collection to put up a Rossini statue, Rossini was both amused and amazed at the cost. "I'll tell you what," he said. "Just give me the money instead, and I'll stand on the pedestal myself."

**Figure 5-1:**
Gioachino
Rossini, the
most
popular
opera
composer
of his day.

Despite this adoration, Rossini abruptly stopped composing shows at age 36. For the last 40 years of his life, he was an opera retiree. For years, scholars and opera buffs have tortured themselves, trying to guess why Rossini stopped writing opera. Here are some of the more scholarly theories:

- Rossini worked his head off to create his last opera, *William Tell;* he felt that it was his masterpiece. When it was a commercial flop, he felt so burned that he never wrote another opera.

- He was often sick — plagued by unbelievably painful gallstones.

- He was insecure; younger musicians were taking Rossini's own developments in opera and running with them, creating a different kind of show that he didn't feel secure competing with.

But if you ask us, the most plausible reason Rossini stopped writing operas is much simpler: He didn't *feel* like it! Rossini was an enormous fat guy, rolling in money, who loved life, loved to cook, loved to eat and drink, and most of all, loved lolling around and doing nothing. "I can think of nothing more admirable than eating — and I mean *really* eating," he once said. "Appetite is for the stomach what love is for the heart . . . Eating, loving, singing, and digesting are the four acts of the comic opera known as life."

With such distractions as Italian food all around him, Rossini was by no means Mr. Motivated when it came to composition. At least once, his producers had to lock him in a room just before opening night, forcing him to write an overture — handing pages out the window as he finished them — so that the show could go on. "Nothing primes inspiration more effectively than the sight of a producer tearing out his hair," Rossini once said. "In my time, all the producers in Italy were bald at age 30."

The story goes that once, while composing an opera overture, Rossini dropped his sheet of music paper on the ground. Rather than reach down and pick it up, he took a fresh sheet of paper and began composing the piece again. In fact, Rossini's laziness was so great that he often used the *same* overture over and over again, tacking it onto one opera after another — until that opera became famous enough that he thought people would recognize the overture.

We think that if Rossini could hear what the experts are theorizing about his retirement, he'd be rolling in his grave — if it weren't so much effort.

# Gaetano Donizetti

One of Italian opera's more prolific figures was Gaetano Donizetti (1797–1848), who wrote *incredibly* quickly, tossing off melodies almost without thinking. Once a friend asked him whether he believed that Rossini had really composed *The Barber of Seville* in 13 days. "Oh, I absolutely believe it," he answered. "Rossini has always been unbelievably lazy!"

Donizetti ("doe-neet-SETT-ee"), in fact, composed over 70 operas by the time he was 50, including such perennial hits as *The Elixir of Love, The Daughter of the Regiment,* and *Don Pasquale.* One of his most serious works, *Lucia di Lammermoor,* is a surprisingly deep character study. You can read about it in Chapter 12.

Critics snipe that most of Donizetti's operas follow the same formula, don't show much variety, and are light on dramatic insight. But hey, they were entertaining. One of his earliest efforts, *Viva La Mamma,* features a man-in-drag role, foreshadowing the movie *Tootsie* by about 150 years.

Unfortunately, Donizetti didn't live very long. Shortly after writing *Don Pasquale,* Donizetti developed syphilis; depression, paralysis, and insanity quickly followed. They put him in an asylum — and then he died.

# Vincenzo Bellini

If Donizetti's music was sometimes tossed-off and formulaic, that's not the case with his fellow composer Vincenzo Bellini (1801–1835), who slaved over every note he wrote. Bellini ("bel-LEE-nee") composed passionate, deeply felt, soaring melodies with an unmistakably "Italian" sound. His vocal music was extremely lyrical and smooth; it helped bring about the style of opera singing called *bel canto* ("beautiful song"). This technique, taught to singers even today, emphasizes breath control, a beautiful tone, agile leaps from note to note, and great flexibility in dynamics (going quickly from loud to soft, for example). After decades of more declamatory, speechy singing, the sweetness and beauty of *bel canto* singers were a big hit with audiences.

We'll never know just how far Bellini may have gone with his development of opera, however — after finishing ten operas, he died at age 34. Fortunately, he left behind some great shows: *La Sonnambula* (*The Sleepwalker*), *I Puritani* (*The Puritans*), and *Norma*.

Meanwhile, a few miles away, one of the greatest opera composers who ever lived was just getting started: the galactically renowned, fantastically gifted Joe Green.

Of course, most people know his name in Italian: Giuseppe Verdi.

# Giuseppe Verdi

Opera fans will forever disagree on who wrote the greatest opera ever. Some say Mozart, some say Wagner, and some say Verdi (shown in Figure 5-2). But for *consistent* composing on the highest level of music, plotting, character, entertainment, suspense, and so on, it's no contest: Verdi (1813–1901) takes the cake.

Verdi ("VAIR-dee") didn't write for opera snobs. He wrote music for regular, honest-to-goodness people. "From the beginning," he once said, "my best friends have been the common people."

If the old saying that you have to suffer to be a great artist is true, then this guy must be the greatest of all. When he was two, Russian soldiers massacred his entire town — Verdi and his mom survived only by hiding in a bell tower. He was dirt poor as a kid, earning only pennies a week in his job as an organist. He was rejected by the Milan Conservatory as being "insufficiently talented." And his wife, whom he married when he was 23, bore two kids, each of whom died, and then she died herself. Verdi was devastated.

The only thing that kept him going was the sympathy of his friend Bartolomeo Merelli, who happened to be the producer at the most famous opera house in the world, La Scala in Milan. Merelli bugged Verdi, "C'mon, Joe, write me an opera!"

The result, in 1842, was Verdi's first big hit: *Nabucco*. The famous chorus of Hebrew slaves, *"Va, pensiero,"* was so stirring that in the first rehearsal, everyone in and around the building — even workmen pounding away on the roof — suddenly became silent when it was sung, and broke into a spontaneous, enthusiastic *bravo* when it was over. (You can hear this

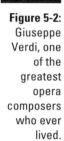

**Figure 5-2:**
Giuseppe
Verdi, one
of the
greatest
opera
composers
who ever
lived.

chorus on the CD that came with this book.) There was something forceful and desperate in the music, which both the public and critics loved. *"Va, pensiero"* became an unofficial Italian anthem, and *Nabucco* became an international success.

For an opera composer, half the battle is choosing a good play to adapt, and Verdi made some great choices. One play by Victor Hugo and another by Alexander Dumas led to two of Verdi's all-time most popular operas, *Rigoletto* and *La Traviata* (*The Fallen Woman*).

But most of his operas were successes precisely because of Verdi's emphasis on real, human emotions (love, greed, jealousy, desire) . . . and, of course, his glorious music. He had all of Italy humming.

By the time he was 57, Verdi was well known enough throughout the world that fans could send a letter to the address, "Maestro Verdi, Italy," and it would reach him. At about this time, the king of Egypt contacted Verdi and commissioned a new opera. Verdi saw an opportunity for one big, last operatic blowout before retiring to his farm, where verdant Verdi vineyards and contented cows awaited him. The opera that resulted became one of the most loved shows ever: *Aïda* ("ah-YEE-dah"). The story, described in Chapter 12, had romance, courage, loyalty, and patriotism — all the elements that got Verdi going.

Not only was *Aïda* filled with great, passionate melodies and ingenious orchestra sounds, but it was also spectacular in scale. It's written for full orchestra, solo singers, a huge choir, ballet, an elaborate set . . . and did we mention elephants? Today, it's one of the most oft-performed operas in the world.

# The best bad review he ever got

A famous critic came to call on Verdi just as the great composer was finishing up his opera *Il Trovatore.*

Verdi sat down at the piano and played some of the music from the opera. "What do you think?" he asked.

"That's terrible," the critic replied.

"Well, what about this?" Verdi asked, playing another number.

"That's even worse!" shuddered the critic.

"All right, just one more. . . ." And Verdi played the "Anvil Chorus."

"Oh, my goodness! Absolutely horrible!" cried the critic, covering his ears.

Verdi, smiling broadly, got up from the piano and threw his arms around the critic. "Oh, thank you so much!" he cried, "I've been writing an opera for the common people of Italy. If you, the eminent and refined critic, had liked it, then nobody else would have. But if you hate it, that means the whole world will love it!"

After *Aïda,* Verdi headed home to his cows, confident that he'd exited the world's opera stage at just the right time for him. But his publisher, who'd found a really talented young libretto writer named Arrigo Boito, began needling Verdi about the possibility of writing even more operas.

Good thing, actually. The result of this new collaboration was a pair of outstanding Shakespearean shows, *Otello* and *Falstaff,* two of Italy's best operas ever. On the opening night of *Otello,* Verdi was cheered everywhere he went. He was called to the front of the stage time after time, and after the performance a huge, wild, and enthusiastic crowd accompanied him all the way back to his hotel.

Through all the fame and glory and various attempts to elevate him to an official royal position, Verdi remained the simple, common man he wanted to be. "Musician I was born, and musician I remain," he said.

# Giacomo Puccini

If anyone was Verdi's successor, it was Giacomo Puccini (1858–1924), shown in Figure 5-3, who likewise was Italian, likewise cared more for the real than the metaphysical, and likewise captured the hearts of his audience.

Puccini ("poo-CHEE-nee") wrote some of the most often-performed, well-loved, and imitated operas of all time. For example:

- *La Bohème* (means "The Bohemian," but nobody ever refers to the opera that way; premiered in 1896): Talk about not being about Greek mythology! Starving-artist boy meets girl; boy loses girl; boy gets girl just as she dies of tuberculosis. Popular, heartbreaking, and full of gorgeous melodies that guaranteed Puccini's immortality. Adapted for the Broadway musical *Rent.*

- *Tosca* (premiered in 1900): Evil police chief says that if Tosca will sleep with him, he'll free her boyfriend. She pretends to agree, but — well, we won't ruin it for you until Chapter 12. A shocking dual-surprise ending. Famous songs, great action.

- *Madame Butterfly* (premiered in 1904): Gut-wrenching tragedy. Opening night was awful (see the "Bagging a butterfly" sidebar). This opera is the basis of the Broadway show *Miss Saigon,* which changed the locale from 1900 Japan to Saigon during the Vietnam war. The heartless cad in both cases is an American officer.

- *Turandot* (premiered in 1926, two years after the composer's death): This exotic tale of a staggeringly beautiful Chinese princess and her hopeless suitors actually has a happy ending — well, in the opera, anyway. In real life, Puccini died before finishing it. At the premiere in Milan, conductor Arturo Toscanini suddenly stopped conducting right in the middle of the third act. He laid down his baton, turned to the audience, and said: "Here the maestro laid down his pen."

**Figure 5-3:**
Giacomo Puccini, the most popular opera composer in the world.

## Bagging a butterfly

The first performance of Puccini's opera *Madame Butterfly* at La Scala in Milan was one of opera's all-time worst flops.

Back when everybody still thought that opera was fun, nobody was silent at an opera. Operagoers were there to register their opinions; they either loved it or they hated it. Whenever a character expressed himself, people either cheered or booed — just like talk-show audiences today.

To complicate things, composers sometimes hired a group of people to cheer their works — or to boo the works of their rivals. This group, called a *claque*, was a common feature at European opera performances.

There was definitely a claque in the balcony at this performance.

The audience appeared unappreciative of the beautiful arias at the beginning of the opera. And when Butterfly herself entered, the audience displayed its displeasure. "That sounds just like *La Bohème!*" people yelled — a reference to Puccini's earlier hit. They yelled this even during the love duet, which, let's be honest, sounds nothing like *La Bohème.*

In the second act, things got worse. At one point, wind blew in from the theater wings, inflating the kimono of the Japanese heroine. "Butterfly is pregnant," somebody yelled. And someone else answered, "With the conductor's child!" (Apparently, this soprano had been sleeping with the conductor, and now all of Milan knew it.)

Between the second and third acts was a short musical interlude with bird calls. The audience imitated the birds, throwing in some donkeys, cows, sheep, and goats as well. The third act was also full of animal noises, hisses, and boos.

That was the temporary end of *Madame Butterfly* — which went on to become one of the best-loved operas in history.

# ... And Friends

Puccini was the biggest star in Italian opera during his lifetime, but not the only one. Pietro Mascagni wrote a one-act opera called *Cavalleria Rusticana* (*Rustic Chivalry*), filled with noble sentiments about honor and death. This opera was Mascagni's only genuine triumph, which he could never surpass — even when he wrote *Isabeau,* an opera about Lady Godiva, in which the soprano had to ride naked on a horse.

In most performances, *Cavalleria Rusticana* is paired up with another short opera, *I Pagliacci* (*The Clowns*) — an opera that features a crying clown who, among other things, stabs his wife and her boyfriend. (You can read about both these operas in Chapter 12.) This opera was written by Puccini's friend Ruggiero Leoncavallo.

*I Pagliacci* provided Leoncavallo with at least one experience that he would never forget. He was visiting a small town and learned that his opera was being performed there. He decided to go to the performance incognito. He sat next to a lovely young lady, who noticed that he didn't applaud at all.

When she asked why not, he responded that the whole opera was rubbish, that it was entirely unoriginal, and that every catchy phrase had been stolen from one great composer or another. The woman was stunned, but asked, "Is that your honest opinion of *Pagliacci*?" "Absolutely," he replied.

The next morning, when he read the local newspaper, his eye was attracted by a big headline: "Leoncavallo Speaks Out on His Own Opera, *I Pagliacci.*"

# Chapter 6

# The French Connection

*I*f you've read Chapter 5, you know that opera was born in ancient Greece and raised in Italy. But one by one, other countries adopted opera as their own, taking it in new and different directions.

France was one of the first countries to try its hand at opera. In the 16th and 17th centuries, musical pageants were regularly composed for important French events — royal birthdays and weddings, visits by foreign dignitaries, and so on — just as they had been in Italy.

But it took a transplanted Italian to *really* get things started.

## French Opera Gets Patented

Many people consider Jean-Baptiste Lully (1632–1687) to be the father of French opera. Born in Italy, he wrote or cowrote nearly 80 ballets and operas, and his influence on French music was enormous. Everyone was a Lully wannabe.

Somebody ought to write an opera about *this* guy's life. Lully ("lew-LEE") came to Paris at age 14. He was a dancing (and violin-playing) fool — energetic, ambitious, and self-promoting enough to be noticed by the young Louis the 14th (a fellow dance fanatic), who immediately hired him as a violinist. Being the Sun King's special buddy wasn't so bad; Lully soon gained complete control of all court music. In fact, by the time Lully was 42, he'd managed to *patent* his new "invention" — opera — so that no opera could be performed in France without his permission.

Lully eventually teamed up with France's most famous playwright, Molière. Together, Lully and Molière developed a new kind of show called the *comédie-ballet:* a funny musical play with dancing. Amazing — this guy even invented the Broadway musical!

## The Lully aftermath

For nearly a hundred years, Lully's formula for creating an opera *was* the French formula. This kind of opera put less emphasis on the aria (the big musical number) than Italian operas, but much more emphasis on dances. In fact, 200 years later, French audiences still demanded the big middle-of-the-show ballet number, even in operas imported from other countries.

After inventing ballet, musical comedies, and the two-man writing team, Lully invented one more thing — and it was ultimately his undoing. In his efforts to keep the orchestra playing together, he pioneered the concept of the conducting stick. Unfortunately, his first baton prototype was, in fact, a heavy six-foot staff, which he banged on the ground in time to the music.

We say "unfortunately" because in 1687, while conducting a concert to celebrate the Sun King's return to health after an illness, Maestro Lully missed the ground entirely and slammed the staff into his own foot, which became gangrenous, ultimately killing him.

## Meyerbeer makes it grand

Put Lully's brand of opera into a historical crock pot, set on simmer, and let sit for a couple of hundred years — and the result is *French grand opera*. Its most successful composer was Giacomo Meyerbeer (1791–1864).

Meyerbeer ("MY-er-bear"), shown in Figure 6-1, was either very resourceful or an opportunist, depending on your point of view. Born in Germany as Jacob Beer, he tried to make a living writing German operas, but had no success. He moved to Italy, changed his first name to Giacomo, and had meager success. Finally, he moved to France, started writing French grand operas, changed his last name to Meyerbeer, and had *great* success.

If operagoers came out of Verdi's shows humming the tunes, they came out of Giacomo Meyerbeer's shows humming the *sets*. Meyerbeer wasn't one of the world's best composers, but patrons sure got their francs' worth in entertainment. His operas put the "grand" in the term *French grand opera* — the sets were lavish and realistic, the machinery was breathtaking, and the musical forces (choruses and orchestras) were designed to blow the audience away.

**Figure 6-1:**
Giacomo
Meyerbeer,
composer of
monumental
operatic
spectacles.

His most well-known opera, *The Huguenots,* has some beautiful music and powerful drama. But it's not easy to take that opera seriously when it comes from the same guy who dreamed up a skating ballet in his opera *The Prophet* (predating Andrew Lloyd Webber's *Starlight Express* by more than a century) and a ballet of defrocked nuns for his opera *Robert the Devil.*

Meyerbeer's operas are almost entirely neglected today because they're far too costly to produce — and because each one requires the five greatest opera singers in the world.

## *Hector Berlioz*

Hector Berlioz (EK-tor BARE-lee-o's — 1803–1869), shown in Figure 6-2, was one of opera's true iconoclasts. During his career, he put every aspect of music under his microscope — the rules of harmony, the structure of an opera, the way to write a melody, the number of players in an orchestra, and so on. If he felt that these rules helped express what he wanted to express, he kept them. If not, he broke them; public be damned.

Berlioz's grandest opera was *Les Troyens (The Trojans)*; many critics believe that it was the most important French opera of the 19th century. But it's hardly ever performed in its entirety — it's over five hours long, if you include time for intermissions and scene changes. And because of the opera's wealth of major and minor singing roles, outrageously elaborate sets, and special effects, the first producer had to get a hefty stipend from the French government just to put on a *condensed* version.

The condensed version was good, but Berlioz was unsatisfied. He had fought bitterly for years trying to get his masterpiece performed, and he couldn't stand to see it cut. He became disillusioned, resolved never to write another opera, and died three years later.

**Figure 6-2:**
Hector Berlioz wrote highly imaginative, but unappreciated, French operas.

*Les Troyens* finally got a complete, uncut performance — 21 years after Berlioz's death — in Germany. And it wasn't until 1935 that anybody performed the whole thing in French.

Fortunately for posterity, Berlioz had an alternate career as a composer of superb nonoperatic music, such as symphonies. (You can find a greater discussion of Berlioz, and his life as a neurotic nut case, in *Classical Music For Dummies*.)

## Charles Gounod

Though he's known today primarily for just two operas, Charles Gounod (1818–1893), shown in Figure 6-3, has an important place in French opera history. Gounod ("goo-NOE") composed in a style that was wholly French. His music is graceful, harmonically traditional, and full of good tunes — without any remnants of the Italian mannerisms that had been a part of French opera from the beginning.

Gounod, like so many of the composers that the world remembers, had a horrible temper that flared up especially in his encounters with intimate acquaintances. His mistress (and landlady) tells of one such encounter:

> "Don't touch me," he shrieked, "it is you who have incited your husband to insult me, to outrage me, to defy me. I will die," he shrieked, "and all shall perish with me!" I was terrified. The thought struck me that he meant to set the place on fire, but I followed him with my eyes, hoping that my looks might subdue him. He rushed like a madman to the cupboard where the orchestral score of [his opera] *Polyeucte* was carefully stowed away. He seized hold of it, crying out, "*Polyeucte* first; *Polyeucte* shall burn!". . . .

**Figure 6-3:**
Charles
Gounod,
composer
of *Faust* and
*Romeo and
Juliet.*

> With strength lent me by the horror of despair, I threw myself on
> Gounod with all my weight; I knocked him down; I rolled on him; we
> tussled violently for possession of the treasure. I tore it from him; I
> flung it on the sofa; I suddenly picked myself off the floor; I sat upon it
> and screamed, "You shall kill me first, but you shall not burn *Polyeucte!*". . . .
> Thank God, the score to *Polyeucte* was saved.

She might have saved herself the effort. Today, nobody performs *Polyeucte*.
The operas of Gounod that do get performed are *Faust* and *Romeo and Juliet*.
Of these, *Faust* has been more successful (see the sidebar "The ticket scam
of 1859"); it's considered one of the best of the French operas, and it was
even chosen to open the Metropolitan Opera House in 1883. You can read
more about it in Chapter 12.

## Jules Massenet

Jules Massenet (1842–1912) followed in Gounod's footsteps with a tuneful,
graceful, consummately French musical style. Many of his operas have
exotic settings, with colorful, descriptive music to match.

Massenet (pronounced "mahss-NAY") was the ultimate flatterer, a "yes-man
par excellence," in the words of one famous singer. His music, too, aims to
please. What he wanted, more than anything else, was to be loved — and he
succeeded. His career spanned over 30 years of success after success.

In his 27 operas, Massenet wrote some spectacular arias that show off the
human voice to the utmost. He launched the career of many a soprano.
(Some say that he did more than that to them.) Today, Massenet is best
known for his operas *Manon* and *Werther* — both of which you can read
about in Chapter 13.

FOR COCKTAIL PARTIES

## The ticket scam of 1859

*Faust* is the opera that introduced Charles Gounod to the opera-loving world. But he might not be known at all if not for the genius of a scheming impresario.

A few days before opening night of the new opera, tickets weren't selling. Only a few dozen seats had been sold for a total of four performances. So the producer took matters into his own hands: He gave away the remaining tickets for the first three performances to people who lived out of town. Then he advertised in the local newspaper that the first three performances were sold out.

Wondering what all the fuss was about, a curious public snatched up tickets to the fourth performance. At the end of the show, the crowd went crazy, confident that it had witnessed the world's greatest spectacle. Gounod came out onstage for curtain call after curtain call. The show was held over for many successive nights, as the whole city clamored to get in. *Faust* was a hit. (We're surprised that producers don't pull this stunt more often.)

*Faust* went on to become one of the most-performed operas, receiving thousands of performances over the next few decades.

# *Georges Bizet*

Though he was composing operas at the same time as his countrymen Gounod and Massenet, Georges Bizet (1838–1875) was a different case entirely. Bizet's music is more adventurous; he was capable of a much wider range of melodic, harmonic, and orchestral effects. The characters in his operas come more vividly to life.

Bizet ("bee-ZAY"), shown in Figure 6-4, was another victim of OCMEDS (Opera Composers' Mysterious Early Death Syndrome) — like Bellini and Mozart, he died in his mid-30s. Yet, like those masters, he managed to squeeze out a few great ones in his short career. His last work is one of the most often performed operas of all time: *Carmen*.

ON THE CD

*Carmen* turned heads when it premiered in 1875, for an important reason: It showed a gritty, seamy underbelly of life. Bizet was unafraid to depict smuggling, betrayal, and cruelty, not to mention a very sexually active title character (who you can hear crooning her seductive Habanera on your free CD). At the premiere, the audience didn't know what to make of this kind of drama, and the reception was far from enthusiastic.

Georges himself died just three months after the premiere; he went to his grave thinking that his final opera was a flop. Little did he know that it would eventually receive hundreds of performances a year all over the world. (More on *Carmen* in Chapter 12.)

**Figure 6-4:**
Georges
Bizet,
composer
of *Carmen*.

# Jacques Offenbach: Opera goes funny

While Bizet and his buddies were busy creating serious French operas, a different kind of composer came along. Jacques Offenbach (1819–1880) grabbed the concept of opera, made it funnier and frothier, added spoken dialogue, and almost single-handedly created the *operetta*.

As you probably know, *-etta* or *-ette* at the end of a word means "little." A *kitchenette* is a little kitchen; a *cigarette* is a little cigar; an *Irish setta* is a little dog. An *operetta* is often shorter than a real opera, and it's always lighter-hearted and designed more for entertainment than for catharsis. Whereas most operas are made of 100 percent singing, operettas feature *talking* scenes between songs. If you saw an operetta, in fact, you'd probably think that you were attending a Broadway musical comedy.

Jacques Offenbach, most hilarious of Catholic French composers, was originally neither Catholic nor French. His actual name was Jakob Eberst; his actual heritage was Jewish; and his actual place of birth was Cologne, Germany. (In later years, he signed his name O. de Cologne.)

His transformation into France's satire king began at age 14, when his dad took him to Paris for cello training. Newly renamed Jacques was a true prodigy on the cello, but he was easily distracted from his studies — especially by the rich theater life of Paris in the springtime. He found that he had a talent for composition, and he set about composing his own operas.

He tried to break into the circle of Parisian theaters, but in vain; Napoleon rigidly controlled their schedules and offerings. Expecting to get his shows mounted there was akin to aiming for Broadway today. ("Sure, son. Got $10 million?")

Frustrated, Jacques took his talent elsewhere: to unofficial, back-room theaters and non-theaters. He supported himself by performing every musical task anyone offered: conducting, copying music by hand, producing shows, and even acting as stage manager for other peoples' shows.

As you may recall from Chapter 5, it was a rite of passage for young composers to write an opera based on the Greek tale of *Orpheus*. For Offenbach, though, this was not a duty but an opportunity — to completely ridicule that overdone myth. His *Orpheus in the Underworld* is a screamingly funny spoof of all the serious operas based on that same myth, sort of a *Saturday Night Live* edition. He put on the show in a tiny wooden theater that he had taken over in 1855, and it was a smash hit.

Soon Offenbach was spoofing not just one particular opera, but opera itself — a worthy subject for satire, because grand opera had become so grand that it was about to burst. His *The Beautiful Hélène* (1864) was a takeoff on the Trojan War (and of grand opera, of course), and *The Parisian Life* was a satire of cosmopolitan Paris, featuring that ever-popular high-kicking dance number, the Can-Can.

Interestingly, Offenbach wrote only one serious opera — yes, a genuine grand opera — called *The Tales of Hoffmann*. This show was a tremendous success and remains so even today. Surprisingly, it holds its own with the best operas ever written. You can read all about it in Chapter 12.

Unfortunately, Offenbach died a few months before the opening night of *Hoffmann.* One of his actor friends, hearing that he had been ailing, visited Offenbach's apartment. When greeted by the servant, the actor asked, "How is he?"

"Monsieur Offenbach is, unfortunately, dead," was the servant's reply. "He died very peacefully, without knowing anything about it."

"Oh," the actor replied. "Will he ever be surprised when he finds out!"

# Beyond Offenbach

French music in the 20th century took a very different turn, into the realm of the modern. In our handy companion volume, *Classical Music For Dummies,* we go into more detail about this phenomenon. But for the purposes of *this* book, two composers command our attention: Claude Debussy (1862–1918) and Francis Poulenc (1899–1963).

## Claude Debussy

Debussy ( pronounced "de-bu-SEE," or "WC" if you say it really fast) was one of a group of composers we call *Impressionist.* He tried to portray in music the *impressions* created by sights, sounds, fragrances, and tastes, much the way that such painters as Monet and Renoir depicted blurry fields of dappled light, Paris in the rain, and so on.

To create such impressionistic sounds, Debussy needed a new musical language. The tried-and-true harmonies and chord structures weren't enough anymore. He needed different chords — and different progressions of chords — to produce his delicate and subtle special effects.

As you might imagine, Debussy flunked composition at the Paris Conservatory, where weirdo harmonies were frowned upon. In fact, several years later, another Conservatory student was expelled just for having a Debussy score in his possession!

Debussy's opera *Pelléas and Mélisande* is a big deal for opera fans. Based on a drama by the Belgian poet Maurice Maeterlinck, the opera — called an "Impressionistic tone picture" — tells the story of a romance between Pelléas, a young man, and Mélisande, a mysterious young girl.

Unlike most opera composers, Debussy didn't hire a librettist to adapt the play; instead, he just used it as it was, omitting a line or two here and there. But the playwright hated the opera with a passion — mainly, we think, because his opera-singer girlfriend wasn't chosen to sing the lead role.

The audiences in Paris took a long time to get used to Debussy's radical new musical sounds. What we hear as lush and sensual today struck them as utterly strange and chaotic.

# Francis Poulenc

Francis Poulenc is another French composer whose work gets appreciated more and more as time goes on. Poulenc ("poo-LANK") was famous for witty, high-spirited, even sarcastic-sounding works, like his two-piano concerto. But he was also capable of high seriousness, and he displayed it in the opera for which he is best known among opera buffs: *Dialogues of the Carmelites*.

Like Debussy, Poulenc used an existing play for his libretto — a powerful story about a flock of nuns who get beheaded during the French Revolution for refusing to give up their faith. You can read all about this opera — along with many other great French operas — in Part IV.

# Chapter 7

# English Channels

*W*hile the French and Italians were furiously racing around devising new forms of musical entertainment, opera in England was always more reserved, less innovative, and less apt to involve smoke machines, flying harnesses, or crashing chandeliers (at least until Andrew Lloyd Webber came along). Few shows from other countries infiltrated the sheltered world of British opera in the 1600s.

Still, not all was quiet on the British front. Young composer Henry Purcell ("PER-sull," 1659–1695) inadvertently wrote, in 1689, an extremely important English-language opera, *Dido and Aeneas.* Believe it or not, he wrote it as the drama production for a local girls' academy. ("Mom, can I stay after school to try out for what will eventually be considered one of the most famous operas of all time?")

As you'd imagine for a school musical, *Dido and Aeneas* (perfectly ordinary names, by the way — for Greeks) is short (about an hour long) and easy to sing. But compared with the fancy-sounding music of the day, Purcell's tunes were simple, natural, and evocative; his score included drunken sailors singing a sea chantey, witches chanting, and a heart-rending lament by a grief-stricken Dido that still stands as a musical masterpiece.

As Purcell's career proceeded, he began to study the explosively popular Italian opera format, borrowing its most interesting elements (such as, of course, recitative). As things turned out, he could have just waited until the turn of the century, and a lesson in Italian opera would have come to *him* — aboard the fertile brain of George F. Handel.

# The Italian Invasion

Even before 1700, a few Italian influences were seeping into the hermetically sealed British opera scene. Translated versions of hit Venetian productions showed up here and there. But when German-born, Italian-speaking Handel moved to London, the British had the rare opportunity to go see true Italian operas, in Italian, without so much as booking a flight to Venice.

Turns out they hadn't the least bit of interest.

George Frideric Handel (1685–1759), shown in Figure 7-1, was one of the leading composers of the Baroque era (about 1650–1750). Handel ("HEN-dle," to be perfectly proper) was born in Germany and trained in Italy — which explains, of course, why he's considered one of the greatest of the *English* composers. Try not to think too hard about this.

**Figure 7-1:**
George Frideric Handel was German, moved to England, and wrote Italian operas there. Got it?

Actually, there's logic here. Handel was the son of a German barber-surgeon (not the kind of guy you'd want to do your tummy tuck). With Dad spending his days removing one vital body part after another, it's no surprise that the young George Frideric took up the organ. At 18, he left home for the big city — Hamburg, where he found work as a composer and performer.

Handel knew that Italian opera was going to be the next big thing in Europe. And so, at 22, he went off to Italy to learn how to write in the Italian style. He got to meet the superstar composers of the day, whose works he emulated. After a stint back in Germany, Handel ditched his homeland and moved to London.

As a composer of serious opera, Handel was far more talented than his adoptive countrymen, and he knew it. (Once, when he was caught in the act of passing off another composer's aria as his own, he replied, "Yes, but it was far too good for him!") Unfortunately, few Britons ever discovered his opera talent; in keeping with the grand tradition of starving-artist composers, Handel had to do without funding from any royal court figure.

Instead, the 36 Italian-style, Italian-language operas that he wrote during 30 years in London were produced by a group of rich amateurs who hadn't a clue about how to make money in theater. (Clue number 1, perhaps, would have been: Try producing operas in a language the audience understands.) The London audiences just didn't get these operas, and sometimes they booed Handel's work mercilessly. They just couldn't Handel it.

Finally, Handel gave up trying to sell masterful Italian operas to uncomprehending Britons, and he switched to writing *oratorios* ( long choral pieces that usually use Bible quotations as lyrics) — in English. He became instantly successful.

The most famous of his oratorios was *Messiah,* first performed in 1742. It became so popular that gentlemen were encouraged to attend performances without their swords, and ladies without their hoops, so as to make more room. Even today, there's a performance of his oratorio *Messiah* in every major city in the United States every Christmas season, and everywhere else in the world at Easter.

Besides these oratorios, Handel is also extremely well known for his purely instrumental compositions, which are beautiful and a lot of fun to listen to. If you'd like to know more about them, we'd like to suggest a book — just a little book; nothing special really. We're embarrassed to even mention it. It's called *Classical Music For Dummies.*

# Gilbert and Sullivan

After Handel died, a century passed before England again made its mark on the world opera scene. Its next dramatic contribution was the celebrity author-composer team: William Gilbert and Arthur Sullivan.

If you've seen the word *operetta* elsewhere in this book, and you've been muttering, "Hey, what about Gilbert and Sullivan?" nonstop, we understand. In the English language, G & S *are* operetta. Although they hated each other's guts, fought incessantly, and split up a couple of times, their 14 shows are side-splittingly funny even today. They feature some of the wittiest dialogue (and catchiest tunes) ever to float across the Atlantic.

After a couple of early so-so efforts, every single G & S collaboration became a success, spawning touring companies worldwide (sometimes unauthorized). London theatergoers eagerly awaited each new show: *H.M.S. Pinafore, The Pirates of Penzance, Patience, Iolanthe, Princess Ida, The Mikado, Ruddigore, The Yeomen of the Guard,* and *The Gondoliers.* And each made merciless fun of the stuffy British government, political shenanigans, and artistic pretensions.

Through it all, Arthur Sullivan (1842–1900) gnashed his teeth, intensely frustrated that the world was ignoring his *real* music, his *serious* music. That his light, bubbly, *funny* stuff was internationally worshipped, while his serious music was utterly ignored, drove him wild. Meanwhile, William Gilbert (1836–1911), who wrote the words, was frustrated in his own ways — first, by the fact that Sullivan was constantly in acute agony from ulcers and unable to work for weeks at a time, and second, because Sullivan was knighted by the Queen, before he (Gilbert) was. (And no wonder: Would *you* be eager to knight a guy who dedicated his career to making fun of you?)

In 1890, after a screaming, blowout fight, Gilbert and Sullivan vowed that they'd never again collaborate. (Why do great groups always *do* that? The Beatles . . . Monty Python . . . the original cast of *Cheers.* . . .) For three years, the adoring public begged G & S to get back together. At last, in 1893, they made a couple of feeble attempts at new shows, but the magic was gone. Sullivan turned full-time to his serious composing and died from exhaustion (and ulcers); Gilbert drowned by throwing himself into a lake — not to kill himself, but to save a drowning swimmer.

# Benjamin Britten

Speaking of water, there's plenty of it in the operas of Benjamin Britten (1913–1976) — surely one of the best composers England has ever known. Britten dominated the British opera scene for much of the 20th century.

Britten's first wildly successful opera was *Peter Grimes,* the story of a fisherman whose assistants have a funny habit of dying. From the beginning, the public hailed this opera as a masterpiece — and there were many more to come: *Billy Budd* (another sailing story), *A Midsummer Night's Dream* (based on the Shakespeare play), *Noye's Fludde* (based on the Bible story of Noah, intended for performance in a church), and *Death in Venice* (a re-creation of Thomas Mann's novel), among others. Many of these operas have entered the standard repertoire. You can read about some of Britten's work in Part IV.

Great Britain has had other outstanding composers since Benjamin Britten — Michael Tippett, Thea Musgrave, and Peter Maxwell Davies, to name a few — but none have found the enormous, appreciative worldwide audience that Britten has.

# Chapter 8

# Opera with a German Accent

## In This Chapter

▶ Gluck fathers an art form

▶ Wolfgang Amadeus Mozart, child genius

▶ Beethoven's only opera

▶ Weber creates German Romantic opera

▶ Richard Wagner, genius and louse

▶ A couple of Strausses, and how to tell them apart

▶ Alban Berg's atonal toe-tappers

*I*f you want to see how opera history works, just look at Germany and Austria. Over the centuries, one composer influenced the next in a direct and powerful way. Take the big names of the classical music world, for example — Bach, Haydn, Mozart, Beethoven, Brahms, and Mahler, to name a few. Each of these composers followed in the musical footsteps of his predecessor, taking classical music further and further in the process. (And each one is described in loving detail in *Classical Music For Dummies*.)

In the German and Austrian *opera* world, most of the names are different — but the same rules apply. You can trace a clear musical lineage from Gluck to Mozart, to Beethoven and Weber, to Wagner, to Richard Strauss, and to Alban Berg.

Here's the scoop on the composers who put Germany and Austria on the opera map.

## Christoph Willibald von Gluck

The founder of German opera was Christoph Willibald von Gluck (1714–1787), shown in Figure 8-1. Gluck ("glook") was born in Germany but moved to Vienna in 1747, probably because of the other kids calling him "Willibald" all the time.

**Figure 8-1:**
Christoph
Willibald
von Gluck,
the father of
German
opera.

Gluck was a purist: He believed that opera should tell stories in a simple and direct way. He disliked all the flowery mannerisms that had grown up around opera over the years. More than once, he came out against the prevailing Italian opera style of the day: "It's all very well and good, but it simply doesn't draw blood!"

Gluck's *Orfeo ed Euridice* must have tickled Rousseau pink. Emotional, pure, simple melodies replaced the fancy trills and vocal fireworks being per-formed in other operas. And although he originally wrote it with a castrato hero, he later revised the opera (with the French title *Orphée*) so that the hero was a bona fide tenor — much more realistic, you'll agree. (Convincing the gods that you want to go down to Hades and pick up your lost wife is really difficult when you've been castrated.)

Gluck went on to become one of the most famous figures among opera composers. Some of the really big opera daddies of all time, such as Mozart and Wagner, were influenced by Gluck's less stylized, more realistic shows.

There's a great story about a scene in Gluck's opera *Iphigénie en Tauride,* in which Orestes sings, *"Le calme rentre dans mon coeur!"* ("My heart becomes calm again!") In the first rehearsal, Orestes got to this line just as some of the strings in the orchestra began playing a wild, excited musical passage. The orchestra stopped playing, thinking that there must be some mistake: How could the music sound so frenzied on a tranquil lyric like that? But Gluck motioned for the orchestra to continue. "He's lying. He killed his mother. Keep on playing!"

# Mozart Arrives!

Wolfgang Amadeus Mozart (1756–1791), shown in Figure 8-2, lived at the height of the Classical period in music history — a time of elegance, beauty, refinement, and grace. He wrote 22 operas — 10 of them as a teenager. Although many operas written by other composers during that time seem out-of-date and stilted, Mozart's still appear remarkably fresh to today's audiences.

**Figure 8-2:** Wolfgang Amadeus Mozart — composer of some of the greatest operas of all time.

German-born Mozart ("MOAT-sart") was one of the best opera composers who ever lived — and many consider him to be the greatest composer, period. From the very beginning of his short life, Mozart mastered music with a natural grace and facility that blew people away. He was the Tiger Woods of composers.

With his dad's nurturing, young Wolfgang was composing piano concertos by age 4. Shortly thereafter, he wrote his first symphony. And he wrote the opera *Bastien and Bastienne* when he was 11.

## Mozart joins the circus

Wolfgang probably would have been happy to stay at home and compose operas for fun. But Mr. Mozart, Wolfie's father, had other ideas. To show off his genius son, he packed up young Wolfgang and his older sister, Nannerl, and toted them all over Europe. Everywhere they went, Leopold touted his son as a scientific phenomenon. One of his posters in England said: "To all lovers of sciences: The greatest prodigy that Europe, or that even Human Nature has to boast of is, without contradiction, the little German boy Wolfgang Mozart." (No pressure, Wolfie.)

The young Mozart displayed such stunts as improvising at the keyboard, performing difficult pieces he had never seen before at first sight, and playing with his hands hidden under a cloth so that he couldn't see the keys. Nannerl helped out, too, wowing the public with her harpsichord playing. Together, they were a traveling circus act.

By age 13, Wolfgang found a job as concertmaster of the orchestra and organist of the court of the archbishop of Salzburg, where he worked for 12 years. But his constant traveling and angling for better jobs irked the archbishop. Finally, with absolutely no clue how politically incorrect he'd look to future generations, the archbishop fired Mozart.

When he grew up, Mozart moved to Vienna to seek his fortune. Vienna was a center of musical activity, and he had been successful on tour there as a child prodigy.

But Mozart wasn't a child prodigy anymore — and he had a hard time finding steady work. Without a steady job, Mozart sustained himself in Vienna by writing operas.

During this time, Mozart married a young woman named Constanze Weber. Perhaps to commemorate this happy occasion, he used the name Constanze for the heroine in his exotic, comic-rescue opera, *Die Entführung aus dem Serail* (known in English as *The Abduction from the Seraglio*). This opera had everything: great tunes with trendy Turkish-sounding effects, a wacky story, harems and other exotic attractions, and great escape scenes (see Chapter 12).

It had something else, too: It was in German, the language of the people for whom it was written — rather than in Italian, like most operas. Mozart believed in communicating directly to the people; and he was supported by the emperor of Austria-Hungary, Joseph II.

To make the opera even more down-to-earth, Mozart used spoken dialogue rather than recitative — kind of like an operetta, or a Broadway show of today. An opera like this was called a *Singspiel* (pronounced "Zing-shpeel") — literally, "sing-play."

## Ease and beauty

Mozart was a natural. Music flowed freely from some hidden realm directly into his head, as if he were taking dictation — all he really had to do was write it down!

Mozart was especially good at opera. His melodies were simple, graceful, and full of feeling. He loved writing parts for several onstage characters to sing simultaneously — and managed to make all the words clear. He also mastered the orchestra's *colors,* using cleverly chosen groups of instruments to create special effects and sounds.

Furthermore, Mozart had a knack for picking the right plays to turn into operas. One of his best picks was a play by Pierre de Beaumarchais called *The Marriage of Figaro,* a hilarious (and very controversial) sendup of contemporary society and politics. We consider Mozart's 1876 opera version — for musical, comic, and dramatic reasons — to be one of the best operas ever written. (You can hear the buoyant, sparkling overture on Track 1 of the CD that comes with this book.) This opera offers great examples of the kind of realistic motivations that drive Mozart's characters. For details, see Chapter 12.

One year after the premiere of *Figaro,* the city of Prague commissioned Mozart to write an opera to celebrate the marriage of the emperor's niece. And what solemn story did he choose to musicalize for this sacred union? The tale of Don Juan, the sleaziest sex maniac of them all. The opera was *Don Giovanni.* It was a smash hit. You can read all about it in Chapter 12.

## The minuteman

Tales of Mozart's speed in writing music became legendary. When a beggar approached him on the street, for example, he found himself without his wallet — so he whipped out a sheet of paper and wrote a new composition in a couple of minutes. He gave it to the beggar and sent him to a music publisher, who purchased it on the spot. (We suspect that Mozart would have less luck with this technique in today's New York City.)

This kind of composition speed went along with Mozart's hyper personality. In the middle of a conversation, he'd suddenly burst out laughing, jump up and down, turn somersaults, and leap tall tables and chairs in a single bound.

## Lorenzo da Ponte, Mozart's lecherous librettist

Of course, Mozart doesn't get all the credit for his sensational operas; after all, he *only* composed the music. The rest of the credit goes to the guy who wrote the words (the *libretto*). Mozart's best librettist was Lorenzo da Ponte (1749–1838), who first appears in Chapter 2 of this book.

Lorenzo, as you can read in Chapter 2, had no shortage of girlfriends. Perhaps they were the inspiration for his famous lyrics to the "Catalogue Aria" from Mozart's opera *Don Giovanni,* in which you learn about the more than 2,000 women Don Giovanni supposedly slept with. This aria is on Track 2 of the CD that came with this book, if you'd like a taste.

Together, Lorenzo and his buddy Wolfgang wrote three famous operas: *The Marriage of Figaro, Don Giovanni,* and *Così fan tutte.* These three Mozart-da Ponte productions were the high point of what they called, in Italy, *opera buffa* — a kind of farcical musical comedy — and, essentially, the end of it. Time had marched on, and the standard formulas were getting stale.

In the year of his death, Mozart composed *The Magic Flute.* Like his earlier hit *The Abduction from the Seraglio,* it is a German *Singspiel* — it has spoken dialogue between songs. *The Magic Flute* is a story about good and evil, redemption through virtue, immature bird catchers, and a Queen of the Night who owes no apologies to the Wicked Witch of the West. (See Chapter 12 for the full story.) In this opera more than any other, Mozart tells a story honestly and directly — proving himself a true descendent of Gluck. It remains a favorite even today.

Mozart died very shortly after the premiere of *The Magic Flute,* at age 35. For years afterward, the rumor (perpetuated in recent times by the movie *Amadeus*) circulated that Mozart had been poisoned by Antonio Salieri, a jealous fellow composer. But most likely, he simply died from exhaustion.

Since his death, the music world has never seen anyone with Mozart's combination of musical genius, compositional facility, and seemingly divine inspiration. His music is the essence of the Classical style: elegant, graceful, refined, high-spirited, and unsentimental, but with a deep vein of emotion.

# Ludwig van Beethoven

One of Mozart's most fervent admirers was Ludwig van Beethoven (1770–1827), pictured in Figure 8-3. Though Beethoven didn't concentrate on the realm of opera, he had an enormous effect on classical music as a whole. Practically by himself, this one man dragged music into a new world, kicking and sreaming.

Born in Bonn, Germany, Beethoven ("BAY-toe-ven") was the son of a court musician named Johann. Like Mozart's dad, Johann tried to turn his son into a famous child prodigy. Unlike Mozart's dad, Johann did it the hard way, beating his son when prodigyhood was too slow in coming.

Like so many composers of his day, Beethoven eventually moved to Vienna to be where the musical action was (and also, perhaps, to be as far away from Dad as possible). There he lived mostly by writing pieces commissioned by rich patrons and producing public concerts of his own compositions.

**Figure 8-3:**
Ludwig van
Beethoven
wrote
only one
opera —
but he
wrote it
three times!

Both Beethoven and his music were fiery, impulsive, and impetuous; people loved to watch and listen as he played his piano compositions with an impassioned delivery. Offstage, however, his fiery personality got him into fights with his landlords and girlfriends; Beethoven wasn't a long-term kinda guy, either in apartments or relationships.

## Composition for the hearing-impaired

At 31, Beethoven began to lose his hearing — the worst thing that can happen to a musician. The approaching deafness had a deeply disturbing effect on Beethoven, and he responded to this tragedy by throwing himself headlong into the creative process. Beethoven's compositions bear the mark of a *humanist,* a man desperately trying to rip his fate from the grasp of an uncaring universe. When you're aware of his condition at the time, his music makes much more sense.

## Fidelio: the opera

"Of all my children, this is the one that caused me the worst birth pangs, the one that brought me the most sorrow; and for that reason, it is the one most dear to me," Beethoven wrote about his one and only opera, *Fidelio.* He struggled with this work for 11 years, revising it over and over again, throwing out version after version. He even wrote five different overtures for the show in an effort to get it right. The opera was finally produced in 1803, just as Beethoven's deafness was plunging him into depression.

*Fidelio,* if produced as a movie today, would star Demi Moore as the clever, driven wife of a guy (played by Bruce Willis) who has been unjustly imprisoned. Demi dreams up a plan: She'll dress herself up as a man, call herself Fidelio, and bust her hubby out of jail. And that's just what she does. (More on this opera in Chapter 12.)

No stodgy old royalty figures dominate this plot, and no Greek myths are enacted. It's a testimony to the creative daring of Beethoven the humanist that he chose a story about a common man and woman with uncommon principles and bravery. In *Fidelio, they* are the ones who direct their fates — not a god, or gods, or the horoscope in the newspaper.

# Carl Maria von Weber

Carl Maria von Weber (1786–1826), shown in Figure 8-4, lived during the time of Beethoven. Weber (pronounced "VAY-ber") is more famous for his operas than for his instrumental compositions; in fact, he is known as the father of German Romantic opera.

In the Romantic style of classical music, the rules of logic and reason take a back seat to emotion. Romantic works — like the composers who wrote them — are expressive, passionate, and highly dramatic.

**Figure 8-4:**
Carl Maria von Weber was the father of German Romantic opera.

Weber's parents belonged to a traveling opera troupe, so Weber got to hear a lot of operas as a kid. He tried his hand at the art form early on — he wrote his own first opera when he was 14.

His most important opera, though, was *Der Freischütz* — which roughly means "The Free Shooter." It's the story of a hunter who makes a deal with the devil in order to procure some magic bullets, win a shooting contest, and get the girl. (Chapter 12 offers a somewhat more detailed synopsis.) In composing his music for this show, Weber transformed the nature of the art and created the first German Romantic opera.

How did he accomplish this feat? Well, first, Weber was a master of moods. In *Der Freischütz,* he created some stunning atmospheric effects, including a shivering, shuddering, devilish Wolf's Glen scene, in which the magic bullets are forged. It was a lot like Gothic horror; in fact, it *was* Gothic horror. This was the same period when Mary Shelley wrote her classic, *Frankenstein.*

Second, Weber made use of some pretty far-out literary themes — like the forces of good and evil. *Der Freischütz* introduced mysticism, the supernatural, and even Satanism to opera. We're talking 18th-century *X-Files.*

Actually, these themes weren't completely new; Mozart had used some of them in *The Magic Flute.* But in perpetuating the German-Austrian musical line, Weber took the themes further, going where no man had gone before.

In fact, he achieved something even more monumental: With *Der Freischütz,* Weber paved the way for the most mystically, spiritually, supernaturally plotted series of operas in the world — the *Ring* cycle, by Richard Wagner. Read on.

# Richard Wagner

For many opera fans, the Big Daddy of Them All was Germany's Richard Wagner (1813–1883), shown in Figure 8-5.

How do you assess a person like Richard Wagner ("REEKKH-art VOGG-ner")? He was an arrogant, dishonest, jealous, hypocritical, racist, sexist, and passionately anti-Semitic human being. In fact, Hitler adopted him as a hero for his beliefs — and until very recently, Wagner's music has been banned in Israel.

**Figure 8-5:**
Richard
Wagner
revolu-
tionized
opera.

Yet Wagner's music is innovative, imaginative, lush, powerful, intense, thrilling, and gorgeous. That's the paradox; musicians and other human beings over the last century have had to come to grips with the fact that a *person* like Wagner could have *composed* like Wagner.

Wagner was born in Leipzig, Germany, and from the beginning, he loved the theater. When he was 20, he got a job playing piano for rehearsals for an amateur opera company. This first-hand look at the innards and outards of opera-making inspired him to try his own hand at it.

Trust us on this: That hand was shaky at first. Wagner couldn't persuade anyone to even put on his first opera, *The Fairies.* And his second, *The Ban on Love,* was an utter disaster. On opening night, the singers didn't know their parts; the orchestra was out of tune and out of sync; and the prima donna's husband got so upset with the tenor's amorous behavior toward his wife in the opera that he jumped up on the stage to punch him in the face. (Apparently, he took the title of the opera literally.)

## Man without a country

But Wagner had the bug; he was too persistent (or too foolish) to give up. If Germany wasn't going to appreciate him, maybe another country would — such as, oh, say . . . *Latvia.* Wagner stayed in Latvia for two years, long enough to write a third opera, called *Rienzi,* which got a half-decent production. Although his attempts at opera were improving, his attempts at earning money were not. After two years, with creditors literally chasing him out of the country, he jumped onto a ship bound for London.

# Bad luck

Here's an interesting tidbit for numerologists: Wagner's entire life seems to have been dominated by the number 13.

For example, the name Richard Wagner contains 13 letters. He was born in 1813. (Those digits also add up to 13.) He was exiled from Germany for 13 years.

His opera *Tannhäuser* received its first performance on the 13th of April, and its disastrous Paris premiere took place on March 13. The *Ring* cycle was first performed beginning on August 13.

Wagner wrote 13 operas. He died on February 13, in the 13th year of the new German government.

And you wonder why the guy was unlucky?

Wagner wasn't what you'd call a boat person, however, and the stormy, violent crossing left an indelible mark on him. As he lurched miserably about in his cabin, the seed of a new opera came to him: *The Flying Dutchman,* based on the legend of a sea captain condemned to sail the seas forever. Listen to the cruel, raging sea sounds the orchestra makes in this opera, and you'll understand what Wagner's ship ride was like. (Plot details in Chapter 12.)

Next stop: Paris. Wagner spent two-and-a-half miserable years there, barely scraping by, writing piano arrangements of other peoples' operas. But while in Paris, Wagner was bitten by a second bug: German medieval poetry. He found in these legends fantastic tales of spiteful gods, stolen gold, and incest — perfect opera material.

Back he went to Germany, confident in his next operatic efforts: *Tannhäuser* and *Lohengrin,* based on those ancient German stories. Unfortunately for him, he'd also been active in political protests — enough to get him fired from his job, get a warrant out for his arrest, and force him to leave the country. (He wasn't allowed to go home for 13 years.)

After a few years of hanging out in Switzerland as a multinational reject, Wagner returned to Paris in 1861 to oversee a production of *Tannhäuser.* But the French audiences turned the premiere into a fiasco. (See the sidebar "A famous fiasco.")

## A famous fiasco

Few opera premieres have caused such a fiasco as Wagner's *Tannhäuser*. And yet, few premieres have started so promisingly.

Wagner had come to Paris looking for success; but there, as everywhere else, success had been elusive. After half a life of failure and financial ruin, Wagner was stunned and overjoyed to find that Napoleon II had ordered the Paris Opéra to produce his opera *Tannhäuser*. To Wagner, this was the world's greatest opportunity: a major-league opera house, fabulous singers, a world-class orchestra, and a blank check for sets, costumes, and staging.

The only problem was one of Parisian convention. For as long as anyone could remember, every show performed at the Paris Opéra had to have a ballet in the middle of the second act — as close to 10 p.m. as possible. The reason? A particularly exclusive, high-class group of opera snobs, who called themselves the Jockey Club, loved to watch ballerinas. On opera nights, they would eat at a fancy restaurant, stay for a leisurely dessert, and then amble over to the opera, arriving right around ten. They expected the ballet to start when they got there.

Wagner, being Wagner, rejected this custom. But the Opéra's director was upset. It would be impossible, he said, for any opera to succeed in that theater without a ballet in the second act. The Jockey Club simply would not allow it.

Wagner got to thinking: "You know, this opera really could use a ballet — at the *beginning*." So for the Paris production, he added a ballet to the *first* act. He was thrilled at the idea that the Jockey Club would miss it completely.

Furious at being spited, the Jockey Club arranged for the premiere to be a flop. They tramped in at the appointed time, as loudly as they could, and proceeded to boo the whole thing. Wagnerians in the audience tried to defend their master, but to no avail. Eventually, everyone was booing, hissing, yelling, laughing, and throwing things.

Still, plenty of audience members were impressed by the opera. So on the second night, with a much larger and more curious audience, the Jockey Club had to be more creative: They showed up with *whistles* and tweeted all the way through the performance. The third performance got whistled, too, and by then Wagner had had enough. Even though the opera was beginning to show some staying power (after all, it takes a lot to survive the Jockey Club), he ordered it withdrawn.

Wagner didn't hear *Tannhäuser* performed again for over 30 years.

## The call of Mad Ludwig

But fate finally smiled on Wagner; his persistence at opera-writing finally paid off on that bright day in 1864 when he met King Ludwig II of Bavaria. The king was a huge fan of Wagner's, and he sent a messenger to bring the composer to his castle, promising to satisfy his every need and publicize his operas throughout the land.

By most accounts, young Ludwig (shown in Figure 8-6), whose outlandish, ostentatious castles you can still visit, was a certifiable nut case. (He eventually went completely berserk and drowned himself in a lake.) In other words, he was the perfect patron for Richard Wagner.

**Figure 8-6:** King Ludwig II of Bavaria (1845–1886), known as "Mad Ludwig," was a famous nut case, and also supported Wagner.

Flush with funding from Ludwig, all of Wagner's influences, dreams, and theories about opera began to coalesce — and his opera career exploded. In 1865, Munich heard the premiere of *Tristan and Isolde,* a tale of two star-crossed lovers as tragic as Romeo and Juliet. Three years later came *The Master-Singers of Nuremberg (Die Meistersinger von Nürnberg),* which was supposed to be a cute little comic opera but wound up being one of the longest operas in the world. (Whoops.) You can hear excerpts from both of these momentous operas on your free CD.

The following year marked the premiere of Wagner's hugest creation: the *Ring* cycle (or *The Ring of the Nibelungs*). This cycle of four gigantic operas, based on medieval folk tales, ultimately made Wagner world-famous, just as the three *Star Wars* movies put George Lucas on the map.

You can read much more on the *Ring* cycle in Chapter 12. This *tetralogy* (a four-part trilogy) includes

✔ *The Rhine Gold* (known in German as *Das Rheingold*), which premiered in Munich in 1869.

   ✔ *The Valkyrie (Die Walküre),* which debuted in 1870. The most famous music from this show is the "Ride of the Valkyries," which has been used about a million times in movies and TV shows. (Remember in *Apocalypse Now* when the U.S. soldiers blast menacing music from their helicopter loudspeakers to terrorize the Vietnam jungle? That's it.)

   ✔ *Siegfried* and *Twilight of the Gods (Götterdämmerung),* first produced together in 1876.

Wagner realized very early on that in order to do justice to the *Ring,* he was going to have to build a special theater. In 1871, he picked out a site in the town of Bayreuth ("BUY-roit"); and for the next five years, he gave concerts all around Europe, raising money to realize his dream.

Once the money was raised, Wagner built the opera house to his exact specifications, including the world's only invisible orchestra pit. (A curved shield hides the musicians from the audience.) The now-famous Festival Playhouse (shown in Figure 8-7) opened with a complete *Ring* cycle in 1876. Bayreuth became the first summer opera festival in the world; and to this day, the Playhouse puts on the entire *Ring* every year.

Until you've heard the four operas of the *Ring,* you can't imagine how huge, complex, and sweeping they are. They're filled with enough sex, symbolism, and philosophy to keep psychiatrists busy for decades.

**Figure 8-7:**
The Fest-
spielhaus in
Bayreuth,
the opera
house
designed by
Wagner.

For Wagner, the *Ring* cycle wasn't just *opera* — it was, as he called it, an "artwork of the future." He didn't want his *Ring* operas to be about music alone; he wanted to unify all forms of art — music, poetry, drama, and design — into a single, all-encompassing new art form. He wanted the effect on the audience to be not just entertaining, but almost religious in impact.

Wagner did this by changing everything about opera as the world knew it: the story, the morality, the audience, and even the opera house itself.

## *The rules are broken*

To create this powerful "new art form," Wagner junked the existing rules of opera structure. Previous operas had consisted of a distinct alternation of *arias* (the main songs) and *recitatives* (free-rhythm, speechlike singing). In the *Ring* cycle, however, you hear a never-ending combination of both (or neither). That is, all the singer's notes are written out, and every note gets a syllable, but the effect is flexible and amorphous.

You generally can't even tell at what point a Wagner "song" begins or ends, because he didn't write the music in logical, recurrent chunks (such as the repeating verses and choruses that make, say, "Oh, Susannah" so easy to remember). Learning a Wagner opera isn't a cakewalk for the singers, either, because he didn't write simple *tunes;* he wrote complex, meandering melodies for the voice, as if it were a virtuosic orchestral soloist.

Plenty of people can't stand Wagner's music. If you're one of them, you're in good company. The Italian opera composer Gioachino Rossini said, "Wagner has some good moments," he said, "but some horrible quarters of an hour." And the poet Baudelaire wrote: "I love Wagner . . . but even more, I love the sound a cat makes when it's hung outside a window by the tail, and it tries to stick to the glass with its claws."

Wagner knew very well that his music wasn't built on traditional forms. So to lend *some* structure to the music, Wagner dreamed up the *Leitmotif* ("LIGHT-mo-teef," meaning "leading theme") — a little musical lick that's associated with a particular character in a story. Every time that character comes onto the stage, that little melody is played by the orchestra.

Once you understand how the technique works, go see *Star Wars.* Composer John Williams pulled exactly the same stunt in the movie music, providing a different musical theme for Princess Leia, Luke Skywalker, Obi-Wan Kenobi, and even Yoda.

## *The ride of the control freak*

Wagner threw his entire being into his operas. Perhaps inspired by the dismal productions that began his career, Wagner became the ultimate control freak and stage mother, overseeing every detail of every production: sets, lights, and even the theater itself. (We don't envy the set designer who was given the task of creating flying horses for the Valkyrie women, or simulating underwater swimming by the Rhine-maidens.)

Yet despite all his efforts to create perfectly balanced multimedia experiences, it's the *music* that continues to wow the crowds 125 years later. Like the opening of *The Rhine Gold,* for example: a single chord, repeated over and over for several minutes in undulating ripples by the orchestra, depicting the depths of the Rhine river. Or the mighty "Ride of the Valkyries." Or the Magic Fire Music at the end of *The Valkyrie.* Or Brünnhilde's stunning self-immolation scene in *Twilight of the Gods.* You just can't beat those moments for atmosphere and high drama. They make your hair stand on end.

As his reward for such an unusual combination of character and music, Wagner occupies a unique honor: More books and articles have been written about him than any other person in history except Jesus (and possibly O.J.).

Visit Chapter 12 (and Tracks 9 and 10 of this book's CD) for much more on Wagner's earth-shaking operas.

# *Johann Strauss, Jr.*

Meanwhile, back in the world of *funny* operas, a star was rising in Austria: Johann Strauss, Jr. (1825–1899), shown in Figure 8-8.

You're forgiven if your eyebrows just shot up. "Strauss? Not *the* Strauss? The one who invented blue jeans?"

No, no, the *other* Strauss: the one who wrote (and also performed) all those incredibly catchy Viennese waltzes, such as *The Blue Danube.* With his big bushy muttonchops, his violin always at the ready, "The Waltz King" flamboyantly conducted his touring orchestra all over Europe for adoring audiences, leaving a wake of love letters and swooning young women everywhere he went. Strauss's waltz concerts were the Woodstock of the 19th century, with police roping off meadows to contain the tens of thousands of dancing, humming groupies.

Strauss also managed to write 16 operettas — including his most famous of all, *Die Fledermaus (The Bat),* a funny, frothy, sparkling, tuneful work that appeals to opera beginners and opera snobs alike. His second most famous operetta is *The Gypsy Baron;* both are still performed today.

**Figure 8-8:**
Johann
Strauss Jr.,
known as
"The Waltz
King,"
wrote the
most
popular
German-
language
operetta
ever: *Die
Fledermaus
(The Bat).*

If you guessed that Strauss's shows are filled with waltzes, you're right —
which helps explain their great box-office draw. But the humor in these
operettas isn't as pointed and barbed as Offenbach's satire; the jokes target
classes of people in *general* rather than *particular* people.

# Richard Strauss

Just when you thought that you'd gotten your Strausses straight, here
comes Richard (no relation to "The Waltz King"). In the scheme of things,
Richard Strauss (1864–1949), shown in Figure 8-9, was actually a much more
important composer than Johann. Talk about talent: Richard (you have to
say it in German: "REEEKKHH-art") was composing and performing as a
mere tot. His first symphony was performed when he was just 14.

## Thus spoke Strauss

As an adult, Strauss firmly believed that after the age of Wagner, making
music in the old, established forms was no longer possible. For Strauss, the
future was in opera and in *tone poems:* orchestra pieces that tell a specific
story. (For the whole scoop on tone poems, see our modest little book,
*Classical Music For Dummies.*)

**Figure 8-9:**
Richard
Strauss
took
Wagner's
heroic
scale into
the 20th
century and
expanded
on it.

Richard Strauss's most famous tone poem is the monumental *Also sprach Zarathustra (Thus Spoke Zarathustra),* better known as the opening theme from the movie *2001: A Space Odyssey.* Remember when the proto-cavemen are looking at the giant black rectangle from outer space? You hear three long notes for trumpet, followed by a huge crash ("DA-Daaaaaaaah") for the entire orchestra and the roaring pulse of the kettledrums.

Strauss wasn't thinking about outer space when he wrote that piece. He was trying to depict, in tones, the sudden revelations of the legendary, ancient prophet Zarathustra. Can you think of any better way to depict in music a realization so cataclysmic that it affects the entire nature of the universe? (If so, please contact our toll-free number, 24 hours a day: 1-888-ZARATHUSTRA.)

Strauss claimed that he could describe extremely specific physical objects with musical notes. He once said about his tone poem *Don Juan,* "If you cannot hear from my music that Don Juan's second lover has red hair, then I have failed."

(Actually, *we* hear more of a dirty blond. But we digress.)

## Strauss goes operatic

Just as masterful as Strauss's tone poems are his 15 operas, in which he did his darnedest to emulate the sweeping scale, orchestral *Leitmotifs,* and all-arts-unified theory of his hero, Richard Wagner. One of his most famous was the mind-blowing shocker *Salome,* set in biblical times.

*Salome* was based on an Oscar Wilde play that was banned in England; maybe Strauss should have taken the hint. Anyway, it's about a highly neurotic, nearly nymphomaniac princess, Salome. When the imprisoned John the Baptist is brought before her, smelly, ratty, and filthy, she's filled with lust (she sings the immortal line, "I'm enamored of your hair") and begs to kiss him right in front of everyone. Her bodyguard, quite reasonably, immediately kills himself in disgust.

And that's just the *opening number.*

As you can imagine, this was heady stuff in 1905; the Germans absolutely loved it. Britons and Americans, however, were completely grossed out. The Metropolitan Opera in New York banned the opera for 27 years. (Much, *much* more on *Salome* in Chapters 2 and 12.)

You'd think that Strauss would have taken the hint, but in his next opera he didn't back off at all. Based on Greek mythology, *Elektra* (1909) is the story of a brother and sister (probably incestuous) who plot to kill their evil mother and stepfather. Composed during the time of Sigmund Freud, the score to this psychological drama often sounds completely chaotic, as it echoes the psychoses of the characters. *Elektra* is a primal scream, calculated to blow you out of your seat.

But then came 1911's *Der Rosenkavalier (The Knight of the Rose),* which many consider to be Strauss's masterpiece; instead of incest, murder, and filthy hair, this romantic comedy features lots of tuneful waltzes along the lines of *Johann* Strauss's greatest hits. (We guess that it'd be unsporting to tell Richard that in 1740 Vienna, where this opera is set, waltzes had not, in fact, been invented yet.)

The music in Strauss's shows, even the light, funny ones, never lost the stamp of a Wagner worshiper. The melody lines are often incredibly complex, with lots of musical ornaments and runs, and the orchestration is *thick,* with lots of instruments playing most of the time. In fact, Strauss's music has the reputation of being incredibly difficult to perform — and as a result, his pieces make some of the most-demanded *audition* pieces for orchestra-player candidates.

Strauss was also a prominent conductor, which may explain why he was one of the rare composers to get rich and famous while still alive. He regularly conducted his own music, as well as pieces by his hero, Wagner. Though he was a musical genius, you'd never know it from his conducting. He conducted sitting down, sober, expressionless, clear but passionless, his baton moving unemphatically through the air. He once proclaimed that a conductor's left thumb never needs to leave the pocket of his waistcoat. (Generations of future conductors, not knowing what a *waistcoat* is, have searched in vain for a place to stick their left thumbs ever since.)

# Alban Berg

Strauss's thick, complex music had a great influence on the operas of Alban Berg (1885–1935) of Vienna. If Strauss approached chaos in his wildest scores, Berg ("BEARg") attained it completely. If you're used to the hummable melody, toe-tapping rhythm, and satisfying harmonies of traditional classical music, this guy's stuff will freak you out.

Like many other composers at the beginning of this century, Berg experimented with music that was *atonal* — not in any particular key. Atonal music is *dissonant;* it sounds as if all the notes are wrong. For Berg and his contemporaries, this musical language reflected the chaos and destruction of post-World-War-I Europe.

Berg employed the alien strangeness of this new musical language to explore some of the same dark subjects of human psychosis and despair that Strauss had explored. He managed to create two well-known operas, *Wozzeck* (1925) and *Lulu* (1935). More on these smiley little nightmares in Chapter 13; for now, we'll just say that these operas are filled with sex, illegitimate children, sadism, violent murders, and suicide.

Do you wonder any longer, Dear Reader, why people love opera?

# Chapter 9

# The Russian Evolution — and the American Way

- - - - - - - - - - - - - - - - - - - - - - - - - - - - - - - - - -

### In This Chapter

▶ Mikhail Glinka, the guy who made Russian music Russian

▶ Peter Tchaikovsky, best of the Russians

▶ America: opera's late bloomer

- - - - - - - - - - - - - - - - - - - - - - - - - - - - - - - - - -

*A* curious trend shaped the opera world well into the last century. Since the time of Mozart, many composers throughout the world had sought to master the "Vienna sound," a style of composing with characteristics as recognizable as pop music's "Motown sound" (though markedly different). Then, after Rossini and friends made a big splash in Italy, the "Italian sound" became equally popular abroad. Everywhere, composers wanted to *sound* European — even if they weren't.

Opera in Russia, like everywhere else, began with decades of such Europe-worshiping. The first opera ever performed in Russia was imported from Germany by Tsar Alexis around 1650. Later, Empress Catherine the Great created a little Italian opera company in St. Petersburg, and she commissioned a new opera (to her own libretto) on the occasion of her coronation. The opera, called *The Victory of Minerva,* took a full two weeks to perform. No wonder it didn't do so well at the box office.

In the 19th century, however, composers worldwide rediscovered the folk tunes of their own native countries — the unique sounds they'd heard growing up. Suddenly, composers began rejecting the Austrian-German and Italian traditions in favor of their homelands' native styles.

Soon the wave of *Russian nationalism* began as well. And the surfer atop the crest of that wave was Mikhail Glinka.

# Mikhail Glinka and Friends

So what makes a Russian opera sound Russian? Just ask Mikhail Glinka ("GLEENG-ka"; 1804–1857), shown in Figure 9-1, nicknamed "the Father of Russian Music." (The Mother of Russian Music has not been identified — but she sure wasn't Glinka's wife, who complained that Mikhail was wasting money buying music paper.)

**Figure 9-1:**
Mikhail Glinka (1804–1857), considered to be the father of Russian music.

As demonstrated by Glinka's most famous operas, *A Life for the Tsar* (1836) and *Ruslan and Ludmila* (1842), real Russian music is painted in broad, bright strokes and dramatic, soaring melodies. The rhythms are based on the inflections of Russian speech, and the simple, hummable melodies were no doubt a refreshing change from the complex musical motifs that were filling German operas at the time.

## The Mighty Fistful

Glinka was hailed as a hero by other Russian composers of the day. In emulation of Glinka, a group of five composers, called the Mighty Five, or the Mighty Fistful, decided to banish western European influence from their music, embracing Russianness to the max. The individual fingers of the Mighty Fistful were Mily Balakirev (1837–1910), who first got the group together but didn't actually write any operas himself; Cesar Cui (1835–1918); Alexander Borodin (1833–1887); Modest Mussorgsky (1839–1881); and Nicolai Rimsky-Korsakov (1844–1908).

All of them were decent musicians, but only one of them (Balakirev) had originally entered music as a profession. Cui was a professor of military engineering; Borodin was a chemist; Mussorgsky was a civil servant;

Rimsky-Korsakov was a naval officer. Of all these composers, the sailor became the most accomplished in the symphonic realm, and the civil servant became the best opera composer.

## Rimsky-Korsakov: the one-man team

When we were kids, we thought Rimsky-Korsakov was a songwriting team, like Rodgers and Hammerstein or Lerner and Loewe. Not only were Rimsky and Korsakov the same person, that wasn't even his *entire* name; his first name was Nicolai.

Rimsky-Korsakov's music is elegant, polished, and colorful, with a real Russian flair. He wrote operas based on Russian folk stories. His most famous effort is *The Golden Cockerel;* somewhat less well known are *Sadko, May Night* and *The Snow Maiden.* You can read much more about his life and work in *Classical Music For Dummies.*

One of R-K's other famous marks on history was helping out his friend Modest Mussorgsky. Although he was a highly imaginative musician, Modest had trouble finishing his pieces, partially because he lacked compositional technique and partly because he was a roaring drunk. Rimsky, recognizing his friend's rough genius, completed several of his compositions for him.

Good thing, too — today, Mussorgsky is considered one of the most important Russian opera composers. In fact, his 1874 opera *Boris Godunov* is considered *the* Russian nationalist opera. You can read all about it in Chapter 12.

What makes *Boris Godunov* unique is that the standard Italian opera formula goes out the window. The plot arrives in self-contained historical panels called *tableaux* instead of the traditional dramatic scenes; and instead of fancy arias and polished, European-sounding phrases, the music has a coarser, folksy style.

# Peter Tchaikovsky

The best Russian composer of them all was not a member of the Mighty Fistful. He was, however, a self-absorbed, neurotic, vulnerable, intense guy whose entire life consisted of suffering. So give him a break.

Peter Ilyich Tchaikovsky ("chy-KOFF-skee"), shown in Figure 9-2, was another of the great nationalists. Though he was well-versed in western European forms, his music exudes an unmistakable Slavic warmth.

**Figure 9-2:**
Peter
Tchaikovsky,
one of the
greatest of
Russian
opera
composers.
He was
even more
successful
as a
composer of
symphonies
and ballets.

Tchaikovsky's musical career didn't begin until after a sincere but miserable attempt at parent-induced law school; his next stop was the St. Petersburg Conservatory of Music. Eventually, Tchaikovsky (1840–1893) learned enough to get a job as professor of music at a new conservatory being formed in Moscow. He was, however, flat broke.

Luckily, fate smiled on him at least once in his life. A woman named Nadezhda von Meck, the wealthy widow of a railroad entrepreneur, became enamored of his music. She probably became enamored of *him,* too, which was something of a no-no in the days of wealthy widows of 19th-century railroad entrepreneurs. Therefore, she added a peculiar condition to her financial support: If she and Tchaikovsky ever met, the money would stop. Needless to say, they never met. Tchaikovsky was exceedingly grateful for her funding, and he even dedicated his Fourth Symphony to her, with the words, "To my best friend."

## Nobody knows the trouble I've seen

The Nadezhda effect eased Tchaikovsky's financial worries, but new troubles loomed — mainly because he was gay. Homosexuality was a crime in Russia, punishable by exile to Siberia. For most of his life, Tchaikovsky was forced to conceal his true nature in misery and despair. Many historians even believe that his eventual death — ostensibly of cholera — was actually a suicide. In any case, it's easy to imagine that the soaring, longing melodies of Tchaikovsky's music reflect the agony of having to live a secret life.

At one stage, Tchaikovsky honestly believed that he could "cure" his torment. He married a former student who had professed her undying love for him (a good start, we always say). But the marriage was disastrous, leaving him miserable, divorced, and worse off than before.

## The music of a pained soul

Despite his private-life soap opera, Tchaikovsky's symphonies, ballets, operas, and overtures became immensely popular, and his fame spread around the world. He even conducted at the gala opening concert of New York's Carnegie Hall in 1891.

Why was Tchaikovsky so popular? In a word, *melody* — Tchaikovsky's greatest gift. In the tradition started by Glinka, Tchaikovsky wrote *entire* melodies into his music. And *what* melodies they were — soaring, passionate, and glorious.

Two factors make Tchaikovsky seem like the perfect opera composer. First, his famous symphony and ballet music is *extremely* dramatic (for example, the love theme from his *Romeo and Juliet,* which plays soaringly in the background every time you see a kiss on TV or in a movie). Second, his whole *existence* was extremely dramatic, including, as it did, marriage to a daft groupie and a tormented secret life.

Yet of his ten operas, only two were ever heard from again: the passionate, lyrical *Eugene Onegin* (1878) and *The Queen of Spades* (1890). The more successful of the two is *Onegin,* which you can read about in Chapter 12. And if you'd like to know about the nonvocal works of this incredible composer (such as his *Nutcracker* ballet or his *1812 Overture*), we refer you, blushingly, to *Classical Music For Dummies.*

# Later Russian Masters

Russian opera did not end with Tchaikovsky. Two later masters deserve mention in this book. The first is Igor Stravinsky (1882–1971), well known for his ground-breaking, scandalous ballet, *The Rite of Spring.* Stravinsky's opera *The Rake's Progress* is still performed everywhere.

The second master is Dmitri Shostakovich (1906–1975), the best composer of the former Soviet Union. As a young man, he achieved great success with his compositions — until he wrote his modernistic opera, *Lady Macbeth of Mtensk*. Stalin condemned the opera as "chaos instead of music," and Shostakovich became a musical outcast overnight, officially branded an *Enemy of the People.* It took an abject (and insincere) apology to rehabilitate himself in the eyes of the totalitarian regime. Today, *Lady Macbeth of Mtensk* is one of the most beloved and often-performed operas in Russia.

## Czech mates

While all the operatic triumphs you've been reading about were happening in western Europe and Russia, another little country was producing hits of its own. Bohemia (the area now known as the Czech Republic) produced three outstanding operatic composers — Smetana, Dvořák, and Janáček.

Bedřich Smetana ("BED-r-zhikh" SMEH-ta-nah" — hey, nobody said that opera was going to be easy) was one of the first nationalist composers. Smetana (1824–1884) created truly Bohemian-style music, incorporating traditional folk tunes and rhythms. His comic opera *The Bartered Bride* remains a favorite in Bohemia and all over the world. Read about it in Chapter 13.

Smetana influenced Antonín Dvořák (1841–1904), another Bohemian hero. Dvořák ("da-VOR-zhak") wrote lots of beautiful, tuneful instrumental music, and his opera *Rusalka* — a Czech *Little Mermaid* tale — continues to delight audiences whenever it is performed. It's also described in Chapter 13.

Dvořák, in turn, influenced Leoš Janáček (1854–1928), who mingled his Bohemian influences with a bold new musical style of his own. His operas include *Jenůfa, Katja Kabanová, The Makropulos Case*, and *The Cunning Little Vixen*. You can read about *Jenůfa* in — you guessed it — Chapter 13.

# The United States of Opera

One reason opera has only recently become the rage in the United States is the fact that, from an American's point of view, all the most famous operas are in foreign languages. The average American can be forgiven for asking, "Why aren't more operas written in good old American English?"

*Answer:* Europe had a 1,000-year head start.

As a result, in the early American years, singers, conductors, and producers were imported from Europe to strut their stuff for the New World. And when U.S. composers did begin writing operas, their first attempts were designed to sound European. Furthermore, even the first native U.S. operettas were written by transplanted Europeans, such as Sigmund Romberg (1887–1951) from Hungary, who wrote *The Student Prince* and *Desert Song;* and Victor Herbert (1859–1924) from Ireland, who was well known for *Naughty Marietta,* among others.

But those early operettas were set in exotic, escapist locales: medieval France, North Africa, and other times and places far removed from the modern United States. This country had its own stories to tell and its own problems to confront. Eventually, African-American music, jazz, and movies with soundtracks helped create a distinct American sound, and a blossoming of native U.S. talent.

## Opera swings

Take George Gershwin (1898–1937), for example. (See Figure 9-3.) Most of his shows were proper musicals, such as *Girl Crazy, Of Thee I Sing, Let 'Em Eat Cake, Funny Face,* and *Oh, Kay!*

**Figure 9-3:** George Gershwin was one of the first composers to successfully combine classical and jazz elements in the concert hall and the opera house.

But another work of his belongs in this book: *Porgy and Bess.* Though heavily infused with jazz and other U.S. musician influences, this was a real opera — and, because its main characters were poor, downtrodden African-Americans, it was both powerful and controversial. You can read our copious comments on this masterpiece in Chapter 12, and listen to an excerpt on Track 13 of your free CD.

The American ragtime composer Scott Joplin (composer of "The Entertainer," "The Maple Leaf Rag," and other tunes that found their way into the movie *The Sting*) wrote two operas a couple of decades before Gershwin's *Porgy and Bess.* The first one has disappeared, but the second, *Treemonisha,* occasionally receives enthusiastic revivals.

Two of America's greatest composers were Samuel Barber and Aaron Copland. Barber's lush and lovely opera *Vanessa,* which won the Pulitzer Prize in 1958, is considered one of the staples of the modern opera repertory. (His only other opera, *Antony and Cleopatra,* was written for the opening of the new Metropolitan Opera in New York — and it's as grand as opera gets. But because of its enormous production costs, it gets performed much less often.) Copland's *The Tender Land,* which takes place on an American farm during the Depression, receives periodic revivals in the United States and abroad.

# U.S. opera is alive and well

After World War II, the surging American optimism (and booming economy) helped give birth to a different breed of opera: the *musical*. In musicals, dialogue scenes and musical numbers are equally important, and the lyricists are just as important as the composers.

Think of all the great shows that began life in New York City: *Show Boat, Oklahoma, The Sound of Music, Guys and Dolls, My Fair Lady, West Side Story,* all of Stephen Sondheim's stuff . . . the list is practically endless. Then there are the recent musicals that approach opera in their grand, monumental treatments and unending musical flow: *Sweeney Todd,* for example, or *Rent,* or *Les Misérables.* In fact, some people believe that the Broadway musical has been the United States' real contribution to opera. But hey — that's the topic for a different *...For Dummies* book.

Even as musicals blossomed on Broadway, traditional American operas continued to sprout. Carlisle Floyd's *Susannah* (1955) — a homespun folk opera filled with hymns, Appalachian square dances, and folk tunes — remains among the most frequently produced American operas. 1956 brought Douglas Moore's *The Ballad of Baby Doe,* another folk-influenced opera — based on the true story of an American silver-mine owner who lost his fortune but found love in the arms of a miner's wife. The authentic American dialect and highly melodic folk tunes made this miner opera a major one.

More recently, John Adams set the music world abuzzing with his minimalist opera, *Nixon in China.* (*Minimalism* is a type of music involving very repetitive snippets of music, with subtly shifting rhythms and harmonies that tend to lull the listener into an altered state — known in some circles as *sleep.* We love this music, but it's definitely a matter of taste.) Another minimalist composer, Philip Glass, has written four fascinating operas so far: *Einstein on the Beach, Satyagraha* (sung in Sanskrit, about Gandhi's nonviolent resistance movement), *Akhnaten* (about the forward-looking Egyptian pharaoh, Nefertiti's husband), and *The Voyage* (an opera that combines Columbus's voyage with space travel, specially commissioned by the Metropolitan Opera in New York).

Yet another extremely gifted American composer, William Bolcom, recently composed an opera called *McTeague,* the story of a very unusual dentist. And John Corigliano composed a wildly successful opera, also commissioned by the Met. Called *The Ghosts of Versailles,* it shifts effortlessly among time periods and places, involving the characters from *The Marriage of Figaro* in a hilarious, atmospheric time-travel sendup — and bringing us full circle.

# Part III
# A Night at the Opera

The 5th Wave                    By Rich Tennant

"Funny—I just assumed it would be Carreras, too."

## In this part . . .

Attending a live opera isn't quite as simple as popping a CD into your stereo and hitting Play. But no worries: If you've never attended a live opera, you've come to the right place. Chapter 10 takes you into the strange traditions of the opera house. Chapter 11 contains a guided tour of the CD that comes with this book, to give you some practice in listening to the greats. And the Intermission that follows takes you backstage — into the fascinating world of singers, conductors, orchestra musicians, choruses, and stage directors.

# Chapter 10

# How to Go to an Opera

## In This Chapter

▶ How to get the best ticket deals

▶ What to wear, what to eat, and where to sit

▶ How to decipher the program book

▶ How to survive the intermission — and maybe even enjoy it

*I*f you've read the first two acts of this book, you now know what a libretto is, what opera is, and how one gets turned into the other. You've read a little bit about the history of opera, the composers who wrote it, and the people who sing it. Now it's time to experience an opera performance — live.

At this point, your average beginner's-guide-to-opera book would probably tell you to sit back, relax, and have a great time. But why on earth should you relax? Do you relax just before you go skydiving for the first time? Do you relax before your first night of passionate romance? *Do you relax before hiking through a swamp full of anacondas?*

Of course not. You're doing something new, dangerous, and exciting. Opera isn't a sedative — it's a kick!

So please: Be afraid. Be very afraid. *We,* your intrepid authors, are relaxed. We'll get you through this in one piece.

## Buying a Ticket

Before you can go to the opera, you have to get yourself a ticket. This section gives you five tips for the most successful ticket-buying experience.

## Buy in advance

When a big opera star comes to town, tickets go fast — especially the good seats. Most big opera houses put their tickets on sale four to six weeks in advance of the show. Call the box office and check.

## Understand the opera house floor plan

The inside of a professional opera house is *huge.* Depending on where you sit, your experience can vary enormously. Every opera hall is unique, but most have these elements in common:

- ✔ **The orchestra section** is the ground floor — the expensive seats in front of the stage and the orchestra pit. In England, these seats are called the *stalls.*

- ✔ **Tiers** is a fancy word for balconies, especially the ones that stretch all the way around the sides of the auditorium. These tiers usually have creative names like First Tier and Second Tier; you may also hear names like Dress Circle, Balcony, and (at the Met) Family Circle. Generally speaking, the higher they are, the cheaper they are. The high tiers are really, *really* high; if you're acrophobic, consider the orchestra section instead, or pack a parachute.

- ✔ **Boxes** are sectioned-off groups of seats. Within each box, the chairs may be freely moved around (unlike regular auditorium seats, which are bolted to the floor). Boxes often have anterooms, where you can hang your coat and sneak in and out of the auditorium without bothering anybody.

- ✔ **Standing room,** available in some opera houses, is a limited area in the back of the orchestra section for standing. Standing for an entire opera is uncomfortable, but tickets are very cheap.

- ✔ **Partial view, no view:** Many opera houses offer seats whose view is blocked by pillars and other obstructions. They're usually 30 to 75 percent cheaper than the full-view seats. But unless you're visually impaired anyway, what's the point? The satisfaction of knowing that you saved big bucks can't make up for the frustration of not being able to see what's going on.

If you're buying tickets to a particular opera house for the very first time, we suggest that you actually *go* to the box office, where you can examine a seating plan of the auditorium. That way you know what you're buying.

## Don't hide your innocence

Let the box office know that you're buying a ticket for your first opera ever. Most box-office attendants have at least a little pride in their organization, and they want to make sure that you enjoy the experience enough to come back. They'll gladly explain the different sections of their particular opera house to you — including the seats that have the best view, the best sound, the best access to the rest-room, and so on. They can also alert you to good deals, discounts, or special offers.

## If the box office doesn't have what you want, don't give up

At most opera companies, most tickets are sold by mail or by phone. Those tickets may reside in the actual box office itself — or they may be in a separate part of the building, where those mail or phone orders are processed. It's quite possible that the tickets sitting at the box office on the day you visit represent just a fraction of the tickets *available* for sale!

So if they don't have what you want at the box office, try ordering by mail or by phone. And if *that* doesn't work, keep trying. Usually, somebody turns his ticket back in — and you're in luck.

## Consider subscribing

If you're beginning to get the feeling that this opera thing is for you, consider buying a subscription series, consisting of anywhere from two to ten (or more) operas. The advantages of becoming a subscriber are substantial:

- ✔ **You get first crack at the best seats.** Tickets always go on sale to subscribers before the general public. And if you like your seat, you can renew it year after year.

- ✔ **You get invited to special events** — the Opera Ball, for example, or the Pavarotti gala concert.

- ✔ **You get a discount.** The cost of a series of five operas is almost always less than the cost of five separate operas.

The disadvantages of subscribing are few, but significant:

- ✔ **You may not like all the operas.** After all, in most subscription series, the opera house chooses the operas that you're going to hear.

- ✔ **You may have a schedule conflict.** Unless you plan your life around the opera, you may not be able to make it to all the performances. In that case, you're not saving any money by subscribing; buy single tickets instead.

- ✔ **You may not like your seat.** If you buy a subscription series, you'll sit in the same seat for every opera. If you don't like that seat, it's too late to change until the following season.

# How to Save Money at a Bulgravian Opera House

Most opera companies these days have financial worries. If they're not actually running a deficit, they're just scraping by. All opera companies need and deserve moral and financial support. We'd feel extremely guilty giving you tips on how to save money at an opera house in *this* country.

So instead, we're going to give you tips on how to save money at a Bulgravian opera house. In Bulgravia, as you probably know, opera companies are funded by an autocratic government; we don't particularly care whether it makes profits on its operas.

*Fact number one:* From a sonic point of view, the best seats are not necessarily the most expensive. In many opera houses, the best *sound* is in the back of the top balcony; there, you can sometimes hear sound reflected at you from the ceiling, sounding as if you're right next to the singers. On rare occasions, you can even hear their whispers. Furthermore, seats right in front of the stage, where the bigwigs sit, often have the *worst* acoustics; sitting there is like eating *knotchpanitchki* with too much garlic and not enough onion. You get too much of one thing and no blend. Let the flavors mix by sitting farther back.

*Addendum:* On the other hand, watching singers is an awful lot of fun, and you can watch them best if you sit up front. So what to do? Well, binoculars are good. (If you don't own a pair, you can rent them at the opera.) You might also consider buying a cheap ticket up in the top balcony, and (at some point during the first act) scanning for empty seats down front. After intermission, take any unclaimed seat. This way, you get the best of all possible worlds: superb acoustics in the first act, a great view in the second (or third or fourth) act, and a cheap ticket.

***Addendum to the addendum:*** What if you take an unclaimed seat and then someone shows up to claim it? Take out your own ticket, appear surprised, and use the following phrase:

| | |
|---|---|
| *Hôppla! et hèlá plàta Orkêstu A-1?* | Oh, is this seat Orchestra A-1? |
| *Jôt dümal shto bîla Tritja Balkôn ZZ-49!* | I thought it was Third Balcony ZZ 49! |
| *Jôt toka requalá.* | I'm so sorry. |

Or, better yet:

| | |
|---|---|
| *Môy bônaful! Et hèlá Sámôdi?* | My goodness, is this Saturday? |

Actually, just a smile will do nicely. You always have your own ticket to fall back on.

***Fact number two:*** You may find scalpers standing in front of opera houses. Some of these people may try to rip you off, but most are quite honest. They can't use their tickets, but they don't want them to go to waste. Sometimes they ask the original price; sometimes they offer a discount; and sometimes they just *give* them away! Look friendly and respectable, and try to avoid being spotted by the Secret Police.

***Fact number three:*** If you're *really* hard up for cash, consider arriving at the first intermission. (The intermission time varies widely according to opera; call the opera house to find out when it starts.) You can always find some folks who leave at intermission, because they have a headache, they have an early day at the collective farm tomorrow, or whatever. Usually, they're delighted to give you their tickets. Just stand outside on the front steps (or in the lobby) and ask politely. That's all it takes. In our student days, we did this occasionally. Now we do it all the time.

***Addendum to fact number three*** (and remember, you didn't hear this tip from us): In many Bulgravian opera houses, tickets are almost never checked as people return from the intermissions. And that's all we're going to say about *that.*

# For Lovers Only: Which Operas to Attend — or Avoid — on a Date

An opera is a wonderful event for lovers. Opera has been synonymous with romance and beauty for centuries. Just think: Sets! Costumes! Huge, powerful sopranos!

Well, okay — sets and costumes.

If you want to impress your date with your taste, culture, and romantic instinct, you simply can't do better than an evening of opera. This well-planned evening of romance won't lead to *further* romance, however, unless you take certain things into account.

First, what kind of opera company are you going to hear? If it's an established opera company or national tour, you almost can't go wrong. The voices will be good, the sets will be impressive, and the orchestra will be first-rate. If it's a small, professional, college, or conservatory production, you may be in for some uneven vocal and instrumental quality, but overall high standards. And if it's an amateur community group, all bets are off.

Next, consider what style or period of music you're going to hear. You can use the Opera Timeline (Appendix B) to see what period each composer on the program belongs to, which will give you some clue as to the character of the opera you're about to hear. *Baroque* music is expressive, but in a highly stylized way. *Classical-period* music is lovely and gracious, yet somewhat emotionally reserved (great for the first date with the daughter of an oil magnate). *Romantic* music is lush, gorgeous, and very expressive. *Modern* music can range from harsh and dissonant to all of the above.

Finally, investigate what the opera's *about.* Because some of the stories can be embarrassing in romantic situations, you may want to avoid certain operas on a date (especially if you don't know each other very well). For example, beware of the following operas:

- ✔ ***Don Giovanni*** (by Wolfgang Mozart, 1787): A brilliant and charming opera featuring Don Juan, the lover and rapist, who slept with 2,065 women. The opera begins with a murder and attempted rape, chronicles various seductions, features a brutal pistol-whipping, and ends when the screaming Don gets dragged down to Hell.

- ✔ ***I Pagliacci*** (by Ruggiero Leoncavallo, 1892): Another masterwork, one of the standards of the repertoire. It's about a pathetic clown who laughs on the outside, cries on the inside, and stabs his wife and his wife's boyfriend.

- ✔ ***Wozzeck*** (by Alban Berg, 1925): A happy little toe-tapper of a musical about a dimwitted soldier (with an illegitimate child) who drowns himself after murdering his tramp of a girlfriend. Better wait until you're going steady before you see this one.

On the other hand, depending on the relationship, some of these operas may be just the ticket.

# How to Prepare for It — or Not

All right then. You've bought your tickets and invited your date. Now you want to get ready for the experience. In this section, we tell you what steps you should take to prepare.

## Learn something about the opera

You don't need to spend months studying an opera in advance of a performance. But the better you know something, the more you tend to enjoy it. So after spending up to $100 on an opera ticket, you may want to spend a little bit of time preparing for the experience. Here's what we recommend:

- ✔ **Listen to a recording of the opera you're about to hear.** The more you listen, the more you'll get out of the opera, guaranteed.

- ✔ **Read the libretto.** While you're listening, follow along with the libretto (the little book that has all the words in the opera, complete with translation). A libretto is enclosed in almost all opera CDs.

That's plenty of preparation, unless you want to be like the hard-core opera lovers who actually buy the printed score and study the music. (If you decide to do *that,* let Chapter 3 be your guide.)

## Sleep tight

Get a good night's sleep before an opera performance — or better yet, a good *day's* sleep. A little nap in the afternoon before an opera will make you blazingly awake for the performance.

## Can I wear a toga to Julius Caesar?

People often get uptight about what to wear to an opera. And well they should! How can ordinary people like us be expected to know what to wear to the opera?

The truth is, you can wear whatever you want. Absolutely no dress requirements or dress codes are in force at the opera house. We, your radical authors, feel that informal dress makes it much easier to relax and really get into the music.

But wait, you say. What about all those men dressed like waiters? And the women with pearls draped around their necks and hair piled up to the third balcony?

Well, some of them, to be sure, enjoy the opportunity to step into their most magnificent finery a few times a year (and if you are one of them, here's your chance). But a small percentage of these elegant dressers — oh, say, about 90 percent — are bowing to peer pressure. They feel that they're *expected* to dress up at an opera. If they don't dress up, what will their friends think?

We want you to be comfortable with your environment, not intimidated by it. So for handy reference, here's what you're likely to see at an opera:

- ✔ A small segment of the audience — especially the younger crowd — dresses casually.

- ✔ The largest segment wears business attire: a suit and tie for men, a dress (or business suit) for women.

- ✔ The elite crowd takes this dressing up to an extreme, wearing a tux or pearls (or even *both*). ***Note:*** At the opening night of an opera or a benefit performance, *most* of the audience dresses this way.

Custom varies widely from place to place. For example, Europeans tend to dress up more than Americans. And within the United States, the East Coast (and especially New York) dresses more formally than the rest of the country.

By the way, if you do decide to wear theme clothes to a concert (a toga and so on), you'll probably be alone. You'll get funny looks, but you won't be asked to leave; some people will assume that you're doing publicity for the opera, and they'll be delighted.

We now come to a very important point on the subject of dress. If anyone, at any time, shows disapproval of your dress, do the following: Turn to the person, smile, and ask, "What did you think about that absolutely stunning resolution of the suspended dissonance by means of an arpeggiation of the tonic triad toward the end of the exposition in the overture?" This tactic always works.

You're usually best off waiting, however, until after the orchestra has played something.

## *The gourmet guide to pre-opera dining*

Here's the rule in pre-opera dining: Avoid creating a situation in which you're constantly walking out of the auditorium to use the facilities. The list of foods to avoid includes, for example, deep-fried cheese curds, baked-bean casserole, a Double Whopper with Cheese, and a Big Gulp.

At an opera, you're being entertained by live human beings who must maintain focus, concentration, and composure for long periods of time. It's conceivable that you, standing up, sidling your way past 44 sets of audience-member knees, and ducking for the exit, could disturb the performers (and rile the audience).

***Warning:*** The line for the ladies' room at today's opera houses often stretches for several city blocks. This situation is a result of a simple mathematical relationship:

- ✔ The average opera house holds upwards of 2,000 people.
- ✔ The average ladies' room holds six.

Believe it or not, many opera houses have been forced to lengthen their intermissions for precisely this reason.

If you're a woman, we offer two suggestions for avoiding the Opera-House Ladies' Room Nightmare:

- ✔ Don't overindulge in the liquid department before the opera.
- ✔ Dress as a man.

What all this boils down to is a solution that experienced operagoers have known for a long time: Eat light beforehand — and pig out *after* the opera.

# *Arriving at the Opera House*

Now comes the big moment when you actually set foot in the opera house for the first time. It's a confusing and intimidating place, made all the more intimidating by the fact that everyone else seems to know what's going on. Here's what we suggest:

- ✔ **Arrive early.** Many opera houses won't admit latecomers until the first intermission — and that could mean a one-hour wait (or even *two* hours, in extreme cases).
- ✔ **Check your coat in the winter.** If you keep a thick winter coat with you at your seat, you'll regret it. That coat will hang on you all night like a bear rug. You can check it safely near the entrance for a couple of bucks — a little money for a lot of comfort.
- ✔ **Use the restroom beforehand.** Trust us on this one.
- ✔ **Find the right seat.** Don't be lulled into a sense of security by the fact that your ticket says "Seat B-4." Each section, tier, and balcony of the auditorium is likely to have its *own* seat B-4! If you're not sure where your seat is, ask an usher for help.

> ✔ **Turn off anything that beeps.** The sound of 3,845 watches simultaneously beeping the hour can be disconcerting to an opera singer — not to mention the audience.

# A Peek at the Opera Program

The program booklet is critical to enjoying the opera you're about to experience. You can expect to see all the following elements in any self-respecting opera program book:

> ✔ A list of the opera characters, and who plays them

> ✔ A list of the acts and scenes of the opera

> ✔ A short summary of the plot, including some history

> ✔ A roster of the players in the orchestra and the singers in the chorus

> ✔ An advertisement for Rolex

Many opera houses offer for sale at least two printed items beyond the program book itself. One is a *deluxe* program book, complete with gorgeous color pictures, a history of the opera (including all past performances at that particular opera house), critical essays on the meaning of the opera, and a description of the characters and the action in each scene. The other book is a copy of the libretto itself, both in the original language and in translation, in case you'd like to follow along.

## The orchestra pit

If you haven't been to an opera before, you may not know what an *orchestra pit* is. Technically speaking, it's a pit with an orchestra in it.

The orchestra pit is a relatively new development. In the last century, people discovered that seeing and hearing the singers onstage was a whole lot easier when the orchestra musicians weren't blocking their view.

So in most opera houses, the area under that stage, and slightly in front of it, is hollowed out for the orchestra. During an opera, much of the audience can't see these subterranean music-makers at all — except for the conductor, whose head sticks up so that he can cue the singers onstage.

If the orchestra piques your curiosity, check out our companion volume, *Classical Music For Dummies*. It covers all aspects of classical music, with several chapters devoted to the instruments of the orchestra.

These books can cost an arm and a leg, but they're great to have; the deluxe program book is neat to look at (and to remember the production by, even years later); and the libretto can help you understand what's going on in the story. (Of course, you won't need it at all if surtitles are provided. See "Surtitles to the Rescue" later in this chapter.)

# A simple example

We're now going to take you through a simple opera program, representative of many of the programs you may encounter at an opera today.

What a great program you see on the next page: Helpful, informative, and efficient, it does its job wonderfully. At the top of the page is the name of the company that's putting on the opera — in this case, Tri-Counties Opera, Inc.

Below the name of the company is the one ambiguous aspect of the program page. Are you going to hear the opera *Don Pasquale* by Gaetano Donizetti? Or is it *Gaetano Donizetti* by Don Pasquale? You can find out if you turn the page to read about the composer. (**Hint:** Donizetti's the composer.)

Next is a list of six dates on which the opera will be performed. Note that there are five days off between performances! That's because singing an opera takes a lot of vocal strength and stamina, and even the most seasoned professionals need time off between performances to rest their voices. It's a rare opera company indeed that schedules two performances of the same opera, with the same cast, on two consecutive nights. The Tri-Counties Opera, Inc. is following in a proud tradition that allows the singers to be at their best at every performance.

Still, *five days* between performances is a bit extreme. Then again, just look at the singers — they're all either world-class or dead. So give them a break.

After the dates comes the cast of characters. This opera includes only five singing roles. Beside each character is the name of the singer hired to play that part, and what vocal part (soprano, tenor, and so on; see Chapter 4).

Finally, this admirable little program page gives the name of the conductor and a description of the opera's setting. You're ready to roll.

## The Tri-Counties Opera, Inc.
Furioso Sabado, Artistic Director

Robert Louis Stevenson Elementary School Auditorium
Farfalloo, Wyoming

Gaetano Donizetti
# Don Pasquale

*September 1, 6, 11, 16, 21, and 26, 1998*
*8:00 p.m.*

*Cast of Characters:*

| | |
|---|---|
| Don Pasquale, *an old bachelor* | Fyodor Chaliapin, bass |
| Ernesto, *his nephew* | Leo Slezak, tenor |
| Norina, *a young widow* | Adelina Patti, soprano |
| Dr. Malatesta, *a physician* | Cornell MacNeil, baritone |
| A Notary | Luciano Pavarotti, tenor |

*Furioso Sabado, Conductor*
*Sung in Italian with English supertitles*
*The action takes place in Rome early in the 19th century.*
*(For the purposes of this production, the scene has been updated to Woodstock, 1969.)*

## A more complex example

But not all operas are that simple, and neither are all program books. Consider a more complex example. In fact, take a look at the most complex example of all: Wagner's *Ring* cycle.

Suppose that your local opera company is putting on the complete, four-opera *Ring* cycle, and you were able to nab tickets to the whole thing. You've already seen the first three operas in the cycle: *Das Rheingold (The Rhine Gold)*, *Die Walküre (The Valkyrie)*, and *Siegfried.* And now you're ready for the five-and-a-half-hour home stretch: *Götterdämmerung (Twilight of the Gods).* The program page might look like the one on the following page.

Below the dates and times you can see Richard Wagner — the guy who wrote the opera, music *and* words. Next comes the complete name of the cycle of four operas. *Der Ring des Nibelungen* means "The Ring of the Nibelungs" — that's the full English title. (*Ring* cycle is just a nickname.) *Nibelungs* are little mythical gnomes . . . but that's a long story (*18 hours* long, to be exact). See Chapter 12 for details.

 Below this title is a major clue that you are in for a long evening: "Opera in a prologue and three acts." Most operas are divided into acts, with intermissions between them. In the case of Wagner, who was never exactly what you'd call concise, you can guess that each act will be well over an hour long.

After the roster of exalted administrative staff comes the list that's most likely to interest you: the cast of characters. Note that they're listed in order of who *sings* first.

After the cast of characters comes yet *another* roster. Here's a thumbnail sketch of what they do:

- **Chorus master:** Teaches the chorus its notes and the pronunciation of foreign words.

- **Musical preparation:** Refers to the people who play the piano for rehearsals and coach the singers.

- **Assistant Stage Director:** Brings the director her coffee and notes, and he diagrams every bit of stage action the director comes up with, in case he needs to take over for her occasionally in rehearsal.

- **Stage Band Conductor:** Conducts the band that sits offstage. *Note:* Most operas don't have a band offstage — or even onstage, for that matter. But if the opera plot calls for an offstage (or onstage) band for a special effect, that band needs a conductor.

- **Prompter:** Sits in a little box near the footlights of the stage with a copy of the score in case a singer forgets the lines. Some singers like the prompters to be continuously busy, whispering line after line for security. Smaller opera houses often have *no* prompters, panicking singers who are used to them.

- **Surtitles:** Refers to the person who wrote the English translation for the surtitle slides, or the person who gives the cues for each slide to be flashed.

- **German diction coach:** Teaches the singers good German pronunciation.

- **Painted slides:** Refers to the person who paints the backdrops that are projected onto the scene.

More titles follow. As you read, the gist of the whole program gradually becomes clear: that the Suburban Opera Company must be one heck of an organization to have its own Wig Department.

THE SUBURBAN OPERA COMPANY
April 3, 1998, 6:00–11:40 p.m.
April 13, 1998, 6:00–11:40 p.m.
April 23, 1998, 6:00–11:40 p.m.

Richard Wagner

DER RING DES NIBELUNGEN

 Götterdämmerung

Opera in a prologue and three acts

| | |
|---|---|
| *Conductor:* | Nello Divine |
| *Production:* | Otto Gift |
| *Set and Production Designer:* | Ralph Longbarrel |
| *Costume Designer:* | Gandolf Taylor-Siemsstress |
| *Lighting Designer:* | George Changeman |
| *Stage Director:* | Pavel Müller |

*Characters in order of vocal appearance:*

| | |
|---|---|
| *First Norn* | Betty Spenden |
| *Second Norn* | Michaele Olds |
| *Third Norn* | Françoise Genfer |
| *Brünnhilde* | Gertrud Nase |
| *Siegfried* | Franz Messerschmidt |
| *Gunther* | Albrecht Hero |
| *Hagen* | Matthew Lachs |
| *Gutrune* | Marie Antoinette |
| *Waltraute* | Norma Schwartzkopf |
| *Alberich* | Lech Walesa |
| *Woglinde* | Jaye Manner |
| *Wellgunde* | Joan Burrell |
| *Flosshilde* | Wendy Brite |

| | |
|---|---|
| *Chorus Master:* | Ronald Wilford |
| *Musical Preparation:* | Bill Tausend and Richard Masterson |
| *Assistant Stage Director:* | Shalom Thompson |
| *Stage Band Conductor:* | Greg Bookman |
| *Prompter:* | Donna Reed |
| *Supertitles:* | Francesco Rozzi |
| *German diction coach:* | D. Deutsch Lehrer |
| *Painted slides by:* | Robin Williams |
| *Assistant to Mr. Taylor-Siemsstress:* | Todd Allson |
| *Scenery, properties, and electrical props constructed and painted in:* | Suburban Opera Shops |
| *Costumes executed by:* | Suburban Costume Department |
| *Wigs executed by:* | Suburban Wig Department |

On the next page of the program, you're likely to see something like this:

**Synopsis of Scenes**

**PROLOGUE:** The rock of the Valkyries

**ACT I**

**Scene 1:** The hall of the Gibichungs

**Scene 2:** The rock of the Valkyries

*Intermission*

**ACT II**    The banks of the Rhine

*Intermission*

**ACT III**

**Scene 1:** A forest clearing

**Scene 2:** The hall of the Gibichungs

This list makes several things clear: how many acts there are, where each scene takes place, and when you can go to the bathroom. The three acts are like three courses in a meal — appetizer, entree, and dessert — except that the dessert is bigger than the entree and takes 85 minutes to eat. But otherwise, it's exactly the same.

# Enter the Conductor

You're settled into your seat, and you've read your program book. You've elbowed your snoring neighbor. You're ready for the opera to begin.

Now the lights dim. The orchestra tunes. A hush falls over the opera house. Suddenly, the conductor enters. You can barely see him, way down there in the pit. Only his head, shoulders, and white bow tie are visible. He plows through the orchestra like a velociraptor through tall grass. After he reaches his podium (the raised box at the front of the orchestra), he motions for the orchestra to stand. He smiles and nods to the audience, confident that, for all you know, he could be wearing no pants.

Don't be ashamed if you find yourself wondering what the big deal about the conductor is. Musical novices wonder. Audience members wonder. Even the musicians sometimes wonder. You can find out the entire scoop on the conductor in the Intermission after Chapter 11.

Now he turns his back to the audience, raises his baton, and the orchestra comes to attention. Suddenly, with a snap of the wrist, the conductor gives a downbeat, and the orchestra begins to play.

# Silence of the Hams: The Overture Begins!

The *overture* is the one part of the opera in which you won't hear any singing. It's played while the curtain is down to get the audience into the mood of the opera. An overture by any other name (*Prelude,* for example, or *Introduction*) is the same deal.

Many opera overtures — especially those of early Italian composers, such as Gioachino Rossini — begin with a loud crash from the entire orchestra. There's a reason for this tradition. Opera in centuries past was a bustling, boisterous free-for-all. People went to the opera house to shmooze, gossip, and enjoy each other's company, with a little background entertainment thrown in. It took the first two chords of the overture — the musical equivalent of "TA-DAAA" — to grab everybody's attention. And then it often took the rest of the overture to quiet everybody down.

These days, you can expect a reverent silence from the audience during the overture. In recent times, the music has become just as important as the shmoozing.

Overtures can last from 2 minutes (as in Mozart's very early *Bastien et Bastienne*) to 15 minutes (as in Wagner's preludes to *Parsifal* and *Tannhäuser*). Some do little more than establish the mood of the first scene, or of the opera as a whole. Others (such as Johann Strauss's *Die Fledermaus* or Donizetti's *Don Pasquale*) tease you with all the great tunes from the opera — just like the overture of a Broadway musical. Still others (like the overture to Weber's *Der Freischütz* or Wagner's *The Flying Dutchman*) present a musical synopsis of the entire opera.

Some operas (Puccini's *Tosca,* for example, or Gershwin's *Porgy and Bess*) have no overture at all; the action begins almost immediately. Some overtures (such as Mozart's *Don Giovanni*) slide right into the opera itself, but most come to a brilliant, triumphant end.

Now the curtain rises. If it's a half-decent set, the audience, which probably clapped at the end of the overture, generally begins clapping again. Fortunately, many opera sets *are* breathtaking. A good set designer can make you feel like you're on the prow of a ship, on the streets of Paris, or on the rock of the Valkyries — sometimes all at once.

# Surtitles to the Rescue

Now you're watching the opera. But here's an age-old problem: The opera's in Italian, and the audience speaks English. What to do? Sing the opera in Italian and leave the English-speaking audience in the dark? Or sing it in English and forfeit the composer's intent, mangling the poetry in the process? (See Chapter 2 for more on this dilemma.)

Thankfully, technology has provided a solution in the form of *surtitles* (also known in some parts as *supertitles*). Surtitles are slides projected above the stage; each time a character sings something in a foreign language, the English translation magically appears overhead.

Opera snobs, arguing that surtitles are distracting, object to these attempts to make opera comprehensible. But more and more opera companies realize that surtitles present the best compromise between authenticity and comprehension. The Metropolitan Opera in New York has actually gone to the trouble of installing a personalized titles screen on the back of *each seat* so that each patron can choose whether or not to view them.

Furthermore, whether in live performance or on video, most of today's surtitles are designed to minimize distraction. You'll see no surtitles at all, for example, when the meaning is obvious, or when words are simply being repeated.

# The Weirdness of Applause

If one question has nagged more first-time operagoers in history than any other, it's *when to clap.*

You'd think that the answer would be easy: When a singer finishes singing, clap. (Especially if the last note was really high.) But unfortunately, that kind of practice will earn you stares and dirty looks throughout much of the opera world.

In German operas, the general custom is not to clap until the *end of each act.* In fact, Richard Wagner made it clear that he didn't want the audience to clap *at all* until the end of his opera *Parsifal.* Although Wagner broke his own rule by cheering his own music, these days, people still don't clap after the first act. They do clap at the end of the second and third acts, though — if they're still awake.

In French and Italian opera, the rules are much more flexible. It's probably best not to leap to your feet every time you hear a high C, but go ahead and clap at the end of a big aria or chorus — the rest of the audience will clap, too.

## Behind the screens

Flashing surtitles correctly is an art. The projectionist has to project the slides that explain important plot twists at just the right moment so that the audience gasps at the right time. And he or she must time the punch line of the joke just as the soprano sings it so that people laugh appropriately.

One of your present authors, in his youth, had a job running surtitles for a large national opera company. Actually, "running surtitles" is exaggerating: The job involved following the action of the opera while simultaneously scrutinizing the musical score, and saying "Now" into a headset at the precise instant that the next surtitle was supposed to flash above the stage. On the other end of the headset sat a union projectionist, whose job consisted of pushing a button whenever he heard the word "Now."

On more than one occasion, your present author caused a punchline to flash above the stage too soon. Just a *second* too soon, you understand — but enough to cause the audience to erupt into hysterics, completely obliterating the world-famous soprano's priceless high E-flat.

That's why your present author is now writing books.

The best general rule is this: When in doubt, don't applaud. It will become clear soon enough whether you're expected to clap or not.

## "Bravo! Brava! Bravi! Brave!"

Weird Audience Behavior Number Two is the strange assortment of syllables that otherwise sane operagoers emit during the applause. What the heck are they yelling?

It's usually a variant on the word *bravo* ("BRAH-voe," in case you've never heard it). Bravo is Italian for brave, clever, or skillful. In opera houses, however, it means "Yeeeeeeaaaaaaahhhhhh!"

What's odd about Italian adjectives is that they're different for men and women. So, to be perfectly correct about it, you'd yell *bravo* for a man, and *brava* ("BRAH-vah") for a woman. If a woman sings a stunning aria and you yell *bravo,* you'll be stared at. (**Hint:** If somebody *does* stare at you, look that person directly in the eye, assume a posture of indignance, and say, "You didn't know? She's actually a guy.")

It gets worse. If you want to cheer for two or more singers, you have to use the plural form of *bravo,* which is *bravi* ("BRAH-vee"). Except when the group consists solely of women, in which case you yell *brave* . . . ("BRAH-vay").

Got it?

Actually, only snobs get themselves worked up about this stuff. If you're not sure what to yell, just clap *really* loudly. Or go, "Yeeeeeeaaaaaaahhhhhh!"

## About booing . . .

A further variant of the audience-response thing is *booing* to express disapproval. You may be surprised to observe booing in an opera house, *even by people wearing tuxedos!*

Booing has its own grand tradition — it's been around almost since the beginning of Italian opera. Italian audiences have always been very honest with their emotions, and that's commendable. But we don't recommend booing: It just makes the performers nervous, and then they sing even worse. If you don't like the way somebody sang something, just don't clap. You won't be alone.

## . . . and whistling

Here's a *very* important tidbit for Americans: Don't whistle as a sign of appreciation, as you might at a baseball game. Italian singers will think that you hate them. In Italian, a whistle means "Booo!"

# The Snobfest Known as Intermission

Ah, intermission. Twenty-five minutes of high society. The chance to show off your finest attire, hobnob with the illuminati, and look down your opera glasses at the hoi polloi. Personally, we always seize the opportunity to run across the street for some Chicken McNuggets.

But if the intermission is your bag, we've got a few tips for you:

- ✔ The intermission usually lasts between 15 and 25 minutes in the United States, and longer in Europe (where it's not uncommon to have a meal between acts). Plan accordingly.

- ✔ Intermission is a great time for people watching. The people in pearls who paid $100 for their tickets are great entertainment, especially the ones who slip into a corner of the lobby and scarf down a pastrami sandwich from a paper bag.

- ✔ All opera houses sell refreshments (wine, champagne, soft drinks, and assorted nibbles) during intermissions. Be warned: These refreshments are often exceedingly expensive, and the lines are long.

✔ If you've been itching to strike up a conversation at the opera, this is the time. Opera fans love to expound on what they've just heard, even with someone they don't know. Be prepared to hear strong opinions. And don't feel bad if you don't understand what they're saying. It could be the champagne talking.

✔ About halfway through intermission, you'll hear a series of bells, chimes, or gongs over the loudspeaker. The opera house, in its innocent optimism, is hoping that you'll sprint right back to your seat at this point. But experienced operagoers wait a few more minutes for the bells, chimes, and gongs to signal a second time — *then* they mosey back in.

# After the Opera: Meeting the Singers

It's perfectly possible to go backstage after an opera and meet the singers who just sang for you — but as with everything else in the opera house, you should know the protocol.

If you're interested in meeting a singer or two, get busy *before* the opera ends — during one of the intermissions, for example. First, find the stage door. If you need directions, ask any official-looking person in the lobby.

When you find the stage door, you'll run into a guard. Don't be intimidated: His whole reason for being there is to have encounters with people like you. Tell the guard that you'd like to leave your name for the singer(s) of your choice. If your singer wants to meet you, she'll put your name on her "list." Believe it or not, she may well do that, even if you're a total stranger. You might improve your odds if you also tell the guard your reason for coming: "This was my first opera, and I want to thank Miss Belcanto for making it great," or "I've been a fan for years," for example.

After the show, come back to the stage door again. If you find your name on the list, you can go inside to the backstage area. If not, you're out of luck.

We hope that the singer puts you on her list, for two reasons. First, she's probably a fascinating person, and you'd have a lot of fun talking to her. Second, if you get to go backstage, you'll witness a fascinating world: soldiers with spears dashing around, singers undressing, stagehands scrambling over one another, enormous set pieces lurching this way and that.

But if you don't get in, don't be discouraged; you can always take a *virtual* backstage tour in the Intermission following Chapter 11.

# Chapter 11

# A Spin through Your Free CD

........................................................

........................................................

*O*pera is an incredibly diverse art, teeming with different styles. This chapter offers an introduction to the styles of the major opera composers, from the Classical era through the beginning of the 20th century. You can listen to what we're talking about, too; all you need is a CD player.

The CD that comes with this book isn't a "greatest hits" CD; our intention is to introduce you to each famous opera composer. We've chosen each track to be as representative of a composer's style as possible.

If, on first hearing a particular track on the CD, you're not enjoying yourself, for goodness' sake, switch to another track. We're not here to torture you; we want to show you what we love. Then again, if you're having trouble liking one track, try putting it on again in a week or so. Something interesting happens when you become more and more familiar with a piece of music: It tends to grow on you.

*Note:* As we go along, we'll identify particular moments in the music by using time codes: **1:34**, for example, means that you can use your CD player's fast-forward button to scan to 1 minute, 34 seconds into the track. (Or better yet, just *listen* until the music reaches that point.)

## 1 Mozart: Overture to The Marriage of Figaro

The *Opera For Dummies* CD begins as most operas do — with an *overture,* an introduction for the orchestra alone, without singers.

But this isn't just any overture; it's the Overture to *The Marriage of Figaro,* which musicians consider one of the best. This overture is a regular fixture in symphony orchestra concerts worldwide.

When you hear this piece, you'll know why. It's brisk, bubbly, catchy, funny, and full of spirit and energy and variety. No wonder — it's by Mozart, the prodigy genius whose life story graces the pages of Chapter 8 (and whose music graces the first three tracks of the CD). This overture is a great example of Mozart's clear-thinking, witty style.

This overture has a specific structure. It's a modified version of *sonata form,* an immensely important three-part format used regularly by composers for the last 250 years. If you panic at the mere mention of musical structure, we humbly refer you to *Classical Music For Dummies* for a clear and painless explanation. There's a reason that music people make a big deal about structure, though — it helps you understand what's going on in the music.

**0:02** The music begins with a low, bubbling theme in the strings and bassoons. The woodwinds and horns enter with a quiet commentary on the theme, and then — BOOM! — the whole orchestra comes crashing in with a high-spirited musical punctuation. We know already that this opera isn't going to be anything heavy and brooding.

**0:16** The same thing again. But if you listen carefully, you can hear the high oboe and flute playing a little add-on melody along with the bubbling theme.

**0:30** With a series of emphasized chords in the orchestra, the violins play a series of descending scales — each beginning higher than the last. Then the violins repeat a high note over and over, while the lower instruments take over the melody for the moment. At **0:49**, we've reached an important moment; it sounds like one section has ended and another is about to begin.

**0:50** A new section, which we'll call the transition, begins here. Unbeknownst to us, Mozart has smoothly and cleverly changed *keys,* and the purpose of this new section is to make us feel at home in our new surroundings. The music is quick and sprightly, but much quieter. The orchestra gives us a series of little shocks at **1:04**, **1:06**, and **1:08**, preparing us for a little melodic lick in the lower instruments at **1:13**. The violins take up that melodic lick at **1:21**, and with a quiet flourish, the transition is complete.

**1:33** This gentle melody in the violins and bassoon is the second main theme of the overture. At **1:39**, the flutes join in. More orchestral accents shock us at **1:45**, as the melody rises and rises, reaching a climax at **1:54**. Now the melody falls all the way back down again, and we're back at the beginning.

**1:59** This is an exact repeat of the music at **0:02**.

**2:13** Just as at **0:16**, the low bubbling theme repeats with an add-on melody in the high oboe and flute. But can you hear that at **2:15**, the music goes off in a new direction? That's Mozart adding variety to the music.

**2:27** Here's the transition from **0:50**. Tiny shocks at **2:41**, **2:43**, and **2:45** prepare us, as before, for the melodic lick in the lower instruments at **2:50**. And again, at **2:59**, the violins take over that melody, finishing up the transition.

**3:10** And here's the second theme, quiet and gentle as before. But at **3:22**, something different happens. Instead of the series of accents from **1:39**, we hear a kind of perpetual motion machine, fueled by a repeating bunch of notes in the violins, and pumped by a repeating low note. (Listen carefully for that repeating note — it plays over and over for 15 seconds, a very long time in the context of this piece.)

As the note repeats, more and more instruments join in, and the orchestral sound grows. This *crescendo* (or growing sound) sweeps us powerfully into the musical flow. (After Mozart, a crescendo like this became a regular fixture in the overtures and operas of Gioachino Rossini — as you can hear on Track 4.)

**3:37** The music reaches another climax, and with a series of flourishes, the overture comes to a buoyant close. This is Mozart — impossible to resist!

# 2 *Mozart: Don Giovanni — Leporello's Catalogue Aria*

This aria is more pure Mozart — you'll probably recognize the style from Track 1. We've selected this piece for several reasons. First, it's an amazing demonstration of how a composer can capture human psychology in music. Second, it's a perfect example of a *basso buffo* aria (sung by the funny stock servant character known as the "buffoon bass," so common in Italian operas of the 18th century, as you can read in Chapter 5). Third, it comes from *Don Giovanni*, which is on almost every opera nut's Top Ten List (and on plenty of people's Top One). And finally, it's famous in itself — mainly because it's so funny.

As you can read in the complete synopsis in Chapter 12, Don Giovanni (aka Don Juan) has spent his life loving and leaving young women. One woman is Donna Elvira, whom he now runs into again by chance. When he realizes that she's one of his previous one-night stands, he bolts, leaving his servant Leporello to clean up the mess. Leporello tries to comfort Elvira with the fact that she is not alone — in fact, she's one of over *2,000* ex-girlfriends. He helpfully recites from his catalogue exactly how many women from each country Don Giovanni has slept with.

| | |
|---|---|
| *Madamina: il catálogo e questo delle belle che amò il padron mio; un catálogo egli è, che ho fatto io;* | Dear lady: this is a catalogue of the beauties my master has loved; it's a catalogue I've made; |
| *osservate, leggete con me!* | look at it, read it with me! |

**0:19** Here Mozart adds what can only be described as a musical laugh. The violins play a quick downward scale, with super-short notes, and the flutes join them with a flourish. As Leporello begins to sing again at **0:22**, the oboes and horns play a hilarious, boisterous repeating snippet.

| | |
|---|---|
| *In Italia seicento e quaranta;* | In Italy, 640; |
| *in Almagna duecento e trent'una;* | in Germany, 231; |
| *cento in Francia, in Turchia novant'una;* | 100 in France, 91 in Turkey; |

**0:35** And now, the bubbling motion of the music comes to an abrupt halt, as Leporello exclaims, in effect, "But wait — you've got to hear *this!*" At **0:49**, the music seems to shrug in mock innocence, as if to say, "Who, me?"

| | |
|---|---|
| *ma in Ispagna son già mille tre!* | but in Spain there are already 1,003! |

**0:51** Now then; back to the matter at hand. The music picks up where it left off as Leporello looks at his catalogue again. This is a perfect example of the kind of music you find in almost any *basso buffo* aria — low, short, and fast notes. Composers have long known that the combination of those three qualities makes music sound funny.

| | |
|---|---|
| *V'han fra queste contadine, cameriere, cittadine,* | Among these there are countrywomen, chambermaids, citywomen, |
| *v'han contesse, baronesse, marchesane, principesse,* | there are countesses, baronesses, marchionesses, princesses, |
| *e v'han donne d'ogni grado, d'ogni forma, d'ogni età. . . .* | and there are women of every rank, every shape, every age. . . . |

**1:09** Over a new accompaniment of quick notes falling down the scale in the violins (and bubbling back up again in the cellos and basses), Leporello recites his numbers again, and repeats the entire text from that point.

| | |
|---|---|
| *In Italia sei cento . . .* | In Italy, 640 . . . |

**2:03** The aria seems to be over. But actually, the second half is yet to begin. At **2:06**, the music becomes slower and gentler, with three beats to the measure. Leporello's voice, sung here by Samuel Ramey, sounds almost mournful. Can Leporello be apologizing for his master's behavior?

| | |
|---|---|
| *Nella bionda egli ha l'usanza di lodar la gentilezza,* | With a blondes it is his custom to praise her gentleness, |
| *nella bruna la costanza, nella bianca la dolcezza.* | with a brunette her constancy, with a white-haired one her sweetness. |
| *Vuol d'inverno la grassotta, vuol d'estate la magrotta.* | In winter he wants a plump one, in summer a lean one. |

**2:57** As he sings about the majesty of the tall woman, the music becomes more and more majestic, reaching a climax at **3:13**.

| | |
|---|---|
| *È la grande maestosa;* | The tall woman is majestic; |

And as he sings about the tiny girl at **3:22**, the music gets faster and — well — *cuter.*

| | |
|---|---|
| *la piccina, la piccina . . . e ognor vezzosa. . . .* | the little tiny girl . . . is always charming. . . . |

In the following phrase, listen closely to the music as Leporello reaches the word *lista* ("list") at **4:00**. Notice the almost ominous shift in harmony in the orchestra, pointing out (a) that Leporello knows there's something wrong with Don Giovanni's behavior, and (b) that the Don's gonna get it in the end.

| | |
|---|---|
| *delle vecchia fa conquista, pel piacer di porla in lista.* | he makes conquests among old women for the pleasure of adding them to the list. |
| *Sua passion predominante e la giovin principiante;* | His outstanding passion is the youthful beginner; |
| *non si picca se sia ricca, se sia brutta, se sia bella. . . .* | he doesn't care if she's rich, if she's ugly, if she's beautiful. . . . |

**4:28** Now the music becomes even gentler, softer, more hesitant — almost sad. Leporello is *really* apologetic. But with one final statement of the last line at **5:31**, he brings the aria to a majestic end.

| | |
|---|---|
| *purche porti la gonnella, voi sapete . . . quel che fa. . . .* | As long as she wears a skirt, *you* know . . . what he does. . . . |

# **3** *Mozart: Don Giovanni — Final Scene*

We've included another scene from *Don Giovanni* on this CD: the final climax of the opera. This piece demonstrates a mastery of dramatic pacing; Mozart keeps us hanging onto every word. This finale also demonstrates a special feature of opera that you don't find in any other art form: We learn what several characters are thinking simultaneously.

For the full scoop on this opera, check out Chapter 12. But here's the scene: At the very beginning of the opera, Don Giovanni killed the Commendatore (Commander), who had been trying to protect his daughter's honor. Later, in a graveyard, the statue on the dead man's gravestone *spoke* to Don Giovanni, who laughed it off — and even invited the statue to dinner. As the track begins, the statue shows up to claim his dinner — and Don G. is the main course!

**0:00** Two momentous chords begin this selection, as dramatic an entrance as anyone can make. At **0:15**, the statue speaks; note the agitated accompaniment of the strings. Mozart punctuates each of the statue's lines with a somber, quiet trombone chord — a nice touch. Trombones in that era were inextricably linked with certain religious rites, particularly the Requiem for the dead.

**Statue:** *Don Giovanni! A cenar teco m'invitasti! E son venuto!*

Don Giovanni! You invited me to dine with you! And I have arrived!

Just after Don Giovanni begins his reply, at **0:42**, the strings play a quickly undulating, insinuating, nervous-sounding figure. Though Don Giovanni speaks with panache and brash confidence, the musical undercurrent is extremely insecure.

**Don G:** *Non l'avrei giammai creduto; ma farò quel che potrò. Leporello! Un'altra cena! Fa che subito si porti!*

I should never have believed it; but I'll do what I can. Leporello! Another dinner! Have it brought immediately!

**0:57** Leporello, on the other hand, has no qualms about appearing nervous. He's mortified. The violins speed up in agitation as he speaks.

**Leporello:** *Ah, padron! siam tutti morti!*

Ah, master! we're all dead!

**Don G:** *Vanne, dico!*

Go to it, I say!

**1:07** The orchestral sound grows to a huge climax, as the statue speaks again.

**Statue:** *Ferma un po'!*

Hold it!

**1:14** As he sings, the trombones play along. Twice the rest of the orchestra enters suddenly (at **1:20** and **1:34**), with shuddering accents in the strings.

*. . . non si pasce di cibo mortale, chi si pasce di cibo celeste!*

. . . one who partakes of celestial food does not partake of mortal food.

**1:41** Now a scary violin melody goes up and down the scale. (Mozart certainly meant it to go up and down your spine.)

*Altre cure piu gravi di queste, altra brama quaggiù mi guido.*

More serious matters than dinner brought me down here.

**2:10** Now we hear a great example of what opera can do. As the statue finishes his last note with ominous force, Leporello begins singing. His music — nervous, repeating *triplets* (groups of three notes) — continues as Don Giovanni begins to sing brashly and defiantly. All three contrasting moods, with their different motivations, simultaneously come through loud and clear to the audience. Try *that* in a movie or play!

| | |
|---|---|
| **Leporello:** *La terzana d'avere mi sembra, e le membra fermar più non so.* | I seem to have a fever, and I can't stop shaking. |
| **Don G:** *Parla dunque! che chiedi? che vuoi?* | *To Statue:* Speak, then! what do you ask? what do you want? |
| **Statue:** *Parlo: ascolta! più tempo non ho.* | I speak: listen! I don't have much time. |
| **Don G:** *Parla, parla, ascoltando ti sto.* | Speak, speak, I'm listening to you. |

**3:02** Now we hear a short orchestra *vamp* (a repeated snippet), as all action seems to stop. We're in limbo; we're hanging . . . what's gonna happen? Then, at **3:09**, a huge full-orchestra chord accompanies the first note of the statue.

| | |
|---|---|
| **Statue:** *Tu m'invitasti a cena, il tuo dover or sai,* | You invited me to dinner, you know your obligation now; |
| *rispondimi, verrai tu a cenar meco?* | answer me, will you come to dine with me? |

**4:01** Always one to provide comic relief in moments of terror, Leporello jumps in with predictably quick notes, echoing his agitation.

| | |
|---|---|
| **Leporello:** *Oibo, oibo; tempo non ha, scusate.* | Oh, oh; he hasn't got time, sorry. |
| **Don G:** *A torto di viltate tacciato mai sarò.* | I shall never be accused of cowardice. |

**4:22** A big chord accents each of the statue's next two lines. Leporello, too agitated now for singing, simply *yells* his next line.

| | |
|---|---|
| **Statue:** *Risolvi!* | Decide! |
| **Don G:** *Ho già risolto!* | I have already decided. |
| **Statue:** *Verrai?* | You will come? |
| **Leporello:** *Dite di no!* | Say no! |

**4:38** As the Don gives his bold response, the violins play a swaggering musical phrase. On the last syllable of his final word *verrò,* Don Giovanni and the orchestra sound a decisive low note (at **4:50**) that's particularly powerful and edgy.

| | |
|---|---|
| **Don G:** *Ho fermo il core in petto, non ho timor, verrò!* | My heart is steady in my breast, I am not afraid; I'll come! |

**5:01** On the next line, listen to the horrific, scary orchestral outburst on the word *pegno*.

| | |
|---|---|
| **Statue:** *Dammi la mano in pegno!* | Give me your hand as pledge! |

**5:08** Now, as Don Giovanni gives the statue his hand, Mozart signals the moment where he suddenly feels its icy coldness (between *Eccola* and *Ohimé!*). Listen carefully — can you hear the sudden change of harmony and the shuddering of the strings?

| | |
|---|---|
| **Don G:** *Eccola! Ohimé!* | Here it is! Oh, my God! |
| **Statue:** *Cos' hai?* | What is the matter? |
| **Don G:** *Che gelo e questo mai?* | It's so cold! |

**5:14** More huge chords, as the statue, extremely threatening, commands Don Giovanni to repent.

| | |
|---|---|
| **Statue:** *Pentiti, cangia vita, e l'ultimo momento!* | Repent, change your life, it is the last moment! |
| **Don G:** *No, no, ch'io non mi pento, vanne lontan da me!* | No, no, I do not repent, go away from me! |
| **Statue:** *Pentiti, scellerato!* | Repent, villain! |
| **Don G:** *No, vecchio infatuato!* | No, stupid old man! |
| **Statue:** *Pentiti!* | Repent! |
| **Don G:** *No!* | No! |
| **Statue:** *Si!* | Yes! |
| **Don G:** *No! No!* | No! No! |

*The Commendatore's statue begins to move toward the door . . . roaring flames begin to surround Don Giovanni.*

**5:53** Suddenly, the music is quiet again, but fast, repeated notes in the violins keep up the agitation in the air. Then, at **6:03**, more loud accents illustrate Don Giovanni's mounting horror.

| | |
|---|---|
| **Statue:** *Ah! tempo più non v'è!* | Ah! There is no more time! |
| **Don G:** *Da quel tremore insolito sento assilir gli spiriti! dond'escono quei vortici di foco pien d'orror?* | My muscles are trembling! where did these horror-filled whirlpools of fire come from? |

**6:14** A full chorus of demon voices begins singing. Don Giovanni, Leporello, and the chorus sing three different things at once. The atmosphere is utter chaos as the Don gets his just dessert — just before dessert.

| | |
|---|---|
| **Demon Voices:** *Tutto e tue colpe è poco! vieni! c'è un mal peggior!* | All this is nothing compared to your crimes! Come on! Worse is in store for you! |

| | |
|---|---|
| **Don G:** *Chi l'anima mi lacera? Chi m'agita le viscere? Che strazio, ohimé, che smania! Che inferno, che terror!* | Who's tearing my spirit? Who shakes my guts? What twisting, my God, what frenzy! What hell, what terror! |
| **Leporello:** *Che ceffo disperato! Che gesti da dannato! Che gridi! Che lamenti! Come mi fa terror!* | What a despairing grimace! What gestures of a damned soul! What shouts! What wails! How terrified it makes me! |

*Don Giovanni utters his final cry, is enveloped by flames, and sinks to Hell. Leporello echoes the Don's shout.*

The orchestra concludes the scene with an incredibly powerful wall of sound.

In the full opera, a happy little scene follows in which the other characters enter to moralize, saying, "Look what happens when men behave badly." But for many years, performances of this opera ended with the scene you just heard.

## 4 Rossini: The Barber of Seville — Duet of Rosina and Figaro

We chose this piece for several reasons:

- It's a quintessential example of Rossini's music.
- It illustrates what the *bel canto* style was all about — a style of singing meant to exalt the beauty of the human voice. (You can probably hear the contrast between this track and the previous one, in which the *drama* was by far the most important element.)
- It demonstrates the concept of *coloratura* — light, agile vocal pyrotechnics — more than anything else you're likely to hear.
- It's a beautiful recording of Maria Callas, one of the most famous opera singers (as you can find out in Chapter 4), who almost single-handedly brought about a *bel canto* revival in the 20th century.
- It documents Callas's remarkable and sympathetic partnership with a baritone named Tito Gobbi, with whom she worked time and time again.

In this recording, Gobbi plays Figaro, the multitalented Barber of Seville himself, and Callas is the lovely young girl, Rosina. You can read the complete, mind-twisting story in Chapter 12, but here's the background: Rich, good-looking Count Almaviva is in love with Rosina, even though they've never met. He hires Figaro to help him woo Rosina away from her lecherous old guardian. To avoid the guardian's suspicion, Figaro proposes that the Count dress as a drunken soldier seeking shelter. Figaro tells Rosina the plan; but instead of revealing that her admirer is a count, he tells her that it's an average guy named Lindoro. (The Count wants to be loved for who he *is,* not for his title.) Excited, Rosina gives Figaro a love letter, with instructions to bear it to Lindoro.

**0:00** Maria Callas begins alone with a short *recitative* — a talky style of free, out-of-rhythm singing with very little going on in the orchestra. The music as Rossini composed it was simple and unornamented, but at **0:13**, Callas displays her famous vocal agility.

| | |
|---|---|
| **Rosina:** *Dunque io son . . . tu non m'inganni?* | Then I am . . . you're not deceiving me? |
| *Dunque io son, la fortunata?* | Then I am the fortunate one? |

**0:18** The next line expresses her fluttering heart. Notice how lightly Callas sings, using her *head voice.* (See Chapter 3 for a discussion of chest voice and head voice.) If you have trouble following this text, it's because Rossini repeats certain words and combinations of words again and again; remember, the point of the *bel canto* style is to show off the singer's voice above all else.

| | |
|---|---|
| *Già me l'ero immaginata: io sapevo pria di te.* | (to herself) I had already guessed it: I knew before you did. |

**0:50** With an orchestral background that's typical of Rossini's lighthearted style, Figaro starts to tell his part of the story in a chatty manner. His notes and rhythm are simple, giving Gobbi the chance to prepare for his show-off passage.

| | |
|---|---|
| **Figaro:** *Di Lindoro il vago oggetto siete voi, bella Rosina.* | Lovely Rosina, you are the object of Lindoro's affections. |

**1:08** And here is that passage, just like Rosina's — sung in a light, "heady" tone to facilitate the speed and accuracy of the line. Rossini uses these difficult vocal runs to express Figaro's own excitement.

| | |
|---|---|
| *O, che volpe sopraffina,* | (to himself) Oh, what a cunning little minx, |
| *ma l'avra da far con me.* | but she will have to deal with me. |

**1:23** For the next few moments, Rosina and Figaro "speak" clearly, enunciating every syllable, so that the audience grasps the plot.

| | |
|---|---|
| **Rosina:** *Senti, senti . . . ma a Lindoro per parlar come si fa?* | Listen, listen . . . how do I arrange to speak to Lindoro? |
| **Figaro:** *Zitto, zitto, qui Lindor per parlavi or or sarà.* | Hush, hush, Lindoro will be here soon to talk to you. |
| **Rosina:** *Per parlarmi? . . . Bravo! bravo!* | To talk to me? Wonderful! terrific! |

| | |
|---|---|
| *Pure venga, ma con prudenza;* | Let him come, but prudently; |
| *io gia moro d'impazienza!* | I'm dying of impatience already! |
| *Ma che tarda? . . . cosa fa?* | But what's the delay? . . . What's he doing? |
| **Figaro:** *Egli attende qualche segno,* | He's waiting for some sign, |
| *poverin, del vostro affetto;* | poor chap, of your affection; |

**1:56** Suddenly, the orchestral accompaniment comes to a halt. Figaro assumes a tone of macho guy as he becomes the tutor, instructing Rosina what to do.

| | |
|---|---|
| *sol due righe di biglietto* | send him a note of only two lines |
| *gli mandate, e qui verrà.* | and he will come. |

**2:19** The lively music starts up again. Rosina coyly demurs, and Figaro becomes increasingly insistent.

| | |
|---|---|
| **Figaro:** *Che ne dite?* | What do you say to that? |
| **Rosina:** *Non vorrei . . .* | I shouldn't . . . |
| **Figaro:** *Su, corraggio.* | Come, courage! |
| **Rosina:** *Non saprei . . .* | I wouldn't know how . . . |
| **Figaro:** *Sol due righe . . .* | Only two lines . . . |
| **Rosina:** *Mi vergogno . . .* | I'm ashamed . . . |
| **Figaro:** *Ma di che? Ma di che? . . .* *si sa!* | But of what? But of what? . . . He knows! |

*(He brings her to the writing desk.)*

**2:33** A sudden loud burst in the orchestra as Figaro pushes her to write the letter. Notice that on the word *presto,* Figaro sings much faster than before.

| | |
|---|---|
| *Presto, presto; qua il biglietto.* | Quick, quick; here's the note. |

*(Rosina calls him back, pulls a letter out of her pocket, and gives it to him.)*

**2:37** Listen to the way Rosina sings her next line. This moment depends on good acting, and Callas is up to the job.

| | |
|---|---|
| **Rosina:** *Un biglietto? . . . eccolo qua.* | A letter? . . . Here it is. |

**2:44** Figaro realizes that Rosina knows exactly what she's doing. He sings the next phrase (at **2:46**) with indignation, and the strings accompany him in unison.

| | |
|---|---|
| **Figaro:** *Già era scritto?* | *(to himself)* It was already written? |
| *Ve', che bestia! Il maestro faccio a lei!* | See, what a fool I am! And I play teacher to her! |

**2:55** Rosina sets the pace of the rest of the duet. With another coloratura display, she expresses her anticipation and excitement.

| | |
|---|---|
| **Rosina:** *Fortunati affetti miei!* *Io comincio a respirar.* | How fortunate I am in my affections! I'm beginning to breathe again. |

**3:04** Following her lead, Figaro imitates her coloratura passage almost note for note — but with a markedly different attitude!

| | |
|---|---|
| **Figaro:** *Ah, che in cattedra costei* *di malizia può dettar.* | Ah, that woman could deliver a lecture on cunning. |

**3:11** Rosina shows us her true character: charming, lustrous, and completely feminine.

| | |
|---|---|
| **Rosina:** *Ah, tu solo, amor, tu sei* *che mi devi consolar!* | Ah, you alone, my love, are the one to bring me consolation! |

**3:31** As at the beginning of the duet, Rosina repeats the same words over and over again. This ingenious device gives Callas an opportunity to display her talent without having to worry about pronunciation of the text.

| | |
|---|---|
| **Figaro:** *Donne, donne, eterni Dei,* *chi vi arriva a indovinar?* | Women, women, eternal gods, who can figure you out? |

**3:47** Here the composer makes one of the *crescendos* for which he became famous: the music gets louder and louder. Meanwhile, Rosina and Figaro have the following exchange, which is almost obliterated by the orchestra:

| | |
|---|---|
| **Rosina:** *Senti, senti . . . ma Lindoro!* | Listen, listen . . . but Lindoro! |
| **Figaro:** *Qui verrà, fra momenti* *per parlavi, qui sarà.* | He'll be here in a few moments to talk to you, he'll be here. |
| **Rosina:** *Venga pur, ma con prudenza.* | He should come, but carefully. |
| **Figaro:** *Zitto, zitto, qui verrà.* | Hush, hush, he'll be here. |

**3:59** Rosina repeats some of the earlier words, with new and even more impressive coloratura:

| | |
|---|---|
| **Rosina:** *Fortunati affetti miei!* *Io comincio a respirar.* | How fortunate I am in my affections! I'm beginning to breathe again. |

Now it's time for the real fireworks — Maria Callas pulls out all the stops. She even adds a few extra high notes that are not in the sheet music — but that's what this style is all about. (Even when the composer writes a complicated line full of fast notes, many *bel canto* artists embellish the line further.) Meanwhile, Gobbi the tenor, a true gentleman, gets out of her way, singing the exact notes written by Rossini.

| | |
|---|---|
| **Rosina:** *Ah, tu solo, amor, tu sei* *che mi devi consolar!* | Ah, you alone, my love, are the one to bring me consolation. |

**Figaro:** *Donne, donne, eterni Dei,* | Women, women, eternal gods,
*chi vi arriva a indovinar?* | who can figure you out?

**4:50** Here's a Callas specialty: a perfectly sung high D. She holds it forever — seven seconds, to be exact. For pure vocal excitement, you can't beat this ending.

# 5 Verdi: A Masked Ball — Renato's Aria

If you've read Chapter 5, you know that Giuseppe Verdi (1813–1901) is one of the giants of the opera world. His works consistently combine great music, ingenious plotting, well-developed characters, and high drama.

We've selected this aria to represent Verdi's unique style. It's written for a baritone, Verdi's favorite voice type. It was Verdi who first imagined that this kind of voice was capable of an incredible expressive range — and demanded it. In fact, as you can read in Chapter 4, the Verdi baritone is a voice category unto itself.

You can find the whole story of *A Masked Ball* in Chapter 12. But in short: Renato, the governor's secretary, suspects that his wife Amelia is having an affair with his boss. He threatens to kill Amelia; even though she denies the affair, she agrees to die. But then Renato realizes that his greatest anger is reserved for his boss. He looks at the governor's portrait on the wall and addresses it.

**0:04** The baritone on this recording is Tito Gobbi, the same one who sang opposite Maria Callas on Track 4. But how different he sounds here! The light, fast singing from the last track is replaced with a sustained, full, passionate tone. Listen to the beauty of his voice — and the melody itself.

*Eri tu che macchiai quell'anima,* | You're the one who ensnared and defiled my love,

*La delizia dell'anima mia* | spoiled the joys of my soul.

**0:27** There's a discernible change in the vocal "color" — the character of the sound quality — as Gobbi expresses the next thought. Listen to the snarl in his pronunciation of *esecrabile*. Gobbi was famous for color changes like this one.

*Che m'affidi e d'un tratto esecrabile* | You inflicted me with most treacherous villainy;

*L'universo avveleni per me!* | You've poisoned the universe for me!

*Traditor! Che copensi in tal guisa . . .* | Traitor! This is your way of rewarding . . .

**0:58** The orchestra slows down and stops. Again Gobbi's tone changes quite noticeably, as he momentarily relents in his anger and, instead, recalls his own past friendship and fidelity to his boss.

| | |
|---|---|
| *Dell'amico tuo primo la fe'!* | The dear friend who is first in faithfulness! |

**1:15** The orchestra takes over from the soloist and begins a beautiful interlude: an expressive flute melody with harp accompaniment. Renato's resolve softens as he remembers Amelia as his beloved wife, not as the adulteress he has condemned to die.

**1:40** Now Gobbi takes over the flute's melody. What was easy for the flute is very challenging for a baritone; within a short section, he has to sing two high Fs and a long-held high G. Gobbi again goes for a completely different vocal color, singing with the sweetness and pathos of a true Verdi baritone.

| | |
|---|---|
| *O dolcezze perdute! o memorie* | Oh, the sweetnesses lost! O memories |
| *d'un amplesso che l'essere india!* | of embraces that raised me to Heaven! |
| *Quando Amelia si bella, si candida* | When Amelia so beautiful, so innocent |

**2:22** Listen for the sadness in his voice as he sings *brillava d'amor,* the last two words.

| | |
|---|---|
| *Sul mio seno brillava d'amor!* | Lay beside me and gave me her love! |

**2:35** He repeats those last few words, more intensely this time.

**2:56** Now, with a swell in the violins, the sweet memories retreat, and Renato is faced with his demons once again. Once again, baritone Gobbi alternates between colors, snarling one moment and caressing the next.

| | |
|---|---|
| *È finita, non siede che l'odio* | It's all over, and nothing is left for me but hatred |
| *e la morte nel vedovo cor!* | and death in my sad widowed heart! |

**3:23** The orchestra becomes hushed. The flute and harp enter as before, as he sings:

| | |
|---|---|
| *O dolcezze perdute!* | Oh, lost sweetnesses! |

The orchestra slows down to accompany Gobbi as he sings, rising beautifully to a high F. Notice how his voice continues to grow on the last note.

| | |
|---|---|
| *O speranze d'amor, d'amor, d'amor!* | Oh, hopes of love, of love, of love! |

Verdi chose to end Renato's aria of desolation on these hopeful words —
and in a major key, too! All this gives us the feeling that perhaps there is
some hope for Amelia. After all, Renato has directed his fury not at her, but
at the governor, her supposed "seducer." Guess who dies in the end?

# 6 *Verdi: Nabucco — Chorus of Hebrew Slaves*

We wanted to include a chorus by Giuseppe Verdi on this CD, because his
choruses are among the most beautiful ever written. But which one? Verdi
wrote several opera choruses, each lovelier than the last. After much
wringing of hands and gnashing of teeth, we finally selected this one from
*Nabucco.* It's among the most heartfelt of them all.

In Chapter 5, you can read about the circumstances surrounding this opera,
and Chapter 13 acquaints you with the plot. But in brief: The story occurs in
ancient times, and Babylon has defeated and enslaved the Hebrews. Now the
slaves sing of their homeland, alternately nostalgic for it and fiercely determined to return. In Verdi's day, this chorus struck a chord among the Italian
people, who saw it as a reflection of their own political oppression. It
became an unofficial Italian anthem, and it continues to have a special
significance to Italians today.

**0:00** The orchestra begins softly. The tempo is slow, and the mood is
somber. At **0:23,** a lone flute enters. It's the musical embodiment of the
flying "thought" that the chorus is going to sing about.

**0:30** A huge orchestral outburst follows, perhaps describing the Hebrews'
desperate plight. This music sounds very similar to the statue's entrance in
the last act of *Don Giovanni,* which you can hear at the beginning of Track 3.

**0:46** The mood suddenly becomes sweet again, and the flute brings us into a
major key, full of hope. At **1:00,** the strings begin to play a repeating snippet,
and at **1:04,** the chorus enters with its beautiful melody.

Have you noticed that the entire chorus is singing the exact same melody?
Nobody sings harmony, as you'd hear in a barbershop quartet or a church
choir. This technique has two effects: It implies the simplicity and purity of
the slaves as they reminisce about their homeland, and it underscores their
solidarity.

*(The banks of the Euphrates)*

**Ebrei:**                                  **Hebrews** *(In chains, at forced labor):*

| | |
|---|---|
| *Va, pensiero, sull'ali dorate;* | Fly, thought, on wings of gold; |
| *va, ti posa sui clivi, sui colli,* | go settle upon the slopes and the hills, |
| *ove olezzano tepide e molli* | where, soft and mild, the sweet airs |
| *l'aure dolci del suolo natal!* | of our native land smell fragrant! |

**1:55** As the chorus sings its next phrase, the melody changes. Notice the very short notes and descending line on *torri atterrate* — "toppled towers." Verdi is using *word painting* to illustrate the towers falling down.

| | |
|---|---|
| *Del Giordano le rive saluta,* | Greet the banks of the Jordan, |
| *di Sionne le torri atterrate.* | and Zion's toppled towers. |

**2:18** The voices swell as they sing the words *O mia patria* — "Oh my fatherland." Notice how they sing loudly on *si bella* ("so lovely") but then become hushed on *e perduta* ("and lost").

| | |
|---|---|
| *O, mia patria si bella e perduta!* | Oh, my fatherland so lovely and lost! |
| *O, membranza si cara e fatal!* | Oh, remembrance so dear and so full of despair! |

**2:47** If you could hear that the Hebrew slaves were singing in *unison* (all on the same melody) until now, you'll certainly notice a difference here. Suddenly, they break into harmony, supported by the full orchestra. At **3:00**, they become hushed, singing the second line almost under their breath. And they repeat this pattern over the next two lines — alternately wailing and stifling their lament.

| | |
|---|---|
| *Arpa d'or dei fatidici vati,* | Golden harp of the prophetic seers, |
| *perchè muta dal salice pendi?* | why do you hang upon the willow? |
| *Le memorie nel petto raccendi,* | Rekindle our bosom's memories, |
| *ci favella del tempo che fu!* | and speak of times gone by! |

**3:37** As the chorus continues, the solo flute that we heard at the beginning comes back, floating like a free spirit over their earth-bound cries.

| | |
|---|---|
| *O simile di Solima ai fati* | Mindful of the fate of Jerusalem, |
| *traggi un suono di crudo lamento,* | either give forth an air of sad lamentation, |

**3:50** Notice the quick rising line in the violins as the chorus holds the last syllable of *lamento*. The violins express the slaves' longing and powerful resolve.

| | |
|---|---|
| *o t'ispiri il Signore un concento* | or else let the Lord imbue us with |
| *che ne infonda al patire virtù!* | fortitude to bear our sufferings! |

**4:22** The chorus repeats this last line twice more, to different music. Then, at **4:48**, they repeat the last three words, fading out to nothing. This quiet conclusion, so full of hope and sadness, is more moving than a triumphant ending could ever be.

# ▉7 *Puccini: La Bohème — Rodolfo's Aria*

When it comes to the most well-known arias of Giacomo Puccini, Rodolfo's aria is certainly one of the Big Three. But we chose it because it's so typical of its composer. It's a great melody, it's hummable, and it gives the soloist the chance of a lifetime to show off his voice. No wonder it's one of the favorite arias of tenors everywhere.

Puccini always specified exactly the kinds of liberties he wanted singers to take with his music. Many opera singers use Puccini's notations only as a starting point and go much further — or ignore the markings completely. But not Nicolai Gedda, the singer in this recording. Gedda takes Puccini's wishes seriously, presenting the aria as the composer wanted.

The background for this aria, detailed in Chapter 12, is simple. Rodolfo, a poor Parisian poet, is alone in his garret when beautiful, sickly Mimì enters, asking for a light (for her candle). She passes out in a fit of coughing, and Rodolfo revives her. He then "accidentally" blows out his own candle. When Mimì drops her key, they both get down on the floor to look for it in the moonlight — and their hands brush together. He's about to fall in love — hard.

**0:01** The aria starts with a single note in the orchestra — and an important one, at that. This is the note that Rodolfo must begin singing.

The script indicates that Rodolfo should hold Mimì's hand and sing with a voice full of emotion. Nicolai Gedda sings, as softly and tenderly as possible, the first of two memorable melodies in this song.

| | |
|---|---|
| *Che gelida manina,* | What a frozen little hand, |
| *se la lasci riscaldar.* | would you let me warm it? |
| *Cercar che giova?* | What's the good of searching? |
| *Al buio non si trova.* | We won't find it in the dark. |

**0:26** The orchestra now echoes the melody of his last line, with a short section of "moonlight music" played by the harp and strings. At **0:36**, Gedda warms up his voice, singing more strongly:

| | |
|---|---|
| *Ma per fortuna è una notte di luna . . .* | But luckily it's a moonlit night . . . |

**0:44** Puccini is very clear about how the next phrase should be sung. In the sheet music, he writes: "Freely, then slowing down with individual note stresses for each syllable of *'e qui la luna';* speeding up for the beginning of *'l'abbiamo vicina';* and slowing down on the last syllable."

| | |
|---|---|
| *e qui la luna, l'abbiamo vicina.* | and we'll have the moon near us here. |

*(Mimì tries to withdraw her hand.)*

**0:53** Now Rodolfo quiets down, repeating the melody from the beginning of the aria. He has her attention now.

| | |
|---|---|
| *Aspetti, signorina, le dirò con due parole . . .* | Wait, miss, and I'll tell you in a couple of words . . . |

**1:02** Rodolfo now thinks that it is time to reveal his growing affections for Mimì — as you can hear, as he lets his voice blossom on *chi son* ("who I am"). Notice the sound of the orchestra on this second *chi son*. You don't have to understand much about music to hear that there's a new sound here — a warm entrance of several brass instruments, with harp, and a chord that you haven't heard in this aria before. It's a striking moment.

| | |
|---|---|
| *Chi son, chi son, e che faccio, come vivo.* | Who I am, who I am, and what I do, how I live. |
| *Vuole?* | Would you like that? |

*(Mimì is silent. Rudolfo releases her hand. Drawing back, she finds a chair into which she sinks, overcome by emotion.)*

**1:26** As Rodolfo gets ready to express his thoughts about his life and who he is, he again sings *Chi son?* twice, first simply (as if musing, wondering how to answer), and then strongly. He continues with the quiet phrase, *Sono un poeta,* and sings loudly again on *Vivo.* It's an unusual thing to be a poet, and he's proud of his profession.

| | |
|---|---|
| *Chi son? Chi son? Sono un poeta.* | Who am I? Who am I? I am a poet. |
| *Che cosa faccio? Scrivo. E come vivo? Vivo.* | What do I do? I write. And how do I live? I live. |

**1:51** Rodolfo introduces himself as a man rich in spirit and inspiration (though poor in the IRS sense). He acknowledges his poverty simply and quietly, but his voice grows to the hopeful millionaria.

| | |
|---|---|
| *In poverta mia lieta scialo da gran signore* | In my poverty, I feast as gaily as a grand lord |
| *rime ed inni d'amore.* | on rhymes and hymns of love. |
| *Per sogni e per chimere e per castelli in aria,* | For dreams and fancies and castles in the air, |
| *l'anima ho millionaria.* | I have a millionaire's soul. |

**2:25** Now comes the second catchy tune of the aria, the one that guaranteed its worldwide success, brought Puccini untold fame, and made Cher cry in the movie *Moonstruck.* From here to the end, Puccini directs the singer (in the sheet music) to "sustain broadly," to "slow down," to "sing extremely sweetly," to "stretch," and then to "slow down again." As before, Gedda complies beautifully.

| | |
|---|---|
| *Talor dal mio forziere ruban tutti* | Now and then, two thieves rob all the jewels |
| *gioielli due ladri: gli occhi belli.* | from my strong box: two beautiful eyes. |
| *V'entrar con voi pur ora,* | They came in with you just now, |
| *ed i miei sogni usati,* | and my old dreams, |
| *e i bei sogni miei tosto si dileguar!* | my beautiful dreams quickly dissolved! |

**3:14** The next phrase is sung warmly and freely, with great joy.

| | |
|---|---|
| *Ma il furto non m'accora,* | But the theft doesn't hurt me, |

**3:19** As the tenor pauses for a moment, the orchestra swells and takes over the melody. The tenor enters a few seconds later, and with great emotion, sings his famous high C (an *incredibly* high note for a guy — and especially difficult to sing beautifully).

About this high C: *Puccini didn't write it.* For generations, tenors have added one here just to show off, and audiences became accustomed to it. This, of course, poses a problem for tenors who *can't* always hit that note. In fact, the expectation has caused many a challenged tenor to ask for the whole aria to be played in a lower key — just so he can manage to hit a note that Puccini never asked for! However, in this recording, you get to hear the real C — for six long seconds.

| | |
|---|---|
| *poichè . . . poichè v'ha preso stanza la speranza!* | since . . . since hope has taken its place! |

**3:45** The orchestra quiets down again; the wave of great emotion has passed. Rodolfo, having said his piece, sets the mood for Mimì to tell him about herself. He begins very sweetly and softly again; then makes his voice swell as he insists that she share her story. Finally, he fades to almost nothing on *Vi piaccia dir* ("Please tell!").

| | |
|---|---|
| *Or che mi conoscete, parlate voi,* | Now that you know me, |
| *deh! Parlate! Chi siete?* | come, you speak. Who are you? |
| *Vi piaccia dir!* | Please tell! |

Then it's Mimì's turn — but you'll have to see the opera (or read Chapter 12) to find out what she says.

# 8 *Puccini: Tosca — Final Scene*

Be warned — we're about to give away one of the most shocking surprise endings in all of opera.

We've included the end of *Tosca* on this CD to illustrate the *verismo* style: the documentary-like, reality-based type of drama made famous by Puccini, along with such composers as Ruggiero Leoncavallo and Pietro Mascagni. As we explain in Chapter 5, the word *verismo* literally means "truthism" — and the term applies to other arts as well, such as filmmaking.

Unlike *bel canto* operas, *verismo* operas don't put the greatest emphasis on the beauty of the human voice. What are important are drama and action, perfectly illustrated in this excerpt.

The story of *Tosca* is in Chapter 12. For the purposes of this track, though, know this much: Floria Tosca is in love with Mario — who has been imprisoned by supervillain Scarpia and sentenced to be executed for his political beliefs. Scarpia promised Tosca that if she slept with him, he'd save her beloved Mario's life ( by filling the firing squad's rifles with blanks). Tosca agreed; but before Scarpia could have his way with her, she stabbed him.

Nobody knows yet that Scarpia's dead. As we join the story, it's time for the mock execution to take place — high atop a fortress in Rome. Tosca has explained the plan to Mario and instructed him to act really, really dead after he's "shot" so that nobody will suspect that he's actually alive. From there, she tells him, they'll be free to live a long and joyous life together.

*(The platform of Castel Sant'Angelo. It is still night: This gives way slowly to the uncertain grey twilight that precedes dawn.)*

*Mario is about to face the firing squad, and Tosca instructs him how to fake his death.*

**0:00** The track begins with a slow, almost lugubrious march. The melody, begun in the strings, is highlighted by the flutes playing very low in their range. The march continues under the following action.

*(Mario follows the officer, after first bowing to Tosca, who positions herself in such a way that she is able to observe the platform. She sees the officer and the sergeant lead Mario over to the wall facing her. The sergeant offers to blindfold him; he refuses, with a smile. These gloomy preliminaries exhaust Tosca's patience.)*

**0:22** Tosca sings over the same march, as it continues.

| | |
|---|---|
| *Com'è lunga l'attesa!* | What a time they are taking! |
| *Perchè indugiano ancor? Già sorge il sole. . . .* | Why are they still delaying? Sunrise already. . . . |
| *Perchè indugiano ancora?* | Why are they still delaying? |
| *È una commedia, lo so . . .* | It's all acting, I know . . . |
| *ma questa angoscia eterna pare!* | but still this waiting makes me frantic! |

**0:56** The march becomes more insistent as the scene moves to its first climax.

*(The officer and the sergeant draw up the firing squad, giving the appropriate orders.)*

The orchestra's playing gets thicker, louder, and more and more intense, growing continuously. The brass play an ominous chord as Tosca sings the word *armi.*

| | |
|---|---|
| *Ecco! . . . apprestano l'armi. . . .* | There! . . . They're raising their rifles. . . . |

**1:22** A huge drumroll as we wait for the shots to be fired.

| | |
|---|---|
| *Com'è bello il mio Mario!* | How handsome he is, my Mario! |

**1:22** The shots ring out!

| | |
|---|---|
| *Là! muori!* | There! die! |

*(Seeing him on the ground, she sends him a kiss with her hands.)*

| | |
|---|---|
| *Ecco un artista!* | Now *there's* an artist! |

**1:28** As she sings *artista,* the cymbals crash. Again, we hear the lugubrious march melody; but instead of low flutes, we can hear high horns, blasting the melody at full force. What was ominous before is now terrifying.

*(The sergeant goes up to the crumpled body and inspects it: Spoletta has also gone over; he draws the sergeant away, preventing him from giving the coup de grace, then covers Mario with a coat. The officer lines his men up: the sergeant relieves the sentry and all go off down the stairs, led by Spoletta.)*

**1:41** Now the music returns to the original, quiet version of the march.

*(Tosca is intensely agitated, watching all that goes on in a panic lest Mario, out of impatience, move or speak too soon.)*

**1:48** As Tosca (played by Renata Scotto in this recording) begins to sing, notice how "realistic" she sounds. She's trying to make her singing sound like speech.

| | |
|---|---|
| *O Mario, non ti muovere . . .*<br>*S'avviano. . . .* | Oh! Mario, don't move . . . They're going now. . . . |
| *Taci! Vanno . . . scendono . . .*<br>*scendono . . .* | Quiet! They're going away . . . they're going down . . . they're going down . . . |

The orchestra continues to play softer and softer as the firing squad disappears.

*(As soon as they have left the platform, she goes to listen at the entrance to the stairway. Breathless with fear, she suddenly thinks that the soldiers are returning to Mario again, and she says in a low voice:)*

| | |
|---|---|
| *Ancora non ti muovere. . . .* | Don't move yet. . . . |

*(She listens. They have all gone. She runs to Mario.)*

**2:21** Two more halting notes in the orchestra, and the soldiers are gone. Tosca sings without the orchestra, still almost speaking the words.

| | |
|---|---|
| *Presto! Su, Mario! Mario! Su, presto; andiamo!* | Quickly! Up, Mario! Mario! Quickly! Let's go! |
| *Su! Su! Mario! Mario!* | Up! Up! Mario! Mario! |

*(She bends down to help Mario to his feet. Suddenly, she gives a choked cry of shock and horror, and looks at her hands, with which she has lifted up the coat. She kneels, tears off the coat, and then leaps to her feet again, pale and stunned.)*

**2:38** As she screams, the orchestra screams with her: a huge brass chord, followed by a dramatic, heart-pounding, rhythmic punctuation. It's all a trick! Mario's dead! The firing squad's rifles weren't loaded with blanks after all! Evil Scarpia has had his revenge, even from the grave — he lied to Tosca from the beginning.

| | |
|---|---|
| *Morto! . . . morto!* | Dead! . . . dead! |

*(Uttering broken words and sobs of grief, she throws herself on Mario's body, unable to believe what has happened.)*

| | |
|---|---|
| *O Mario . . . morto? Tu? Così? Finire così?* | Oh Mario . . . murdered? You? Like this? Finished like this? |
| *Povera Floria tua!* | Your poor Floria [Tosca]! |

*(Meanwhile, from the courtyard below the parapet and up the small stairway, the confused voices of Spoletta, Sciarrone, and a number of soldiers are heard approaching.)*

**2:47** Under this confusion of voices, the music changes to a quick pulsing undercurrent. It's hard to hear the words here, but you can figure out what's going on. The police have discovered Scarpia's corpse, and they know that Tosca is the one who killed him. They're after her now!

| | |
|---|---|
| **Sciarrone:** (off stage) *Vi dico, pugnalato!* | I tell you someone's stabbed him! |
| **Voices:** *Scarpia?* | Scarpia? |
| **Sciarrone:** (off stage) *Scarpia!* | Scarpia! |
| **Spoletta:** (off stage) *La donna è Tosca!* | That woman is Tosca! |
| **Voices:** (closer) *Che non sfugga!* | Don't let her get away! |
| **Spoletta:** (off stage, but closer) *Attenti . . . agli sbocchi delle scale!* | Keep watch . . . at the bottom of the staircase! |

*(A great noise is heard from downstairs.)*

**2:57** The music continues to build, culminating at **3:02** in a brutal, stomping rhythm. The strings tremble.

*(Spoletta appears from the stairs, while Sciarrone behind him points at Tosca and shouts.)*

| | |
|---|---|
| **Sciarrone:** *È lei!* | It's her! |
| **Spoletta:** (rushing at Tosca) *Ah! Tosca, pagherai ben cara la sua vita. . . .* | Ah! Tosca, you will pay most dearly for his life. . . . |

*(Tosca leaps to her feet and, instead of fleeing from Spoletta, pushes him violently away, answering:)*

| | |
|---|---|
| **Tosca:** *Colla mia!* | With my own! |

*(Spoletta staggers back with the unexpected force of Tosca's resistance, while she quickly runs across to the parapet.)*

**3:10** A driving musical snippet repeats four times, rising ever higher, before Tosca screams, without the orchestra:

| | |
|---|---|
| *O Scarpia, avanti a Dio!* | Oh Scarpia, we'll meet before God! |

**3:24** The orchestra overwhelms us in sound. At this spot in the score, Puccini wrote, *"Tutta forza con grande slancio"* ("Pull out all the stops — let's hear what you've got").

*(Tosca hurls herself off the parapet. Sciarrone and a few soldiers, emerging from the staircase, rush to the parapet and look down. Spoletta is left dumbfounded and horror-stricken. Quick curtain.)*

# 9 *Wagner: Tristan and Isolde — Isolde's Love-Death*

No opera could be more different from *Tosca* than *Tristan and Isolde* by Richard Wagner, and no heroine could be more different from Tosca than Isolde. When Tosca sees her beloved die, she flings herself off a parapet; when Isolde sees *her* beloved die, she hallucinates that he is still alive, sings for seven minutes, and is transformed into the truest form of love before dying herself.

Wagner wasn't aiming for realism, as Puccini was. As you can read in Chapter 8, Wagner saw his operas as complete art works, uniting music, storyline, drama, scenery, and action in one glorious whole. He usually chose legendary subjects that lent themselves to grandiose treatment. The opera we've chosen for this track is a perfect example. *Tristan and Isolde* isn't about love; it's about *Love.*

You get to hear Wagner's trademark composing style in this recording: The music builds and builds, always seeming just about to reach a climax; then it backs off, and builds up again, time after time, until . . . well, maybe you'd better just listen.

Chapter 12 has the complete story of this opera; read it before listening, if possible. This excerpt contains the famous *Liebestod* ("Love-Death") that ends the opera. In it, you hear only one character: Isolde. Her beloved Tristan has just died — but she's so deeply in love and in grief that she imagines that she sees him reviving.

**0:01** The orchestra plays as quietly as possible as Isolde (played here by Helga Dernesch) begins singing. Note the first four notes she sings on *mild und leise;* we'll call that the "Rocking Melody." She sings that melody again, higher this time, on the words *wie das Auge.*

| | |
|---|---|
| *Mild und leise wie er lächelt,* | Mildly and gently he is smiling, |
| *wie das Auge hold er öffnet!* | see, his eyes he softly opens! |

**0:30** Now Isolde sings a new melody, but listen! Under her words, the horn continues the four-note Rocking Melody she began with. She reaches her first mini-climax on the word *leuchtet.*

| | |
|---|---|
| *Seht ihr, Freunde, seh't ihr's nicht?* | See, my friends, don't you see it? |
| *Immer lichter wie er leuchtet,* | How he, bright and brighter burning, |

**0:57** Now the music backs off a bit and the cello takes over, always rising, as she sings the following line:

| | |
|---|---|
| *sternumstrahlet hoch sich hebt?* | streaming starlight, heaves himself up? |

**1:11** The orchestra backs off, changes key, and seems to begin again. Now the Rocking Melody can be heard all over the orchestra, in one instrument after another, until Isolde sings it herself on *muthig schwillt.*

| | |
|---|---|
| *Seht ihr's nicht? Wie das Herz ihm muthig schwillt,* | Don't you see how his heart swells with courage, |
| *voll und hehr im Busen ihm quillt?* | welling up strong and pure within him? |

**1:41** Again, the orchestra plays the Rocking Melody, but now Wagner adds a beautiful embellishment, first heard in the clarinet at **1:52**. (Eventually, Isolde gets a chance to sing it, too.) In fact, Isolde's melody almost seems less important than the orchestra's part here.

| | |
|---|---|
| *Wie den Lippen, wonnig mild* | From his mild lips, the breath he breathes to me |
| *susser Athem sanft entweht.* | is so soft and sweet. |
| *Freunde!* | Friends! |

**2:30** Together, Isolde and the orchestra share a short melodic interlude, as Isolde presses her friends, who are on hand to witness this tragic ending, to agree that Tristan lives. The music reaches another mini-climax at **2:40**.

| | |
|---|---|
| *Seht!* | See! |
| *Fühlt und seht ihr's nicht?* | Don't you see it? Don't you feel it? |

**2:44** Again the orchestra backs off. Isolde and the orchestra return to the Rocking Melody; and at **3:11**, she sings the same embellishment first played by the clarinet at **1:52**.

| | |
|---|---|
| *Hore ich nur diese Weise,* | Don't any of you hear the music, |
| *die so wundervoll und leise,* | so soft and full of wonder, |
| *wonne klagend, alles sagend,* | sweetly ringing, everything singing, |
| *mild versöhnend aus ihm tönend,* | swelling from him, foretelling peace, |

**3:32** In the next phrase, Isolde and the violins gradually rise in pitch, one note at a time — a device that keeps the tension and anticipation of the phrase mounting.

| | |
|---|---|
| *in mich dringet, auf sich schwinget,* | growing around me, flowing through me, |
| *hold erhallend um mich klinget?* | sounding around me? |

**3:53** Here's the first *real* climax of the piece — or so it seems.

| | |
|---|---|
| *Heller schallend, mich umwallend,* | Blowing clearer, surrounding me, |

**4:06** Now we hear a classic Wagnerian phrase: long, rising lines, continuously mounting tension, an endlessly delayed climax. The playing and singing are gorgeous, but it's the tension that draws us in. This phrase is Wagner in a nutshell — it's what makes his music great.

| | |
|---|---|
| *sind es Wellen sanfter Lüfte?* | are they waves of soft air? |
| *Sind es Wolken wonniger Düfte?* | Are they clouds of perfume and pleasure? |
| *Wie sie schwellen, mich umrauschen!* | How they swell, how they overwhelm me! |
| *Soll ich athmen, soll ich lauschen?* | Dare I breathe them, dare I hear them? |

**4:35** Suddenly, the orchestra backs off yet *again*. Wagner uses this hushed moment to regroup before the final push to the real climax. Listen to the beautiful tone that Helga Dernesch injects into the line, *"soll ich schlurfen."* You can imagine the beautiful young Isolde, rhapsodically willing Tristan to breathe again.

| | |
|---|---|
| *Soll ich schlurfen, untertauchen,* | Shall I drink them, dive among them, |
| *süss in Duften mich verhauchen?* | Sweetly bury myself in their fragrance? |
| *In dem wogenden Schwall,* | In their billowy well, |
| *in dem tönendem Schall,* | in their resonant spell, |

**5:01** This is it. The big climax of the aria — and of the entire opera.

| | |
|---|---|
| *in des Welt Athems wehendem All* | with the world's life breath, breathing over all |

The orchestra's climax seems to last for quite a while, and — to tell the truth — almost drowns out Helga Dernesch completely. As conductors ourselves, we can tell you how difficult it is to keep the orchestra restrained at this moment. First, it's not easy to hear a singer when 105 musicians are playing *any* music; second, this particular music just *wants* to be loud. Little wonder that this *Liebestod* is often performed in concert — without the singer!

**5:26** Now the music sinks, beginning to fade away. The orchestra conjures up many images in these last few phrases: a sunset, birds singing, and Isolde's transformation into pure sound. We almost feel happy for the two lovers that they unite in death.

**5:59** Isolde's final note — on the word *Lust* ("desire") — is completely ethereal and seems to emanate from heaven.

| | |
|---|---|
| *ertrinken, versinken, unbewusst,* | to drown, to sink, unaware — the |
| *hochste Lust!* | highest desire! |

*(Isolde, as if glorified, sinks gently down upon Tristan's body.)*

The final moments played by the orchestra create a perfect summation of the aria. It's a moment of pure peace and acceptance.

# ⑩ *Wagner: Die Meistersinger von Nürnberg — Final Monologue and Chorus*

If Wagner glorified love in Tristan and Isolde, he glorified the old German traditions in his comedy *Die Meistersinger von Nürnberg* (*The Master-Singers of Nuremburg*). The longest opera regularly performed today, it tells the story of an inexperienced young singer, Walther, who hopes to win beautiful Eva's hand by winning a singing competition. (For full details, see Chapter 12.) Eventually, he wins, and he's invited to join the sacred guild of master-singers. At first he refuses this honor, irked by their rude treatment of him when he was a beginner. But Hans Sachs, cobbler and master-singer extraordinaire, lectures him on the glorious importance of Germany's singing tradition. Walther finally agrees, and everyone rejoices.

**0:01** The final section of the opera begins with a strongly stated melody played by the orchestra in unison. Hans Sachs begins with a declamatory instruction to Walther.

**Sachs:** *(Grasping Walther by the hand)*

| | |
|---|---|
| *Verachtet mir die Meister nicht, und ehrt mir ihre Kunst!* | Don't disdain our Masters like that; honor their art! |

**0:24** The orchestra now plays a sweet melody, as Hans Sachs begins to tell his story, still in a somewhat declamatory style. He explains to Walther that his poetry and singing have earned him respect, not his wealth or physical power. Furthermore, says Sachs, Walther should be grateful to the Masters from whom he learned this art.

| | |
|---|---|
| *Was ihnen hoch zum Lobe spricht,* | What they love and prize the most |
| *fiel reichlich euch zur Gunst.* | has made them support you. |
| *Nicht euren Ahnen, noch so werth,* | It wasn't your father's name and worth, |
| *nicht euren Wappen, Speer, noch Schwert,* | nor your weapon, spear or sword, |
| *dass ihr ein Dichter seid;* | it was your poet's art; |
| *ein Meister euch gefreit,* | a master freed you, |
| *dem dankt ihr heut' eu'r höchstes Gluck.* | you must thank *him* for all your bliss. |

**1:01** In the next few phrases, Sachs's music becomes more songlike:

| | |
|---|---|
| *Drum, denkt mit Dank ihr d'ran zurück, wie kann die Kunst wohl unwerth sein, die soche Preise schliesset ein?* | So think back with thankfulness, how could an art be unworthy that brings such a noble prize? |

**1:21** The orchestra briefly slows down, stating a more martial-sounding accompaniment. Then, at **1:41**, the orchestra picks up the lyrical tune once again. As you might have noticed from the previous track, Wagner often has the orchestra play the melody while the singer "accompanies" it — exactly the opposite of what an Italian opera composer would do.

| | |
|---|---|
| *Dass uns're Meister sie gepflegt,* | Our Masters guarded this art well, |
| *grad' recht nach ihrer Art,* | they knew its real worth, |
| *nach ihrem Sinne treu gehegt,* | and they stayed true to its spirit, |
| *das hat sie echt bewahrt:* | and protected it: |
| *Blieb sie nicht adlig, wie zur Zeit,* | And even when it was not honored, |
| *wo Höf' und Fürsten sie geweiht,* | when courts and kings told of its glories, |
| *im Drang der schlimmen Jahr'* | throughout the strife of the hardest years |
| *blieb sie doch deutsch und wahr.* | it remained German and true. |

**2:04** As the orchestra continues with the melody, the soloist has the difficult task of pronouncing 40 million consonants within a short time. Phrases like this really test the singer, who has to keep the vocal line flowing while simultaneously transmitting truckloads of information.

| | |
|---|---|
| *Und war sie anders nicht geglückt,* | And though our art was even less honored, |
| *als wie wo Alles drängt und drückt,* | throughout the years of storm and stress, |
| *ihr seht, wie hoch sie blieb in Ehr'!* | you see, it is highly honored still! |
| *Was wollt ihr von den Meistern mehr?* | What more could you want from the Masters? |

**2:22** The orchestra grows to a loud, barking outburst. Sachs gets to the gist of his monologue. The orchestra underscores its importance with trembling strings, and punctuates his points with accents.

| | |
|---|---|
| *Habt Acht! Uns drohen üble Streich';* | Take heed! Evil times now threaten us; |
| *zerfällt erst deutsches Volk und Reich,* | and if we should fall away, |
| *in falscher wälscher Majestät* | and false outsiders should rule us |
| *kein Fürst dann mehr sein Volk versteht;* | no king would understand his people; |
| *und wälschen Dunst mit wälschen Tand* | and foreign rule and foreign ways |
| *sie pflanzen uns in deutsches Land.* | would be planted in our land. |

**3:12** The orchestra writing becomes very sparse as Sachs sings with a rather tender tone, reminiscing about something he considers almost lost.

| | |
|---|---|
| *Was deutsch und echt wüsst' keiner mehr,* | What is truly German would soon be forgotten, |
| *lebt's nicht in deutscher Meister Ehr'.* | if they did not live in the German Masters' art. |

**3:29** For the next several seconds, the orchestra plays a new rhythm. Listen to Sachs's voice on the word *Meister* (at **3:43**): With a huge leap down from one note to another, he really makes his point.

| | |
|---|---|
| *Drum sag' ich Euch:* | I say to you: |
| *ehrt eure deutschen Meister;* | Honor your noble Masters; |

**3:44** As if that huge leap were a cue to the orchestra, it now begins a much quicker motion. Woodwinds and high strings run circles around the melody.

| | |
|---|---|
| *dann bannt ihr gute Geister!* | thus you will keep bad luck away! |
| *Und gebt ihr ihrem Wirken Gunst,* | If you hold them close to your heart, |
| *zerging' in Dunst* | even if the Holy Roman Empire |
| *das heil'ge röm'sche Reich,* | dissolved away into dust, |
| *uns bliebe gleich* | we'd still have at home |
| *die heil'ge deutsche Kunst!* | our sacred German art! |

**4:26** On Sachs's word *Kunst* — "art" — the orchestra reaches a climax, and the chorus enters. The violins and violas twist and turn around the new melody — a common Wagnerian trick. This is the big tune first heard in the overture of the opera — over five hours ago! The chorus enters, and the music takes on a religious fervor. It sounds like the glorious final moments of a spiritual declamation.

*(During the Finale, Eva takes the wreath from Walther's head and crowns Sachs with it. He takes the chain from Pogner [Eva's father], and hangs it around Walther's neck. After Sachs has embraced the pair, Walther and Eva remain one on each side of him leaning on his shoulders. Pogner kneels as if in homage before Sachs. The Master-Singers acclaim Sachs with upraised hands as their leader.*

*While the prentices clap hands and shout and dance, the people wave their hats enthusiastically.)*

| | |
|---|---|
| *Ehrt eure deutschen Meister:* | Honor your noble masters, |
| *dann bannt ihr gute Geister!* | thus you will keep bad luck away; |
| *Und gebt ihr ihrem Wirken Gunst,* | If you hold them close to your heart; |
| *zerging' in Dunst* | even if the Holy Roman Empire |
| *das heil'ge röm'sche Reich,* | dissolved away into dust, |
| *uns bliebe gleich* | we'd still have at home |
| *die heil'ge deutsche Kunst!* | our sacred German art! |
| *Heil Sachs! Hans Sachs!* | Hail Sachs! Hans Sachs! |
| *Heil Nürnbergs theurem Sachs!* | Hail Nuremberg's poet Sachs! |

# 11 Strauss: Arabella — Duet of Arabella and Zdenka

*Arabella* was one of Richard Strauss's later operas, and in it he gave up the harsh musical sounds of such earlier operas as *Salome* and *Elektra*. We've chosen this track because it contains one of the best examples of Strauss's later style — and one of the most ravishing tunes he ever wrote.

You can read the synopsis of this opera in Chapter 13; but in short, young Arabella is waiting for Mr. Right to come along, and she muses on what their first meeting will be like. Meanwhile, her sister Zdenka, whose parents have raised her as a boy — don't ask — expresses both her affection for Arabella and her sadness at being left out of the romance picture.

**0:03** The singer playing Arabella in this recording, Elizabeth Schwarzkopf, was a great interpreter of Strauss's music. Here she begins simply, almost speaking the first two phrases with a breathy tone, as she describes the man she knows she'll meet someday.

You can tell from the first note that Strauss is portraying a mature character in love. The music rises and falls in a measured way; it seems to express an understanding of the two sides of love — joy and sorrow.

| | |
|---|---|
| **Arabella:** *Aber der Richtige, wenn's einen gibt für mich auf dieser Welt,* | But if there's a man who's right for me in this world, |
| *Der wird eimal dastehn, da vor mir,* | he will stand before me one day, |
| *und wird mich anschaun und ich ihn,* | he will look at me and I at him, |
| *und keine Zweifel werden sein und keine Fragen,* | and there will be no doubts and no questions, |

**0:37** On the word *selig* (literally, "blessed"), Schwarzkopf's voice takes a beautiful flight, spinning the melody ever onward. This is Strauss at his best.

| | |
|---|---|
| *und selig, und selig werd' ich sein und gehörsam wie ein Kind.* | and I will be happy and as obedient as a child. |

**1:16** Now little sister Zdenka begins to sing. Her music is much different: much faster and less ethereal. Her words and melody press forward as she tries to make sense of what Arabella is expressing. (Zdenka doesn't yet understand the yearning and sadness that come with love.) But on the word *helfen* (at **1:45**), her melody echoes some of Arabella's flight of fancy.

| | |
|---|---|
| **Zdenka:** *Ich weiss nicht, wie du bist;* | I don't really know you; |
| *ich weiss nicht, ob du Recht hast;* | I don't know whether you are right; |
| *dazu hab ich dich viel zu lieb!* | I love you too much for that! |
| *Ich will nur, das du glücklich wirst mit einem,* | All I want is for you to be happy with someone, |

| | |
|---|---|
| *der's verdient! Und helfen will ich dir dazu.* | who's worth it! And I want to help you in this. |

**1:52** Now Zdenka speaks to herself, and Strauss indulges himself in some beautiful *word painting* (making the music act out the words). On the word *Licht* ("light," at **2:05**), the violins soar upward. And on *hinab ins Dunkel* ("down into the darkness"), the music becomes hushed and falls precipitously, cloaked in the somber robes of funereal trombones.

*(speaking more to herself than to her sister)*

| | |
|---|---|
| *So hat ja die Prophetin es gesehn:* | This is just how the fortune teller saw it: |
| *sie ganz im Licht,* | her up in the light, |
| *und ich hinab ins Dunkel.* | and me down into the darkness. |

**2:25** But all this was only a quick aside. Now the original melody comes back as Arabella repeats her opening words and melody.

| **Arabella:** | *(aside)* |
|---|---|
| *Aber der Richtige, wenn's einen gibt für mich,* (etc.) | But if there is a man who is right for me, *(etc.)* |

**2:31** After a moment, Zdenka joins her sister — and reflects Arabella's hopeful mood in her vocal line and poetry. The two soprano voices entwine and soar around each other.

| **Zdenka:** *Sie ist so schön und so lieb. . . .* | She is so fair and so kind. . . . |
|---|---|
| *ich werde gehn,* | I will go, |

**3:00** Here, as before, Arabella soars on her word *selig* — but now Zdenka joins her, soaring on the similar word *segnen*. If more heavenly music exists, we haven't heard it!

**3:26** At the end of the duet, Zdenka thrills us with a high C, before they both end on the same note.

| | |
|---|---|
| *und noch im Gehn werd' ich dich segnen,* | and even as I go I will bless you, |
| *meine Schwester!* | my sister! |

Very few composers wrote for this particular combination of voices. Strauss obviously loved the sound of sopranos soaring together, and he wrote soprano duets and trios into quite a few of his operas. Another spectacular example is the famous trio from *Der Rosenkavalier*. If you enjoy this *Arabella* duet, check it out.

# 12 Bizet: Carmen — Habanera

No introduction to opera would be complete without Georges Bizet's *Carmen* — and no performance of *Carmen* would be complete without the Habanera, one of the most famous arias in all of opera. A *habanera* is a Cuban dance (from Havana, to be exact) that may remind you of a tango.

We've chosen this piece for another reason, too: It demonstrates the sensuality of the French language — especially when put to use by the right singer. The Carmen in this recording is Victoria de los Angeles, who combines her perfect French pronunciation with a fiery Spanish soul.

You can read the complete synopsis in Chapter 12, but here's the scene: Outside a cigarette factory in Seville, a bunch of soldiers hang around to shmooze with the lovely ladies. Enter Carmen: seductress, vamp, cigarette-factory worker. As she comes to work, she flirts shamelessly with the guys. She teases, in particular, the handsome (but already romantically spoken-for) corporal, José.

This piece has a simple musical structure: a brief introduction followed by a verse, a refrain, another verse, and a repeat of the refrain.

**0:02** The introduction is a short *recitative* — quasi-spoken words, sung in a free rhythm, that advance the plot. The orchestra tosses in a chord at opportune moments.

*Introduction:*

| | |
|---|---|
| *Quand je vous aimerais? ma foi, je ne sais pas. . . .* | When will you have my love? who knows, it's hard to tell. . . . |

**0:10** Now Carmen sings the beginnings of a real melody as she plays with the guys' hopes.

| | |
|---|---|
| *Peut-être jamais! . . . peut-être demain!* | Perhaps never . . . perhaps tomorrow! |

**0:24** And now, back to the *recitative* style.

| | |
|---|---|
| *Mais pas aujourd'hui, c'est certain.* | But not today, that's for certain. |

**0:31** Now begins the familiar Habanera itself. The orchestra *vamps* (repeats a snippet over and over) for several seconds before Carmen enters at **0:37**. Listen to the way Victoria de los Angeles makes her voice sensual and coquettish as she sings the words. She does this partly by creating a particular tone color, and partly by sliding mischievously between notes.

*Verse 1:*

| | |
|---|---|
| *L'amour est un oiseau rebelle* | Love is a bird that will live in freedom |
| *Que nul ne peut apprivoiser,* | That no man ever learned to tame, |
| *Et c'est bien en vain qu'on l'appelle,* | And in vain men may call her |
| *S'il lui convient de refuser!* | If she feels like refusing! |
| *Rien n'y fait, menace ou prière,* | Nothing they do, threatening or pleading, |
| *L'un parle bien, l'autre se tait;* | The one speaks well, the other is quiet; |
| *Et c'est l'autre que je prefère,* | And it's the other that I prefer, |
| *Il n'a rien dit, mais il me plaît . . .* | He says nothing, but it pleases me . . . |

**1:09** As Carmen finishes this verse, the other cigarette girls and boys chime in. They repeat Carmen's verse softly and lightly, as Carmen herself hovers above them with the word *l'amour* ("love").

**1:25** Now on to the refrain. Carmen sings it alone, to the same habanera accompaniment from the orchestra.

*Refrain:*

| | |
|---|---|
| *L'amour est enfant de Bohème,* | Love is the child of the Gipsy, |
| *Il n'a jamais, jamais connu de loi,* | It has never known the law, |
| *Si tu ne m'aimes pas, je t'aime;* | If you don't love me, then I love you; |
| *Mais si je t'aime, prends garde à toi!* | But if I love you, then watch out! |

**1:41** Suddenly the entire chorus, supported by full orchestra, jumps in with *Prends garde a toi!* ("Watch out!").

Now Carmen repeats her lines. Notice how she glides sensuously down on the word *t'aime* (at **1:52**). The chorus jumps in again, even louder this time. Carmen finishes the chorus alone, singing in a gutsy *chest voice* (see Chapter 4). (See if you can hear that powerful tone at **2:06**.)

Now the others chime in, and the whole last section is repeated. At **2:39**, Carmen holds a high note. The composer has written a *fermata* over the note, a marking that tells the singer to hold it for as long as she feels comfortable. Victoria de los Angeles makes herself comfortable for about five seconds.

**2:44** The orchestra starts again, and we're off to the second verse. Can you hear the moment where it changes from a *major key* to a *minor key?* (It's at **2:51**, precisely the spot where Carmen begins singing again, even more sensuously than in the first verse.) Now the melody is the same as before, but the words are new:

*Verse 2:*

| | |
|---|---|
| *L'oiseau que tu croyais surprendre* | But this bird that you thought you had taken |
| *Battit de l'aile et s'envola:* | Has flapped her wings and flown away: |
| *L'amour est loin, tu peux l'attendre;* | When love's gone you sit there waiting, |
| *Tu ne l'attends plus . . . il est là!* | You stop waiting and it's right there! |
| *Tout autour de toi, vite, vite,* | All around you, quickly, quickly. |
| *Il vient, s'en va, puis il revient;* | It comes, it goes, then it returns; |
| *Tu crois le tenir, il t'évite;* | You believe you've caught her, then she escapes; |

And now listen to Victoria de los Angeles's delicious, mischievous, and seductive use of chest voice as she slows down to attack the word *tient*.

| | |
|---|---|
| *Tu crois l'éviter, il te tient.* | Think you've escaped, and she's caught you. |

**3:27** Again, softly and lightly, the men and women repeat the verse as Carmen floats above them with the word *l'amour* three times. At **3:42**, the refrain repeats, and Carmen ends with a triumphant *Prends garde a toi!* (Watch out, indeed!)

# 13 Gershwin: Porgy and Bess — "It Ain't Necessarily So"

The most well-known American opera is George Gershwin's *Porgy and Bess*. This "aria" will make you understand why. As you can read in Chapter 9, Gershwin had one foot in Tin Pan Alley and one foot in the concert hall. His genius was his ability to combine both styles into a completely new American style.

You can read the complete synopsis in Chapter 12. Here's the scene: Most of the residents of poor Catfish Row, South Carolina, have gone to a picnic on Kittawah Island. There the character named Sportin' Life, a tenor (who later goes on to lead Bess, the heroine, astray), holds a mock sermon. The crowd gathers around him, cheering him on.

In this recording, Damon Evans captures the cheeky irreverence of Sportin' Life. Though Evans is a trained singer, he doesn't try to sound operatic in this show. Sportin' Life's music would sound very wrong if sung with the usual opera-singer sound!

In this number, Gershwin's aim was to write in an American gospel style. At the beginning of each verse, Sportin' Life yells out a line, and the choir repeats it. True to the style, Evans improvises freely, changing Gershwin's notes here and there as the spirit moves him. The conductor on this track, Simon Rattle, understands the style, too — and has instructed the chorus to repeat whatever Evans sings, however he sings it. As a result, this recording takes on a feeling of joyous, spontaneous improvisation unlike anything else on the CD.

The piece opens cheerfully, with plenty of laughing and back-slapping. The orchestra plays a quiet, relaxed vamp (a repeated snippet) for several seconds before Sportin' Life begins to sing.

**0:09** Evans has an edgy, focused, somewhat nasal tone. When the chorus imitates Sportin' Life's lines, it imitates his voice quality as well.

**Sportin' Life:** *(Happily, with humor)*

It ain't neccessarily so,
It ain't neccessarily so,
De t'ings dat yo' li'ble to read in de Bible,
It ain't neccessarily so.
L'il David was small but, oh my!
He fought big Goliath who lay down and dieth!
L'il David was small but, oh my!

**0:48** Suddenly, the full orchestra bursts in, playing a quick, loud, jazzy, toe-tapping rhythm — and Sportin' Life goes to town. The soloist's vocal choices in this section are just as virtuosic as anything that an operatic singer might display — but in a very different style. Again the chorus imitates him.

Wadoo,
Zim bam boddle-oo,
Hoodle ah da wa da,
Scatty wah.
Yeah!

**1:02** And now the orchestra takes us back to the original, slow, relaxed rhythm of the song. Again, the chorus imitates each line exactly as Damon Evans sings it.

Oh, Jonah, he lived in de whale,
Oh, Jonah, he lived in de whale,
Fo' he made his home in dat fish's abdomen.
Oh, Jonah he lived in de whale,
L'il Moses was found in a stream,
L'il Moses was found in a stream,
He floated on water till ole Pharaoh's daughter
She fished him, she says, from that stream.

**1:42** Once more, a big, fast orchestral outburst, as Sportin' Life goes wild.

Wadoo, (etc.)

**1:49** Listen to how long Damon Evans holds the word "Yeah!" Gershwin has notated a *fermata* (a hold) on the word — just as Bizet did for Carmen at the end of her habanera on the previous track. Evans takes advantage of this opportunity to show off his voice and charisma, holding the word for a full 11 seconds. The chorus shows its appreciation. As Sportin' Life continues, the orchestra quiets back down to its original vamp.

It ain't necessarily so,
It ain't necessarily so,
Dey tells all you chillun de debble's a villun,
But 'tain't necessarily so.

**2:19** Now Sportin' Life sings a contrasting melody, a kind of musical bridge leading us back to the final repetition of the main tune (at **2:37**).

To get into Hebben don' snap for a sebben!
Live clean! Don' have no fault.
Oh, I takes dat gospel whenever it's pos'ble,
But wid a grain of salt.
Methus'lah lived 900 years,
Methus'lah lived 900 years,
But who calls dat livin' when no gal'll give in
To no man what's 900 years?

**2:57** Sportin' Life concludes his number with a little summation, and the chorus gleefully joins in.

I'm preachin' dis sermon to show,
It ain't nessa, ain't nessa, ain't nessa, ain't nessa,
ain't necessarily so.

If you enjoy this song, check out all of *Porgy and Bess* — the whole opera is filled with music in this fresh, delightful, 100 percent American style.

# Intermission

# Backstage Tour

· · · · · · · · · · · · · · · · · · · · · · · · · · · · · · · · · · · · · · · · · · · · · · · · · · · ·

· · · · · · · · · · · · · · · · · · · · · · · · · · · · · · · · · · · · · · · · · · · · · · · · · · · ·

*T*he next time you find yourself at an opera with nothing to ponder, watch the stage and the orchestra pit. Everything seems to run so *smoothly,* doesn't it?

You'd never guess that a drama is going on backstage — and it's just as compelling as the drama onstage. On any given evening, the production staff, the orchestra, the conductor, and the singers are engaged in a hilarious human comedy. Of course, opera companies won't tell you that. But that's what *we're* here for.

## Divas and Their Dressing Rooms

Foremost on the opera staff are the singers — they won't let you forget that. Most are nice people, but they do have certain needs that must be fulfilled. Take, for example, the singer's dressing room. Here's where the singer spends most of his time at the opera house: before the opera, during intermissions, and afterward.

The dressing room needs to be the kind of place where a singer can relax, warm up the voice, mentally prepare, focus on his character, and indulge in non-opera-related pleasures if necessary. Well aware of these requirements, opera companies provide dressing rooms that are functional, well equipped, and private whenever possible.

## Special rooms for special people

What does *functional* mean? At minimum, a dressing room usually has the following:

- ✔ A table with a big, lighted mirror (and preferably lighted side mirrors as well) for putting on makeup
- ✔ A bathroom with a shower for *removing* makeup, among other things. Some singers also use the shower to create steam, which can be helpful in (a) preparing the vocal chords for singing and (b) other fun activities.
- ✔ A couch or lounge for relaxing
- ✔ A piano
- ✔ General Foods International Coffees (optional)

Some singers have more unusual needs, which opera houses try to accommodate if possible. If a singer says that he absolutely requires a bowl of Grey Poupon mustard (chilled) and a spoon in order to sing *Otello* at his best, someone on the staff makes sure that it's provided.

But occasionally a singer — or conductor, or other guest artist — demands *more* than a little special treatment. If this person is famous enough, the opera company does its best to please. We know of one company that had to rebuild a dressing room overnight (including all the air-conditioning ducts) to please an artist who wanted his room over *here,* not over *there.*

### The Last Super

As you delve deeper into the world of opera, certain questions are bound to nag at you late at night. For example, how the heck do they provide dressing rooms for the cast of thousands milling about onstage?

They don't. Those warriors, courtiers, exiles, slaves, spear carriers, witches, and citizens of Paris, Cairo, and Thebes aren't considered important enough to get their own rooms. In fact, anyone who doesn't have a significant number of solo lines to sing is considered an extra. Extras usually share one big dressing room, or one for the men and one for the women. In the opera world, extras are called *supernumeraries* — and everybody calls them *supers.*

One of your present authors remembers his days running supertitles for a large American opera company. Imagine his delight in encountering an enormous dressing room, complete with 32 well-lit mirrors, with the word *SUPERS* in big letters on the door. Imagine his dismay when he discovered that the big room wasn't for the *supertitle* operator at all.

## The payoff

When we first heard that a top singer was going to get $20,000 to appear in a production of *Carmen,* we were stunned. "Twenty grand to sing for a couple hours a night for a week?" we asked. "A part she already has memorized? That's *crazy!*"

We were wrong. The fee wasn't $20,000 for the week — it was $20,000 for *each performance.*

In fact, the fees go even higher. In Tokyo, Japan or Bilbao, Spain, a top singer can command up to *$30,000* for one night. Interestingly, the more prestigious the opera house, the less it has to pay to get these stars. The opera houses in Vienna and Munich regularly pay close to $20,000, and the Metropolitan Opera in New York pays even less.

To these opera companies, the singers are well worth the price. They draw an immense crowd that pays through the nose for the privilege of seeing and hearing their favorite stars.

But still. $30K per night? Maybe we'll start taking voice lessons again.

# Auditions: Behind the Screams

Even the biggest stars were little once. And before they came to the public's attention, they had to go through a highly competitive audition process.

To show you how the audition process works, we're going to tell you the story of a friend of ours, a really superb soprano. We'll call her Mimi (although her real name is Lucia Jerkins, 31 Walnut Court, Gainesville, FL 32606; phone 352-364-9287, fax 352-364-9942; e-mail larynx@diva.net).

"Mimi" had originally moved to Gainesville to take a part-time job in the music department at Alachua County Community College, teaching voice to non-majors three days a week. On the side, she sang Gilbert and Sullivan operettas in a tiny community group called the AriaGators (not their real name). But still, she felt unfulfilled. She dreamed of getting real opera experience, and she had what it takes to succeed in the opera world: a gorgeous lyric soprano voice, flawless technique, and a body to match.

Unfortunately, Mimi had plenty of competition — a *lyric soprano* is the most common kind of opera singer in the world. There are far too few jobs for them all, even for the great ones.

## *The notice*

Mimi subscribed to the *New York Opera Newsletter,* the main source of information about opera auditions. The pages of each issue are crowded with audition announcements from opera companies and festivals around the world. Mimi was leafing through the latest issue when the following notice caught her eye.

---

# The Tri-Counties Opera, Inc.

Furioso Sábado, Artistic Director

announces auditions for its

## Young Artist Apprentice Program

Operas to be performed in the coming season:

*Carmen*

*Die Fledermaus*

*Tosca*

*The Marriage of Figaro*

Auditioning singers must provide their own transportation and accommodations. Participants must be prepared to rehearse in Farfalloo for a small stipend.

Send one-page résumé, photograph, and birth certificate to:

Tri-Counties Opera, Inc.
c/o Robert Louis Stevenson Elementary School
Attendance Office, Room 121-B
33 Grossman Drive
Farfalloo, WY 82505

Audition information will not be provided over the phone.

---

A *young artist apprentice program* at an opera house is a type of internship, where young singers get valuable professional experience. They *cover* some of the major roles — that is, they act as understudies, filling in if a star gets sick. They sometimes get cast in minor roles. And they sometimes get to perform operas for kids in public schools, in sharply scaled-down traveling versions.

Mimi knew that the competition for *this* audition would be especially tough. Small companies receive an inordinately large number of applications because of a peculiar unwritten law in the opera world: Singers are discouraged from auditioning for opera houses more than *two levels above* their current level of experience. (Doing so is considered highly presumptuous.) The Tri-Counties Opera was on a higher level than anything Mimi had done before, but not so high as to risk professional backlash for applying.

## The documents

Mimi searched her apartment for her most current résumé, an old photograph, and a copy of her birth certificate. She clearly remembered the words of her teacher at the conservatory: "As early as you can, take as many years off your age as possible."

Among unknown singers, youth is a requirement. No significant vocal competition or apprentice program considers women older than about 30 — even though the soprano voice often doesn't peak until the late 40s. If you're a lyric soprano, and you haven't established your career by 30, forget it; so the saying goes.

Mimi was 34. So she did what many self-respecting sopranos around the world do: She forged her birth certificate.

"Forge as many documents as you can," her teacher had said. "First, make photocopies of your passport, birth certificate, and driver's license. White out all the numbers. Then find the right kind of typewriter, line everything up, and put the new numbers in place. Photocopy the photocopy a few times, until the new numbers look right at home."

Mimi took six years off her age. Now, as far as anyone knew, she was 28 — a perfectly respectable age for an unknown, highly talented lyric soprano.

Her next step was to falsify her résumé. No opera company takes a soprano seriously unless she has several important opera roles under her belt. But where can a glut of lyric sopranos gain experience? Time to make something up.

"For goodness' sake, be careful!" her teacher had said. "You have to make up the name of a *small* opera company. If you say that you sang the role of Donna Anna in *Don Giovanni* at the Met, they'll check up on you. But if you say that you sang Donna Anna with a community opera company in a *church* somewhere, who's gonna check?"

Her teacher had also advised her to stretch the truth a little. "Let's say that you sang one of Fiordiligi's scenes from *Così fan tutte,* with piano accompaniment. Well, for goodness' sake, write down that you sang the 'role of Fiordiligi.' That makes it sound like you sang the *whole darned opera with full orchestra.*"

As Mimi knew, there were other ways to get experience, too. Several New York companies offer singers experience — for a fee. You pay $500 for the opportunity to sing half a performance of an opera. Another soprano sings the other half. The next night, another two sopranos, and so on. Each gets to list the starring role on her résumé, and the company gets rich. Mimi had "starred" in two such productions.

As for the photograph: It was seven years old.

Mimi hated this deception with all her heart. But she was also realistic: Without it, her chances were zero.

## The list

Mimi sent off her package to Farfalloo and waited for a response. Two weeks later, she received word: She was one of 50 singers accepted to audition! The letter told her to submit a list of her five chosen arias in advance.

She pondered her options. The four operas being presented next season had several roles that she could sing — including Micaela in *Carmen,* Rosalinde in *Die Fledermaus,* and the Countess in *The Marriage of Figaro.* But Mimi guessed that the opera house had probably already given those parts to no-name singers from New York with good agents. Still, Mimi felt that the audition was worth her time and money. She had already made the first cut, and — who knows? — the opera house might ask her to be a *cover.* Even a cover role is good for the résumé, if it's with an opera company that actually pays.

Mimi chose five representative arias to sing: Musetta's Waltz from *La Bohème,* Micaela's aria *"Je dis que rien ne m'épouvante"* from *Carmen,* the Countess's aria *"Dove sono"* from *The Marriage of Figaro,* Violetta's famous aria *"Ah, fors'è lui"* from *La Traviata,* and Pamina's aria *"Ach, ich fühl's"* from *The Magic Flute.* She typed the titles of these pieces on a separate sheet of paper and sent the list to Farfalloo.

## The trip

Mimi arrived at the Farfalloo International Airport the day before the audition. She checked into the Motel 6, had dinner, and went to bed. The next morning, she got up early and began to *vocalize* (warm up her voice with singing exercises). She continued singing in her rental car as she followed her map to Robert Louis Stevenson Elementary School. Because it was Saturday, school wasn't in session, but she counted at least 30 singers waiting in the foyer — 25 were sopranos.

A nice old woman ushered her into a classroom. "This is your dressing room," she said. "You can warm up here if you like. You sing in 30 minutes — call if you need anything."

## The switch

No sooner had the woman left than there was a loud, hurried knock on the door. Peering through the thin window, Mimi saw a distraught-looking singer, hair piled high, makeup piled even higher, an unlit cigarette hanging from her lips, waving her hands wildly. Mimi opened the door.

"Oh, thank Gawd," the singer gushed. "I'm supposed to sing in an hour — but I'll miss my plane to New Yawk!" She stopped to catch her breath and looked at Mimi with panic-stricken eyes.

"Yes . . . ?" Mimi answered politely, not understanding.

"Do you think I could trade places with you and sing first?" the woman asked. "Then I could make my plane."

"Sure, I don't see why not," Mimi replied. She could use the extra half-hour going over the music in her head, here in the dressing room.

"Great," the distraught singer said. "So can I have the dressing room, then? You'll have another half-hour when I'm done."

This development took Mimi by surprise. "I . . . suppose. . . . Okay," she faltered, trying (and failing) to think of a nice way to refuse. She gathered her music and stepped out of the room.

## The wait

Alone in the hallway, Mimi heard the other singers vocalizing from other rooms: humming and noodling seemed to come from everywhere at once. Then the distraught singer in Mimi's dressing room began to warm up, too — singing some of the same arias that Mimi had prepared. Mimi began to feel nervous.

Just off the hallway was the door to the cafetorium where the auditions took place. Mimi put her ear to the door. She heard a beautiful singing voice — a tenor. A moment later, the door opened, and the tenor emerged. Mimi smiled. "That was beautiful," she said.

He beamed, showing a perfect row of teeth. "Thanks! I do my best!" He was tall, fresh, very strong-looking, and slightly older than Mimi (although not according to his birth certificate). "Are you next?"

"Well, I would have been," she replied. "But I'm letting another soprano switch with me, because she has a plane to catch."

"Oh, really?" he replied. "She asked to change her time?" He frowned. "I wonder if she *really* has a plane to catch. I'll bet she just doesn't want to sing right after another soprano. She switched with you so that she could sing after a baritone! How much d'ya wanna bet?"

"Really?" asked Mimi, bewildered.

"Sure. That way, the audition committee won't compare her to the singer before her. Happens all the time," said the tenor. "By the way, I'm Rod."

The other soprano emerged from the dressing room, totally transformed. The unlit cigarette was momentarily gone. Bold and glamorous, she looked as if she had walked straight out of the first act of *La Traviata.* "Thanks so much," she said to Mimi with a half-smile. "By the way, what arias are on your list?"

"Actually, I think we have pretty much the *same* list," Mimi answered, blushing. "I'm planning to start with Musetta's Waltz."

"Oh, *really?*" said the soprano, eyeing her up and down. "I never would have imagined you in that role. You look too . . . sweet, too innocent." She looked at Mimi again. "Oh, no, they'd *never* cast you in that." And she disappeared into the cafetorium.

"Now I *know* what that lady's up to," Rod said. "She's trying to psych you out."

"She's succeeding," said Mimi.

## *The tryout*

The other soprano finished singing and came out of the cafetorium beaming broadly. Nervously, Mimi entered the room herself. She found herself onstage — alone except for an accompanist, who sat at a beautiful baby grand piano. He smiled at her. The audition committee, five people, sat about 20 yards away on tiny little cafetorium chairs.

"Good morning," one of them said. "What would you like to start with?"

Mimi had been all set to start with Musetta's Waltz, but at that moment she changed her mind. Maybe the other soprano was right: Maybe she *did* look too innocent. "I'd like to start with Micaela's aria from *Carmen,*" she said.

The committee let Mimi sing all the way through the opening recitative, and one verse of the aria. She sang beautifully, and her French was impeccable. She made appropriate dramatic gestures with her hands as she sang. Everything was wonderful . . . except . . .

. . . *the committee members weren't looking at her at all!* They were reading her résumé. Two of them, engaged in conversation, didn't even seem to be listening. Mimi was angry. All her singing and acting classes, years of private lessons and vocal coaching, and $893 in plane fare and hotel . . . for this? With steely resolve, she hurled her climactic notes right out to the committee.

After one verse, they stopped her abruptly. "Thank you very much." *Well, at least I got in one high B,* Mimi thought. *Now what will they ask for?*

"*'Dove sono,'* please."

She knew it — the Countess's aria from Mozart's *Figaro.* Nothing is more difficult than Mozart: Although the notes aren't particularly hard to sing, they must be perfectly in tune, with a pure sound and beautiful delivery.

They let her sing the aria all the way through — a good sign, Mimi thought. "That will be enough, thank you very much," someone said as soon as she finished. The audition was over.

## *The outcome*

Back in the hallway, Rod the tenor was waiting. "Beautiful job!" he said. "I stayed to hear you sing, and I was *very* impressed."

She blushed. "Thanks. When do we find out?"

"They'll write to us in a week or so — *if* they're interested, that is. Otherwise, we might not hear from them at all."

"Oh well," sighed Mimi, "at least this was a nice break from Gainesville life."

"Gainesville!" he exclaimed. "I'm from Tampa!" In fact, they were booked on the same flight home.

That evening they met for a quick bite at the airport bar before the flight. Out of the corner of his eye, Rod spied the distraught soprano who had stolen Mimi's dressing room ten hours earlier. Her cigarette was lit now, and she no longer looked the least bit distraught. "Look!" he whispered, pointing. "Over in the smoking section."

"Well, what do you know?" said Mimi. "She wasn't in such a hurry to get back to New York after all."

## The aftermath

We wish we could tell you that Mimi won her audition, but she didn't. Besides, if she'd won, we wouldn't have accomplished our purpose of showing you a *typical* audition experience.

But ten days later, Mimi got a call from a man in Oklahoma, who had sat in with the committee in Farfalloo. "I must say I was impressed with your interpretation of Micaela's aria," he said. "I'm sorry the committee stopped you after just one verse; I would have liked to have heard the end of the piece. I'm producing *Carmen* next spring with a very small opera company here in Oklahoma. All the parts are cast already, but we don't have our cover for Micaela yet. Are you interested?"

Mimi was ecstatic. As a *cover* (an understudy), she may never get to sing the role in performance, but at least she could add something *real* to her résumé. She happily agreed.

Something else came of her audition experience as well: Mimi kept in touch with Rod. He told her that he had been accepted into Farfalloo's apprentice program, covering the part of Don José in *Carmen*. After a few phone calls, Mimi and Rod decided to get together. Rod made the short trip to Gainesville, and a week later Mimi visited him in Tampa. At this very moment, they are in the first phases of a fiery Florida fling.

# Sets! Costumes! Wigs!

As you can read in Chapter 5, people have always flocked to operas for the spectacle. Even in Renaissance times, flying gods and swimming nymphs livened up many a show. Today, the spectators at any major opera house still expect to be blown away by what they see, not just what they hear. In recent years, opera sets — like Broadway sets — have continued to reflect the latest improvements in technology. The results have been awesome.

Some of the most celebrated sets have come from the mind of director Franco Zeffirelli, also well-known for several beautiful movies. He has directed operas all over the world, including some legendary Metropolitan Opera productions. In many cases, he re-created, onstage, full-scale replicas of famous scenes: a street in Paris for *La Bohème* (complete with kids, horses, and falling snow), and three actual Roman buildings for *Tosca.* The audience went nuts.

For the most part, sets are not built onstage, because the stage is already in use for another show. Big opera houses usually have impressive set-building workshops a level or two *below* the stage. Sets are built down there and brought up by elevator, piece by piece.

If you go backstage at a huge opera house like the Met, you'll see an amazing thing. There's enough room backstage for several complete sets: one to the left of the main stage, one to the right, one behind — and sometimes, one underneath as well. With the push of a button, these stage setups can move from back to front, from side to side, and sometimes up and down. Between scenes, the scenery moves as a whole; the *entire stage* is pushed off in one direction, and another one comes on.

This capability can make for some spectacular scene changes *during* the action of an opera. We've seen a production of *Tosca* where, after the opening of the third act, the whole set slowly rose in the air, revealing an underground jail cell with a singing tenor in it — provoking gasps, swoons, and cries of "Bravo!" from the audience. When the tenor was finished with his aria, he disappeared underground again. Gone are the days when the audience could leave the theater to take in a meal, or put up some siding, and return in time for the next scene.

Wherever you find great sets, you usually find great costumes, too. Burrowed deep in the crevices of the opera house is the costume workshop. In the big opera houses, these workshops are constantly busy, with a team of full-time seamstresses. And the *really* big opera houses even have their own *wig* departments.

We're not in Farfalloo anymore.

# *Unsung Heroes: The Opera Orchestra*

An orchestra is a world unto itself, made up of practically every kind of instrument you can name. It's also a fascinating microcosm of the human race, containing every personality type imaginable. Orchestra life has its great excitements, its challenges, and its amazing frustrations. And you can read about them in detail in *Classical Music For Dummies.*

The orchestra is the *star* of a classical music concert, but in the opera house, it's relegated to the role of accompanist. Audiences often undervalue the contribution of the players, who sit hidden from view and take care not to drown out the singers.

The opera orchestra doesn't just back up the singers, though; it fulfills a psychological function as well. If the soprano sings "I love you" to the tenor, the orchestra's music may tell you that she really wants to rip him to shreds. If the character thinks that he's going to survive the "fake" execution, but we know he won't, it's the orchestra that tells us so. The music tells us what's *really* going on in the drama — just like the narrator of a play, the voice-over in a movie, Lassie in *Lassie,* or the thought bubbles in *Beetle Bailey.*

If orchestra life has its rigors, *opera* orchestra life is over the top. Regular orchestras perform for about two hours per concert. But opera orchestras keep going — three or four hours, or as long as it takes until the opera is done. Furthermore, unlike the singers onstage, the orchestra never gets to exit after a difficult scene. It plays *all* the time.

# Unstrung Heroes: The Opera Chorus

The *supers* (an opera's extras) we described earlier in this Intermission (see the sidebar "The Last Super") often have a musical role to play as well — they're the opera chorus. (See Figure IM-1.)

As you might guess, the musical goals of a chorus member are completely different from those of an opera star. Whereas a star has to be able to fill an auditorium with her voice alone, a chorus singer must blend her sound with the rest of the group. A singer with a diva voice could never *be* a chorus member — she'd always stick out. Similarly, a good chorister would have a hard time changing into a prima donna.

Choruses are divided into four major voice parts — soprano, alto, tenor, and bass. In preliminary chorus rehearsals, each singer usually sits together with the other singers of his part. That's a great arrangement for learning; if you lose your place in the music, you have ten voices around you singing your part.

**Figure IM-1:**
The opera chorus — one of the most challenging jobs in the opera house.

But in performance, this seating arrangement is impossible. First of all, the chorus members are standing most of the time onstage. Second, they're not only standing; they're probably also *walking*. Third, they may be *fighting*. Or dancing. Or rioting. Or drinking. And singing nonstop, all the while.

Sure, the *main* characters in an opera have to do all these things, too. But there's a major difference: When a tenor soloist simultaneously sings and fights the dragon, the conductor and orchestra can bend to accommodate any rhythmic imprecision that the fighting may have caused. But no matter what the singers in the *chorus* are doing physically, they must always sing their notes together, perfectly in rhythm and perfectly in tune — from opposite sides of the stage.

# Opera Conductors and Semi-Conductors

Throughout dozens of rehearsals (appropriately known in French as *répétitions*), the opera stars, chorus, dancers, orchestra musicians, and prompters learn their parts inside and out. But in performance, one person controls it all: the conductor.

## From coach to maestro

*Classical Music For Dummies* offers great detail on the instrumental conductor, what the little stick is for, and what the job entails. The conductor's art is a complex one, partly musical and partly political. But opera conductors are a breed apart from instrumental conductors. Instead of studying the symphonies and concertos of old, most of them spend their youth playing opera music at the piano. They become intimately acquainted with the great operas, learn several foreign languages, and spend their days helping singers prepare for their operatic roles. Of course, they also have to learn conducting technique and develop a clear beat.

## Float like a butterfly, sting like a bee

During an opera, the conductor must give the signal for the orchestra to begin, set the tempo (or speed) at which the musicians play, vary it when necessary, cue the entrances of the orchestra (or the singers), and constantly adjust the balance between orchestra and vocalists, so that one doesn't drown out the other.

The conductor's most difficult job, though, is *following the singers*. Yes, that's right — in opera, the notion that the *conductor* directs the music falls apart. If a tenor feels like lingering on a particular note in his aria, the conductor's job is to make certain that the orchestra lingers there as well. If the tenor needs to stop singing for a second to take a big breath of air, the conductor must make the orchestra pause. And if the tenor speeds up the end of his line because he's running out of wind, the conductor must speed up the orchestra, too. The best opera conductors can actually *anticipate* the singers' wishes, guessing where the singer wants to go musically — and arriving there at precisely the same time.

In short, the conductor is like a professional boxer, constantly bobbing and weaving, sometimes following, sometimes leading, and always listening with great intensity.

# *The Stage Director: Master of Them All*

The person who rules an opera production, though, is not the conductor *or* the prima donna. It's the stage director. Although she doesn't do a thing during the performance itself, she determines — more than anyone else — what the audience experiences at the opera house.

The stage director does exactly what the director of a movie or play does: figures out how to present the drama to the audience. On the simplest level, she tells the singers when to move across the stage, and where to stop. On a more complex level, she provides the singers with "motivations" for their lines and actions, to help make them convincing. And on the highest level, she creates an overall "concept" for the production — an artistic idea that unifies all the elements of the opera.

The favorite concept of many stage directors is to change the time and place of the opera's action. After all, what makes a great opera great is its universality: Whether it takes place in ancient Egypt, or aboard a British sailing ship, or in the streets of Rome, its themes and emotions are universal. When a stage director shifts the action of a favorite opera to a completely new time and place, she succeeds in (a) commenting upon this universality and (b) drawing attention to herself.

Take the brilliant young stage director Peter Sellars, for example. He up-dated Mozart's *Così fan tutte* to a contemporary greasy spoon diner, and changed Don Giovanni into a criminal from inner-city New York. Another director junked the set locations in *Carmen* and staged the entire show in a bull ring, changing Carmen's job description from "cigarette-factory employee" to "matador."

Personally, we love the bold visions of stage directors like these. Though they may not always be completely convincing, they keep expanding the frontiers of this ancient art form — showing us that grand old opera can be *new* at the same time.

# Part IV
# A Guide to the World's Most Beloved Operas

The 5th Wave    By Rich Tennant

Porky and Bess

B'da b'dab'dab- Bess, ♪ ♩ you is my woman ♫ m'naminaminaminam'NOW...

## In this part . . .

All the rest of this book is about opera in *general* — the people, the art form, the orchestra, the music, the words. But opera is more than words and music; operas are *stories*. If you listen to an opera on your car stereo, you're missing exactly 50 percent of the experience.

This part, then, is the fattest part of the book. Chapter 12 contains plot summaries of the 50 operas we think you're most likely to encounter — in live performance, on TV, in the record store, or in the library. And the next chapter has 24 more — shorter summaries of the next operas you're likely to see.

# Chapter 12

# The 50 Big Kahunas

This chapter is the fattest part of the book. It has plot summaries of the 50 operas we think you're most likely to encounter — on TV, in the record store, at the library, or in live performance. Chapter 13 has 24 more — shorter summaries of the operas you're next most likely to see.

We've designed this chapter to serve you in three ways:

✔ To help you choose an opera to see (on videotape or in person)

✔ To help you prepare for an opera you're *about* to see by flagging the most important musical numbers, events onstage, character entrances, and so on, as points of reference

✔ To provide several months' worth of bedtime stories

As for the names of these operas: Some are in English, and some are in the original languages. We chose a title language for each opera based on the way *most* people refer to it. And what, you may well ask, is the criteria for selection? There *is* none; some operas are known by their English titles, and some by their non-English titles, and that's that.

Either way, though, you can't lose in this chapter — we've listed operas both ways, providing cross-references to the primary listings.

# The Abduction from the Seraglio

**Title translation:** *Die Entführung aus dem Serail.* **Music by:** Wolfgang Amadeus Mozart. **Libretto:** In German by Gottlieb Stephanie, based on another opera. **First performed:** Vienna, Austria, 1782.

**What to look forward to:** Mozart's first successful opera — a rescue comedy in three acts. *The Abduction from the Seraglio* ("sir-AHL-yo") is more of a musical than an opera; all the actual plot takes place in spoken dialogue scenes, just as in a musical — only the big emotional moments are sung. The German word for this kind of musical is *Singspiel* (which means "sing-play").

**Astonishing trivia:** The heroine of this show is the pretty Constanze. Mozart, while writing the music, was himself engaged to a pretty woman named Constanze, whom he married just after the opera opened. Coincidence? You decide.

**Act I:** Turkey, the 1500s. Belmonte, a young tenor nobleman from Spain, is poking around the mansion of the evil Count Selim. (*Pasha* is Turkish for *count,* so that's what we'll call him henceforth.) The pasha has kidnapped Belmonte's pretty soprano girlfriend, Constanze; her maid, Blondchen; and Belmonte's servant, Pedrillo.

Osmin, the harem manager, has fallen in love with Blondchen — over the protests of servant Pedrillo, who loves her too (and he was there first). Osmin chews out rival Pedrillo, who's now employed as a gardener.

Hero Belmonte, however, is thrilled to see Pedrillo, who tells him that the pasha has been putting the moves on Constanze. Belmonte's more determined than ever to rescue his beloved Constanze: *"O wie ängstlich, o wie feurig"* ("How anxiously, how ardently!").

The pasha and Constanze arrive by boat to a choral welcome. Pedrillo introduces Belmonte to the pasha as a promising young architect; after some conniving, Belmonte and his servant enter the palace.

**Act II:** Blondchen rejects the advances of big oaf Osmin. The pasha's not getting anywhere with Constanze, either; she rejects him in *"Martern aller Arten"* ("Endless torture"). Pedrillo sets the escape plan into motion; in the duet *"Vivat Bacchus"* ("Long live the god of wine!"), Pedrillo gets Osmin completely sloshed. The couples are ready to escape, ending the act with a joyous quartet.

**Act III:** As Pedrillo sets up ladders, Belmonte impersonates Pedrillo's nightly singing to Blondchen to divert suspicion. Belmonte and Constanze slip away, but Pedrillo is caught. Osmin gloats with a crazed song of triumph, as Belmonte and Constanze are also hauled in.

Constanze pleads with the pasha, and Belmonte adds that his father is a rich Spaniard who'll pay quite a bit in ransom. Oops — should have kept his mouth shut; the rich Spaniard is the pasha's lifelong enemy. Faced with death, the lovers fearfully sing *"Welch' ein Geschick!"* ("What a fate!").

Fortunately, the pasha has a quick change of heart (it *is* getting to the end of the show, after all) and decides to set his captives free. Everyone's happy except Osmin, who interrupts to vent his rage before returning to the onerous work of supervising a palace full of sexy women.

# Aïda

**Music by:** Giuseppe Verdi. **Libretto:** In Italian by Antonio Ghislanzoni. **First performed:** Cairo, Egypt, 1871. **What to look forward to:** A heart-rending, ancient-Egypt tragic love triangle in four acts. *Aïda* is Verdi's most popular opera — in fact, it's one of the most performed operas *ever.* The show is expensive to produce, requiring gigantic sets, but worth it; pure human passions and French-style spectacle make for fewer boring parts than any other opera.

**Astonishing trivia:** The show was commissioned by the Khedive of Egypt for $20,000. When it opened in Italy a year later, conducted by Verdi himself, it was such a crazy hit that the audience's standing ovation lasted for *32* curtain calls.

**Act I:** The evil Ethiopians are advancing on Memphis! Country music is threatened forever! No, no, strike that; this would be Memphis, capital of *Egypt.*

Good-looking tenor Radames prays that he'll be chosen to defend Egypt. Becoming a hero would make Radames look good to the slave girl he adores — Aïda (a soprano — "ah-EE-duh"). Radames sings the classic aria (don't ask why a young Egyptian is singing in Italian):

| | |
|---|---|
| *Celese Aïda, forma divina,* | Radiant Aïda, beauty resplendent, |
| *Mistico serto di luce e fior, del mio pensiero,* | mysterious blending of flowers and light, |
| *tu sei regina,* | Queen of my soul, |
| *tu di mia vita sei lo splendor.* | You are the bright splendor of my life. |

Man, they don't write love songs like *that* anymore.

Anyway, two wrinkles complicate this little love setup. First, the king's daughter Amneris has a raging secret crush on Radames. Second, Aïda is *Amneris's* personal slave girl. In the trio *"Vieni, o diletta,"* Amneris slyly sings to her slave (as Radames anxiously watches), "Come, dearest friend, come near to me; slave I no longer call you — my *sister* I proclaim you!"

Radames has been chosen to lead the Egyptians into battle. And guess who's leading the *enemy* army? A guy named King Amonasro — as Aïda sings, "My father!" Talk about coincidence!

The complications aren't lost on Aïda. If she roots for Radames, she's hoping that her own father gets wiped out; if she roots for Dad, she's cheering for her lover to die. The crowd shouts *"Ritorna vincitor!"* ("Return victorious!"); Aïda sings her famous aria: *"Numi pietà, del mio soffrir!"* ("Pity, kind heaven, to you I fly; there's no hope in my woe!"). The first act ends with an elaborate Egyptian dance number in which Radames prepares for battle.

**Act II:** Radames has triumphed, wiping out most of the evil Ethiopians. The stage fills with soldiers, prisoners, trumpets, elephants, and all the regalia of Radames returning from battle. The congratulatory Egyptian king offers him anything he wants. Radames resists, blurting out, "I'd like to marry your daughter's slave girl, please."

Radames sets free all the prisoners of war except Aïda and her father, Ethiopian King Amonasro, cleverly disguised as a common officer. As his "reward" for defeating the enemy, Radames is given Princess Amneris's hand in marriage. The crowd goes wild, singing *"Gloria all' Egitto!"* ("Glory to Egypt!"). Everyone's happy — except, of course, Radames and Aïda.

**Act III:** At a temple by the moonlit Nile River, Aïda arrives, hoping for a secret rendezvous with Radames. Before Radames arrives, however, Aïda's father shows up. In an impassioned duet, he persuades her that she should learn from Radames how he plans to continue the battle against the Ethiopians. He goes crazy, telling her that if she doesn't help, Radames will wipe out the remaining Ethiopians, including Aïda's family and friends. Aïda reluctantly agrees.

Radames finally shows up. In a dreamy duet, Aïda suggests that he run away with her: *"Fuggiam gli ardori inospiti"* ("Ah, fly from this bare, burning desert"). Radames falls for it, even suggesting how they can escape without being noticed: "Why, we'll just take the [unguarded] pass of Napata!" Oops, he just gave away the strategy he was going to use in battle tomorrow.

King Amonasro bursts out of his hiding place, having heard all — and then Princess Amneris bursts out of *her* hiding place, having heard still more. Radames turns himself in for having unwittingly aided the enemy.

**Act IV:** Princess Amneris offers to see what she can do to get Radames off the hook. But he won't hear of it. *"Sol bramo di morir,"* he says ("I wish only to die"). The priests condemn him, repeatedly singing, "Traitor!" and punctuating Amneris's desperate song of love and pity.

The show ends with a famous double scene: The stage is split into two levels. Above, the temple, where Princess Amneris throws herself sobbing on the stone that has sealed the tomb. Downstairs, the underground dungeon in which Radames has been permanently sealed alive. Radames looks up to see his beloved Aïda emerge from the shadows; anticipating his sentence, she has hidden in the dungeon so that they may be together at last, if only in death (and in one more fantastic duet).

*Andrea Chénier . . . See Chapter 13*

*Arabella . . . See Chapter 13*

# Ariadne auf Naxos

**Title translation:** *Ariadne at Naxos.* **Music by:** Richard Strauss. **Libretto:** In German by Hugo von Hofmannsthal. **First performed:** Stuttgart, Germany, 1912; revised and expanded for Vienna, 1916.

**What to look forward to:** A one-act, intimate comedy, a spoof of the Greek myth of Ariadne. (Background: Theseus, King of Athens, kills the half-man, half-bull Minotaur with the help of Crete's Princess Ariadne. He fell in love with her and carried her away, but got bored with her and abandoned her on the island of Naxos.) *Ariadne auf Naxos* is a comic opera *about* a serious opera being presented in a rich guy's house. If you can get that much straight, you're home free.

**Astonishing trivia:** Although this opera is only one act (plus a Prologue), it was originally *really* short — designed, in fact, as a thank-you note, a mini-mini-opera for the producer of the composer's previous opera.

**The plot:** In Vienna during the 1800s, a wealthy homeowner has commissioned a new serious opera to be put on for his guests. In the *real* opera's prologue, the actors, singers, and stage crew bustle about in readiness for the first performance of the new (fictional) opera. The stress is high, because after the opera there's to be a Harlequin clown show, and after *that*, at 9 p.m., fireworks will begin — whether or not the first two entertainments have finished.

But the rich host has an idea to avoid running late: The opera and the Harlequin show will be performed *simultaneously*. The composer is nearly apoplectic, but the director assures him that his clowns will fit themselves into the opera smoothly.

In despair, the composer lets the fictional opera-within-an-opera begin.

Now we're on a desert island, where soprano Ariadne is awaiting death in a cave, watched over by a trio of nymphs. The clown troupe tries valiantly to cheer her up with sprightly songs, but to no avail — Ariadne mutters that only death can rescue her now.

Zerbinetta, the lead clown-ette, tries her secret cheer-up weapon: an unbelievably difficult, complex super-aria (no joke — it's about the most difficult-to-sing piece of opera music ever written). In it, she explains to Ariadne that there's no point mooning over one lost guy; Zerbinetta's philosophy boils down to "Love the one you're with."

The young, good-looking God, Bacchus, now approaches the island. Ariadne, thinking that he's Theseus, or perhaps death, runs out happily. But it's better than death — it's Bacchus, who falls in love with her and takes her into the cave for a little cheering up. Zerbinetta pops her head back onto the stage to summarize — "We women are conquered the minute a new god comes along!"

## *Un Ballo in Maschera . . . Look under A Masked Ball*

# *The Barber of Seville*

**Title translation:** *Il Barbiere di Siviglia.* **Music by:** Gioachino Rossini. **Libretto:** In Italian by Cesare Sterbini. **First performed:** Rome, Italy, 1816.

**What to look forward to:** A riotous romantic comedy in two acts, based on a play by the French playwright Beaumarchais. Nonstop funny, fast action, pranks, and a first-act finale of musical chaos and hilarity that you have to see, not just listen to on CD. (These characters will return in the sequel, Mozart's *The Marriage of Figaro*.)

**Astonishing trivia:** Rossini was a big fat guy who did much to establish the stereotype of the *lazy* big fat guy. He didn't even bother writing an overture for this opera; instead, he just tacked on the overture left over from a previous, less successful show.

**Figure 12-1:**
*The Barber of Seville:* (left to right) Thomas Allen in the title role, Frank Lopardo as Count Almaviva, Nicola Ghiuselev as Basilio, Claudio Desderi as Bartolo, Cynthia Lawrence as Berta, Frederica von Stade as Rosina, Lyric Opera of Chicago, 1989–90. (photo: Tony Romano)

**Act I:** Count Almaviva has arrived in Seville, Spain, to woo the woman he loves: the beautiful, rich Rosina. He's aided by his old friend Figaro, local barber, handyman, and general wise guy. (You'll probably recognize the famous tune Figaro sings as he appears: *"Largo al factotum della città"* ["Make way for the city's jack of all trades, La la la la la laaa!"]).

Rosina is the ward of the crusty old Dr. Bartolo, who intends to marry Rosina for her money. Figaro proposes that, to avoid suspicion from Dr. Bartolo, the Count dress as a drunken soldier seeking shelter. Now, the Count wants to be loved for who he *is,* not for his title; so when Figaro tells Rosina the plan, he claims that her ardent admirer is an average guy named Lindoro. Rosina, excited, gives Figaro a love letter with instructions to bear it to Lindoro. (This duet is on your CD; see Chapter 11 for lyrics.)

When the "drunken sailor" shows up, Bartolo nearly throws him out of the house. During the scuffle, Almaviva manages to pass a love letter of his own to Rosina. When the police burst in, Dr. Bartolo demands that they arrest the "drunken soldier" — but Almaviva whispers his actual identity to the police, who, respectful of his rank, back out. All express their amazement and amusement as the curtain falls.

**Act II:** Count Almaviva returns, introducing himself this time as Don Alonso, the substitute music teacher; he explains that the real music teacher is ill. Now comes the famous music-lesson scene, in which the Count pretends to teach the super-diva Rosina how to sing, as Figaro, supposedly on hand to give Dr. Bartolo his daily shave, sneaks off to find the key to unlock the balcony doors so that Rosina can escape later in the evening. Everything goes well until the *actual* music teacher, Basilio, shows up — quite healthy. Figaro and the Count, aided by a wad of money, manage to persuade Basilio that, come to think of it, he really isn't feeling so hot.

The disguised Count and Rosina exchange plans for a midnight elopement, but Bartolo overhears them. He vows to dash their plans by marrying Rosina that very night, and goes off to get the police so that he can arrest Figaro and "Alonso" as thieves when they arrive for the elopement.

When Count Almaviva finally reveals his identity, Rosina, thrilled that her admirer is not only cute but a count as well, agrees to elope with him. The notary arrives to sign the marriage between Rosina and *Dr. Bartolo* — but a gun to the head persuades him to marry Rosina to the Count instead.

By the time Dr. Bartolo returns with the police, it's too late; Rosina and Almaviva are newlyweds. So that the opera may end happily for every character on the stage, however, they're nice enough to give Bartolo what he really wants — a big fat check.

*Billy Budd . . . See Chapter 13*

# Bluebeard's Castle

**Title translation:** *A Kékssakállú Herceg Vára.* **Music and libretto by:** Béla Bartók (in Hungarian). **First performed:** Budapest, Hungary, 1918.

**What to look forward to:** Sorry, kids: This isn't the swashbuckling, seagoing Bluebeard the Pirate you're expecting — this is a dark, psychological fairy tale in one act, so none of your whining. Don't expect to walk out humming the tunes; don't expect to *find* any tunes. This music has been described as harsh, jarring, and slashing. There are no breaks or intermissions or places where you can clap.

**Astonishing trivia:** From the time it was composed until 1948, this opera was produced fewer than 12 times. Since World War II, however, it's become extremely popular, possibly because (a) it requires only two singers and (b) it's only an hour long.

**The plot:** We see seven big doors in a big room in a big castle. Bluebeard, a big bass, and his new wife Judith, a mezzo-soprano, enter. (That's all the characters, so you shouldn't have much trouble following the synopsis.)

Judith wants to find out what's behind the seven doors. Reluctantly, Bluebeard gives her a key.

When she puts the key in Door Number One, the castle makes a spooky moan, but she goes ahead and opens the door. It's . . . *a new car!* No, really, it's just a torture chamber, walls wet with blood.

Bluebeard asks if she's afraid, but Judith is one tough cookie. She opens Door Number Two, and reveals . . . *a home entertainment center!* Just kidding. It's a room full of weapons. Covered with blood.

Behind Door Number Three is . . . *all of Bluebeard's treasure!* (We're serious this time.) Judith picks out a crown and a jeweled cloak, but they're covered in blood. What's with this blood? The real estate agent never even *mentioned* it.

She moves on to the fourth door, behind which is the garden, but the leaves are covered in blood. Behind the fifth door, she can see all the land that Bluebeard owns, but it has this sort of bloody hue to it. Behind the sixth door is a big lake. "The water is tears," says Bluebeard. (What? No blood?)

Now Judith begins to think that the rumors she heard about Bluebeard (that he keeps the bodies of his late wives in his castle) are true, and that they must be behind Door Number Seven. Sure enough, there are his three late wives, but they're not dead. They're . . . well, the opera never quite explains *what* they are, but they're gorgeous and fully mobile.

Bluebeard tells Judith that his wives find the treasures and water the garden, and that his land is their land, and the tears are their tears. He sings that he met the first wife in the morning of his existence, the second at noon, the third in the evening — and Judith, the fourth, on a dark night. As Judith joins the other wives through Door Number Seven, the door closes behind her.

Left alone on stage, Bluebeard sings, "And now it will be night forever." Hey, *you* figure it out.

# La Bohème

**Title translation:** The Bohemian. **Music by:** Giacomo Puccini. **Libretto:** In Italian by Giuseppe Giacosa and Luigi Illica. **First performed:** Turin, Italy, 1896.

**What to look forward to:** A bittersweet tragedy in four acts — one of the five best-loved operas in the world. The precursor to *Friends:* Funny, wonderful roommates trying to handle true love when it hits. Puccini's first smash hit. A real weeper, but also sweet and funny.

**Astonishing trivia:** The critics savagely blasted *La Bohème* on opening night, complaining that the music was too simplistic, and that there wasn't enough action. Little did they know then that *La Bohème* would go on to be the second most-performed opera in the world.

Figure 12-2: *La Bohème:* Vyacheslav Polozov as Rodolfo, Katia Ricciarelli as Mimì, Lyric Opera of Chicago, 1986 (photo: Tony Romano).

**Act I:** Four best-friend guys — artistic, idealistic, and poor as dirt — hang out together in an attic apartment in Paris. It's Christmas Eve. In the freezing garret, not having paid the utility bills, Rodolfo the tenor-poet volunteers to sacrifice his latest play manuscript to the stove for heat. After cheerfully putting off their landlord, they head out for dinner.

Rodolfo stays behind to finish an article he's writing. A knock at the door: It's Mimì, a beautiful, frail soprano with a hacking TB cough, from a neighboring apartment. She announces that her candle has gone out.

In the moonlight, they look for her key, which she's dropped. Falling for her in a big way, Rodolfo grabs her hand, singing the famous *"Che gelida manina! Se la lasci riscaldar"* ("Your hand's frozen! I'll warm it up"; this aria is on this book's CD). The *La Bohème* love theme soars. They sing a passionate love duet as only two broke twentysomethings can, then run out to join the boys for dinner.

**Act II:** In the intersection next to the café, the Christmas passersby bustle, shop, and sing in perfect harmony. Marcello the painter's gorgeous, high-maintenance ex-girlfriend Musetta (a soprano, of course) approaches with an old, rich companion. Sitting at a nearby table, she sings one of the best-known melodies in all of opera — "Musetta's Waltz" — flirting with Marcello right under the nose of her rich old companion:

| | |
|---|---|
| *Quando m'en vo soletta per la via,* | As I walk alone through the streets, |
| *la gente sosta e mira, e la bellezza mia tutta ricerca in me,* | People ogle me, see how great-looking I am, |
| *ricerca in me da capo a piè.* | Check me out from head to toe. |

A military drum corps enters the square, to the crowd's delight, and the four buddies carry Musetta home on their shoulders. Her sugar daddy gets stuck with the bill and collapses in a chair. Now *that's* comedy.

**Act III:** Two months later. Outside a tavern in the dead of winter, Mimì, sicker than ever, tells painter Marcello that her relationship with Rodolfo is on the rocks. And Rodolfo confides in Marcello, and rattles off a litany of commitment-phobic Gen-X guy complaints: Mimì's boring. I'm not good enough for her. She's got TB and she's gonna die. And *"Mimì è una civetta"* ("Mimì's a flirt"). They break up in a duet that ends, *"Addio, senza rancor"* ("Goodbye — no hard feelings, okay?"). Meanwhile, Marcello and Musetta are having their *own* argument. They, too, decide to break up. The act ends with a quartet of mutual dumping.

**Act IV:** Back in the attic, Rod and Marc are missing their girlfriends in a big way. Musetta, all serious, bursts in and announces that she's just found Mimì collapsed on the stairway; the boys rush to carry her onto a bed. Springing into action, Musetta rips off her earrings and tells Marcello to sell them to buy some medicine. Colline rushes out to sell his "venerable coat" for food. And Musetta tears out to find a muff for Mimì's frozen hands.

Alone with Rodolfo, Mimì opens her eyes and tells him weakly:

| | |
|---|---|
| *Ho tante cose che ti voglio dire,* | I've so many things to tell you, |
| *o una sola ma grande come il mare,* | or one thing — huge as the sea, |
| *come il mare profonda ed infinita . . .* | deep and infinite as the sea: |
| *Sei il mio amor . . . e tutta la mia vita.* | I love you . . . you're my whole life. |

They remind each other of that first incredible night when the lights went out, singing snippets of their earlier arias: *"Te lo rammenti"* ("Do you remember?"). The roommates return. Rodolfo puts the muff on Mimì, but she's too far gone to even feel it. Mimì closes her eyes; Rodolfo is the last to realize that she's dead. He throws himself on her body, sobbing: "Mimì . . . Mimì!"

If *this* show doesn't choke you up, something's wrong with your emotion glands.

# Boris Godunov

**Music by:** Modest Mussorgsky. **Libretto:** In Russian, or, rarely, in Italian, by Mussorgsky, based on a drama by Alexander Pushkin. **First performed:** St. Petersburg, Russia, 1874.

**What to look forward to:** A passionately tragic drama in four acts, based on the true story of coups and infighting for the throne of Russia. Heavy-duty hallucination and death scenes for Boris; hair-raising Russian choral numbers.

**Astonishing trivia:** *Boris Godunov* is Mussorgsky's only completed opera in about ten attempts. Perhaps that's why he's better known as the composer of the instrumental and very scary *Night on Bald Mountain* and the piano suite *Pictures at an Exhibition.*

Mussorgsky kept tinkering with the scenes' order, and Rimsky-Korsakov later made several show-doctoring attempts of his own. Because of its checkered history, there's no telling which of the many versions of this opera you'll see. Mussorgsky's first attempt was rejected by the St. Petersburg Opera in 1870 for having no central female role, no ballet scene, unusual-sounding music, and a lead role that wasn't a tenor. After the poor guy spent four years rewriting, they rejected the opera *again.* After still more revisions, the SPO finally put on the opera (in 1874) but pulled it after 25 performances.

**Act I:** Russia and Poland, 1598–1605. Dmitri, son of the Tsar (that is, the president of Russia), has been murdered. As a result, when the Tsar himself dies, there's a receding heir line. Little do the frenzied crowds know that Boris Godunov, the Tsar's distant relative, was Dmitri's murderer. In front of the Kremlin, Boris is crowned; a Tsar is born. Meanwhile, when young tenor monk Grigori learns that he's about the age Dmitri would have been now, a plan forms in his mind.

**Act II:** Two alcoholic friars come into a little inn on the border to Lithuania, followed by ex-monk Grigori. The police are hot on Grigori's tail for having defected from the monastery, but he escapes out the window.

Tsar Boris tells his teenage son, Feodor, to keep up the good work, because he'll be Tsar someday. Then, in a powerful monologue, Boris mutters to himself about how awful the five years of his reign have been, and how guilty he feels for killing Dmitri.

Boris's advisor, Prince Shuisky, warns Boris that somebody in Poland is raising an army, claiming to be the old Tsar's son Dmitri! Boris, starting to unravel, distinctly remembers *killing* Dmitri. At this point, Boris is a few clowns short of a circus; when he thinks that he sees Dmitri's ghost, he comes apart at the seams in one of opera's most powerful mad scenes.

**Act III:** The beautiful Polish princess, Marina (a mezzo-soprano), has her sights set on "Dmitri" (actually Grigori), whom she plans to marry and thus become the Tsarina of Russia. She persuades him to march on Moscow immediately in exchange for her love.

**Act IV:** Russia is in a chaotic state of poverty and famine. (What else is new?) In a forest near Moscow, the peasants torment Boris supporters and the village idiot (a tenor, naturally). "Dmitri" and his soldiers march on Moscow — leaving behind the simpleton, who sings a tragic song of trouble to come.

At the Kremlin, the Russian senate is meeting to discuss what to do about Dmitri the Pretender. Boris rushes in as though he's seen a ghost; when an old monk reports that a blind shepherd has just had his sight restored at the *tomb* of Dmitri, superstitious Boris, already a little jumpy, promptly has a heart attack. Dying, as the crowds rush in, Boris pleads for mercy, finally screaming, "Here's your Tsar!", pointing at his son Feodor. He dies and falls down the steps. The crowd remarks: "He dies."

# Carmen

**Music by:** Georges Bizet. **Libretto:** In French by Henri Meilhac and Ludovic Halévy. **First performed:** Paris, France, 1875.

**What to look forward to:** A tragedy of obsessive love, with dialogue, in four acts. (In some productions, the dialogue is set to music, but it's not by the original composer; accept no imitations.) Stay tuned for the hair-raising finale, with Carmen's terror and violent death superimposed on the cheers from inside the bull ring.

**Astonishing trivia:** *Carmen*'s premiere was one of the most famous flops of all time — not because the audience threw tomatoes or anything; it was just your run-of-the-mill failure. Bizet considered this show to be his masterpiece and died three months later in abject depression. Ironically, *Carmen* went on to become one of the most loved, most performed operas in the world.

**Act I:** The show opens at, of all things, a *cigarette factory* in Seville, Spain. Soldiers are hanging out outside, when a pure, pretty, soprano peasant named Micaela comes looking for her boyfriend from back home, a corporal named José ("zzhoe-ZAY"). The bell rings to signify the beginning of the work day. As the good-looking young factory women enter the building, they flirt with the soldiers, laugh, chat, and sing in perfect harmony.

**Figure 12-3:**
*Carmen:*
Plácido
Domingo as
Don José,
Alicia Nafé
in the title
role, Lyric
Opera of
Chicago,
1984 (photo:
Karen
Engstrom).

The most gorgeous man-magnet of all is Carmen, a mezzo-soprano of Gypsy descent. On her way in to work, she pauses long enough to sing what's possibly the most famous aria of all time, *"L'amour est un oiseau rebelle"* ("Love is a rebellious bird"). (You can hear this song on the CD that came with this book.) Carmen directs this song at hunky José, but he pretends to ignore her come-on.

Micaela returns; she brings José news from home: *"Parle-moi de ma mère"* ("Tell me: How's mom?"). Suddenly, shrieking erupts from inside the factory. What could it be? News of an anti-smoking bill? A grisly industrial accident? No, it's only Carmen, who has slapped another girl's face. The captain orders José to arrest her. But José, not exactly thinking with his brain, is so overwhelmed by Carmen's sexiness that he unties her wrists. Carmen throws off the rope, shoves the guards aside, and runs off, to the delight of the townies.

**Act II:** In a local bar, a month later, Carmen hangs out with a couple of her Gypsy friends. They sing *"Les tringles des sistres tintaient"* ("When the guitars are playing"), complete with castanets, increasingly violent dancing, and a "Tra la la la" refrain that needs no translation.

Having won the big fight in the local bull ring, buoyed by the cheering crowds, Escamillo the bullfighter sings the *other* most famous opera song of all time, *"Toréador en garde!"* ("Toreador, be careful!"). Carmen has the hots for him instantly.

As the bar closes, a couple of smuggler friends of Carmen's arrive. When the bugle blows to command José back to the barracks, Carmen suggests that he join her for tonight's smuggling run. Suddenly his boss, Zuniga, bursts in (he, too, is hoping for a date with Carmen). José and Zuniga fight over her with swords. The smugglers take Zuniga away at gunpoint. "And *now* will you come with us?" Carmen asks. By drawing his sword on his commanding officer, José has pretty much just downsized himself out of a career; reluctantly, he joins Carmen and her crew in the mountains.

**Act III:** In their mountain hideaway, the merry Carmen (plus Gypsy girl-friends) and smugglers sing away. (Telling fortunes with her girlfriends, Carmen is dealt the Death card. "What does it matter?" she says, having seen many an opera; "You can't avoid your fate!") Only José is miserable. Carmen is showing about as much affection for him as a grapefruit.

The smugglers post José as a sentry; he fires his gun at a man coming up the hillside. "An inch lower, and you would have hit me!" cheerfully shouts Escamillo the bullfighter, looking for Carmen. José, blind with jealousy, lunges at his rival with his knife. "Don't be mad, soldier," an unharmed Escamillo teases José. "We'll meet again."

Micaela comes up the mountain to find José; she tells him that his mother is dying, and he reluctantly agrees to return home.

**Act IV:** Just outside the bullfight ring, the happy, happy villagers dance and sing and sell oranges. Escamillo enters, with Carmen on his arm, to the cheers of the crowd. For good luck before the fight, they sing a love duet: *"Si tu m'aimes, Carmen"* ("If you love me, Carmen . . .").

José appears — haggard, desperate, a hollow shell of a tenor. She tells him (in case he hasn't figured it out) that it's over. The fanfare inside the stadium heralds the beginning of the bullfight, and the crowd cheers Escamillo. José, a couple sandwiches short of a picnic, plunges his knife into Carmen's back.

The crowd bursts out of the arena. José turns himself in to the nearest policeman. As the crowd watches in horror, he throws himself over her body and cries, "Carmen! My beloved Carmen!"

Some guys just don't get it.

# *Cavalleria Rusticana*

**Title translation:** *Rustic Chivalry.* **Music by:** Pietro Mascagni. **Libretto:** In Italian by Giovanni Targioni-Tozzetti and Guido Menasci. **First performed:** Rome, Italy, 1890.

**What to look forward to:** A tragic drama in one act. This opera is in the *verismo* style — harsh and meant to be realistic. (See Chapter 5 for details.) Pulsing passion, rich melodies, an easy-to-grasp plot (man loves other man's wife, dies in a duel).

**Astonishing trivia:** Starving piano teacher and compositional hopeful Mascagni wrote this one-act opera for an opera competition, hoping to pull himself out of poverty. Disgusted with his efforts, he gave up — but his wife secretly mailed the opera to the judges. Mascagni won the contest, plus worldwide fame and fortune, but he never wrote another hit.

**The plot:** The action takes place in 19th-century Sicily. (Many of the children in this piece grow up to appear in *The Godfather.*)

From offstage, we hear the voice of Turiddu, a tenor soldier, singing of his love for Lola in the famous "Siciliana": *"O Lola, bianca come fior di spino . . ."* ("Oh, Lola, pretty as the smiling flowers"). He sings of the days when he was engaged to her, now married to someone else. He concludes, *"Ah, ah, ah, ah"* ("Ah, ah, ah, ah").

Pretty Santuzza asks Mamma Lucia where her son Turiddu is. Mamma Lucia invites her into the house, but Santuzza refuses because she's been declared an outcast (*"Sono scomunicata!"*). Alfio, the baritone cart driver, pulls up, singing of his love for his adoring wife Lola; "Who's happier than a cart driver?" sing the townspeople.

Alfio suggests that everyone go to church. Left alone, Santuzza gives Mamma the whole story, singing the famous aria *"Voi lo sapete"*: While Turiddu was away in the wars, his fiancée Lola married Alfio, the driver. Depressed, Turiddu slept with sweet Santuzza, disgracing her. But recently, Turiddu has again been sleeping with married Lola.

Turiddu comes home. Santuzza accuses him of still loving Lola, but vows to love him no matter what. "Why do you follow me around?" Turiddu shouts, shoving her to the ground. She curses him, sobbing. When Alfio the driver shows up, Santuzza tells him about the illicit affair his wife has been having. He thanks her, crying, *"Vendetta!"* ("Vendetta!"). Sweet music plays to an empty stage — the now-famous "Intermezzo," a favorite of classical music concerts.

After church, Turiddu, with Lola on his arm, leads the crowd in a big, happy drinking song, *"Viva il vino spumeggiante"* ("Long live red wine!"). Alfio challenges Turiddu to a duel. To show his acceptance, Turiddu bites Alfio ceremonially on the ear, just as they do in gangster movies. Turiddu runs off. A moment later, a woman runs in, screaming: *"Hanno ammazzato compare Turiddu!"* ("Somebody killed Turiddu!"). Mamma Lucia and Santuzza faint.

# Così fan tutte

**Title translation:** *All Women Are Like That.* **Music by:** Wolfgang Amadeus Mozart. **Libretto:** In Italian by Lorenzo da Ponte. **First performed:** Vienna, Austria, 1790.

**What to look forward to:** A comedy in two acts about two fickle, vain, dimwitted women. The title places this show very low on the list of Favorite Feminist Operas. Less emphasis on big arias than on brilliant *combos* — duos, trios, quintets, and so on.

**Astonishing trivia:** Many opera directors have succeeded in bringing out the serious, moving side of this tale — but for generations, certain Mozart lovers considered the libretto too fluffy to deserve Mozart's amazing music. As a result, several writers in the 1800s actually tried to write entirely new words (and a new plot) to fit Mozart's music. Predictably, these attempts resulted in pure theatrical dreck.

**Act I:** Two handsome young officers are engaged to a pair of sisters. Ferrando, the tenor, is engaged to Dorabella; his baritone buddy Guglielmo is engaged to Fiordiligi. Anyway, you'll never, ever get these names straight just by reading this synopsis, so we'll call them Couple A and Couple B.

Boyfriends A and B are having lunch with their cynical bachelor pal Alfonso. They're arguing heatedly about women, particularly the betrothed sisters: Are they fickle airhead twits, easily drawn to whichever guy is handiest (Alfonso's belief)? Or are they truly in love, a love that can remain steadfast even in the fiancés' absence?

In a musically amazing trio of trios, Alfonso makes a bet with his pals. Pretend to go out of town, he tells them; dress up as a couple of Albanians; and see if you can seduce *each others'* girlfriends. Ferrando and Guglielmo are confident that their fiancées will remain faithful; Alfonso isn't so sure.

Cut to Girlfriends A and B. Alfonso bursts in and announces that Boyfriends A and B have been called into army duty. The women are shattered. After their beaux's departure, Alfonso sings a pretty harsh condemnation of women in general. Clearly, this guy's got some issues.

Despina, the Girlfriends' chambermaid, is every bit as cynical. Alfonso slinks in and explains the whole experiment to her; she agrees to help perpetrate the stunt. Boyfriends A and B now appear, disguised as Albanians. Boyfriend B (Guglielmo) wastes no time in flirting with Girlfriend A (Dorabella) with his aria, *"Non siate ritrosi"* ("Don't be shy!") — but even before he's finished, the indignant women march out of the room. "Okay, you've won the first round," Alfonso tells them, "but the game isn't over yet."

With the azure blue sky overhead and scenic Naples in the background, the "Albanians" burst into the sisters' garden. To prove the desperation of their love, they guzzle bottles of "poison" and "fall into a coma." When Despina, dressed as a doctor, treats them, the guys magically revive, wonder if they're in heaven, and ask the "goddesses" (A and B) to kiss them to complete the cure. Women A and B decline, harrumphing offstage.

**Act II:** Despina tries to persuade her employers that they're missing a great dating opportunity during their betrotheds' absence. Women A and B agree that there's nothing wrong with *talking* to these guys.

In the seaside garden, the "Albanians" turn on the charm spigot to full blast — they've even hired a barge full of professional serenading musicians. Boyfriend B gives Girlfriend A a heart-shaped locket (and removes from her neck her existing locket, containing Boyfriend A's portrait) — to a very hearty, pit-a-patting aria, *"Il core vi dono"* ("This heart I'm giving you"). But Boyfriend A serenades Girlfriend B (Fiordiligi) to no avail, despite the fact that his famous aria (*"Ah, lo veggio"*) has a bunch of incredibly high notes. Girlfriend B responds with a dazzling showpiece song, *"Per pietà, ben mio, perdona"* ("Forgive me, my dear").

Girlfriend B suggests that they dress up as soldiers and go off to the war, to rejoin their proper boyfriends. But Boyfriend A bursts in, overhearing, and swears that he'll kill himself if she leaves. Falling for her "Albanian's" awesome tenor voice, she melts into his arms, and they sing of their future together. Looks like Alfonso has won the bet. (Let's not ponder too hard why the Boyfriends have worked so mightily to *lose* their own bet).

Boyfriend B, meanwhile, has watched his own fiancée falling for Boyfriend A, and he's furious. "To the Devil with her!" he exclaims. Alfonso gloats. "Repeat after me," he sings: "All women are like that!" (*"Così fan tutte"*).

To prove his point, the maid enters and reports that the women have decided to marry the Albanians on the spot; Boyfriends A and B are quietly seething at their fiancées' fickleness. Maid Despina, disguised this time as a notary, brings the wedding contracts and sings a fast patter song filled with phony legalese.

There's a burst of music: Uh-oh, it's the return of the *original* boyfriends! The "Albanians" are rushed out, the women fall to pieces, and (after a quick costume change) the men appear as themselves once again. Alfonso tells the "returning" men about their fiancées' infidelity, showing them the marriage contracts. But after torturing Girlfriends A and B just long enough, the beaux reveal the game by singing snatches of the "Albanians'" arias.

All is forgiven (it's a musical; it's not *supposed* to be realistic), and the lovers are reunited — but whether As marry Bs or vice versa, the script doesn't say.

*Das Rheingold . . . Look under Ring Cycle*

*Der Freischütz . . . Look under F*

*Der Rosenkavalier. . . Look under R*

*Die Fledermaus . . . Look under F*

*Die Meistersinger von Nürnberg . . . Look under M*

*Die Walküre . . . Look under Ring Cycle*

# Don Giovanni

**Title translation:** *Don Juan.* **Music by:** Wolfgang Amadeus Mozart. **Libretto:** In Italian by Lorenzo da Ponte. **First performed:** Prague (now in the Czech Republic), 1787.

**What to look forward to:** Two hard-to-classify acts. On one hand, there are plenty of funny parts; but on the other, the story *is* about a rapist-murderer-sex maniac who gets a grisly and terrifying punishment. Absolutely sublime music, especially the group numbers, during which several characters sing separate thoughts simultaneously with interwoven melodies.

**Astonishing trivia:** Surveying the cast lists (and the titles) of many operas, you're probably thinking that Italians in 1787 were pretty hard up for baby names — every guy is named Don, and every woman is Donna. Actually, *Don* and *Donna* are Italian for "Mr." and "Miss," or "Sir" and "Madam," or "Lord" and "Lady" — yes, the world's greatest lover's actual name is *Mr.* Juan.

**Act I:** Giovanni's servant, Leporello, complains about the difficulty of having such a sneaky and restless sex machine of a master. Giovanni bursts out of a house, hotly pursued by the woman he's just attempted to rape, Anna. Her father, an old soldier, challenges Giovanni to a sword duel; Giovanni kills him. Anna's fiancé, Ottavio, tries to comfort her and vows revenge. He and Anna become Vengeful Victims No. 1 and No. 2.

**Figure 12-4:**
*Don Giovanni:* Samuel Ramey in the title role, Lyric Opera of Chicago, 1988–89 (photo: Tony Romano).

Giovanni soon spots another prospect: a young woman sobbing. The woman's name is Elvira, and she immediately recognizes Giovanni as the one-night-stand creep who dumped her the morning after — Vengeful Victim No. 3. Leporello tells Elvira that she shouldn't take a Giovanni dumping personally. In fact, in his famous "Catalogue aria" (on the CD with this book), he informs her that Giovanni has slept with, to date, 640 girls in Italy, 231 in Germany, 100 in France, 91 in Turkey, and 1,003 in Spain. (Because Giovanni is supposed to be 22 years old, that means that he has slept with 3.9 women *every weekend since puberty.*)

Near Giovanni's house, several miles away, a group of happy peasants celebrate the upcoming wedding of Zerlina, the gorgeous country girl, and her fiancé, Masetto. Don "Mr. Hormones" Giovanni is instantly interested in Zerlina. He orders servant Leporello to invite the whole crowd *except* Zerlina up to the Giovanni house for a party, handily getting fiancé Masetto out of the way.

Alone at last, Giovanni and new conquest Zerlina sing a gorgeous duet, *"Là ci darem la mano"* ("You'll lay your hand in mine, dear"). Unfortunately, Elvira (Vengeful Victim No. 3) suddenly arrives, bursting his little love bubble. She warns Zerlina about him. To make matters worse, Vengeful Victims 1 and 2, Anna and beau Ottavio, now arrive. ("Everything's going wrong today!" sings Giovanni. Man, he's got *no* idea.) Anna sings of her horrible evening with Giovanni, in one of opera's most shocking and difficult dramatic recitatives:

| | |
|---|---|
| *Tacito a me s'appressa,* | Silently he came nearer, |
| *E mi vuol abbracciar; sciogliermi cerco,* | And grabbed me; When I tried to get away, |
| *Ei più mi stringe, grido.* | He grabbed me even harder. I screamed! |
| *Non viene alcun! Con una mano cerca* | But nobody came. With one hand, |
| *d'impedire la voce,* | he tried to shut me up; |
| *E coll'altra m'afferra* | With the other, he seized me so hard, |
| *Stretta così, che già mi credo vinta.* | I thought I'd have to give in to him. |

Zerlina's screams come from the bedroom — her relationship with Giovanni has been developing a *bit* too quickly. Worse, three guests remove their masks: They're the three Vengeful Victims (Anna, Ottavio, and Elvira), who have crashed the party to exact their revenge. Thunder roars as they condemn Giovanni in front of the guests.

**Act II:** Hoping to dodge all the furious people now after him, Giovanni suggests that he and his servant swap clothes. An angry mob bursts in, armed with guns. Giovanni, dressed as Leporello, gives the crowd bogus directions for finding "Giovanni." Only Masetto remains behind, and he shows "Leporello" the weapons he plans to use on Giovanni. Giovanni, grabbing the two guns, beats Masetto to a bloody pulp.

Giovanni and Leporello run into each other in a cemetery and bring each other up-to-date — when a statue begins speaking: *"Dell 'empio, chi mi trasse al passo estreme, Qui attendo la vendetta!"* ("I'm waiting for heaven's revenge on the guy who killed me!"). The statue is of Anna's father, the old man Giovanni killed at the beginning of the opera. Giovanni laughs and invites the statue to dinner.

Cut to Giovanni at his dining table. Suddenly, the statue, the ghost of Anna's father, enters and moves implacably toward him, the Ultimate Vengeful Victim. (See Chapter 11 for words to this scene, and follow along on your free CD.)

As the stage is filled with ghouls chanting his doom, a fiery pit opens up right in the middle of the room. Shadowy demons grab Giovanni and drag him down, as he shrieks, "My heart's exploding! My internal organs are thrashing! What torture! Madness! Horror! Despair! *Aauuuggghhh!*" The choir promises that horrors even more dire await him in his newly begun afterlife.

In a final scene that was often cut in the 19th century, the Vengeful Victims rush onstage to tell the moral of the story: Look what happens to men who behave badly.

## Better lay off the punch, Wolfie

The scene: The night before the opening of *Don Giovanni,* Mozart's Italian opera. The problem: With 24 hours to go, Mozart still hadn't written a note of the overture.

His first inclination was to do what anyone in his place would have done: go to a party.

After he returned home, he asked his wife, Constanze, to make some punch for him and to stay up with him. As he worked, she read to him from *The Arabian Nights* and *Cinderella.*

But whenever Constanze stopped reading, even for a moment, Mozart dozed off. After she started reading again, he'd wake up. Finally, at 3 a.m., Constanze convinced him to take a nap.

At 5 a.m., freaking out, Constanze woke her husband again. At last Mozart took the overture seriously and got to work. He finally finished — at 7 a.m. The copyists had the orchestra parts ready on the music stands just in time for the performance.

# Don Pasquale

**Title translation:** *Lord Pasquale.* **Music by:** Gaetano Donizetti. **Libretto:** In Italian by Giovanni Ruffini and the composer. **First performed:** Paris, France, 1843.

**What to look forward to:** A romantic comedy in three acts: Nephew and his girlfriend get delicious revenge on the crusty old geezer who won't let them marry. Though filled with sparkling, charming music, this opera doesn't have any smash-hit big numbers that generations have loved to hum. Don't look for heavy messages or lasting moral implications; it's three solid hours of sparkling entertainment.

**Astonishing trivia:** Donizetti wrote fast and furiously and finished the opera in a matter of days. *Don Pasquale* was his *64th* opera.

**Act I:** Rome, Italy, in the early 1800s. Old, fat, rich, bass bachelor nobleman Pasquale is excited about finally getting married. There's only one obstacle to a lifetime of bliss with his fiancée: He doesn't *have* one.

Pasquale's tenor nephew Ernesto, on the other hand, has *his* bride all picked out: the charming young widow Norina (a soprano). But Norina's not exactly going to bring much money into the family. "Marry her," Uncle Pasquale tells Ernesto, "and I'll disinherit you."

Pasquale's baritone friend Dr. Malatesta, however, is sympathetic to the likable young couple. He dreams up a plot: He announces that his own sister, *"Bella siccome un' angelo"* ("Pretty as an angel!"), is the *perfect* woman for Pasquale — a timid, trusting virgin, brought up in a convent. Pasquale practically splits open with hormonal joy at this prospect, and vows to marry her, sight unseen. (Video dating is still over a century away.) Ernesto, devastated, can't help but launch into the touching aria *"Sogno soave e casto"* ("Fond dream of love, goodbye"). What no one knows, however, is that Dr. Malatesta *has* no sister. He has a master plan — which involves young, pretty widow Norina *posing* as this "sister."

Meanwhile, at home, Norina laughs that "I, too, know the craft of magic!" (*"So anch'io la virtù magica"*) in ensnaring men. Dr. Malatesta arrives to explain the scheme to her: Once married, she's to act like the wife from hell, driving Pasquale into seeking a divorce.

**Act II:** Ernesto, still unaware of the plot, is depressed. Pasquale is dressed to the nines, awaiting his new bride. She finally appears, veiled, coy, and trusting.

The moment they're "married," however, Nun Norina instantly becomes Mrs. Hyde, a nasty, bossy, high-maintenance monster bride. She immediately hires Ernesto to be her personal assistant (because Pasquale, she rudely points out, is too old and fat to help her). Pasquale is thunderstruck. On the spot, Norina hires more servants. Pasquale, choking with rage, sings, *"Son tradito, son tradito!"* ("I've been had!"). A hysterical quartet, including Ernesto's joyous realization that all is not lost, ends the act.

**Act III:** Norina is stingy old Pasquale's worst nightmare. She dresses expensively, orders around expensive servants, and plans for an expensive night at the theater. When Pasquale objects, she slaps him. Pasquale sends for Dr. Malatesta. In a hilarious comic duet, the doctor gives Pasquale his "advice" as they "dream up" a scheme to foist Norina off on Ernesto.

In the garden, meanwhile, Ernesto sings his love song to Norina, *"Com'è gentil,"* the opera's sweetest and must hummable aria ("How sweet is this spring night! No clouds in the sky, bright moon. . . . Why don't you belong to me?"). Pasquale bursts in, accusing Norina of infidelity, and proposes a deal to Ernesto (engineered, of course, by the wily doctor). If Ernesto will marry Norina to get her off Pasquale's hands, Pasquale will write him a fat check. Ernesto agrees. The hoax is revealed, but Pasquale is so relieved to have these nasty young people out of his house that he gives his blessing anyway.

# Elektra

**Music by:** Richard Strauss. **Libretto:** In German by Hugo von Hofmannsthal. **First performed:** Dresden, Germany, 1909.

**What to look forward to:** A violent tragedy in one act. A shocker, based on the Greek myth of Elektra. In what other musical does a brother chop up his mother as his sister screams, "Stab her again!"? The last 15 minutes are particularly gut-wrenching, musically and dramatically. Not what you'd call a laff riot, but amazing orchestral special effects and powerful emotions — an evening you're not likely to forget.

**Astonishing trivia:** Composer Richard Strauss was definitely into screaming emotions and agony. At the dress rehearsal for this opera, at one point he yelled down into the orchestra pit: "Louder! I can still hear the singer!"

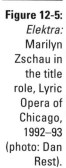

**Figure 12-5:**
*Elektra:*
Marilyn
Zschau in
the title
role, Lyric
Opera of
Chicago,
1992–93
(photo: Dan
Rest).

**The backstory:** There's a long *backstory,* as they say in Hollywood — stuff from Greek mythology that took place before the plot begins. When King Agamemnon returned home from the Trojan War, he discovered that his wife Clytemnestra had been having an affair. Not wishing to hear another of the king's lectures about fidelity, Clytemnestra murdered him and took over the kingdom herself (with her lover). Her son Orestes ran away. Clytemnestra, not exactly Mother of the Year, reduced her daughters, Chrysothemis and Elektra, to semi-slaves, forcing them to eat and sleep with the dogs.

**The plot:** The servants are discussing Elektra, the family basket case, who acts like a cat, howls like a dog, and gets regular beatings. Muttering *"Allein! Weh, ganz allein!"* ("Alone, alas, all alone!") , Elektra enters and madly chatters about revenge on Mommie Dearest. One day, soprano Elektra sings, she'll get together with her AWOL brother Orestes and kill her murderous, adulterous mom. (Soprano sister Chrys isn't quite so bent on revenge.)

Mom appears. "Her sallow, bloated face is pale," the script says. "Her eyelids are unusually large and she seems unable to keep them open without effort." Mmmmm, *nice.* Queen Mom asks Elektra if there isn't some sacrifice she can make to alleviate her months-long insomnia. Sure, Elektra says scornfully — you'll sleep just fine, *when my brother and I kill you!*

Sister Chrys bursts in, sobbing: Brother Orestes has been dragged to death by his own horses! Elektra, clearly not what you'd call a well-adjusted teenager, crawls around on the ground like a wild animal. A shadowy figure appears: It's brother Orestes — not dead after all! In what's called the Recognition Scene, Elektra goes crazy with delirious joy: *"Orest! Orest! Orest!"* They agree to avenge the murder of their father — *right now.*

Orestes disappears into the house. We hear Queen Mom's screams as he hacks her. "Strike, strike again!" screams Elektra, cheering him on, as various palace personnel wake up and wonder what's happening. When Aegisthus (Mom's lover/new husband) appears, Elektra, weirdly turned on, taunts him. He rushes into the palace. A moment later, he appears at the window as he, too, gets Orestes's ax in the back, screaming, "Help! Murder! Does no one hear me?" "My *father* hears you," Elektra exults.

As the palace descends into chaos, Elektra goes off the deep end, dancing on her father's onstage tomb in a demented frenzy as she always said she'd do someday — and then she keels over, dead as a doornail. The opera ends with sister Chrys banging on the palace door, screaming, "Orestes! Orestes!"

Next week: *Oklahoma!*

# *The Elixir of Love*

**Title translation:** *L'Elisir d'Amore.* **Music by:** Gaetano Donizetti. **Libretto:** In Italian by Felice Romani. **First performed:** Milan, Italy, 1832.

**What to look forward to:** A two-act, witty comic opera; a sure winner. Clever plot, bouncy music and a famous tenor aria, *"Una furtiva lagrima."*

**Astonishing trivia:** Donizetti wasn't one to slave over every note, fussily revising and rewriting — he wrote this entire opera in *two weeks.*

**Act I:** In an Italian village in the 1800s, Adina is the kind of soprano we've all met: She's beautiful, rich, demanding, and fickle — a man magnet. Poor tenor farmer Nemorino, among others, has the raging hots for her: *"Quanto è bella,"* he sings ("How beautiful she is!"). When she reads from her book the story of Tristan and Isolde (described later in this chapter), Nemorino wishes that there *were* such a thing as a love potion — especially because his rival is the cocky Sergeant Belcore, a baritone, who now arrives with a bouquet for Adina.

When Dr. Dulcamara, a hilarious traveling salesman/quack, offers a love potion for sale — *"Udite, udite, o rustici"* ("Listen up, folks"), farmer Nemorino forks over his last dollar. The "elixir" is actually a bottle of cheap wine, which Nemorino guzzles. The potion has its effect: Nemorino's drunk, dancing and singing and disgusting Adina enough that she agrees to marry the *other* guy, Sergeant Belcore.

**Act II:** At Adina's wedding, she keeps postponing the moment of truth. Nemorino complains to the quack Dr. D that the potion didn't work. The doctor offers a second bottle, but Nemorino's broke. Sergeant Belcore, ever the military man, suggests that Nemorino enlist in the Army, which pays 20 crowns just for signing up. Nemorino does so, pays Dr. Dulcamara, guzzles down the second bottle of "elixir," and becomes rowdier than ever.

A rumor spreads that Nemorino is newly rich. The town girls pay more attention to him. Adina, naturally, is suddenly interested, too. Nemorino's delighted that the love potion works! He sings to Adina the most famous number from this show, *"Una furtiva lagrima"* ("A secret tear").

Adina buys back Nemorino's enlistment papers from Sergeant Belcore, who takes this rejection like a soldier. She swoons in Nemorino's arms as the triumphant quack Dr. D sells out his entire stock of cheap-wine phony potions to the villagers.

*Die Entführung aus dem Serail . . . See The Abduction from the Seraglio*

# Eugene Onegin

**Title translation:** *Yevgeny Onyegin* (that's his name in Russian). **Music by:** Peter Ilyich Tchaikovsky. **Libretto:** In Russian by K.S. Shilovsky and the composer, based on a poem by Aleksandr Pushkin. **First performed:** Moscow, 1879.

**What to look forward to:** A romantic tragedy of desperate lost love in three acts, the most successful of Tchaikovsky's ten opera efforts. The music in this opera, as with most of Tchaikovsky's work, is *incredibly* soaring, emotional, and full of longing. There's not a lot of action or special effects, but there's plenty of pure, desperate emotion — especially nonstop unfulfilled love.

**Astonishing trivia:** At the beginning of this opera, Eugene misses his opportunity to snatch up the young, pretty teenager Tatiana — and regrets it for the rest of his life. While writing this opera, Tchaikovsky himself was pursued by a girl he'd met while teaching music, who claimed to be desperately in love with him. Under the influence of his own opera, not wanting to make the same mistake as his title character, Tchaikovsky married the girl. (Unfortunately, the marriage was loveless and horrible; see Chapter 9.)

**Act I:** It's the late 1700s, at a country estate in Russia. Soprano beauty Tatiana, age 17, practices a duet with her contralto sister Olga. Olga's fiancé, a tenor named Lenski, arrives, bringing along his neighbor and long-time buddy Eugene.

That evening, Tatiana complains to her nurse that she can't sleep; she's in love! And now the famous Letter Scene: Tatiana writes a love letter, singing occasionally, the orchestra music alone telling us what else she's writing.

*(We won't bother putting the Russian text over here. They use their own wacky alphabet, so it's not like the text would help you recognize the words when you hear them.)*

I behold you with the sweet, and yet fatal look,

Which has wrested my heart . . .

No, no, that's not right. Start over!

The next morning, she asks her nurse to deliver the letter to that baritone hunk, Eugene. He meets her in the garden later, thanks her for the letter, but tells her, point-blank, that he's not interested; he's not into that commitment thing. She's devastated and humiliated.

**Act II:** Tatiana's birthday party. Eugene dances with her, although his heart isn't in it; the guests disapprove of Eugene, whom they consider a cocky jerk. As though to prove it, Eugene starts dancing with Tatiana's sister Olga, much to her fiancé Lenski's irritation. Eugene makes matters worse: "Why don't *you* dance, Lenski? You look like a statue!" They argue, and finally challenge each other to a duel.

The next morning, near a stream in the woods, Eugene and Lenski stand apart and sing a *canon* (like a round, like "Row, Row, Row Your Boat," only *much* more interesting). Eugene shoots. Lenski falls dead.

**Act III:** Eugene has spent six years wandering the wilderness alone, aching over having killed his buddy. He's at a fancy ball, when who should enter but Tatiana, now married to a prince who happens to be Eugene's cousin. This prince chats with Eugene, telling him — in one of bass singers' favorite arias — how much love and beauty she has brought to his lonely prince life. Now that Eugene sees how great Tatiana looks at 23, decked out in a cocktail dress, it's his turn for an aria of hopeless, unrequited love: "Is it she whom I despised? — who one day revealed her crush on me?"

The next day, Eugene pours out his soul to her, begs for forgiveness, begs for a second chance. But through tears, she tells him that it's too late now; she's married, and duty calls. They love each other and sing of what might have been, but ultimately she sends him away, her heart breaking. "I shall not break my pledge! I'll always be faithful to him! . . . Goodbye forever!"

Eugene stands alone, having mucked everything up.

# Falstaff

**Music by:** Giuseppe Verdi. **Libretto:** In Italian by Arrigo Boito, based on Shakespeare's *Merry Wives of Windsor* and *King Henry IV — Part I*. **First performed:** Milan, Italy, 1893.

**What to look forward to:** A lyrical comedy in three acts — Verdi's only successful comedy. Grungy hustler Falstaff hopes to bilk some local women, but they and their husbands get the last laughs.

**Astonishing trivia:** *Falstaff* was Verdi's very last opera; he was nearly 80 at the time he wrote it (which, given the state of medicine at the time, would make him about 167 in today's years). His librettist, Boito, was a composer in his own right; but when his first major opera as composer, *Mefistofele* (1868), was a big flop, he got so depressed that he gave up composing and took up writing librettos for other composers. (In later revisions, *Mefistofele* was more successful, and it is still performed today.)

**Act I:** Windsor, England, early in the 15th century. At a festive inn, Sir John Falstaff, an obese baritone, is hanging out with two scurvy-looking types: Bardolph and Pistol. Decrepit Dr. Caius bursts in and accuses Falstaff of breaking into his house, beating his servants, and stealing his wallet. Falstaff denies all.

Falstaff announces his crush on two rich local ladies, Mrs. Ford and Mrs. Page. He writes a love letter to each. The two women soon discover that they've received identical love notes. They vow revenge (*"Quell'otre! Quel tino!"*) on the gravitationally challenged Falstaff. In fact, just about everyone has it in for him: *Mr.* Ford, robbery victim Dr. Caius, a young man named Fenton, and even Falstaff's two sidekicks, who are sick of being dumped on.

Subplot alert: Young Fenton loves the Fords' daughter, Nannetta. Every time they're alone, they sing a love duet, and this is no exception: *"Labbra di foco! Labbra di fiore!"* ("Kissing is the greatest!").

Mrs. Ford, Mrs. Page, and their friend, Mrs. Quickly, set up a meeting with Falstaff. Fenton and Nannetta sing another love duet, and the vengeful men plot to visit Falstaff in disguise. The hilarity mounts. A giant nonet (song for nine people to sing) results.

**Act II:** Back at the inn, Mrs. Quickly tells Falstaff to visit Mrs. Ford between 2:00 and 3:00, when her husband's out of the house. Falstaff congratulates himself (*"Va, vecchio John, va!"*).

His next visitor is "Master Brook," actually Mr. Ford in disguise. "Brook" offers Falstaff money to help *him* score with Mrs. Ford, who keeps giving him the cold shoulder (*"Quella crudel beltà"*). Falstaff says that he has already arranged a meeting with Mrs. Ford. Unaware that his wife is conducting her *own* anti-Falstaff plot, Mr. Ford rails about the inconstancy of women (*"È sogno? O realtà? Due rami enormi"*). He and Falstaff do a classic "No, after *you,* sir" bit as they try to fit through the door simultaneously.

Back at the Fords', Falstaff arrives, bragging to Mrs. Ford about how *skinny* he was as a lad (*"Degna d'un Re"*) — a likely story. When Mr. Ford arrives, the women hastily hide Falstaff first behind a screen, and then in a laundry hamper. Mr. Ford searches the house, condemning his wife (*"Mi lavi! Rea moglie!"*). Mrs. Ford directs the servants to dump the laundry basket's contents into the river, to the amusement of all.

**Act III:** Back at the tavern, river-drenched Falstaff's bruised ego slowly recovers, with the help of goodly amounts of alcohol. Mrs. Quickly arrives and persuades him to try again with Mrs. Ford. The plan devised by the women conspirators requires that he, dressed as the Black Huntsman, meet her at midnight in the haunted forest glen.

He shows up attired with antlers and heavy cloak. The whole group, dressed as supernatural fairies, flit about the terrified Falstaff, stumbling over him and beating him until he cries for mercy. They all unmask, and everyone's laughing hysterically except Falstaff, who doesn't see what's so funny. Mr. Ford at last allows the young duet-singers, Nannetta and Fenton, to marry. Falstaff leads the crew in a final fugue: *"Tutto nel mondo è burla. L'uom è nato burlone"* ("All the world's a joke, and man was born a fool").

# Faust

**Music by:** Charles Gounod. **Libretto:** In French by Jules Barbier and Michel Carré. **First performed:** Paris, France, 1859.

**What to look forward to:** A supernatural tragedy in five acts, based on the German Faust legend. *You* know that one: Man sells his soul to the Devil in exchange for youth and women, but lives to regret it forever.

**Astonishing trivia:** This *Faust* is one of at least 16 operas based on the Faust legend. It's also one of the most successful operas ever written, having been performed more than 2,000 times in Paris alone by 1934. In the early 1900s, this show was performed at the Metropolitan Opera in New York so often that one critic renamed the Met *Faustspielhaus* (a spoof of *Festspielhaus*, Richard Wagner's Wagner-only opera house in Germany).

**Act I:** Faust, an aging, suicidal philosopher and chemist (and tenor), moans that, despite a life of searching, he'll never know the meaning of life. He curses everybody who's happy or in love, and himself, too, and invokes the name of Satan. With a cry of *"Me voici!"* ("Here I am!"), the wily cad of a Devil, Méphistophélès (a bass), shows up. He offers Faust anything he wants — glory, power, a Mazda Miata, anything! Faust wants only to be young again. The fine print: When Faust is on earth, the Devil will serve him; but down below, Faust will serve the Devil.

When Faust hesitates, Méphistophélès shows him a vision of a beauty named Marguerite at a spinning wheel. Aroused (*"O merveille!"* — "What a wonder!"), Faust signs the contract and drinks a magic potion. And *zingballabing!* He turns into a handsome young hunk.

**Act II (sometimes Scene 2 of Act I):** In the village square, a fair is underway, with students, villagers, and soldiers singing merrily about getting drunk. Valentin and his friend Siebel wander in. Because Valentin is going off to war, he worries about his sister Marguerite in the gorgeous aria *"Avant de quitter ces lieux";* Siebel promises to take care of her.

The Devil begins doing magic tricks and reading palms — the crowd *loves* this guy. He tells Siebel that any flower he touches will wilt, and predicts Valentin's death. For his next trick, Méphistophélès strikes a fake wine barrel that's used as a tavern sign; wine magically gushes out. The Devil tells the delighted crowd to drink, and makes a toast to Marguerite. Valentin (her brother) is furious; the wine bursts into flame. Valentin tries to stab Méphistophélès with his sword, but it breaks. The other men hold up their swords so that they look like signs of the cross in a vampire movie — hokey, sure, but it works. Méphistophélès departs, saying, *"Nous nous retrouverons, mes amis!"* (or, as the Terminator might say, "I'll be back!").

A waltz begins; when Marguerite (a soprano — what else?) arrives in the town square, Faust offers her arm — but she gives him the brush-off.

**Act III (sometimes Act II):** In Marguerite's garden, Siebel picks some flowers — they shrivel, just as the Devil predicted. But when Siebel dips his fingers into a spring of holy water, the curse is removed. He picks a fresh bunch, which he leaves at Marguerite's doorstep just as Faust and Méphistophélès wander in. Méphistophélès, noticing that Faust needs a little help getting the girl, places a box filled with precious gems next to Siebel's flowers.

Marguerite finds Siebel's flowers and thinks they're cute — but the little box of jewels *really* gets her motor revved. In the famous "Jewel Song," she trills away while throwing the jewels all over herself. The Devil puts a spell on Marguerite, who now falls hard for Faust; Faust disappears into her house, as Méphistophélès laughs like the Devil.

**Act IV (sometimes Act III):** Several months later, Marguerite is at her spinning wheel; local girls outside taunt her for having gotten pregnant. (This segment is often cut.) Faust dumped her after their one terrific date, but she loves him nonetheless. In church, she tries to pray, but the voice of Méphistophélès and a demon choir tell her that she's damned to hell. Marguerite passes out.

Valentin, returning from the war, rushes to his sister's house, to find Méphistophélès and Faust. They fight, but Faust has magic on his side; Valentin is roadkill in no time. With his dying breath, he curses his sister. (Like she's not in *enough* trouble?)

**Act V (sometimes Act IV):** Following a nightmarish optional wild ghost ballet, we cut to Marguerite's prison cell; she's there because she went nuts, killed her child, and was sentenced to death. Her brain is so fried that she doesn't even know where she is. She begs:

| | |
|---|---|
| *Anges purs! anges radieux!* | Pure angels! Radiant angels! |
| *Portez mon âme au sein des cieux!* | Carry me to heaven! |

Méphistophélès shouts, "Time's up! Time's up!" as Faust tries to get Marguerite to escape with him. Marguerite "sees" blood on Faust's hands, curses him, and dies. Méphistophélès drags Faust off to hell, while a choir of angels sings, and Marguerite rises up to heaven.

Maybe next time she'll be more careful.

# Fidelio

**Music by:** Ludwig van Beethoven. **Libretto:** In German by Josef Sonnleithner and Georg Treitschke. **First performed:** Vienna, Austria, 1805.

**What to look forward to:** A love-driven rescue story in two acts — with a happy ending! Beethoven, as you may know, is most famous for his thrilling *symphonies* (see *Classical Music For Dummies*). As you may expect, then, much of *Fidelio*'s best is the orchestra playing and the chorus numbers. There is some spoken dialogue in this one.

**Astonishing trivia:** *Fidelio* is Beethoven's one and only opera, but he worked on it enough to have written ten of them. He wrote *16 different versions* of Florestan's first aria, 346 pages' worth of musical notes, and four completely different overtures. Nor did he quit when the show opened; it bombed, so he and his collaborators continued tweaking, combining three acts into two and doing numerous musical rewrites.

The opera was originally called *Leonore,* but it had to be retitled because several operas called *Leonore* were already in circulation. Still, now you know why those first three abandoned overtures are today called *Leonore* Overtures no. 1, no. 2, and no. 3. They're still performed today, especially the popular no. 3. (The fourth and final overture is just called the Overture to *Fidelio*.)

**Figure 12-6:** *Fidelio:* The prisoners' chorus, Lyric Opera of Chicago, 1981. (photo: Tony Romano)

**The backstory:** The time: the 1700s. The place: Seville, Spain. (Funny how the girls in *Carmen's* Seville cigarette factory, the vengeful Sevillian brother from *La Forza del Destino,* and Figaro from *The Barber of Seville* never seem to run into each other downtown. . . .)

Before the opera begins: Florestan is the good guy — a revolutionary Spanish nobleman. To shut him up, evil prison governor Pizarro kidnapped him, threw him into solitary confinement in a dungeon, and spread the rumor that Florestan was dead. But Florestan's feisty, fiercely loyal wife, Leonore, didn't buy it. She dressed up as a man and got hired as a dungeon guard. Her new name: *Fidelio!*

**Act I:** In a dismal Spanish prison, Leonore/Fidelio drags out of Rocco, the jailer, the fact that there's one special prisoner in the deepest cell — and then persuades the warden to take "him" along on his rounds.

The evil fortress governor, Pizarro, reads his mail, which mentions that the prime minister is on his way for a prison inspection. Now's the time to kill off his imprisoned enemy Florestan once and for all. *"Ha! Welch' ein Augenblick!"* ("Ah! What a moment!"), he sings.

Pizarro tells Warden Rocco to go kill Florestan. Rocco declines, perhaps thinking that "merciless murderer" may not look great on his résumé. "Fine, I'll do it myself," snaps Pizarro. "Go dig a grave for him."

Leonore is a tad alarmed — enough to belt out a killer aria:

| | |
|---|---|
| *Abscheulicher! Wo eilst du hin? Was hast du vor?* | Monster! Where are you going in such a hurry? What's up with you? |
| *Was hast du vor in wildem Grimme? . . .* | What puts you in such a rage? . . . |
| *Komm' Hoffnung, lass den letzten Stern der Müden nicht erbleichen.* | Come, hope, don't let the last star abandon the weary. |
| *O komm', erhell' mein Ziel, sei's noch so fern, so fern.* | O come, illuminate my goal, still so far away. |
| *Die Liebe sie wird's erreichen.* | Love will reach it! |

Frantic for a plan, Leonore persuades Warden Rocco that the prisoners should be allowed to walk around in the sunshine for a few minutes. They emerge into the sunshine, blinking, singing as a great all-guy chorus. But since Leonore's husband isn't among the men, she persuades Warden Rocco to let her help with the grave-digging. At last, she'll get to see her husband!

**Act II:** We finally meet Florestan, chained and gaunt, singing Beethoven: *"Gott, welch' Dunkel hier, o grauenvolle Stille!"* ("My God, it's dark in here! And horribly still!"). Leonore, digging the grave with Rocco, spots him — and nearly passes out. It's all she can do to keep from bursting out, "It's *me,* honey!"

Evil Pizarro bursts in, ready to kill Florestan. As he raises his dagger, Leonore throws herself in front of Florestan's body, shouting, *"Töt' erst sein Weib!"* ("First kill his *wife!*") Everyone's astonished (apparently not having noticed that Mr. Fidelio has been singing *soprano* for two years). Pizarro is about to kill *her* when she whips out a pistol: "Another word, and you're dead!"

At this moment, the prime minister arrives. Florestan and his wife sing a joyous duet: *"O namenlose Freude!"* ("Oh, nameless joy!") All secrets are spilled for the prime minister, who turns out to be old friends with Florestan. Needless to say, the PM is horrified to learn about Pizarro's evil deeds. The show ends with a blaze of joyous singing from the chorus as the ecstatic couple looks forward to months of rehabilitation — together.

# Die Fledermaus

**Title translation:** *The Bat.* **Music by:** Johann Strauss. **Libretto:** In German (often performed in English) by Carl Haffner and Richard Genee, based on a comedy by Henri Meilhac and Ludovic Halévy (the guys who wrote the libretto for *Carmen!*). **First performed:** Vienna, Austria, 1874.

**What to look forward to:** A romantic comedy in three acts. Most of the humor comes from (a) drunkenness, (b) mistaken identity, and (c) that old opera standby, men's and women's fickleness. This incredibly popular show is actually an *operetta,* meaning that it's interspersed with dialogue scenes (today we'd call it a musical). Johann Strauss, Jr., is, of course, the Waltz King — the guy who wrote *On the Beautiful Blue Danube* and other super-famous waltzes. You can feel his bubbly, waltzy, lilting spirit in every moment of this cream puff of a musical (especially in the overture, which is famous enough that it's performed at orchestra concerts everywhere).

**Astonishing trivia:** Like many of the greatest operas in history, this one's original production didn't run very long — only 16 performances. In *Die Fledermaus*'s case, however, the short shelf life wasn't because the show was a flop. Instead, on May 7, 1873, the Viennese stock market crashed, and most stock prices fell to zero. *You* probably wouldn't be forking out $75 for a witty, giddy operetta ticket the day *your* nest egg cracked, either.

**Figure 12-7:**
*Die Fledermaus:* André Jobin as Eisenstein, Winifred Faix Brown as Rosalinde, Lyric Opera of Chicago, 1982 (photo: Tony Romano).

**Act I:** Vienna in the late 1800s. As the show opens, we hear only the tenor voice of Alfred, pretty soprano Rosalinde's shameless ex-boyfriend, serenading her from outside.

Rosalinde's maid, feisty Adele, has received an invitation to a fancy costume ball hosted by Russian eccentric Prince Orlofsky. She asks Rosalinde for the night off, claiming that her aunt is sick. But Rosalinde is distracted. Her husband, Eisenstein, is going to jail for eight days for insulting a government official — and the sentence begins tonight. With her husband gone, Rosalinde looks forward to an illicit date with tenor Alfred.

Dr. Falke, Eisenstein's old drinking buddy, appears. He proposes to Eisenstein that they attend the Prince Orlofsky costume bash. Eisenstein can go in costume, he suggests, have one last night on the town, and go to jail the next morning.

Eisenstein is thrilled — forgetting, however, the *last* costume party he attended with Dr. Falke. That night, Dr. Falke dressed as a *bat* and got drunk; Eisenstein left him to find his way home through the streets of town the next morning in that ridiculous getup. Falke has a vengeful prank on his mind: to expose Eisenstein as a philanderer in front of all his friends.

Rosalinde is alone at last for her date with Alfred. He arrives to join his old flame for dinner: *"Trinke, Liebchen, trinke schnell!"* ("Drink, baby, drink it down!"). A knock at the door: It's Frank the prison warden, who drags Alfred off to jail, assuming that *he* must be Rosalinde's husband. Rosalinde does nothing to set him straight.

**Act II:** Prince Orlofsky's bash is a regular animal house, with the costumed guests drinking their heads off and singing catchy choruses. (You may notice that Orlofsky is played by a woman; for the explanation, see "Mezzo-sopranos" in Chapter 4. You may also notice that a Russian in Austria is singing in French; for the explanation, we'd be very grateful.)

Eisenstein gasps at one of the guests — she looks *just* like his own maid, Adele! Ridiculous, Adele says in a waltzy laughing song. Eisenstein does *not* recognize his own wife dressed as a Hungarian countess, however, and he flirts with her outrageously. Dr. Falke suggests that the entire crowd pledge to form a brotherhood forever. The sloshed crowd can't manage words much more coherent than "Du-ee-du" and "La la la," but even those lyrics sound great in a slidey, slow, full-chorus waltz.

As the clock strikes 6:00 a.m., Eisenstein and Warden Frank realize that they're supposed to be at the jail. Unaware of each other's identities, they stagger out together.

**Act III:** When Eisenstein arrives at the jail to turn himself in, he has quite a laugh that some guy (Alfred) has been locked away in his place. Eisenstein borrows his lawyer Dr. Blind's wig, glasses, and legal outfit in hopes of finding out *who* the arrested-in-his-place guy is. But now *Rosalinde* shows up seeking Dr. Blind, hoping to get *Alfred* out of prison. Eisenstein, posing as Dr. Blind, cross-examines everyone in a grandiose trio, drawing out Rosalinde's infidelity and growing angrier by the moment.

Dr. Falke arrives at the jail with the party guests and finally explains his prank on Eisenstein. Rosalinde tells a little white lie: Her date with Alfred, too, was part of the elaborate joke. Eisenstein's perfectly content with that explanation, all are reconciled. With their blood-alcohol levels sky-high, they engage in one final toast, led by Rosalinde, to the reconciling power of champagne. Let's just hope that they don't *drive* home.

# The Flying Dutchman

**Title translation:** *Der fliegende Holländer.* **Music and libretto:** In German by Richard Wagner. **First performed:** Dresden, Germany, 1843.

**What to look forward to:** A grim, grim, grim tragedy in three acts (although the composer wanted it performed in one *long,* uninterrupted act). This was Wagner's first famous opera, and already you can hear some of his famous trademarks. For example, you hear a particular melody (a *Leitmotif*) in the orchestra every time the Dutchman's ship appears, and another every time the Dutchman appears. In professional productions, you may well get to see some great special effects; in every production, you'll hear some amazing sea music, somber and violent and oceany.

**Astonishing trivia:** Wagner was in his 20s when he had to endure a horrific crossing to England during storm season, during which his ship nearly went down three times. Thus were born the seeds for *The Flying Dutchman,* in which the terrifying power of the sea is everywhere in the music.

Desperately in debt, miserable, and having little career success, Wagner sold his *Flying Dutchman* libretto to the manager of the Paris Opera, where it was eventually turned into *another,* long-since-forgotten, opera of the same name (and with the same words). With the money he made from the sale, Wagner bought a piano and set about setting those words to his own music.

**Act I:** Sometime in the 1700s at a Norwegian harbor, Daland, a bass Norwegian sea captain, seeks shelter from a nasty ocean storm, his men shouting *"Ho-jo-he!"* (which is "Heave ho!" in German). He notices another ship pulling up: a strange and grisly ship with blood-red sails and black masts. It's captained by the legendary Flying Dutchman, who sings mysteriously of being cursed to roam the seas forever.

When weird bass-baritone Dutchman learns that Daland has a daughter, he offers all the loot and treasure on his ship if he can marry her. Daland quickly agrees.

**Act II:** At Daland's house, a crowd of girls are merrily singing the now-famous Spinning Song as they spin on their spinning wheels. Senta, Daland's daughter, is there, dreamily gazing at a painting of the legendary Flying Dutchman. Senta's nurse, Mary, and the girls tease her, asking her to sing the "Ballad of the Flying Dutchman" once more.

She complies: The legend goes that years ago, caught in a violent storm, this Dutch captain was trying to sail around the Cape of Good Hope. In desperation, he screamed to the winds that he'd make it around or keep trying forever. The Devil overheard, and, literal-minded creep that he is, condemned the Dutchman to sail the seas until Judgment Day. There's only one loophole: The curse goes away if he can find a woman who'll love him until death. Once every seven years, he's allowed to go ashore to seek such a woman (and, presumably, to get a change of underwear).

Senta tells the girls that *she* plans to be the lucky girl. (That's not such hot news for her boyfriend, Erik.) Imagine Senta's surprise when her father comes home with, of all people, the Flying Dutchman himself. She's enraptured, barely hearing her dad explain the bit about the treasure. Senta and the Dutchman, in a soaring duet, immediately fall in love. Her father's delighted.

Too bad the story couldn't end right here.

**Act III:** Norwegian sailors direct their high-spirited teasing toward the scary-looking Dutch ship parked next to their own, but they get no response — until suddenly, the ocean whips into a frenzy, dark blue flames flare up in the rigging, and the spooky crew of Dutch ghost-sailors sing a chilling chantey of their own, which pretty much shuts up the Norwegians.

Erik the Boyfriend argues with Senta over her husband selection, sweetly recounting the good times they've had. The Dutchman, listening, flies into a jealous rage, saying that it's all over between him and Senta — "Once more to the sea I must wander! I cannot trust you! I cannot trust God!" He runs back to his ship. Senta screams after him to wait — she loves him! — but Erik holds her back.

Finally, as the ghost ship prepares to sail, Senta reiterates her promise to love the Dutchman until she dies — and, breaking free from Erik, she throws herself off the cliff into the sea. The Dutchman's ship sinks immediately; the curse is broken. The ghostly images of Senta and the Dutchman, embracing each other, rise from the sea and float away.

# La Forza del Destino

**Title translation:** *The Force of Destiny.* **Music by:** Giuseppe Verdi. **Libretto:** In Italian by Francesco Maria Piave. **First performed:** St. Petersburg, Russia, 1862.

**What to look forward to:** A horrific tragedy in four acts; just about everybody dies. A plot with holes big enough to drive a sport-utility vehicle through, deadly misunderstandings that could have been cleared up in five minutes, and long, rambling sections in which nothing really happens. But there's enough glorious music to hold the thing together (especially the end of the second act).

**Astonishing trivia:** In the original draft of *La Forza del Destino,* absolutely *everybody* dies — even Alvaro, the hero, throws himself off a cliff to make sure that none of the main characters survive. The composer wrote to his librettist: "We've got to think about the ending and find some way to avoid all those dead bodies." These days, you're most likely to see the revised version, in which Alvaro lives on (albeit in the pits of depression).

**Act I:** Seville, Spain (Opera-Plot Central), at the end of the 1700s. Pretty soprano Leonora's father catches her in her bedroom with boyfriend Alvaro, of whom he disapproves. Dad assumes the worst. "Your child is innocent as an angel," tenor Alvaro tries to explain, "behold me unarmed" — and with that, Alvaro throws down his pistol. Unfortunate Coincidence No. 1: The gun goes off and hits Leonora's dad, who curses Leonora before dying.

**Act II:** In a remote Spanish village, a distraught Leonora, dressed as a young man, having lost track of her beau after That Night, gasps to see her brother Carlo at the communal dinner table. After a powerful, magnificent prayer that ranks with the greatest moments of Verdi's music, Carlo (disguised as a student) grills the poor mule driver who brought Leonora to this village.

Leonora runs to a monastery in the moonlight. In the Big Scene, she falls to her knees, praying, with the choir behind her at full throttle, in the powerful *"Madre, pietosa Vergine"* ("Mother, merciful virgin!"). A kindly monk offers to let her live in the nearby caves.

**Act III:** Boyfriend Alvaro, meanwhile, has enlisted in the army under an assumed name. He's wracked with guilt: "Seville! — Leonora! — oh, sad memories!"

Shortly thereafter, he saves the life of another soldier — it's Carlo! That's Unfortunate Coincidence No. 2, although they don't recognize each other; in fact, they become best buddies. Unfortunate Coincidence No. 3: Only a short time later, *Alvaro* is wounded. He assumes the worst. In a now-famous duet, he begs Carlo to perform one final favor before he dies: To burn the sealed letter in Alvaro's duffel bag. Carlo agrees — but he finds, right there with the letter, a picture of his sister Leonora! Alvaro's cover is blown. When Alvaro is better, Carlo challenges him to a duel. Other soldiers separate them.

**Act IV:** At the monastery, the doorbell rings: It's Carlo, dressed up as a monk, looking for "Father Raffaello." ("Father Raffaello"? Could it be Alvaro in disguise? Here? At the very monastery where Leonora is living in the caves? Yes, it's Unfortunate Coincidence No. 4.) Alvaro begs forgiveness of Carlo and even kneels at his feet. But in a major fiery duet, Carlo calls him a coward, and they run offstage to have their duel.

We hear Carlo scream — Alvaro has stabbed him in the duel! Horrified at now having killed his beloved's father *and* brother, wanting to get help for Carlo, Alvaro bangs at the "cave door" (it really says that in the script). Leonora recognizes her long-lost love. Unfortunately, the first words out of his mouth are, "I just killed Carlo," and she runs offstage in horror — only to be stabbed to death by her dying brother Carlo. "In his last hour, he still wouldn't forgive me," she sings, gasping. "He avenged his shame with my blood." As she dies, she tells Alvaro that her father's curse is finally lifted.

Some consolation, huh?

# Der Freischütz

**Title translation:** *The Free-Shooter.* **Music by:** Carl Maria von Weber. **Libretto:** In German by Friedrich Kind. **First performed:** Berlin, Germany, 1821.

**What to look forward to:** A supernatural thriller, with a happy ending, in three acts. This opera is often considered to be the first German *Romantic* opera (characterized by folk-tale-based plots, spooky mystical supernatural elements, interesting and unusual harmonies, and so on). Watch for the Wolf's Glen scene — a spooky Special-Effects-O-Rama.

**Astonishing trivia:** The overture to *Der Freischütz* was the first in history to include complete tunes from the opera itself.

**Act I:** Deep in the forests of Bohemia (roughly where the Czech Republic is today), the forestry staff is having a shooting contest. Tenor Max, normally an excellent marksman, loses the contest to a mere peasant. He's wracked with performance anxiety — especially when Kuno, his bass boss and future father-in-law, tells him: "If you lose *tomorrow's* shooting contest, you can't marry my daughter." That's a horrifying thought to Max, who loves his boss's daughter Agathe more than life itself. (She's prettier than her name.)

Max's friend Kaspar shows up, making a strange offer:

| | |
|---|---|
| *Wie wär's, Kamerad, wenn ich dir noch* | How would you like it, my friend, if I helped |
| *heute zu einem recht glücklichen Schusse* | you make an incredible shot tomorrow — |
| *verhülfe, der Agathen beruhigte und* | a shot so good you'd simultaneously get |
| *zugleich euer morgendes Glück verbürgte?* | Agathe and win tomorrow's contest? |

When Max doesn't get it, Kaspar asks Max to try shooting a passing eagle with Kaspar's rifle. Despite the dark, Max fires, and the eagle plops dead at his feet. A magic can't-miss bullet was responsible, says Kaspar — and if Max will meet him in the legendary Wolf's Glen at midnight, they'll cast seven more bullets just like it for the contest. Max is a bit creeped out by Kaspar's manner, but he agrees. Kaspar ends the act with a difficult-to-sing but properly scary aria: Turns out he's the secret assistant to none other than Samiel, the Devil himself. *Mua-ha-ha-ha-haaaaa!*

**Act II:** Pretty soprano Agathe is feeling strangely moody; praying in the moonlit window, she sings the beautiful *"Leise, leise, fromme Weise!..."* ("Soft, soft, devout melody: Waft up to the circle of stars!") When she sees Max coming home from work, she has an outburst of absolute ecstasy. But he says that he's only stopping by; he's got to go to the Wolf's Glen to, um, pick up a deer he shot. Yeah, that's it — a deer.

Despite the girls' warning that the Wolf's Glen is haunted, Max ventures forth. A chorus of invisible spirits, singing creepy lyrics about "spiderwebs stained with blood" and dead brides, awaits him there — along with Kaspar. Unbeknownst to Max, Kaspar has sold himself to the Devil and hopes to buy himself more time on earth by procuring Max as a new victim.

Accompanied by powerfully gruesome, evil-sounding music, all kinds of ghastly sights appear: Max's dead mother, warning him away; cadaverous ghost animals spitting flames and sparks; Agathe hurling herself off a cliff. But those omens are a bit too subtle for Max; he joins Kaspar, chanting, half-singing, casting the magic bullets.

**Act III:** Max has used up six of his bullets; Kaspar refuses to give him any more. Agathe, meanwhile, is dressed for the wedding, and her bridesmaids sing joyously, everyone obviously expecting Max to win the shooting contest. The whole village is watching. Kaspar has climbed a tree to watch Max lose his soul forever. The prince, in whose honor the contest is being held, challenges Max to shoot a white dove that's flying by. Just as he pulls the trigger, Agathe jumps out from behind a tree and exclaims, "Don't shoot! I am the dove!" (*"Schiess nicht! Ich bin die Taube!"*) Max shoots anyway, probably a bit confused by her metaphor.

She drops to the ground and Kaspar falls out of his tree. The chorus sings ominously. Agathe wakes up — but *Kaspar's* been shot. By some lucky fluke, the seventh evil bullet, meant for Agathe, hit *Kaspar* ("You, Samiel the Devil — Is this how you keep your promise?" shouts Kaspar before dying); Agathe only fainted.

When Max explains that he won the contest by using trick bullets, the prince banishes him from the kingdom. But it's Max's lucky day: A mysterious hermit appears and suggests that, instead, Max just spend a year apologizing and *then* marry Agathe. That solution seems to please everyone.

# Gianni Schicchi

**Music by:** Giacomo Puccini. **Libretto:** In Italian by Giovacchino Forzano. **First performed:** New York, 1918.

**What to look forward to:** A short, one-act comedy — the only genuine comedy Puccini wrote.

**Astonishing trivia:** The story is based on a real guy who lived in Florence in the late 13th century.

**The plot:** Candles burn around the bed of a dead man named Buoso Donati. His relatives' mourning grows all the more miserable when they hear a rumor that the dead Buoso has left all his money to a monastery. The family tears up the house, trying to find the will. Young tenor Rinuccio, one of the dead man's relatives, hopes for an inheritance that will bring him enough money to marry his girlfriend, Lauretta (*"O Lauretta, Lauretta, amore mio"*). Shortly thereafter, he finds the will hidden in a chest.

Old Lady Zita starts to read the will: *"Ai miei cugini Zita e Simone!"* ("To my dear cousins Zita and Simone!"). The rumor was true: They'll receive none of the dead man's money. The young lover, Rinuccio, tells them that there's one guy who can help them: Lauretta's father, Gianni Schicchi.

Gianni Schicchi, arriving with Lauretta, studies the will and gets an idea: He'll impersonate the dead man and dictate a new, more favorable will to a notary. Before the notary arrives, Schicci reminds the relatives of the penalty they'll receive if the little scheme is discovered: They'll be exiled, after having one hand apiece chopped off.

The notary shows up. Gianni Schicchi dictates the "will." But instead of giving the good stuff to any of the family members, "Buoso" leaves it all to his good friend — Gianni Schicchi!

The family is shocked, but doesn't dare say a word. The will is signed. When the notary leaves, everybody jumps on Schicchi, but he beats them back with the dead man's cane. He chases them around the room, and they steal everything they can get their hands on. After the young lovers, Rinuccio and Lauretta, sing another duet, Gianni Schicchi returns. He tells the audience that his double-cross was worth it — because the money will ultimately go to the young couple — and that the audience should find him not guilty. Then he shows the audience how to applaud for him.

# Lohengrin

**Music and Libretto:** In German by Richard Wagner. **First performed:** Weimar, Germany, 1850.

**What to look forward to:** A tragic love drama in three acts. Three *long* acts — this is Wagner, remember; without cuts, you're looking at a four-hour evening. As always with Wagner, lots of powerful, interesting music; and as *almost* always, the plot is set in legendary times. In fact, you might call *Lohengrin* a sequel to Wagner's *Parsifal,* because it concerns the adventures of the *son* of Parsifal, the Knight of the Holy Grail.

**Astonishing trivia:** Wagner wrote this opera during his 13-year political exile in Switzerland (see Chapter 8). Thanks to the promotional efforts of classical music superstar Franz Liszt (see *Classical Music For Dummies*), this opera was presented in Germany to growing success. After several years, Wagner, still holed up in Switzerland, dryly noted that he was the only German who hadn't heard *Lohengrin.*

**Act I:** Germany's King Henry meets with his staff and the nobles of the Brabant family to discuss the impending invasion by Austria. But the Brabants are of little help, torn up as they are by internal family troubles. If you really want to know, here are the details: The dying Duke of Brabant left two kids, Elsa and Gottfried. Gottfried disappeared; Elsa is suspected of having killed him in order to become her dad's successor. Her betrothed, Count Frederick, immediately married someone else: exotic-looking, quietly sinister mezzo-soprano Ortrud, who's an evil sorceress in her spare time.

King Henry doesn't know if Elsa is guilty or not, but he'll let God decide. He proposes a duel between Count Fred and a knight designated to represent Elsa. Who'll it be? Suddenly, a swan-drawn boat appears, bearing a studly knight. *"Leb' wohl, leb' wohl, mein lieber Schwan,"* he tells his boat ("Farewell, farewell, my dear swan"). He agrees to duel for, and marry, Elsa. Lucky Elsa has found that rare quantity — a single guy who's sensitive, smart, and sexy, with no hangups about intimacy — except he won't tell her his *name.* He makes her promise never to ask it.

After due ceremony by King Henry, the duel begins. Lohengrin (*we* know his name) wins, knocking down Count Fred and "proving" Elsa innocent.

**Act II:** Count Fred and wife Ortrud have been banished in shame. But cunning Ortrud isn't finished with Elsa; she's convinced that Mr. Right Knight won the duel by magic, which would dissipate if his name were known. At Elsa's wedding, Ortrud and Fred confront Elsa and her mystery knight, demanding to know his name. "He must have strong motives for not letting you question him," they sing to Elsa. "What foul disgrace is he hiding, anyway?" Lohengrin doesn't answer, of course, but bride Elsa is eaten up with curiosity and doubt.

**Act III:** The wedding is joyous and festive; the famous "Wedding Chorus" plays (the one we all know as "Here Comes the Bride"!); the happy couple sings a tender love duet. But Ortrud's comments have been bugging Elsa; she finally bursts out with the forbidden question: *What's your name?* Before he can answer, Count Fred sneaks into the couple's bridal suite, murderously bent on avenging his shame. Elsa spots him, though, and Husband X kills the intruder. She faints.

Lohengrin realizes that she'll never be happy until she knows his name. As the king and assembled throngs gather, Lohengrin admits that he's a Knight of the Holy Grail, Parsifal's son ("I'm called Lohengrin"), whose power over evil is renewed by the annual visit of a magic dove — but only as long as his name remains a mystery. The assembled crowd gasps.

Having ruined everything, Lohengrin summons his swan boat, ready to leave forever. But newly widowed Ortrud reveals that her own evil sorcery turned Elsa's long-lost brother — the one whom Elsa supposedly killed — *into* that swan boat! Lohengrin's magic is stronger, though. He prays, and magically the white Grail dove flies down to change the swan back into a little boy, the rightful ruler of Brabant. Lohengrin sadly sails away on the dove-powered boat. Elsa cries, "My husband! My husband!" and dies in her brother's arms.

# *Lucia di Lammermoor*

**Title translation:** *Lucy of Lammermoor.* **Music by:** Gaetano Donizetti. **Libretto:** In Italian by Salvatore Cammarano. **First performed:** Naples, Italy, 1835.

**What to look forward to:** A horrific, bloody tragedy of forbidden love in three acts. Features one of the most famous scenes in all theater, the Mad Scene — and one of the most famous group numbers, the sextet of the second act.

**Astonishing trivia:** This Italian opera is based on a novel called *The Bride of Lammermoor* by Sir Walter Scott. The first names have all been Italianized, but the last names remain Scottish, so don't be befuddled by characters with such names as Enrico Ashton and Edgardo di Ravenswood.

**The backstory:** In Scotland, at the end of the 1600s, the Ashton and Ravenswood families have been killing each other off for as long as anyone can remember. At the moment, the Ashton body count is ahead — there's only one Ravenswood left: Sir Edgardo.

**Act I:** Baritone Enrico Ashton has lost all his money, and his only hope is for his sister, Lucia, to marry a rich tenor named Arturo. "Don't count on it," suggests his servant Norman. Lucia, it turns out, is madly in love with Edgardo of Ravenswood! Enrico blows a gasket and vows revenge.

Edgardo (a tenor, of course) tells his lover Lucia that he must travel to France on an errand of diplomacy. In a duet, he tenderly bids her farewell: *"Verranno a te sull' aure i miei sospiri ardenti"* ("My sighs shall be borne on the balmy breeze").

**Act II:** In the Ashton castle, the guests arrive for Lucia's wedding to rich Arturo — never mind that she's never even *met* the guy; the whole thing has been set up by brother Enrico. Furthermore, Enrico been intercepting Edgardo's love letters from France, hoping that Lucia will think her boyfriend has forgotten all about her. Enrico has even forged a letter saying that Edgardo is getting married to someone else!

Enrico shows this letter to Lucia. Horrified, believing that she's been deserted, she sings a duet with her brother, *"Soffriva nel pianto, languìa nel dolore"* ("Suffering in tears, languishing in pain").

The wedding guests sing a cheery chorus. Lucia, not exactly the blushing bride, signs the wedding contract. But the ink hasn't even dried when her true love, Edgardo, bursts in, back from Paris! Lucia starts to faint, but fortunately doesn't — she's needed in one of the most famous sextets in opera. In it, Edgardo sings *"Chi mi frena in tal momento? Chi troncò dell'ire il corso?"* ("What restrains me now? Why don't I just draw my sword?"). Enrico feels bad about his sister and rich Arturo (if you can believe that); everyone else hopes that this wedding from hell will end soon; and Lucia's despairing cries soar above the other voices. Assuming that Lucia has abandoned *him,* Edgardo takes off Lucia's ring and hurls it at her feet.

**Act III:** Enrico challenges Edgardo to a duel (in a scene that's often cut). Meanwhile, Lucia kills Arturo, her new husband, with his own sword!

Lucia enters, her pretty white wedding dress stained with bright red blood, her hair undone — here's the famous Mad Scene, one of the most difficult and breathtaking episodes in opera. (One of its most famous features: During her *cadenza* — a difficult, high, free, solo passage without the orchestra — the flute alone joins her, powerfully representing the voice that she alone hears.) Half-crazy, she seems to think that she's with Edgardo in happier times: *"Il dolce suono mi colpì di sua voce"* ("His sweet voice captured me"). No question about it, she's a few peas short of a casserole. As Lucia falls to pieces, even evil Enrico feels pangs of conscience. Lucia's now singing about going to heaven, where she can wait for her true love.

Some party guests come upon Edgardo and tell him about the Mad Scene. When the church bells chime, the chorus tells Edgardo helpfully, *"Rimbomba già la squilla in suon di morte!"* ("That sad bell means she's dead!"). Edgardo sees only one way to be together with his true love: he plunges his own dagger into his own chest. The wedding guests pray that God will forgive him.

(We assume that the reception is canceled.)

## *Lulu . . . See Chapter 13*

# *Madame Butterfly*

**Title translation:** *Madama Butterfly*. **Music by:** Giacomo Puccini. **Libretto:** In Italian by Luigi Illica and Giuseppe Giacosa, based on a play. **First performed:** Milan, Italy, 1904.

**What to look forward to:** A heartbreaking tragedy in three acts. One of Puccini's three colossal smash hits (the other two are *La Bohème* and *Tosca*); as always, glorious melodies and pure, gut-wrenching emotion. This opera was the basis for the Broadway musical hit *Miss Saigon,* but there's no helicopter in the original.

**Astonishing trivia:** When *Madame Butterfly* was first performed (in two acts), it was a flop of gigantic proportions. As the crowd booed and jeered, Puccini, already suffering because of a car-accident leg injury, stood in the wings, muttering, "Louder, louder, you beasts! You'll see who's right — this is the best opera I've ever written!" Sure enough, after revising it, splitting the lengthy second act in half, Puccini and his collaborators produced the show again three months later to worldwide acclaim.

**Figure 12-8:** *Madama Butterfly:* Catherine Malfitano in the title role, Richard Leech as Lieutenant B. F. Pinkerton, Lyric Opera of Chicago, 1991–92 (photo: Tony Romano).

**Act I:** Lieutenant Pinkerton of the U.S. Navy (a tenor) is about to marry, just for fun, a gorgeous 15-year-old Japanese girl who caught his eye. Her name is Cio-Cio-San (nicknamed Butterfly). He's just leased a Japanese house, which the marriage broker (Goro, a tenor) is now showing. Sharpless, the U.S. Ambassador, thinks that Pinkerton should take his marriage a bit more seriously. But cocky Pinkerton drinks to the day when he'll have a *real* wedding to a real wife, back in the States.

Butterfly (a soprano) arrives with her friends, singing ecstatically of her love for Pinkerton. To demonstrate her commitment to him, Butterfly has even converted to his religion. Wedding guests arrive, chatting about the funny-looking Americans. But the charming wedding ceremony is interrupted by Butterfly's uncle, the Bonze (a bass Buddhist priest), who curses Butterfly for abandoning the faith of her ancestors. Horrified, the guests leave. Butterfly weeps bitterly; Pinkerton soothes her. As the servants get the house ready for the night, Pinkerton and Butterfly sing a hot love duet:

**Pinkerton:** *Ti serro palpitante.*          Quivering, I press you to me.

*Sei mia.*          You're mine.

**Butterfly:** *Sì, per la vita.*          Yes, for life!

**Act II:** Three years later, Butterfly's maid Suzuki doubts that the long-since-departed Pinkerton will ever return. But in a world-famous aria, Butterfly sings passionately about how great it's going to be when he does come back: "One fine day, we'll see on the horizon a thin column of smoke appearing over the sea. And then the ship will appear."

Sharpless finally reads Butterfly the letter from Pinkerton, in which he officially abandons her and encourages her to forget him. But Butterfly presents her little boy, the result of her wedding night with Pinkerton. "And this? Can *he* be forgotten?" she demands.

A cannon is fired in the harbor. Butterfly runs to her telescope — it's Pinkerton's ship! In a frenzy of joy, she and Suzuki decorate the house with flowers, singing, *"Scuoti quella fronda di ciliegio"* ("Shake the cherry tree until every flower flutters down!").

**Act III:** Butterfly has stayed up all night watching for Pinkerton. Sharpless shows up with Pinkerton, who tells Suzuki that the woman in the garden is his American wife, Kate (a mezzo-soprano); the Pinkertons have come to adopt Butterfly's baby.

At Sharpless's suggestion, Pinkerton leaves before the real ugliness begins; *"Addio fiorito asil di letizia e d'amor"* ("Goodbye, happy home, home of love"). Butterfly discovers Kate and has a panic attack, the awful truth dawning. She tells Kate that she'll give up the baby, but asks for half an hour to say goodbye. The Americans leave.

Butterfly, alone, reads the inscription on her father's suicide knife: *"Con onor muore/Chi non può serbar vita con onore"* ("Death with honor is better than life without it"). She sings a heartbroken goodbye, puts her little boy on a stool, and bandages his eyes. She disappears behind a screen — a moment later, we hear the knife fall. Butterfly staggers toward the child and collapses, lifeless. Pinkerton rushes in, destroyed by guilt and shame; Sharpless takes the baby and turns away, as a thundering, solemn Japanese melody plays in the orchestra.

# The Magic Flute

**Title translation:** *Die Zauberflöte.* **Music by:** Wolfgang Amadeus Mozart. **Libretto:** In German by Emanual Schikaneder. **First performed:** Vienna, Austria, 1791

**What to look forward to:** A comic/serious fairy tale, with some spoken dialogue, in two acts. The music is so good that it leaves musicologists and other composers twitching on the floor, drooling helplessly — especially considering that Mozart tossed this stuff off with about as much effort as scratching his nose. The *plot,* however, is something else again. We'll attempt a synopsis here, but it's either (a) completely absurdist nonsense or (b) a thinly veiled gigantic metaphor for a secret men's club (read on) that nobody knows anything about anymore.

**Astonishing trivia:** Mozart and his librettist Schikaneder were both members of the Freemasons, a secret men's club something like the Elks or the Lions or the Rotary Club. Because *The Magic Flute* is so filled with bizarre characters, nonsensical symbols, and peculiar rituals, analysts have concluded that it must actually be a send-up of the Freemasons. For example, the opera includes initiation rites; a woman trying to break up the kingdom (much as an empress in Mozart's day tried to ban Freemason meetings); and even repeated heavy chords in the overture, which experts say represents someone knocking on the door of Mozart's Freemason club lodge. A few historians actually say that Mozart (who died at age 35) was killed for revealing so much about his secret club.

**Figure 12-9:**
*The Magic Flute:* Timothy Nolen as Papageno, Judith Blegen as Pamina, Lyric Opera of Chicago, 1986–87 (photo: Tony Romano).

**Act I:** In ancient Egypt, a tenor prince named Tamino passes out while attempting to escape a huge snake. He's rescued by three ladies in black dresses — servants to someone calling herself the Queen of the Night. When Tamino wakes up, a guy in a feathered costume comes dancing toward him: It's Papageno, the baritone birdcatcher of the Queen of the Night. He claims that *he* killed the giant snake.

At this, the three ladies put a padlock on Papageno's mouth and show Tamino a picture of the queen's daughter, Pamina. He falls in love hard enough to belt out the gorgeous tenor aria *"Dies Bildnis ist bezaubernd schön"* ("This portrait is enchantingly lovely"). Pamina has been captured by the high priest Sarastro, a bass. "Rescue my daughter," the Queen of the Night sings in an explosion of murderously difficult coloratura-soprano fireworks, "and she's yours." To help Tamino on his way, they give him a golden flute, and Papageno-bird a set of silver bells. The two guys set off on their journey, accompanied by three youths (boys played by women).

At high-priest Sarastro's palace, evil Monostatos, a Moor who works for Sarastro, is making the moves on Pamina. Papageno the Birdman scares Monostatos away and assures Pamina that she'll be rescued.

The three youths, meanwhile, have dumped Tamino in a grove containing three temples. A priest in the third temple explains that Priest Sarastro isn't actually the bad guy; the Queen of Night is the *real* evil one. Sarastro himself enters, hailed by the chorus; Pamina accuses Monostatos of making a pass at her; Priest Sarastro punishes him with 72 lashes of the whip. Sarastro now puts the two young lovers into the Temple of Ordeal, where they're supposed to prove that they're worthy of happiness. (We *told* you this doesn't make much sense.)

**Act II:** Guided by the priests, Tamino passes a test in which he's not allowed to speak to women. Pamina passes test of her own — repeatedly escaping the advances of Monostatos. The birdman, meanwhile, meets an old hag who introduces herself as Papage*na,* his future girlfriend — and who later turns into a gorgeous 18-year-old, also in a bird costume. No doubt hopelessly confused by all these characters and plot twists, Pamina contemplates suicide. The youth boys-women comfort her.

Tamino, meanwhile, is facing a test of fire and water. Pamina joins him for this final trial, which seems to consist of walking in and out of two caves, playing the magic flute, and then announcing, "We bravely met the dangers!"

But uh-oh: The evil queen has promised Pamina to the evil Monostatos in exchange for help wiping out priest Sarastro. Fortunately, following the crashing of thunder, lightning, and waterfalls, the evil little band "sinks into the earth." (Talk about convenient!) Priest Sarastro and his priests congratulate Tam and Pam for making it through the plot alive.

*Manon . . . See Chapter 13*

*Manon Lescaut . . . See Chapter 13*

# The Marriage of Figaro

**Title translation:** *Le Nozze di Figaro.* **Music by:** Wolfgang Amadeus Mozart. **Libretto:** In Italian by Lorenzo Da Ponte. **First performed:** Vienna, Austria, 1786.

**What to look forward to:** A boisterous romantic comedy in four acts — proclaimed by many to be the *best opera ever written.* Anyway, it's certainly among the most performed and the most entertaining. A bustling farce involving cross-dressing, sexy servants and their hormonally charged masters, and mistaken identity. (The famous overture begins the free CD in this book!)

**Astonishing trivia:** Mozart's real name was Johannes Chrysostomus Wolfgangus Theophilus Mozart. And you thought *Wolfgang Amadeus* was unwieldy!

**Act I:** We're in Count Almaviva's castle near Seville, Spain, Home of a Million Operas. Reprising their hit roles in Rossini's *The Barber of Seville* are Count Almaviva, his wife Rosina, Basilio the music teacher, Dr. Bartolo the old money-grubber, and the count's wisecracking barber-assistant, Figaro. (See *The Barber of Seville,* earlier in this chapter.)

Figaro's about to marry a fellow servant, soprano Susanna. As the show opens, he's measuring space in their room for a new bed. Susanna's not thrilled with the location of their new bedroom, however, close as it is to the bedroom of Count Almaviva, her employer. It breaks our hearts to say it, but the young, madly-in-love romantics from *The Barber of Seville,* Almaviva and Rosina, have now grown into a platonic middle-aged married couple who don't communicate. And Almaviva has his eye on Susanna, his maid, as his next conquest. Figaro plots revenge, singing, *"Se vuol ballare, signore Contino, il chitarrino le suonerò"* ("If you'd like to dance, dear Count, I'll play the guitar for you").

But Figaro's troubles have just begun. Marcellina, an upper-class soprano of a certain age, *also* wants to marry him. Figaro owes her money, which she uses, in consultation with crusty bass lawyer Dr. Bartolo, as a pretext to force Figaro's hand. Dr. Bartolo is apparently still irked at having been duped in *The Barber of Seville.* *"La vendetta — oh! La vendetta!"* he sings ("Revenge! Oh, revenge!").

Cherubino, a page "boy" (played by a soprano *woman*) is a mass of adolescent hormones. He's been fired for seducing the gardener's niece, and he seeks Susanna's help in getting rehired. Before she can answer, the Count himself enters; Cherubino hides. The Count makes a pass at Susanna — but music-teacher Basilio bursts in. Much hilarity follows as the Count and Cherubino *both* scramble for hiding places.

Now *Figaro* bursts in with a chorus of local folks, hailing the Count, who softens up enough to rehire Cherubino — this time as an officer in the army regiment that the Count leads.

**Act II:** The Countess sings of her misery being married to such a two-timing slickster. She's intrigued to hear Figaro's plot: He'll "let" the Count intercept a letter implying that the Countess is having an affair, thus making him jealous, thus rekindling his affection for her, thus leaving Susanna alone! They'll dress page Cherubino as Susanna; the Count can be counted on to make a pass at "Susanna," and they'll catch him in the act.

But the Count bursts in; Cherubino hides in the closet; more hiding and comedy ensues. The Count runs out to get a crowbar. Cherubino jumps out the window. When the Count pries open the closet, he finds only Susanna inside! The half-drunk gardener arrives, griping about footprints in the flowers outside the closet window. Old Marcellina now arrives, with Dr. Bartolo in tow, to file an official complaint against Figaro for the money he owes her, with the Count serving as judge. The act ends with multiple-singing pandemonium — Mozart's specialty.

**Act III:** Susanna tells the Count that she'll meet him tonight in the garden; he's giddy with joy. On her way out, she tells fiancé Figaro that his legal problems with old Marcellina are over; she's sure that the Count, hot for his date in the garden, will find in his favor.

Unfortunately, the Count overhears her and realizes that he's being manipulated. He vows revenge: He sentences Figaro to marry old Marcellina. Figaro rolls up his sleeve, however, to reveal the only *spatula tattoo* in all of opera. Marcellina gasps: Figaro is her long-lost *son!* Finally, he thinks, his wedding (and the entrapment of the Count in the garden) can proceed.

The Countess, still in love with her husband, sings of the days when they were first married: *"Dove sono i bei momenti di dolcezza e di piacer?"* ("Where have those moments of sweetness and delight gone?"). She dictates a "Meet me in the garden" letter to Susanna, which Susanna will hand to the Count.

Figaro and Susanna's wedding begins. Amid joyous wedding celebrations, Susanna slips the note to the Count.

**Act IV:** Figaro assumes that the note Susanna handed the Count was a *real* love letter and vows revenge on Susanna for being unfaithful. He hides in the garden, planning to watch the rendezvous. *"Tutto è disposto,"* Figaro sings ("Everything's ready").

Susanna, aware that Figaro is listening, has a little fun with him, pretending to be *serious* about this affair with the Count: *"Deh, vieni non tardar"* ("Come on! Don't delay, my dearest jewel"), she pretends to call to the Count.

Don't even think about getting the next part straight. Cherubino, back in male clothes, makes a pass at the Countess, who's wearing Susanna's clothes. The Count, dressed in his own clothes, *also* tries to seduce Susanna, actually his wife in disguise. Figaro spots the *real* Susanna, who's dressed as the Countess. As he begins telling the "Countess" about her husband's infidelity, Susanna reveals herself. Getting it at last, Figaro pretends to make a pass at her (the "Countess"), which naturally makes the Count fly into a jealous rage. The Count calls everybody out to witness his wife's infidelity — and all the costumes finally come off:

| | |
|---|---|
| **Count:** *Il paggio!* | The page! |
| **Gardener:** *Mia figlia!* | My daughter! |
| **Figaro:** *Mia madre!* | My mother! |
| **All three:** *Madama!* | Madame! |

The Count refuses to forgive anyone, but his wife gracefully pardons all. Everyone sings joyously, just happy to have appeared in one of the best operas in the world.

# A Masked Ball

**Title translation:** *Un Ballo in Maschera.* **Music by:** Giuseppe Verdi. **Libretto:** In Italian by Antonio Somma. **First performed:** Rome, Italy, 1859.

**What to look forward to:** A dramatic romantic tragedy; a tale of political intrigue and illicit love.

**Astonishing trivia:** Verdi's opera was originally called *Gustavus III;* it concerned the assassination of a Swedish king. But it hit too close to home for the Italian government — revolutionaries had just tried to assassinate Napoleon III — so the censors banned the opera. Verdi transplanted the setting to 17th-century New England, changing, for example, King Gustavus to the Governor of Boston. Then, for the Paris premiere, Verdi changed the location to Naples — which, of course, required a whole *new* set of names. Nowadays, you may see any of the different versions. (For sanity's sake, we'll stick with the Boston setting.)

**Figure 12-10:** *A Masked Ball:* Renata Scotto as Amelia, Leo Nucci as Renato, Lyric Opera of Chicago, 1980 (photo: Tony Romano).

**Act I:** At the Governor of Boston's party, all guests sing his praises except two basses: Samuele and Tomaso, who plan to assassinate him for his misdeeds. (We're never told *what* misdeeds they'd hold against a city governor. Maybe they were unhappy with the trash pickup schedule.)

The Governor is delighted to see that Amelia is on the list for his upcoming masked ball. *"Amelia . . . ah dessa ancor!"* ("Amelia — dear, sweet name!"). Unfortunately, Amelia's married — to the Governor's faithful secretary, Renato.

A judge asks the Governor to exile a woman for witchcraft; the Governor decides to visit this witch and make up his own mind. He visits her lair, dressed as a sailor, and hides in a corner to watch a sailor get his fortune told. Next customer: Amelia (a soprano), who asks the witch to help her fall out of love — with the Governor. The witch tells her to go collect a special plant (*"una magica erba"*) growing under the gallows. In a thrilling trio, the Governor vows to protect Amelia during her mission; Amelia hopes to get rid of the big love in her heart; and Ulrica promises that the drug really works. The witch also, by the way, tells *his* fortune; she says that he'll be killed by the next person to shake his hand. Secretary Renato promptly walks in and shakes the Governor's hand, which everyone thinks disproves the prophecy because, hey, they're such good friends.

**Act II:** Amelia goes to the gallows looking for the magic plant, singing a heavy-duty aria, complete with high C. She's startled by the Governor's arrival; they sing of their forbidden love in Verdi's hottest love duet. When Amelia's husband, Secretary Renato, arrives to warn the Governor that assassins are on their way, Amelia hides her face under her veil. The Governor leaves just in time; the conspirators Sam and Tom rush in. They lift the woman's veil — it's Amelia! — and they taunt Renato for sneaking off to have a secret affair with his own wife. Renato, murderously angry about the Governor's affair, tells the conspirators that he'll aid in their assassination plot.

**Act III:** At Secretary Renato's house, Renato tells Amelia that he's going to kill her for adultery. She swears her innocence, but agrees to die. Gazing at a portrait of the Governor, he expresses his anger and bitterness in a powerful aria (which you can hear on Track 5 of your free CD). He and the conspirators plot the Governor's assassination.

The governor's big masked ball begins. In the big gubernatorial ballroom, amid much singing and dancing, Amelia warns the governor about the plot; the Governor recognizes her despite her costume, and they sing farewell: *"T'amo, si, t'amo, e in lacrime"* ("Goodbye, goodbye, with tears").

"And here's *my* goodbye!" shouts Secretary Renato (*"E tu ricevi il mio!"*), shooting the Governor at close range. Renato is captured, but his victim performs three final acts as outgoing governor: He forgives Renato, assures everyone that he never touched Amelia, and dies.

# Die Meistersinger von Nürnberg

**Title translation:** *The Master-Singers of Nuremberg.* **Music and libretto by:** Richard Wagner, in German. **First performed:** Munich, Germany, 1868.

**What to look forward to:** A warm-hearted love-story comedy by Wagner, if you can believe that — his only one, and for many, Wagner's most likable show. No gods, no magic, no legends; in fact, this story is based on actual Master-Singer guilds who held singing contests, and an actual shoemaker/poet named Hans Sachs.

A warning: *The Master-Singers* is the longest opera still performed today. If it's performed in its entirety, you're looking at five hours of good music and wry wit. Pack a suitcase.

**Astonishing trivia:** Wagner's most outspoken detractor was an obnoxious know-it-all music critic named Eduard Hanslick. Surprise, surprise: *The Master-Singers* features a nasty, narrow-minded music judge named Beckmesser who hates anything new or innovative. So what makes us think that Beckmesser was Wagner's revenge on critic Hanslick? Well, how about this: In the first draft of the opera, Beckmesser's name was Hans Lick!

**Act I:** Nuremberg during the mid-1500s. Pretty Eva (a soprano), sitting in church, flirts across the pews with a heroic-looking tenor named Walther. Her nurse Magdelene looks on disapprovingly. Unfortunately, Eva's father has promised her to whoever wins tomorrow's big singing contest — and only members of the Singers' Guild may enter the contest. Walther hasn't the slightest idea of how to go about singing in these things.

The judges for the competition arrive, Master-Singers all: Pogner, Eva's dad; Beckmesser, the evil town clerk; and Hans Sachs — bass-baritone, shoemaker, David's employer/voice teacher, and eminently sensible fellow. Walther will first have to go through the prelims. The rules: Beckmesser will tally the singing mistakes on the blackboard; songs must contain the requisite number of stanzas and syllables; the lines must rhyme; no hitting below the belt. Walther does his best, disastrously improvising a song. Beckmesser interrupts to say that he has marked so many mistakes that he doesn't have any room left to write. Cobbler Sachs and Eva's dad Pogner think that Walther has some talent, but they're in the minority. Walther storms out.

**Act II:** The young singer apprentices, including David, put shutters on the windows and sing merrily of the upcoming music contest. David gives girlfriend Nurse Magdelene the bad news about the contest; she rushes home to give the gossip to Eva. Foiled by the unpleasant Singers' Guild experience, Eva and Walther plan to elope. At Hans's shop, she swaps clothes with Nurse Magdelene so that she won't be recognized.

But now, who should arrive but the annoying Beckmesser — here to serenade Eva with his *own* singing-contest song! Just as he starts singing to "Eva" (actually Magdalene at the window), Hans offers to critique Beckmesser's singing, banging his hammer on his workbench only when he hears a mistake. The singing begins and the hammering joins in seconds later — lots and *lots* of hammering. The neighbors rush to their windows to see what the noise is about. When David sees that Beckmesser is singing to *his* love (Magdalene), he rushes out and starts beating the limburger out of Beckmesser. When the crowd hears the watchman approaching, they run home. The watchman, arriving at the now-peaceful square, tells us that it's now 11 p.m. (but this being Wagner, it's really probably 2:15 a.m.).

**Act III:** It's morning in Hans's shop. Hans gives apprentice David a quick singing lesson, sends him off, and then waxes philosophical: *"Wahn! Wahn! Überall Wahn!"* ("Crazy! Crazy! The whole world's nuts!").

Walther, waking, tells Hans that a beautiful song came to him in a dream. Hans writes it down, realizing that it could make a prize-winning song. When they leave the room, Beckmesser pockets the new song for his own use in the contest. Confident that Beckmesser will make a mess of the song, Hans tells him to keep it as a present.

Under the pretense of needing her shoes fixed, Eva arrives to see her boyfriend, Walther. Walther sings her a lick of his song, which makes her melt.

With a ceremonial punch in the head, Hans promotes David to journeyman, which also means that David is now free to marry Magdalene. In a shimmering quintet of happiness, love, and excitement — *"Selig, wie die Sonne"* ("Blessed as the sun") — they head off to the contest.

In a meadow, there's much singing and dancing as the crowd and the Singers' Guild parade by. Hans introduces the first contestant: the icky Beckmesser. But having only half-memorized the song he got at Hans's shop, he crashes and burns. Enraged, Beckmesser claims that, in fact, *Hans* wrote this terrible song. But Hans replies that the song's great if done right — which is Walther's cue to sing:

| | |
|---|---|
| *Morgenlich leuchtend in rosigem Schein,* | The morning light had a rosy gleam, |
| *von Blüth' und Duft* | Perfumed scent |
| *geschwellt die Luft,* | Filled the air |
| *voll aller Wonnen nie ersonnen,* | Bathed in beauteous light |
| *ein Garten lud mich ein.* | A garden lured me. |

The crowd is blown away. They give Walther the grand prize, Eva's hand in marriage, and an invitation to join the Singers' Guild. Still irked about his treatment by the Guild yesterday, he refuses this final honor — until Hans lectures him on the glorious importance of Germany's singing tradition, in a famous finale that you can hear on your free CD. Walther humbly accepts Guild membership. Everybody cheers.

# Otello

**Music by:** Giuseppe Verdi. **Libretto:** In Italian by Arrigo Boïto, based on Shakespeare's *Othello, The Moor of Venice.* **First performed:** Milan, Italy, 1887.

**What to look forward to:** A musicalized version, in three acts, of Shakespeare's famous tragedy. Luscious melodies of love and longing, plus one of the nastiest villains in all of opera. (He gets away, by the way.)

**Astonishing trivia:** *Otello* is widely accepted as one of Verdi's finest operas — not bad for a 74-year-old man — and much credit for the success is given to Verdi's librettist, Boito, a composer in his own right (*Mefistofele*).

**Act I:** On the island of Cyprus, a crowd worries about the ship that's bringing home the Moor Otello, the governor who has just conquered the enemy. But tenor Otello strides in, perfectly safe, singing of his conquest: *"Esultate!"* ("Celebrate!").

Two of Otello's men, however, aren't in any mood to celebrate. Roderigo (a tenor) has fallen in love with Otello's wife, and Ensign Iago (a baritone) has been passed over for the lieutenant's job he so desperately wanted. Instead, the job went to tenor Cassio (no relation to the digital-watch manufacturer). After lighting a cheery bonfire (*"Fuoco di gioia"*), the crowd adjourns to the tavern, where Ensign Iago gets newly promoted Lieutenant Cassio drunk; Cassio promptly gets into a fight and wounds the former Governor.

All this ruckus brings Otello and his soprano wife, Desdemona. Otello fires Cassio, to evil Iago's delight. When the crowd dissipates, Otello and Desdemona sing a famous love duet:

| | |
|---|---|
| *Già nella notte densa* | The night is quiet and dark, |
| *S' estingue ogni clamor.* | All the loudness has gone. |
| *Già il mio cor fremebondo* | The anger in my heart |
| *S' ammansa in quest' amplesso e si risensa.* | Finds absolute peace in your arms. |

Otello kisses his wife three times: *"Un bacio — un bacio — ancora un bacio"* ("A kiss — a kiss — and another kiss").

**Act II:** Iago, still miffed about losing that promotion, slyly suggests that ex-Lieutenant Cassio ask Desdemona for help getting his job back. As Cassio waits for her, Iago reveals his nasty philosophy of life: "I was created in the image of a cruel God."

When Otello spots his wife chatting with ex-employee Cassio, Iago hints that they're flirting. When Desdemona later asks husband Otello if he'll consider reinstating Cassio, Otello is even more suspicious — so much so that when she wipes his forehead with her pretty handkerchief with the strawberries on it, he throws it onto the floor. Desdemona's maid, Emilia — Iago's long-suffering wife — picks it up, but Iago snatches it from her, as Desdemona continues to try to calm Otello down.

Iago continues to work on Otello's suspicions. Otello, losing his temper, throttles Iago and demands proof of the accusations. Iago claims that he has heard Cassio murmuring "Desdemona!" in his sleep. Otello blows a gasket, vowing violent revenge: *"Si pel ciel"* ("Yes, by heaven!").

**Act III:** Otello demands to see the pretty handkerchief with the strawberries on it. Desdemona, of course, can't produce it. She's baffled by her husband's abusive crankiness, but she assures him that she's faithful. Alone, Otello sings about his broken heart and shattered illusions: *"Dio! mi potevi scagliar tutti i mali della miseria"* ("God, you could have inflicted on me all the ills of misery").

Cassio mentions that he found a pretty handkerchief with strawberries on it in his house — and doesn't know *how* it could have gotten there. Otello, never one for getting both sides of a story, has heard enough; he vows to kill his wife. Iago volunteers to kill Cassio himself, and Otello rewards him with a promotion — to the very job Cassio lost in the first act!

A shipful of ambassadors arrive to tell Otello that he's being called back to Venice. And who do you suppose they want to fill in as Cyprus governor while he's gone? Cassio, of all people! In a rage, Otello knocks Desdemona down right in front of everyone, and then faints. The crowds cheer Otello's promotion ("Hail to the Lion of Venice!"), but Iago only gloats over his passed-out boss. "*There's* your Lion," he smirks.

**Act IV:** In her bedroom, Desdemona asks her assistant Emilia to make up the bed with the wedding sheets, so just in case Desdemona should get murdered or something, she might be buried in them.

Otello arrives, kisses Desdemona three times, and then accuses her of having an affair with Cassio. Her denials drive him into a fit of fury; at this point, he's a taco short of a combination plate. He strangles her. Emilia bursts in to report that Cassio has killed Roderigo (who, you may recall, was in love with Desdemona) in a fight. Former Governor Montano arrives to reveal that, before he died, Roderigo spilled the beans about Iago's evil plot; nothing at all has been going on between Desdemona and Cassio.

Otello feels duped and devastated. He stabs himself with a dagger. He kisses his wife's corpse three times again *("Un bacio — un bacio ancora — un altro bacio"),* and falls down dead on top of her.

# I Pagliacci

**Title translation:** *The Clowns.* **Music and libretto:** In Italian by Ruggiero Leoncavallo. **First performed:** Milan, Italy, 1892.

**What to look forward to:** A gory tragedy in two acts — about *clowns.* Features all kinds of Shakespearean elements, such as a character who addresses the audience before the curtain goes up and a play within a play. Also features a classic dramatic device: a miserably unhappy clown, crying on the inside, whose job it is to make people laugh.

**Astonishing trivia:** This was Leoncavallo's only successful opera; his version of *La Bohème* was wiped off the map by Puccini's version, and Leoncavallo abandoned his "Italian *Ring* cycle" (a massive three-opera work comparable to Wagner's four-opera megawork), after the first opera flopped. Leoncavallo was sued for plagiarism by another writer after *Pagliacci* opened. But in court, Leoncavallo claimed that he wrote the opera based on a similar murder that took place in his hometown — and at which his father was the trial judge. Leoncavallo won his case.

**Figure 12-11:**
*Pagliacci:*
Josephine
Barstow as
Nedda, Jon
Vickers as
Canio, Lyric
Opera of
Chicago,
1982 (photo:
Tony
Romano).

**Prologue:** Calabria, Italy, in the late 1860s. A baritone hunchback clown (!) named Tonio explains that what we're about to see is about real emotions in the lives of people we can all understand.

**Act I:** In a small village, the passersby sing excitedly about the arrival of a clown troupe. A donkey cart arrives carrying Canio, tenor and head clown; his soprano wife Nedda; and Beppe, the drum-playing tenor clown. When Hunchback Tonio helps the lady clown down from the cart, Canio, strangely humorless for a clown, gets jealous and punches Tonio. The audience laughs.

The villagers invite the clowns out for cocktails. Tonio declines to join the others, saying that he's got to take care of the donkey. One of the villagers speculates that Tonio's just waiting for his boss to leave so that he can hit on the boss's wife, Nedda. That's plausible; she feels tied to Canio, and longs to be as free as the birds overhead (cue for a breathtakingly beautiful aria).

When hunchback Tonio tells her that he's in love with her, she hits him with a whip; he vows revenge. When Tonio leaves, Nedda's actual boyfriend, non-clown baritone Silvio, begs her to run away with him — an attractive prospect to Nedda, who's had it with clowns. Nedda promises her secret lover that they'll meet tonight after the show and that "tonight and forever after I'll be yours" (*"A stanotte — e per sempre tua sarò"*).

Unfortunately, Tonio has overheard the two adulterers. He returns with his furious boss Canio, who commands Nedda to reveal her lover's name. When she refuses, Canio becomes a killer clown, lunging at her with a knife. Beppe, former drum-playing clown, breaks it up, pointing out that (a) they still have a show to do, and (b) they don't have understudies. Canio, alone, sings the number we all know from cereal commercials on TV:

| | |
|---|---|
| *Vesti la giubba e la faccia infarina.* | Put on the costume, the grease paint, and the powder. |
| *La gente paga e rider vuole quà . . .* | The people pay you to make 'em laugh . . . |
| *Ridi Pagliaccio, sul tuo amore infranto!* | Laugh, Clown, 'cause your love is over! |
| *Ridi del duol che t'avvelena il cor!* | Laugh for the sorrow that poisons your heart! |

**Act II:** The clown-play-within-a-clown-play begins. Nedda, playing a character named Columbina, mentions that her husband, Pagliaccio, will be gone until the morning and that the servant, Taddeo, has gone to market. How convenient! From offstage, we hear her secret lover singing, *"O Colombina, il tenero fido Arlecchin"* ("Oh, Columbina, your Harlequin awaits!") — then hunchback Tonio, as servant Taddeo, comes in with the groceries. Nedda/Columbina rebuffs his advances.

In through the window comes Beppe, now playing the Harlequin/secret lover, who kicks the hunchback and tells him to butt out. Columbina and her lover plot to kill her husband. When Tonio/Taddeo rushes in, yelling that the husband has come home, Harlequin jumps out the window. Nedda/Columbina calls out the same thing she said to Silvio (the real-life lover) in the first act: "Tonight and forever after I'll be yours" (*"A stanotte — e per sempre tua sarò"*), just as Canio (playing husband Pagliaccio) barges in. (Starting to sound a little familiar?)

"Columbina" accuses "Pagliaccio" of drinking. Canio, departing from the script, insists that she give up the name of her lover. Everyone tries to get him to stick to his lines, but he sings *"No, Pagliaccio non son"* ("No, Pagliaccio, no more!") — his honor must be avenged. The audience thinks that the acting is very realistic.

Nedda tells him that if he thinks so little of her, he can set her free. Canio stabs her, over and over again. Silvio, the boyfriend, rushes up to the stage, and Nedda, dying, calls out his name — exactly what Canio wanted to hear — so Canio stabs him, too. The audience attacks Canio, who drops his knife. Tonio turns to the audience and announces, *"La commedia è finita!"* — "The comedy's finished."

That's putting it mildly.

# Parsifal

**Music and libretto:** In German by Richard Wagner. **First performed:** Bayreuth, Germany, 1882.

**What to look forward to:** A religious drama based on the Holy Grail legend — Wagner's last opera — in three acts. Fabulous music (especially the shimmering, radiant prelude) and a great character in Kundry, both hag and sex machine. Don't expect to get home in time for *Seinfeld,* however; this tale takes its sweet time to unfold.

**Astonishing trivia:** Wagner's subtitle for this opera is *Stage-Consecrating Festival Drama* — he wrote it as a dedication for the special opera theater he had built, to his specs, at Bayreuth. Moreover, that's the *only* place he allowed it to play; he demanded that no other opera house be permitted to produce it. With only a couple of exceptions, nobody outside Bayreuth touched this opera until the copyright expired in 1913.

**Act I:** Spain, the Middle Ages. Knights of the Holy Grail awaken in a forest. They check the health of their king, Amfortas, whose grisly wound has kept him on the edge of death for weeks. Suddenly, Kundry, the wild-haired dramatic soprano, bursts in with a little bottle of medicine for Amfortas. Amfortas thanks her, but the others are dubious, because Kundry also works for their evil archenemy Klingsor. Old knight Gurnemanz, a bass, fills us in with a flashback:

Amfortas's father had two holy artifacts: the Holy Grail (a cup that Jesus used at the Last Supper) and the Holy Spear that stabbed Jesus. Amfortas Sr. hired some knights to protect these Ultimate Museum Attractions. One applicant, Klingsor, didn't get the job. Furious, he vowed to use magic to steal the relics. For his first trick, he created a bunch of irresistibly sexy women to lure the knights to their doom.

Sure enough, Lured Knight No. 1 was Amfortas Jr., who fell for the amazingly great-looking Kundry. Klingsor promptly stabbed him with the Holy Spear — producing the wound that wouldn't go away. A dream told Amfortas that only one event could heal him: An "innocent fool" must touch the wound with the Holy Spear. (End of flashback.)

At this moment, a swan falls dying by a lake. The Knights rush to punish whoever shot the poor swan. It turns out to be a young man named Parsifal. He knows nothing of his name or family; *"So dumm wie den erfand ich bisher Kundry nur,"* mutters old Gurnemanz ("I've never met such a dim-witted dolt — except maybe Kundry here"). And when Parsifal learns that swan shooting is forbidden, his eyes fill with childlike tears. *Wait a sec,* thinks old Gurnemanz: *He's innocent . . . he's a fool . . . could it be?*

Kundry, out of the blue, tells Parsifal that his mother has died. In a rage, Parsifal grabs her throat — then, apologetic, faints.

Old Gurnemanz leads Parsifal to the Castle of the Grail, hoping that *this* innocent fool is *the* innocent fool. The knights enter the dining hall to take Holy Communion, conducted by King Amfortas to shimmery, holy-sounding music. King Amfortas's father speaks from the shadows. King Amfortas falls backward in pain from his wound. The Holy Grail is taken out of the cupboard, where a blinding shaft of light illuminates it.

When the religious service is over, Parsifal, although impressed by the special effects, tells old Gurnemanz that he didn't understand any of it. Gurnemanz, annoyed, throws Parsifal out of the castle.

**Act II:** Evil Klingsor stands at a magic flame. He summons Kundry and berates her for helping the knights on her days off. And he gives her a new assignment: to seduce Parsifal. She objects, but his magic is too strong for her, and she leaves. Klingsor, standing in the tower, watches the knights attacking his castle. With a wave of his hand, he makes his entire castle vanish into the earth.

Parsifal is amazed — especially by the bevy of beautiful models (aka Flower Maidens) running around half-dressed. They're every teenage boy's dream:

| | |
|---|---|
| **First model:** *An deinem Busen nimm mich!* | Hug me to your chest! |
| **Second:** *Die Stirn lass' mich dir Kühlen!* | Let me cool your forehead! |
| **Third:** *Lass mich die Wange dir fühlen!* | Let me stroke your cheeks! |
| **Fourth:** *Den Mund lass' mich dir küssen!* | Let me kiss your mouth! |
| **Fifth:** *Nein, mich! Die Schönste bin ich!* | No, me! I'm the best! |
| **Sixth:** *Nein, ich! Duft' ich doch süsser.* | No, me! I smell sweeter. |

Kundry, however, really gets to him, telling him of his mother's death and offering to soothe him with her kiss. Just as they begin making out, however, Parsifal remembers his mission — the Holy Spear! — and pulls away. Evil magician Klingsor flings the Holy Spear at him. Fortunately for Parsifal, the prevailing winds, or magic, or something, makes the spear freeze in space above his head. Parsifal grabs it, makes the sign of the cross with it, and Klingsor, his castle, and his models shrivel up and blow away.

**Act III:** Back at the knights' camp, Kundry (no longer a temptress, her Klingsor curse having been broken) wakes from a horrible dream. A black-armored knight approaches, carrying the Holy Spear. It's Parsifal, back at last after months of difficult journeying. Kundry and old Gurnemanz fill him in: King Amfortas is sicker than ever; his father has died. They treat Parsifal's ailments; Kundry pours some ointment onto his feet and dries them with her hair. Gurnemanz dubs Parsifal an official Knight of the Grail, and Parsifal officially baptizes Kundry — lots of singing and praying and scenery.

In the castle dining hall, King Amfortas, in screaming pain from his wound, begs the knights to kill him. Parsifal touches him with the Holy Spear, and sure enough, the wound heals. The Holy Cup glows, the room fills with heavenly radiance, and everyone — knights and boys' choir — joins in a holy choral hymn. Everyone's happy except Kundry, who falls over dead, free from the clutches of magic forever, as the orchestra reprises the show's best tunes.

## The Pearl Fishers . . . See Chapter 13

# Peter Grimes

**Music by:** Benjamin Britten. **Libretto:** In English by Montagu Slater. **First performed:** London, England, 1945.

**What to look forward to:** A moving drama in three acts, plus prologue and epilogue — one of the first notable English operas since Purcell's *Dido and Aeneas*, 200 years earlier. Just look at all you get: powerful, fresh music; a chilling depiction of the herd mentality of small-town citizens; a not-all-that-likable *anti*-hero; and such a convincing depiction of the sea that sections of the orchestra music are often performed in symphony concerts.

**Astonishing trivia:** Benjamin Britten, a Briton, moved to the very town where *Peter Grimes* takes place — Aldeburgh — shortly after the opera opened. Coincidence? You decide.

**Prologue:** During a fishing trip, the young boy who worked with fisherman Peter Grimes has died. At Peter's trial, the gossipy townspeople mutter and chant, hungry for blood; but Peter claims that his boat was caught in a squall that blew his boat off course for three days; the kid died of exposure. The Coroner gives his verdict: "Your apprentice died in accidental circumstances." But Peter is advised to hire a grown-up apprentice next time. After the courtroom empties, widowed soprano schoolmistress Ellen comforts Peter.

**Act I:** The shops of the town open, with the townsfolk merrily fixing their nets and singing. Ned Keene, baritone druggist, tells Peter that he's found a good apprentice-boy candidate at the local workhouse; Peter's friend Ellen persuades the reluctant cart driver to go get the boy. The townspeople sing their displeasure.

A powerful sea storm is approaching; the townsfolk fasten down the boats and lock up their shutters, singing a chorus that rises like the wind, then rush into the pub. Peter tells Old Cap'n Balstrode about the horrible three days at sea with the dead boy in the boat. He also reveals his long-term personal goals: to catch enough fish to become rich, marry Ellen, and shut up the town's incessant busybodies.

Inside the pub, various locals burst in with reports of storm damage; the cliff by Grimes's hut has slid into the sea, and the road is flooded. When Peter now appears, everyone shuts up. Peter ignores them, however, singing an introspective tune about the mystery of the skies and Fate: "Now the Great Bear and Pleiades, where earth moves, are drawing up the clouds of human grief." As the villagers grow hostile, Keene distracts them with a sea chantey, soon joined by the other townsfolk until three melodies are woven together:

**First tune:** *Old Joe has gone fishing,*

*And young Joe has gone fishing . . .*

**Second tune:** *Pull them in han'fuls, and in canfuls,*

*And in panfuls.*

**Third tune:** *Bring them in sweetly,*

*Gut them completely,*

*Pack them up neatly,*

*Sell them discreetly!*

What are you looking over here for? This opera's in English!

But when Peter joins the round, he makes up new words about finding a *corpse* in the fishing net: "Bring him in with horror! Bring him in with terror!" Ellen and the cart driver arrive, half-drowned by the storm, with the new apprentice boy in tow. Peter takes him home.

**Act II:** It's Sunday morning. Ellen and the new boy, John, chat as the hymns waft from the local church. To her horror, Ellen a bruise on the boy's neck. She questions Peter, but gets a slap in the face for an answer.

The congregation, pouring out of the church, demands to know why Ellen is sympathizing with the no-good Peter. She tries to defend herself, her voice rising, but the townsfolk march off to find out what exactly is going on at Peter's hut.

Grimes hears the angry mob approaching. He hustles the boy out the door, planning to escape down the cliff created by the landslide. "Shut your eyes and down you go!" he tells young John. But the boy slips and falls out down the cliff out of sight, screaming. Peter runs down the cliff after him. The lynch mob arrives at Peter's empty hut, finding nothing amiss. But old Captain Balstrode peers down the cliff, sees something, then carefully closes the door.

**Act III:** Nighttime; much drinking and women-chasing and dancing. But the townspeople have found young John's jersey washed up on the beach; now they're *really* out for Peter's blood.

At this point, Peter is a few planks shy of a dinghy, muttering madly. He doesn't even recognize Ellen when she arrives with Captain Balstrode. Balstrode suggests that Peter sail far out to sea and sink his own boat. Grimes does, sending himself to a watery grave. The next morning, someone reports having seen a sinking boat far out at sea; someone else claims that's just a rumor; soon enough, the townspeople go back to their miserable humdrum lives.

# Porgy and Bess

**Music by:** George Gershwin. **Libretto:** In English by DuBose Heyward and Ira Gershwin. **First performed:** Boston, Massachusetts, 1935.

**What to look forward to:** A dramatic love story in three acts. A pure American opera (Gershwin's phrase: "folk opera"), featuring the styles of jazz, blues, and Broadway. A nearly all-African-American cast performs a tale from a poor section of South Carolina — about as far from Wagner as you can get.

**Astonishing trivia:** This was not Gershwin's first attempt at "folk" opera — he had previously written a one-act opera called *Blue Monday,* set in Harlem, for *George White's Scandals of 1922.*

**Act I:** In poor Catfish Row, it's summertime, and the livin' is easy. There's piano playing, dancing, street selling, and card-playing. Clara (a soprano) sings the lullaby that we all know and love, "Summertime," to her baby. Sportin' Life (a tenor drug dealer) plays craps with Jake (a fisherman). He warns his and Clara's baby that "a woman is a sometime thing."

Porgy (a crippled bass-baritone) enters on a cart being pulled by a goat. The men tease him about having the hots for pretty soprano, Bess, whom the women disdain — "That gal Bess ain't fit for Gawd fearin' ladies to 'sociate with," says one.

When Crown, the nasty baritone, demands some more liquor, despite the fact that he's had quite enough already, his girlfriend Bess takes his bottle away. Big Bad Crown is not pleased. To make matters worse, he loses at dice, buys some "happy dust" from Sportin' Life, the pusher, loses some more, loses control, and kills Robbins the fisherman with a cotton hook. Robbins's wife, Serena, sobs over the body. Bess, Crown's girlfriend, takes some "happy dust" from Sportin' Life to help her over the shakes, but declines Mr. Life's sportin' offer to go up to New York with him. Bess seeks shelter in Porgy's room.

A detective and a cop show up, trying to find out who killed Robbins. Afraid of evil Crown, nobody says a word. Bess cheers everybody up with a rousing chorus of "Leavin' for the Promise' Lan'."

**Act II:** It's morning. Fishermen repair their nets while getting ready for the big picnic. Fisherman Jake and his wife, Clara (of "Summertime" fame), worry about money, but Porgy doesn't worry: "Oh, I got plenty o' nuttin, an' nuttin's plenty fo' me."

Everyone comments on how Porgy seems to have changed for the better since Bess moved in with him. A lawyer tries to sell her a divorce from Big Bad Crown, raising his fee because she was never married to him in the first place: ". . . it take expert to divorce woman what ain't marry." When Sportin' Life tries to pawn some more "happy dust" off on Bess, she declines, and Porgy reinforces her protests by nearly breaking Sportin' Life's arm off. Bess and Porgy sing a duet: "Bess, You Is My Woman Now." (Technically, *he* sings that; she sings, "Porgy, I's yo' woman now.") Everybody heads off for the big picnic on Kittiwah Island, but Porgy must remain home.

The picnic is a ball, with dancing, singing, and Sportin' Life's bogus sermon called "It ain't necessarily so" (which is on the CD with this book). Bess is accosted by Big Bad Crown, who's been hiding out on this island. Bess tries to talk him out of his interest in her: "What you want wid Bess? She's gettin' ole now; take a fine young gal for to satisfy Crown." He encourages her to think about *his* needs, and throws her into a thicket. A week later, Bess is home, but in a delirium. When her fever breaks, she tells Porgy that though Crown is coming for her, she'd prefer to stay: "I loves you, Porgy." He promises to defend her from Crown.

A storm rises. Clara, carrying her baby, worries about her husband Jake, out at sea, and sings "Summertime" again. There's a knock at the door. It's Crown; he and Porgy fight over Bess. Suddenly Clara, the fisherman's wife, screams: she can see her husband's boat overturned. Bess appeals to the men for help, but only Crown has the guts to go.

**Act III:** The storm is finally over — Crown has survived. But when he sneaks toward Porgy's house with no good on his mind, Porgy strangles him.

The white detectives question Serena about Crown's death, because Crown recently killed her husband, but witnesses back up her claim that she's been ill for some time. The detectives now ask the very apprehensive Porgy to come downtown to identify the body. Before he's led away, Sportin' Life tells him that this is how the cops find out who killed someone — when the killer looks at the face of the victim, the wounds start to bleed. With Porgy out of the way, Sportin' Life works his tricks on Bess, getting her to take some "happy dust" and convincing her to accompany him on "A Boat Dat's Leavin' Soon for New York."

A week later, Porgy returns to a rousing welcome. He tells the crowd that he refused to look at Crown, so the cops put him in jail for contempt of court. While he was in the slammer, he won a load of bucks playing craps, so he has presents for everybody. He calls for Bess — "Bess, oh, where's my Bess?" — and he's told that she's gone up to New York with Sportin' Life. He asks for his goat and his cart, vowing to head for the Big Apple to find her, singing, "Oh, Lawd, I'm on my way."

Gotta love the guy's spirit, you know?

## *I Puritani . . . See Chapter 13*

## *Das Rheingold/The Rhine Gold . . . Look under Ring Cycle*

# Rigoletto

**Music by:** Giuseppe Verdi. **Libretto:** In Italian by Francesco Maria Piave. **First performed:** Venice, Italy, 1851.

**What to look forward to:** A dramatic tragedy in four acts about a sarcastic hunchback court jester. Baritones kill for the role of Rigoletto, who goes through a zillion different emotions in the course of this show — after all, the heroes of *most* operas are tenors. The most famous clown tragedy besides *I Pagliacci*.

**Astonishing trivia:** *Rigoletto* was originally based on a Victor Hugo play about treachery in the court of the French King François I. But Italy, under Austria's rule, was in considerable political turmoil; Verdi and Piave ran into trouble with the Italian censors, who felt that the people didn't need a play about a malicious, philandering king. So Verdi and his librettist changed the setting of the opera to Mantua, which was governed by a small-time nobleman.

**Act I:** Mantua, Italy, during the 16th century. At the castle of the Duke of Mantua (a tenor), the most sex-crazed nobleman since Don Giovanni, there's dancing and laughter. The shameless Duke is the original chauvinist pig; one woman's as good as another, he thinks, even if they're married: *"Questa o quella"* ("This woman or that woman"). As though to prove his point, he takes a female guest, Mrs. Ceprano, into the bedroom — right in front of her husband! Snide, hunchbacked jester Rigoletto (a baritone) mocks the furious Mr. Ceprano. But the tables turn when the crowd starts making fun of *Rigoletto,* teasing him about having a secret girlfriend. Ceprano joins them in discussing *"vendetta"* ("revenge") against the unfunny jester.

Rigoletto even makes fun of an old count that the Duke has arrested. As he's dragged away, the old count puts a curse on Rigoletto.

**Act II:** On a dark, deserted street, a creepy hit man named Sparafucile offers his services to Rigoletto. Rigoletto declines — for now, but compares his lot in life to the hit man's in a powerful baritone aria:

| | |
|---|---|
| *Pari siamo! — dio la lingua, egli ha il pugnale:* | We're alike — my weapon is my tongue, his is his dagger; |
| *L'uomo son io che ride, ei quel che spegne!* | I make people laugh, he gives them grief! |

When a fabulous beauty runs out of one of the houses to greet Rigoletto, he cries *"Figlia"* ("Daughter"), and she cries *"Mio padre!"* ("Daddy!"). See? It wasn't a *girlfriend* Rigoletto has been secretly visiting after all, but his daughter, soprano Gilda ("JEEL-da"). Little does he suspect that the *Duke* has been dating Gilda, disguised as a mild-mannered student (who calls himself Walter Maldè). Gilda, madly in love, sings the famous aria *"Caro nome che il mio cor"* ("Dear name that first made my heart beat faster").

Out on the street, Mr. Ceprano shows up, still plotting revenge on the jester who humiliated him at the party. He and his band bump into Rigoletto himself, but they're masked, and it's dark. They claim that they've come to Ceprano's house (adjacent to Rigoletto's) to kidnap *Mrs.* Ceprano for the duke's pleasure. Rigoletto offers to help; he even agrees to be masked like the rest of the gang — but Ceprano and Co. add a handkerchief, blinding and confusing him. They lead Rigoletto to his *own* house and tell him to hold the ladder. As they break in and carry out Gilda, thinking they're kidnapping Rigoletto's *girlfriend,* they laugh about their trick (*"Zitti, zitti moviamo a vendetta"* — "Hush, hush, let's have our revenge"). Rigoletto rips off his mask, finds Gilda's scarf, realizes what has happened, and has a breakdown. He blames the old count's curse: *"Ah! La maledizione!"*

**Act III:** In a rowdy chorus, the kidnappers report to the Duke that they've stolen Rigoletto's girlfriend and brought her to the castle. The Duke, realizing that they've actually captured Gilda, is delighted. Rigoletto searches for her, pathetically trying to keep up his jester work, singing "Tra-la-la," much to the cruel amusement of the courtiers. Rigoletto deduces that she's in the bedroom with the Duke. The guys bar his way, but he stuns them by revealing that the girl is really his daughter.

Gilda rushes into Rigoletto's arms, deeply upset; the nice student she met at church now turns out to be the lust-crazed rapist Duke himself. Rigoletto consoles her in a touching duet, promising that they'll flee the town tonight. They're interrupted by the old count who put the curse on Rigoletto, passing through on his way to be executed for having insulted the Duke. He gripes about his curse not having had any effect, because the Duke is still alive — but Rigoletto tells him that the game isn't over yet.

**Act IV:** Rigoletto and his daughter are outside the rundown bar owned by creepy assassin Sparafucile. Gilda, one of those women who love men who abuse women, still loves the Duke. Rigoletto, to shock some sense into her, makes her peer inside the bar. There, sure enough, is the Duke, singing another Top Ten Chauvinist Pig Hit, *"La donna è mobile"* ("Women are fickle"), a melody so familiar you could probably sing it in your sleep. Gilda watches him make a play for Sparafucile's mantrap sister, Maddalena. In a famous quartet, the Duke and Maddalena sing *inside* as they play their little love game, while *outside* Gilda and her father sing their unhappiness.

Rigoletto tells Gilda to dress as a man and ride off to Verona; he'll catch up later. Rigoletto gives Sparafucile the down payment for killing the Duke. But inside the bar, Maddalena tells brother Sparafucile that now *she's* in love with the Duke and doesn't want anybody killing him. Sparafucile decides that he'll just kill the next guy to come through the front door and deliver *that* body to Rigoletto in a sack instead of the Duke.

But outside, Gilda has overheard everything, even the part about killing the next guy to walk in the door. Making a noble sacrifice for the life of her beloved no-good Duke, she enters the bar — and Sparafucile stabs her.

Rigoletto returns, gloating about his revenge. As a storm rages, he collects the body sack, pays Sparafucile, and heads toward the river for dumping. But when he hears the Duke singing his pig song again (*"La donna è mobile"*), he freezes — the voice isn't coming from inside the sack where the Duke is supposed to be! Rigoletto opens the sack and discovers his daughter, Gilda, dying. She tells him that she gave up her life for the man she loves. Rigoletto can see that: *"Mia figlia! Dio! mia figlia! Gilda!"* ("My daughter! God! My daughter! Gilda!"). Crying over her body, Rigoletto knows exactly why this fate has befallen him: *"La maledizione!"*

# The Ring Cycle (Der Ring der Nibelungen)

**Title translation:** *The Ring of the Nibelungs.* **Music and librettos:** In German by Richard Wagner. **First performed:** *Das Rheingold,* Munich, Germany, 1869; *Die Walküre,* Munich, Germany, 1870; *Siegfried,* Bayreuth, Germany, 1876; *Götterdämmerung,* Bayreuth, Germany, 1876.

**What to look forward to:** Welcome to the Big Kahuna of Opera: *four* more-than-full-length operas, 18 hours total, accompanied by gigantic orchestras, based on complicated Norwegian mythology and symbolism. These operas changed everything; 100 years later, they're still controversial, loved and hated, and analyzed to death. Appreciating Wagner's *music* is made even more complicated because the guy himself was an anti-Semitic, adulterous, egotistical control freak. (See Chapter 8 for more, if you can stand it.)

Wagner didn't write operas in the usual way — with major musical numbers separated by recitative or dialogue. In a Wagner opera, you can't even identify where one song ends and the next begins — it's all a continuous, flowing mishmash. Much of the emphasis in Wagner's stuff is on the orchestra — the characters are occasionally forced to stand there for minutes at a time while the orchestra plays and plays.

What makes that orchestra music interesting, though, are the *Leitmotifs* — little melodies, about 150 different ones, each associated with a certain character, object, or event. When you retire and have plenty of time on your hands, you can start to listen for these recurring licks and admire Wagner's cleverness.

We'll be honest with you: There are some long, drawn-out scenes in these operas. Keep in mind, though, that in Wagner's day, performances began in the afternoon, and between acts — while the set crew took down one set and put up the next — the audience would take a long walk, have a meal, or discuss metaphysics in German; only then would they return, refreshed and ready for more.

**Astonishing trivia:** Wagner wrote these four megalithic operas while hiding out in Switzerland, having been chased out of Germany for his rebellious political views. He wrote the scripts in reverse order — each time he finished one libretto, he realized that another whole opera was required to *precede* it to explain the complex plot. The music, however, he wrote in correct plot order. Writing everything took him 27 years (although he did take time off to write two *other* operas).

## Surviving the *Ring* cycle

Going to an opera is one thing. Going to Wagner's massive, four-opera *cycle* of operas is quite another: 18 hours of German mythology, not-very-melodious tunes, and — for the only time in opera, believe it or not — women wearing horned Viking helmets.

Not everybody gets the chance to see the full set of operas as they're meant to be performed — one each night in a single week. If *you* get the chance, jump at it, but follow these guidelines:

✔ Go before you go. The first acts of some of the operas are *extremely* long, and *Das Rheingold* has no intermission at all. Use the facilities first.

✔ Don't dress up. Even opera snobs won't sneer at you for this. You're going to be sitting there for *hours,* your mind taxed and your muscles limp. Wear something comfy.

✔ Bring food. These operas are so long, they usually begin around 6 p.m., so forget about grabbing dinner after work. Food is usually available at the opera-house bar, but it's going to cost you $7.50 per Milk Dud. Bring a sandwich or pasta salad to wolf down in the lobby; you won't be eating alone.

✔ Clap when the music stops, not when the curtain drops. This is one of those opera-snob rules, but you'd best heed it. If you clap while the music is still playing — even after the curtain has fallen near the end of the show — they'll stare at you like you have pierced nostrils.

✔ Revel in your beginnerhood. You can't win at the *Ring*; no matter how many times you've seen each opera, the guy next to you will have seen it six more times than you. And he'll make it worse by rattling off the famous singers and classic performances he has caught. Smile appreciatively — that's what he wants, after all — and secretly gloat that *you're* about to experience your first *Ring* cycle, which is the most important one of all.

# Das Rheingold

**Title translation:** *The Rhine Gold*

**The plot (in one act):** At the bottom of the Rhine River, three water nymphs called Rhinemaidens swim about, singing *"Weia! Waga!"* (Don't make fun. A certain *American* song ends every line with "Doo-dah, doo-dah.")

Their games are interrupted by an ugly, misshapen baritone gnome named Alberich, who's looking for sex. The nymphs tease and reject him. As the sun sets, Alberich's eye catches a bright golden reflection — the nymphs sing the two-note lick (the *Leitmotif,* get it?), "Rhine gold! Rhine gold!" They explain that they're guarding it, because if melted down into a finger ring, the gold gives its wearer infinite power. There's fine print, however: The wearer must give up love forever. Confident that nobody would be so stupid as to trade love for mere *unlimited control of the universe,* the carefree nymphs continue to gambol. Ugly, misshapen Alberich, however, has never had much in the way of love. He steals the gold, with the maidens and the music rushing after him.

Cut to Mount Olympus (called Valhalla — this is Germany), where one-eyed bass-baritone Zeus (called Wotan) and the other gods are waking. (Why is he one-eyed? You'll have to wait 15 hours to find out.) King Wotan's castle is breathtaking. But in exchange for its construction, King Wotan promised the contractors, a pair of giants, that he'd pay them with Freia, the beautiful soprano goddess of love. And now these giants are at the door claiming payment. Actually, forget about Freia; King Wotan's more worried about her *apples,* the magic fruit that keep the gods young forever — no Freia, no apples.

King Wotan had sent Loge (the tricky tenor fire god) searching the earth for anything good enough to give the giants *instead* of Freia; Loge suggests the magic gold ring that the gnome has been using to amass gigantic riches. Unlimited control of the universe sounds good to the giants, but they'll hold onto Freia until the magic ring is delivered.

Wotan and Loge zoom to the underworld, planning to swipe the ring. There they find Alberich the all-powerful dwarf in mad control: In the sulfurous caverns beneath the earth, he has used his magic to cruelly enslave all the other dwarves — the Nibelungs, which include his own brother — to help amass his fortune. He also has a magic helmet that lets him turn into any other animal or even become invisible. Loge says, "Prove it!" — which the mighty gnome does by turning himself first into a dragon, and then a toad. King Wotan promptly steps on the toad and takes it back to Mount Olympus, where Alberich is forced to give up the magic ring and helmet. Shaking with rage, Alberich curses the ring:

*Gab sein Gold mir — Macht ohne Mass, nun zeug' sein Zauber Tod dem — der ihn trägt!*

Gold that gave me infinite power, now may your magic deal death to each owner!

Wotan's ready to pay the giants. The deal was: In exchange for Freia, the giants receive a pile of gold tall enough to hide her. Yet the pile of Alberich's gold has a gap in it; one more morsel of gold is needed — oh, say, the size of *a ring.* Earth-goddess Erda rises from the mountain and warns direly to give up the darned ring; King Wotan reluctantly does. The ring's curse instantly springs into action, as the two giant brothers fight over it and one kills the other.

Freed of the ring's curse, Valhalla returns to its sunshiny. King Wotan and his wife joyously cross the magic bridge to the new castle. The Rhine-maidens, meanwhile, are still sobbing about the loss of their gold. King Wotan mightily tells them to shut up.

# Die Walküre

**Title translation:** *The Valkyrie*

**The backstory:** The action picks up after *The Rhine Gold* left off, just as in the three *Star Wars* movies. In a long second-act monologue, you'll find out some necessary background material: Namely, that King-of-the-Gods Wotan has been feeling positively naked without that magic ring, now in the clutches of Fafner, the remaining giant. He slips down to earth and makes love to a human woman; the results are the twins Siegmund and Sieglinde. (Wagner has this annoying habit of making all these characters even harder to keep straight because their names all start with the *same syllable* . . . it's only going to get worse. Anyway, Sieglinde is a girl — "zeeg-LIND-a" — and Siegmund is a boy.)

The twins were separated at birth, and now they're all grown up and, in Sieglinde's case, married.

**Act I:** After a prelude depicting a violent storm, we see the humble home of soprano Sieglinde and her hunter husband, Hunding (a bass). Who should burst in out of the storm but her long-lost brother, Siegmund. *"Wess' Herd dies auch sei, hier muss ich rasten,"* he exclaims ("Hey — whoever owns this house, I have to rest here!").

Sieglinde brings him water; he tells quite a tale. As a boy, he returned home one day to find his house burned, mom dead, and twin sister (hmm!) missing. Then just recently, he tried to rescue a girl whose family was forcing her to marry a cruel hunter husband (*hmmmm!*), but he was outnumbered and ran away. Hunter-husband Hunding recognizes Siegmund as the do-gooder he's been pursuing, but he vows to withhold vengeance until morning.

After drugging her evil husband, Sieglinde slips in. Brother and sister fall into each other's arms, and brother sings the famous "Spring Song." Actually, they do more than just sing, which is why some call *Die Walküre* the "incest opera." Siegmund heroically pulls a magical sword from the tree trunk, and they escape the house.

**Act II:** Wotan's nine daughters are called Valkyrie girls (not to be confused with *Valley* girls), and his favorite of all is Brünnhilde, the dramatic soprano. *She,* in case you've wondered all your life, is the one who inspired the ultimate opera cliché, the Fat Lady Wearing a Breastplate and Viking Helmet. She also has a pretty neat flying horse.

King Wotan asks his daughter to help Siegmund out. No problem, she says, and she summons her eight sisters.

Wotan's wife, Fricka, meanwhile, is on a tear, having learned of her husband's tryst with an earth woman. Wotan explains himself, filling her in about siring a hero to recover the ring, but Mrs. Wotan is not to be calmed. Because she *is* the Goddess of the Marriage Vow and doesn't want to look silly in front of her friends, Wotan finally agrees to let son Siegmund be killed as his own punishment for cheating.

Wotan now takes 20 minutes to bring daughter Brünnhilde up-to-date on what's happened so far in the story. But Brünnhilde still wants to *protect* half-brother Siegmund, despite Wotan's new directive to *kill* Siegmund. Wotan rages and leaves.

Back on earth, S & S are running for their lives, with evil husband Hunding in hot pursuit. Sieglinde is hallucinating about death and shattered swords. Brünnhilde appears, offering to protect Siegmund and his cute sister/lover. Siegmund and evil Hunding fight on the mountaintop. King Wotan, after additional nags by his wife, shatters his own son's sword. Hunding kills Siegmund, and Wotan kills Hunding. Sieglinde faints with a wild shriek. Half-sister Brünnhilde carries Sieglinde's body away, and Wotan vows to kill *her* for interfering. (Talk about dysfunctional families.)

**Act III:** We hear the "Ride of the Valkyries," the stormy music that U.S. military man Robert Duvall blasted from his helicopter in the movie *Apocalypse Now,* as Brünnhilde and her eight sisters ride their magic horses to a mountaintop hideaway.

Brünnhilde announces that Sieglinde is pregnant with the greatest hero the world has ever known (apparently unconcerned about the chromosomal effects of incest). Meanwhile, King Wotan catches up with Brünnhilde and grounds her. No, worse: To the accompaniment of *glorious* music, he strips her of her magic goddess powers and chains her in permanent sleep, surrounded by a ring of fire. Sadly, he bids her farewell. Nobody said parenthood was easy.

# Siegfried

**Act I:** Sieglinde has given birth to a baby tenor. Just to make sure that you're as confused as possible, his name is nearly identical to the names of his parents — it's Sieg*fried*. Mime ("MEE-muh"), the tenor dwarf, has raised the baby after its mother's death. Gnarly little Mime has a simple career plan: (1) equip boy Siegfried with a sword with which to *kill* Fafner the Giant (who's now, thanks to the magic ring, Fafner the Dragon); (2) take the magic ring after Fafner's death; (3) become Mime, All-Powerful-Ruler-of-the-Universe Dwarf. Yet Siegfried is so strong that every sword shatters in his hand — and little Mime can't seem to reforge the shattered pieces of Sieg*mund's* sword. Impatient, young Siegfried, singing lustily, reforges it himself, the orchestra providing an exciting fiery accompaniment.

**Act II:** In the dragon's lair, our old pal from the first opera, Alberich the ugly gnome, is still sore about losing his ring. After Wotan comes by to check things out, dwarf Mime and boy Siegfried slink on in their mission to slay the dragon.

When Siegfried imitates the forest bird noises on his horn, he inadvertently wakes the dragon. A grisly battle ensues, and Siegfried triumphs! When he tastes a drop of the dead dragon's blood, Siegfried finds that he can *understand* the birdsongs. In addition to the usual "Hey, let's all have some worms" and "Honey, I'll be away from the nest for a few days," he also hears the full story of the ring and the magic helmet.

No sooner has Siegfried grabbed these two items that *both* gnomes, Mime and Alberich, appear, arguing. Mime offers Siegfried a drink (laced with poison). But Siegfried's too smart for that, and he kills Mime. A little bird tells him about an amazing woman who lies sleeping in a ring of flames, and Siegfried runs off to save her.

**Act III:** Siegfried now runs into Wotan, who's technically his grandfather, and asks directions to Brünnhilde's ring of fire. Wotan tries to dissuade him, mentioning that he, Wotan, is the guy who originally broke the magic sword. Siegfried angrily chops Wotan's spear in half — Wotan's final appearance in these operas — and runs on up the mountain. There he finds Brünnhilde, still in full armored regalia; Siegfried wonders who this powerful soldier man could be. Upon removing her breastplate and helmet, however, what's underneath sets him straight: "That isn't a man!" he exclaims.

He awakens Brünnhilde with a kiss. The orchestra swells to ecstatic bursts of joy and desire, and — after a moment of hesitation on her part as she realizes that she's about to marry a mortal — they passionately fall into each others' arms, singing at the tops of their lungs, utterly in love and lust: a boy and his very special aunt.

# Götterdämmerung

**Title translation:** *Twilight of the Gods*

**Prologue:** We see the three Fate sisters (aka "Norns") passing their ball of Destiny Yarn back and forth and recounting the history of King Wotan. At the foot of the Ash Tree of Life springs the Spring of Wisdom. Young Wotan happily paid the price of an eyeball in exchange for a sip from the spring. As the sisters finish the Valhallan prehistory, the strand of Destiny Yarn breaks. The Fates scream in horror and sink into the earth.

On a mountaintop, in the ring of fire they call home, newlyweds Siegfried and Brünnhilde bid goodbye; he's off for his day of adventures. He gives Brünnhilde the ring for safekeeping. She offers him Grane, her magic horse. They sing an ardent duet, and the orchestra plays "Siegfried's Rhine Journey" for several minutes.

**Act I:** Alberich the Gnome's son, Hagen, lives in the river valley with his half-brother and half-sister, Gunther and Gutrune. (Let's take a moment to thank Wagner in our hearts for such easy-to-distinguish names.) Evil Hagen has a plan that, if successful, will make him the Ruler of the Universe. This plan requires the participation of Siegfried, who, as luck would have it, shows up at this very moment.

Evil bass Hagen prepares a love potion. Gutrune (the female) serves it to Siegfried, who's immediately raging with desire for her — and even suggests that her brother, Gunther, can have Brünnhilde. The potion makes him forget that he's married (and we've all had potions like *that*).

Back on the mountaintop, one of Brünnhilde's Valkyrie sisters drops by with news of the family. Dad (Wotan) is in a funk, slouching around Valhalla with his broken spear. He has chopped down the Ash Tree of Life and stopped eating Freia's eternal-youth apples. Only when that darned magic ring is returned to the Rhine nymphs will the curse of the gods be lifted. But to Brünnhilde, it's no magic ring — it's her wedding ring, and she refuses to give it up.

Now Siegfried bursts into the ring of fire he calls home — but thanks to the magic helmet, he has made himself look like his new best friend Gunther. "Gunther" rips the ring off Brünnhilde's finger, says that he's going to marry her, and carries her into the cave.

**Act II:** The servants prepare a wedding feast for Gunther and his new "bride." Brünnhilde, spotting the ring on Siegfried's finger, lashes out at him. Confused and angry, she even reveals to smarmy Hagen Siegfried's Achilles' heel: his *back*. Gunther has, by this time, figured out that Brünnhilde isn't thrilled about this new marriage. Hagen helpfully points out that if Gunther *kills* Siegfried, widow Brünnhilde will be free to marry again. As the wedding music swells, Brünnhilde and Gunther sing for revenge, and Hagen sings "At last, Alberich my father, you shall be lord of the ring!"

**Act III:** Siegfried, meanwhile, has run into, of all nymphs, the Rhinemaidens. They tell him about the ring: *"Schlimmes wissen wir dir"* ("Evil awaits you") — but he won't give it up. In that case, the nymphs predict, a woman will wind up with the ring by the end of the day — and *will* return it to them. They swim away ominously.

When the G-gang arrives, Siegfried tells them the whole story of his upbringing: *"Mime hiess ein mürrischer Zwerg"* ("Mime was a gnarly old dwarf"). Evil Hagen hands him an antidote to the original love potion, and suddenly Siegfried remembers his love for (and marriage to) Brünnhilde. Hagen finds that this as good a time as any to plunge his spear into Siegfried's back. Stricken with grief, Gunther and the servants carry the body, accompanied by deeply mournful music, back home.

Hagen grabs for the ring, Gunther grabs for Hagen, and they fight. Gunther falls dead. (*Man,* what a body count!) All curse Hagen for the love-potion business. Brünnhilde directs the servants to build a huge fire by the river, upon which she burns Siegfried's body. Then, after singing one of the longest arias ever written (17 minutes!), during which she yells out to the Rhinemaidens to grab the Ring out of the ashes, Brünnhilde jumps on her horse and leaps into the fire herself. The flames fill the stage, only to be put out by the river, which now overflows its banks. (Now you know why it's difficult to put on this show in a high school gym.) Hagen flails in the water, looking for the ring. But the nymphs already have it, and they drag him to a watery death.

The Rhinemaidens swim away joyously — but in the distant background, we can see the red glow of Valhalla, and all the gods who live there, passing away in flames. The Era of the Gods is over; now only love can rule the world.

# *Romeo and Juliet*

**Title translation:** *Roméo et Juliette.* **Music by:** Charles Gounod. **Libretto:** In French by Jules Barbier and Michel Carré, adapted from Shakespeare's play. **First performed:** Paris, France, 1887.

**What to look forward to:** A tragic, tragic tragedy in four acts.

**Astonishing trivia:** The librettists, Barbier and Carré, added a character to this well-known Shakespearean weeper. Stephano, Romeo's page, is their creation and — get this — *he's* a mezzo-soprano.

**Prologue:** We're in Verona in the 14th century, as in Shakespeare's original. The full cast sings *"Vérone vit jadis deux familles rivales"* ("There once were two rival families in Verona") about the world's most famous round of *The Family Feud:* the ongoing fight between the Capulets (Juliet's family) and the Montagues (Romeo's family), and the tragic love affair of their teenage offspring.

**The plot:** The opera's pretty faithful to the Shakespeare play, so we'll just summarize here. Romeo (a tenor) falls hard for the lovely, the radiant, the babe-alicious Juliet: *"Ange adorable"* ("Fair angel. . . . Don't move, sweetest saint!"). When Juliet comes to her balcony, they promise to love each other forever.

Friar Laurence is nice enough to marry two young lovers. Unfortunately, Juliet's cousin Tybalt kills Romeo's friend Mercutio; Romeo kills Tybalt. The Duke of Verona banishes Romeo from the city. Before he departs, R&J enjoy one night, their "wedding night, our sweetest night of love."

To avoid having to marry the guy she was *supposed* to marry, Juliet agrees to drink a vial of vile potion, provided by Friar Laurence, that will make her seem dead for 42 hours. She's laid out to rest in the family mortuary. She sure *seems* dead ( but if you look really carefully, you can see her breathing). But Romeo never gets the message about the plan; he enters the tomb room, sizes up the situation, and believes that Juliet is dead. Unable to face life without her, Romeo opens up a vial of his own — but *his* is *really* poison. He drinks, as luck would have it, just as Juliet wakes up. They sing a gorgeous duet; Romeo falls still.

Juliet can't live without Romeo, so she stabs herself. As they die together, they still find the energy to sing one more time, *"Seigneur, pardonnez-nous"* — "God, forgive us."

# *Der Rosenkavalier*

**Title translation:** *The Knight of the Rose.* **Music by:** Richard Strauss. **Libretto:** In German by Hugo Von Hofmannsthal. **First performed:** Dresden, Germany, 1911.

**What to look forward to:** A sparkling, bittersweet, waltzy romantic comedy in three acts — the most popular German opera of the 1900s. You may recall Richard Strauss as the composer of *Elektra,* a shocker about a murderous teenage-girl psycho, and *Salome,* a shocker about a necrophiliac teenage-girl sicko. In *Der Rosenkavalier,* there's no blood, no murder, and not even one nut-case teenager.

**Astonishing trivia:** Part of *Der Rosenkavalier*'s lasting popularity comes, no doubt, from the lilting Viennese waltzes that float through its score. Yes, that's right, Viennese waltzes — even though (a) *this* Strauss isn't the same guy as *Johann* Strauss, who wrote the famous waltzes, and (b) you're supposed to be hearing these waltzes played in the 1750s, when the opera takes place, long before the Viennese waltz had been invented!

**Act I:** Mezzo-soprano Octavian and soprano Princess Von Werdenberg are deeply in love. (It's not what you think. Octavian is supposed to be a teenage *boy*, although he's played by a woman.) Unfortunately, the Princess is married. As she and Octavian hear footsteps, Octavian hides and dresses up as a maid.

Fortunately, the arrival is only the Princess's cousin, the silly bass braggart Baron Ochs. Even though he's about to get married (to pretty teenage soprano Sophie), he flirts shamelessly with "maid" Octavian, even asking her/him/her out. The Princess has a busy morning: flute concert, hairdresser, chef, poor orphans, Italian tabloid reporters — the usual.

Baron Ochs hands the Princess a silver rose. He asks her to have it delivered to his bride-to-be, as is the tradition. Alone, the Princess sadly muses about her impending middle age — she's 32 — and her inevitable loss of Octavian, who's 17: *"Die Zeit, die ist ein sonderbar Ding"* ("Time is a very strange thing"). Octavian can't understand her sadness and leaves; the Princess sends her page boy after Octavian with the rose, for delivery to the Baron's fiancée.

**Act II:** Beautiful bride-to-be Sophie is excited about her wedding — and the traditional presentation of the silver rose. Octavian presents it to her in a glorious duet, and she, struck by this handsome cavalier, falls madly in love with him. (Oh, yeah — he's wearing his guy clothes now.)

Unfortunately, the Baron walks in on them and challenges Octavian to a duel. They fight; Octavian nicks the Baron's hand, to which the Baron reacts as though he's lost an arm. Sophie's disgusted with the fatuous middle-aged Baron and refuses to marry him. But her father, dollar signs dancing in his eyes, declares that she'll marry him or else enter a convent. Octavian's not finished yet, however; he sets a scheme in motion by delivering a note to the Baron from the Princess's "maid," whom the Baron asked out in the first act. The note promises him a date.

**Act III:** Octavian, in drag once again, has hired some Italian tabloid reporters to rig a hotel room with trap doors, trick windows, and other gadgetry. The Baron shows up for his hot date but rapidly turns into a blob of terrified, superstitious jelly as "ghosts" appear at the windows. The Baron, panicking, calls for the police. But not wanting to seem as though he's cheating on Sophie, he tells the cops that Octavian *is* Sophie. Unfortunately, the *real* Sophie now drops by; the Baron, painted into a corner, claims that he doesn't *know* her! She and her father call off the wedding in disgust.

The Princess arrives to straighten out the mess. Octavian reveals his true gender, to the Baron's great embarrassment, and shyly introduces his new girlfriend to his old, *old* one, the Princess. In a soaring trio, the Princess sings bittersweetly that she has lost Octavian sooner than she expected. She hooks up with Sophie's single father, and the young lovers sing *"Ist ein Traum, kann nicht wirklich sein"* ("It's a dream! It can't really be true!").

The Princess's little page boy runs on, having been sent back to find Sophie's dropped handkerchief. He retrieves it and runs off the stage. What does it mean? You tell us.

## Rusalka . . . See Chapter 13

# Salome

**Music by:** Richard Strauss. **Libretto:** In German by Oscar Wilde (translated by Hedwig Lachmann). **First performed:** Dresden, Germany, 1905.

**What to look forward to:** A one-act, shocking gore-fest. This one's the NC-17 opera — it has incest, striptease, murder, and dismemberment — and music to match. Don't look for a Disney remake anytime soon.

**Astonishing trivia:** As you can well imagine, audiences of 1905 were shocked by the subject matter of this cheery little tale. New York's Metropolitan Opera refused to present this show for 27 years.

**The plot:** It's A.D. 30. Cute, soprano teenager Salome ("ZAH-lo-may") is the ultimate problem child. As she strolls across the plaza of her stepfather Herod's palace, she hears the baritone voice of a prisoner coming from the well in which he's imprisoned. It's none other than Bible celeb John the Baptist. Salome thinks he's cute. She persuades the reluctant guards to let her meet the prisoner, who's even better-looking up close.

Unfortunately, John wants nothing to do with this Valley-of-Death Girl. His guard, madly in love with Salome, can't deal with her attempts to kiss the prisoner and promptly kills himself. Nobody's more irritated with the guard's death than tenor Herod; good help is so hard to find.

To soothe his stress, Herod asks sexy Salome to dance for him. She continues to resist until, desperately in lust, Herod promises her anything she asks. Manipulative Salome now performs the most famous striptease in opera: the "Dance of the Seven Veils." As she dances, she removes the seven scarves in which she's dressed, one by one, reducing Herod to a panting mass of desire. And now she asks her price: She'd like John the Baptist's decapitated head on a silver platter. Herod splutters in disgust. Won't she take jewels? Riches? The car all next week? Not a chance; Salome knows what she wants. Reluctantly, Herod agrees.

The gory head is duly presented to Salome. Just in case there are one or two audience members who haven't yet lost their lunches, she kisses the bloody head's lips and runs her hands over it, singing crazily about how good-looking it is.

Herod has had quite enough. He commands his soldiers to crush Salome to death with their shields, which they're only too happy to do.

Another *Brady Bunch* episode we'll never see.

## Siegfried . . . Look under Ring Cycle

# Tales of Hoffmann

**Title translation:** *Les Contes d'Hoffmann.* **Music by:** Jacques Offenbach. **Libretto:** In French by Jules Barbier and Michel Carré, based on the stories of E.T.A. Hoffmann. **First performed:** Paris, France, 1881.

**What to look forward to:** Three bizarre, back-to-back stories of bitter disillusionment, plus a Prologue and an Epilogue.

**Astonishing trivia:** As you can read in Chapter 6, Offenbach was the satire king, writing side-splittingly funny operettas that mocked prominent French institutions. But he wanted to write one successful serious opera before he died; *Tales of Hoffmann* was it. Unfortunately, he never got to see the show; he died during rehearsals. Someone else finished the rehearsals, doing major restructuring, omitting an act, and generally messing with the thing. Offenbach's original work is often restored, but you may see any of numerous different versions.

**Prologue:** Evil bass Lindorf and a servant come into a bar. The servant bears a letter from a singer named Stella who's performing at the opera house next door. Lindorf buys the letter from the servant for 40 thalers (of course, a thaler went a lot farther in those days). In the letter, Stella invites the poet named Hoffmann up to her room after the show. Lindorf grins evilly.

Rowdy students sing: *"Drig! drig! drig! à nous ta bière, à nous ton vin"* ("Drig! drig! drig! We want more beer, we want more wine"). The students have dropped by the bar between acts of *Don Giovanni,* which is being performed next door. Hoffmann (a tenor) arrives with his friend Nicklausse (a mezzo-soprano — but the character's meant to be male); Hoffmann reveals that he's depressed from seeing his old flame, Stella, onstage.

When the students ask him to sing something, Hoffmann sings a nutty number about Kleinzach, a hunchbacked jester. After much drinking, Hoffmann agrees to tell the crowd about his last three girlfriends (in each of the opera's three acts). The students, riveted, don't even care that they're going to miss the rest of *Don Giovanni.* (In each act, evil bass magician Lindorf appears as a different character, but always evil and always magical. For sanity's sake, we'll keep calling him Lindorf.

**Act I (Olympia):** A mad-scientist type, Spalanzani (a tenor), has a life-sized, wind-up, gorgeous robot doll named Olympia. Our pal Hoffmann falls madly in love with Olympia, despite sidekick Nicklausse's warnings. Creepy Lindorf, vendor of eye-related gadgetry, sells Hoffmann some X-ray specs that make Olympia look even more attractive. Lindorf has also sold Spalanzani a pair of eyeballs for Olympia; Spalanzani writes a check to cover their purchase.

When the party guests arrive, the Olympia doll sings, rather mechanically, the famous *"Les oiseaux dans la charmille"* ("The birds in the bushes"). Lovestruck Hoffmann sings to her, woos her — but when he tries to hold her hand, he inadvertently releases some kind of clutch; she runs around madly. Nicklausse warns him that though Olympia seems like a real doll, she's also a *real doll.*

Evil Lindorf bursts in — Spalanzani's check has bounced! Olympia is dancing, faster and faster, losing control, singing higher and faster, until finally she's put away in her room. Suddenly we hear the sound of machinery breaking. Lindorf emerges from Olympia's room, laughing evilly. Hoffmann runs to Olympia's room in a panic, returning a moment later, heartbroken, carrying a piece of Robo-Olympia. The guests laugh at him.

**Act II (Antonia):** Pretty Antonia Crespel (the same soprano who played Olympia) is, like so many opera heroines, dying of tuberculosis. When she finishes a sad song, her father (a baritone) yells at her (because singing weakens her). Mr. Crespel tries to tell old, deaf servant Frantz (the same tenor who plays every servant) that nobody's allowed to see Antonia.

Hoffmann arrives and joins Antonia in a love duet, which only makes her sicker. Her father enters, accompanied by the evil Dr. Lindorf, who magically makes Antonia start singing high notes. Hoffmann begs her not to sing. But Dr. Lindorf grabs a violin, driving Antonia into more and more frenzied singing — and, sure enough, Antonia dies.

**Act III (Giulietta):** At a party in Venice, from offstage, we hear a tune that has taunted the fingers of third-year piano students for generations — the "Barcarolle":

| | |
|---|---|
| *Belle nuit, ô nuit d'amour* | Beautiful night, night of love |
| *Souris à nos ivresses,* | Smile on our rapture |
| *Nuit plus douce que le jour* | Sweeter than day |
| *Ô belle nuit d'amour* | O beautiful night of love |

Hoffmann's friend Nicklausse enters with a fabulous beauty, Giulietta (whom you may recognize as Olympia), who is, ahem, a "lady of the *nuit.*" When she sits next to Hoffmann, Giulietta's lover Schlemil (a bass) becomes insanely jealous. (He's a real schlemiel.)

Magician Lindorf appears, describing his evil plans: Hoffmann will fall for Giulietta, and Giulietta will somehow cause Schlemil's death. To help him, he'll use his huge, magical diamond: "Shine, diamond, mirror that can capture the lark!"

Using the diamond, Lindorf tells Giulietta to get Hoffman's *reflection* for his collection. Despite his earlier protests, Hoffmann falls hard for her, even agreeing to give away his reflection just so that they can get on to singing a love duet.

Schlemil and Hoffmann fight over the key to Giulietta's room. Because he's using evil Lindorf's sword, Hoffmann kills his opponent and seizes the room key. Unfortunately, it's too late: Giulietta is in a gondola with another boyfriend, sailing slowly away.

**Epilogue:** We're back in the bar. Hoffmann tells the students that that's the end of the story (*"Voilà quelle fut l'histoire"*). Nicklausse figures out that Hoffmann's three loves are really all Stella, the opera singer. Suddenly, the Muse of Poetry (a soprano) arrives — another incarnation of Nicklause, who for a few moments turns into a girl — telling Hoffmann to devote himself to her and his art instead of women.

A stellar beauty, Stella, enters the bar. Sure enough, she's the same woman Hoffmann has idealized in each of his tales. But Hoffmann is nearly comatose with drunkenness. When evil Lindorf walks out of the room with Stella, she tosses a flower to Hoffmann — but he's in too much of a stupor to respond.

# *Tannhäuser*

**Music and Libretto:** In German by Richard Wagner. **First performed:** Dresden, Germany, 1845.

**What to look forward to:** A religious tragedy in three acts. Watch for the ballet to end all ballets at the beginning of the show, and tune in to the lengthy overture, which tells the entire story of the opera in wordless melodies.

**Astonishing trivia:** The story of *Tannhäuser*'s opening night in Paris could be an opera in itself. As you can read in Chapter 6, every opera performed in Paris in the 1800s was expected to feature a ballet in the second act. This ballet was as customary as fireworks on the Fourth of July. The trendy Jockey Club social-group members counted on this ballet beginning just as they returned from dinner, never mind that they'd already missed half the plot.

Wagner grudgingly wrote a big dance number for *Tannhäuser* — but he put it in the *first* act, where it made sense in the story. The wrath of the socialites, who arrived at 10 p.m. to discover that they'd missed the ballet section, was sure and swift; they jeered and booed. The opera closed after three nights and wasn't seen again in Paris for 35 years.

**Act I:** It's the 1200s. In her palace inside the Venusberg mountain, soprano Venus, Goddess of Love, holds the party to end all parties: hunky teenagers, satyrs, fauns, sirens, and nymphs wildly dance, drink, and seduce each other, ignoring the wall-thumping of the neighbors.

Tannhäuser, a singing knight, has been Venus's love toy for some time, but he's growing antsy for the more unpredictable life back down on earth; after all, how much dazzling beauty, unlimited food, great music, and sex with a goddess can a man take? Venus is furious. "You'll be back," she snipes.

Tannhäuser teleports down to earth. In a beautiful valley, Tannhäuser's old friends, led by Hermann, wander in. "Where've you been?" they ask. Tannhäuser mutters something about needing to find himself. Wolfram, a fellow minstrel knight, invites him back home, where Hermann's pretty soprano niece, Elisabeth — Tannhäuser's virtuous ex-girlfriend — would love to see him.

**Act II:** At Hermann's house, competitors are getting ready for a singing contest; the winner gets to marry Elisabeth. (What *is* it with Wagner and singing contests with female prizes?) Elisabeth is delighted to see her ex, Tannhäuser; they sing a rapturous duet.

The contest begins; the choir bids the contestants a noble welcome. Hermann announces the theme of the singing contest: love. After an endless assortment of love songs, though, Tannhäuser bursts out the fatal aria, *"Dir, Göttin der Liebe,"* which boils down to: "Listen, you people don't know what love *is* until you've had sex with Venus!"

The crowd is shocked — *shocked,* we tell you. The men leap forward to kill him. But Elisabeth, though heartbroken, begs forgiveness for Tannhäuser's stupid comment. Hermann says he'll forgive Tannhäuser if the Pope forgives him, too. Feeling sorry already, Tannhäuser starts out for the Pope's place in Rome.

**Act III:** Months later, Elisabeth's still waiting for Tannhäuser's return. Wolfram, Tannhäuser's friend who's always loved Elisabeth from afar, waits with her for the latest group of pilgrims to arrive from Rome. When they appear, Elisabeth scans the group anxiously, but doesn't find Tannhäuser. Broken-hearted, she walks slowly up the mountain to her home. Wolfram sings the famous "Song to the Evening Star," asking the star to guide Elisabeth's way.

Tannhäuser returns, but he's a basket case: haggard and broken, unshaven and grubby. After all the trouble he went to getting to Rome — climbing dangerous rocks and mountains and skipping all kinds of meals — his reward was the Pope's none-too-charitable crack, "Yeah, right — I'll forgive *you,* pal, when my cane sprouts leaves!"

Depressed, Tannhäuser decides that maybe a little unlimited goddess sex will cheer him up; he starts heading back to Venus's place, her face like a vision before him. Wolfram begs him not to go. When he says the name Elisabeth, Tannhäuser pauses. Venus, furious that he'd even consider dating some pathetic earthling, disappears. But ringing bells announce that Elisabeth has died. Tannhäuser, having managed to lose both women simultaneously, collapses and dies. At this moment, who should arrive but a religious group that carries the Pope's cane — covered with bright green leaves. Tannhäuser's off the hook at last.

# Tosca

**Music by:** Giacomo Puccini. **Libretto:** In Italian by Giuseppe Giacosa and Luigi Illaca. **First performed:** Rome, Italy, 1900.

**What to look forward to:** A violent melodrama in three acts. Yes, there's onstage torture, murder, suicide, and betrayal, but it's Puccini — fabulous melodies, full of emotion.

**Astonishing trivia:** At the end of the story, heroine Tosca is supposed to leap to her death from the roof of the prison. Fortunately for the singer, most productions equip the stage floor, behind the set, with a huge trampoline/mattress to cushion her fall so that she may live to sing the next performance. In more than one production, however, a miscalculation involving the bounciness of the trampoline has sent poor Tosca, after leaping to her death, bouncing back into view above the prison wall.

**Act I:** In Rome, 1800, a political prisoner named Angelotti (baritone) escapes from his cell. He makes a beeline for the church where his old friend, Mario Cavaradossi (a tenor painter), works. Mario carries around his neck the picture of his true love, Tosca, whose features have a "strange harmony" (*"Recondita armonia"*).

Fugitive Angelotti asks Mario for help. Mario gives him directions to a hiding place just as girlfriend Floria Tosca, a soprano (no, really — she's a professional singer in this story), arrives. She's suspicious and jealous of the pretty blonde model for his Virgin Mary painting. Nothing to worry about, he tells her in a long (but gorgeous) duet; nobody could be more beautiful than Tosca.

**Figure 12-12:** *Tosca:* Sherrill Milnes as Scarpia, Renata Scotto in the title role, Lyric Opera of Chicago, 1987–88 season (photo: Tony Romano).

The church choir rehearsal is interrupted by the arrival of Scarpia, baritone police chief, who's so loathsome and cruel that he makes Darth Vader look like a soup-kitchen worker. Hot on the trail of escapee Angelotti, Scarpia quickly finds the food basket Mario has provided to the fugitive. Evil Scarpia talks Tosca into believing that Mario is having an affair with the beauty in the painting. Tosca leaves, sobbing. The act ends with an elaborate choral finale (*"Te Deum"*), in which Scarpia vows to capture Tosca for himself.

**Act II:** Scarpia sends a note, as bait, to Tosca; it says that he has news of her boyfriend. *"Ella verrà,"* he gloats ("She will come"). His lackeys capture Mario and bring him in just as Tosca arrives. Evil Scarpia begins torturing Mario, promising to continue until Tosca reveals the fugitive Angelotti's hideout. Horrified by her beau's moans from the torture room, Tosca spills the beans: Angelotti is hiding in an old dried-up well in the garden. Mario is released from torture, but he's furious with her for having squealed.

Scarpia orders his men to shoot Mario before the firing squad — but tells Tosca that if she'll sleep with him, Scarpia will save Mario's life. In her most famous aria, she turns to God, pleading, *"Vissi d'arte, vissi d'amore"* ("I have lived for art and love"); how can she deserve this treatment?

After all this, the fugitive Angelotti turns out to have killed himself to avoid capture, but Scarpia still demands sex from Tosca in exchange for her beloved's life. (That's *one* way to get a date.) She reluctantly agrees. Scarpia instructs his men to arrange a phony execution for Mario. But as he closes in on her trembling body, she stabs him with a knife she'd swiped from the table. *"Here's* Tosca's kiss!" she cries.

With *that* little inconvenience out of the way, Tosca checks her hair, positions candles next to Scarpia's body and a crucifix on its chest, and hits the road.

**Act III:** Mario is told that he has one hour before his execution. But Tosca shows up, fills him in on her date from hell, tells him that the firing squad will be shooting blanks, and instructs him to lie perfectly still as though he's really been shot. They sing a sweet duet about their hopeful future, and then the firing squad does its thing. Mario falls to the ground. *Wow,* is he a realistic actor: *"Ecco un artista!"* ("What an artist!"), Tosca exclaims.

But when the coast is clear, he remains much too lifelike in his lifelessness. Tosca gives an ear-splitting shriek of horror as she discovers that sinister Scarpia has had his revenge from beyond the grave: He told the firing squad to stage a *fake* fake execution — to *actually* kill Mario. Devastated, and with the police running up the stairs to arrest her for Scarpia's murder, Tosca runs to the edge of the rooftop and leaps to her death. (You can listen to this entire exciting conclusion on the CD that comes with this book; see Chapter 11 for all the lyrics and a complete description.)

# La Traviata

**Title translation:** *The Fallen Woman.* **Music by:** Giuseppe Verdi. **Libretto:** In Italian by Francesco Piave. **First performed:** Venice, Italy, 1853.

**What to look forward to:** A romantic tragedy in three acts. *Pretty Woman* meets *La Bohème:* A high-priced prostitute is forced to give up the only man she ever loved, and then she dies of TB. Based on a true story.

**Astonishing trivia:** As with many now-classic operas, *La Traviata* was a dismal failure on opening night. The audience was confused by the costumes, which were modern-day clothing rather than the period garb featured in most operas. The leading tenor lost his voice, and the soprano — meant to play a frail little thing dying of tuberculosis — looked more like the Michelin Tire man. A year later, the opera was produced again in the same city — this time to thunderous applause.

**Act I:** Paris, 1840s or 1700s, or whenever the director feels like. Violetta, a high-class soprano hooker, is hosting some Paris high-lifers at her house. Aside from her occasional hacking coughs that *La Bohème* fans will immediately recognize as tuberculosis, everyone's having a great time. A nice young tenor named Alfredo introduces himself as a longtime fan — more than that, really; he's mad about her. When the party's over, she wonders if he's "the one I've dreamed of" (*"Ah, fors' è lui"*). If so (she sings, launching into an aria that's a celebrity in its own right), maybe now she can finally be free (*"Sempre libera"*) of her present tawdry lifestyle.

**Act II:** Violetta and Alfredo are a match made in heaven, shacking up together in a little country house. But when Violetta sells off horses, carriages, and other possessions to pay for living expenses, Alfredo's horrified and ashamed; he rushes downtown to get money to reimburse her.

Alfredo's father pays Violetta a visit and chews her out for having seduced and ruined a perfectly good young man. This relationship, he says, is scandalizing the family and jeopardizing the upcoming marriage of Alfredo's *sister* to a snooty nobleman. Violetta, through her tears, sings *"Dite alla giovine"* ("Tell your daughter") — she agrees to give up Alfredo for the sake of his family's reputation. (*Clearly* this show could never be plausibly set in the modern-day United States.) She writes a "Dear Alfredo" letter.

When Alfredo returns, he tells Violetta that his father is coming to visit, completely in the dark about her meeting with him. Pretending that she'd rather not be around for the confrontation, she bids him an emotional *"Amami, Alfredo"* ("Love me, Alfredo") and then departs. Now he finds her breakup letter, and he breaks up. His father arrives and consoles him. But when Alfredo finds a party invitation addressed to her, he assumes that she's ditching him to return to her fast-lane lifestyle in the city. His grief turns to anger, and he vows revenge.

Cut to the party itself, in full swing. Violetta, now on the arm of an old boyfriend, Baron Duphol, is shocked to see that Alfredo has burst in and is winning a fortune at cards. He challenges the edgy Baron to a game and wins again: "Unlucky in love, lucky at cards!" Violetta begs him not to make trouble, but, having promised to conceal her real reason for dumping him, pretends that she actually loves the Baron. At this point, Alfredo's a few fries short of a Happy Meal. In front of all the guests, he heaps abuse on Violetta, shouting, "I call on you all to witness that I'm paying her back!" He throws his gambling winnings in her face. She faints. Alfredo's father denounces him. The Baron challenges him to a duel.

**Act III:** Violetta's misery has accelerated her illness. She reads in a letter that the Baron was wounded in the duel and that Alfredo is on the run. Despite the doctor's white lies, the mirror tells Violetta that her days are numbered. "Farewell to the past," she sings (*"Addio del passato"*).

Alfredo bursts in, begging forgiveness. Her strength seems to return, and they plan a quiet country life together, "far from gay Paris" (*"Parigi, o cara"*). Alfredo's father arrives and *finally* realizes that he's responsible for all this misery. It's all a tragic fakeout, however; a moment later, she gives Alfredo a locket containing her picture, encourages him to marry some pure young girl, and dies.

# Tristan and Isolde

**Title translation:** *Tristan und Isolde.* **Music and Libretto:** In German by Richard Wagner. **First performed:** Munich, Germany, 1865.

**What to look forward to:** The most romantic love tragedy on record, in three acts. Based on an actual legend. Overwhelming music of passion and love.

**Astonishing trivia:** As you can read in Chapter 8, Wagner's life wasn't what you'd call a party cruise; for decades, he was broke, exiled, and unsuccessful in everything he touched. At his lowest point, money from a woman named Mathilde Wesendonck tided him over. Wagner fell madly, hopelessly, insanely in love with her — after all, she was beautiful, rich, and married. *Tristan and Isolde* was Wagner's way of channeling the pain and longing of his unattainable love into his work.

**The backstory:** Here's what has gone on before the plot begins. In a battle, Sir Tristan killed a man but got wounded in the process. When he didn't get better, his HMO authorized him to visit a specialist — sorceress Isolde of Ireland. Bad news: The man Tristan killed was her *fiancé.* Good news: She fell in love with Tristan and healed him. They didn't reveal to each other that they were in love, however.

As part of a treaty to end the war between Ireland and Cornwall, soprano Isolde's hand in marriage was given to Cornwall's King Mark — and who should be sent to collect her but Tristan.

**Act I:** Tristan's ship is carrying Isolde back to Cornwall to meet her new husband, King Mark. Horrified at the prospect of a loveless marriage, and livid that tenor Tristan is ignoring her, Isolde is a few peas short of a casserole; she decides that she and Tristan shall both die. She has her servant, Brangäne, bring over her bag of potions, and she picks out a fast-acting poison.

Isolde hands Tristan a beverage, and she suggests that they drink to forgiveness. Instead of falling to the deck as corpses, however, Tristan and Isolde are suddenly all over each other, fueled by raging hormones. Servant Brangäne, thinking she was doing everyone a favor, substituted a love potion for the poison!

**Act II:** Isolde is married to King Mark now, but has been carrying on a delicious affair with Tristan every night. As the act begins, her husband's off hunting. Isolde puts out the torch at her doorway, which is her secret signal to Tristan. Servant Brangäne is nervous — this "hunting trip" could be a ruse planned by Melot, King Mark's evil assistant — but, this being opera,

Isolde doesn't listen. Tristan joins her and, in case we're not yet convinced of their love, they sing a *40-minute* love duet: *"O sink' hernieder, Nacht der Liebe!"* ("Descend upon us, night of love!")

But King Mark returns, lashes into Tristan for his deceit, and stands by as evil Melot runs Tristan through with a sword.

**Act III:** In his ancient castle overlooking the sea, Tristan wakes from a coma. Unfortunately, Tristan doesn't remember anything — except that he loves somebody named Isolde. His servant Kurwenal reassures Tristan that she's on her way. Tristan becomes delirious, imagining that he sees her ship already, and then collapses from exhaustion.

After more bouts of fever, Tristan really *does* see a ship; Isolde is on the deck, waving. Kurwenal goes down to meet her. Isolde enters, but at this point, Tristan doesn't have all his dogs on one leash; he speaks to the *torch* as though it's Isolde. Strength gone, he collapses into her arms and dies with a final heart-rending gasp: "Isolde!" She can't revive him, and she passes out.

But now another ship arrives: It's King Mark's. Assuming that the king has come to attack Tristan's castle for revenge, Tristan's staff prepares a defense. Kurwenal starts by killing evil Melot, then kills other members of King Mark's staff, and then is killed himself.

But King Mark is here on friendly terms, not hostile ones; "Wake up, Tristan! Hear my grief!" he cries. Servant Brangäne finally reveals the truth: A love-potion made them do it. King Mark, abashed and saddened, apologizes profusely. "Hear that, Isolde?" says Brangäne — but Isolde, in a trance, sings the opera's most famous aria — the *Liebestod* ("Love-Death") number that ends the show. (You can hear it right now; it's on this book's free CD. Follow along in Chapter 11.)

She's carried away, transported, as the music swells in intensity and glory — and then she dies, collapsing on Tristan's body.

# *Il Trovatore*

**Title translation:** *The Troubadour.* **Music by:** Giuseppe Verdi. **Libretto:** In Italian by Salvatore Cammarano. **First performed:** Rome, Italy, 1853.

**What to look forward to:** An action-packed romantic tragedy in four acts. Few operas have spawned so many famous melodies, and few move along with so much action, fighting, and emotion. All the good guys die at the end, but hey — it's opera.

**Astonishing trivia:** If the experts agree on anything, it's that *Il Trovatore* has the most convoluted plot in opera. But so many songs from this show have become classics that 150 years of fans haven't cared a bit.

**The backstory:** Decades before the opera begins, a Gypsy stole into a nobleman's house and touched one of two baby boys. The baby grew sick. Thinking that the Gypsy had bewitched him, the nobleman's family burned her at the stake.

Her vengeful daughter kidnapped the sick baby, planning to throw him into the bonfire where her mom had just been burned. But, having been through a horrible 24 hours, she was one Fruit Loop shy of a full bowl, and she accidentally threw her *own* baby into the fire. Whoops.

She raised the Count's baby as her own, still plotting revenge on his family all the while. The baby grew up to become Manrico the Troubador, who little suspects that the wealthy Count di Luna is his separated-at-birth brother. Cut to the present day (15th-century Spain). Each of the opera's acts has its own subtitle.

**Act I (The Duel):** At baritone Count di Luna's palace, beautiful soprano Leonora tells a friend about her new love interest: the mysterious knight in black armor who recently serenaded her — the Troubador.

Unfortunately, Count di Luna also loves Leonora. He demands to know who the heck this Troubadour is. It's Manrico, an officer in the enemy army, forbidden on the palace grounds. Manrico and the Count rush away to have a swordfight. In the time-honored tradition of opera heroines, Leonora faints.

**Act II (The Gypsy):** Around a Gypsy campfire, Black Knight Manrico joins his mother the bonfire-baby-tosser, now an old lady. The other Gypsies, pounding on their metal, sing the tune that you'd recognize if we could hum it to you, "The Anvil Chorus" (*"Chi del gitano i giorni abbella?"*). Dreamily, Manrico's old mom (a mezzo-soprano) tells *her* version of her own mother's horrible death:

| | |
|---|---|
| *Stride la vampa!* | The flames burn fiercely! |
| *La folla indomita* | The wild, eager crowd |
| *Corre a quel fuoco* | Runs forward, yelling and screaming |
| *Lieta in sembianza* | For vengeance. |

Manrico naturally wonders: If mom threw her real son into the fire, then whose son is *he*? She changes the subject, scolding him for not killing Count di Luna in the swordfight.

A messenger brings two news items. First, Manrico's been put in charge of the newly captured Castellor fortress; second, Leonora thinks that he's dead, so she's going to become a nun. Manrico rushes away to stop her. But Count di Luna has had the same idea, also arriving at the convent. The Count's men and Manrico's men fight, and Leonora is carried away by her Knight in Non-Shining Armor.

**Act III (The Gypsy's Son):** Count di Luna's men are attacking Manrico's palace to rekidnap Leonora. Amid the chaos, an old Gypsy woman has been captured — Manrico's mom. In panic, she calls out her son's name (*"O Manrico, o figlio mio"*). Count di Luna realizes that he has caught his enemy's mother and vows double vengeance.

Inside the fortress, Black Knight Manrico and Leonora prepare for their wedding, trying to enjoy their special day despite the army attacking outside. Suddenly, out the window, Manrico sees the Count leading his mother to a stake for burning. The wedding will just have to wait; there's not a moment to spare! First, however, Manrico takes a few moments to sing of his anger, *"Di quella pira"* ("Of that horrible pyre") — before rushing out to rescue his Gypsy mom.

**Act IV (The Torture):** Manrico lost. He and his mother are chained up in the Count's castle, soon to be burned at the stake. Leonora arrives, hoping to rescue her true love: *"D'amor sull'ali rosee"* ("The horrible fire of the pyre"). As preparations are made to kill Manrico, the choir sings a famous funeral chant, *"Miserere."*

Leonora offers the Count the ultimate incentive for releasing Manrico: her hand in marriage. That's an offer he can't refuse; too bad he doesn't see her gulp down poison from her secret decoder ring.

In the dungeon, Manrico's mother dreads dying by barbecue, just like *her* mother. Manrico, in a tender duet, tries to console her, recalling their happy home in the mountains (*"Ai nostri monti"*). She falls asleep.

Leonora bursts in and tells Manrico that he's free. When her poison starts to kick in, he realizes that she's made the ultimate sacrifice, and he's stricken with grief. The Count gets what's happening, too — he's been gypped out of a wife. Leonora dies in Manrico's arms.

The Count drags Manrico away to be beheaded. Manrico's mother wakes up and learns that her son is now the *late* Manrico. She shrieks that, at last, *her* mother is avenged — the Count has just killed his own brother (*"Egli era tuo fratello"*)!

Whoops.

# *Turandot*

**Music by:** Giacomo Puccini. **Libretto:** In Italian by Giuseppe Adami and Renato Simoni. **First performed:** Milan, Italy, 1926.

**What to look forward to:** A romantic happy-ender in three acts, with just a pinch of tragedy.

**Astonishing trivia:** *Turandot* ("toor-ahn-DOTE") was Puccini's last opera. Correction: His last 90 percent of an opera; he died before writing the big final duet. This number was composed by somebody else, just to get the thing finished. At the premiere, Toscanini, the conductor, stopped the music abruptly and told the audience, "Here the Maestro put down his pen."

**Figure 12-13:** *Turandot:* Gabriele Schnaut in the title role, Ben Heppner as Calaf, Lyric Opera of Chicago, 1996-97 (photo: Dan Rest).

**Act I:** There's a crowd at the Imperial Palace in Peking, China. They've gathered to hear how gorgeous Princess Turandot's latest blind date went. This is no idle gossip; if a guy doesn't pass her test, he gets his head chopped off. And *her* tests aren't the usual "What line of work are you in?" and "How's your hygiene?" Instead, she asks three impossible riddles. If the suitor doesn't answer all three correctly, there's no second date — ever.

The news is good from the crowd's perspective: The latest sucker, the prince of Persia, is to be beheaded at moonrise.

Pushing through the crowd is an old blind man and Liù, his slave girl. We learn that he's King Timur, the overthrown king of rival country Tartary. In the middle of the bloodthirsty crowd, King Timur runs into, of all people, his own long-lost son Calaf, whom he'd thought was dead. Yet no one must know; if the evil Chinese learn that King Timur has a son, they'll certainly want to kill him, too.

When Princess Turandot appears to condemn the poor Persian prince to the ax, Calaf is instantly smitten; she's *really* a fox. Over the protests of his father and Liù, Calaf decides to enter the contest for Turandot's love. Three of Turandot's staff, Ping, Pang, and Pong, also try to dissuade him. But Calaf doesn't listen to them. (Would *you* listen to people named Ping, Pang, and Pong?)

**Act II:** In the palace, the princess explains how she got to be such an ice queen. Many years ago, her ancestor was raped by some evil Tartars. Ever since, Turandot has sought vengeance against mankind.

She asks Calaf her three riddles. Don't get your hopes up for anything witty; they're along the lines of, "Question: What's born every night and dies every day? Answer: Hope." Anyway, Calaf manages to answer all three correctly, much to hostile Turandot's alarm. Now she has to — ick — *marry* this guy, and probably even *touch* him.

But Calaf offers her a bonus round. If she can find out his name in the next 24 hours, she gets to decapitate him anyway. No problem for the princess of Sangfroid: She simply rules that nobody in Peking will go to bed until somebody gives up his name.

**Act III:** As Peking becomes the City that Never Sleeps, Calaf sings, *"Nessun dorma"* ("None shall sleep") — an astoundingly famous aria which has become the Three Tenors' most famous encore. He remains confident that nobody, all-nighters or not, will guess his name. The Ping-Pong trio offers him money, women, or an escape route if he'll tell them the answer, but he declines.

Turandot's guards capture King Timur and the slave Liù, having seen them with Calaf, and claim that they'll torture the old man until he reveals Calaf's name. Noble Liù, not wanting her master to feel pain, steps forward: "I know his name, and *only* I know it." They torture her to no avail; finally, at the end of her strength, warm, sweet Liù rips into cold, hard Turandot: *"Tu, che di gel sei cinta"* ("You, encased in ice!") — and then kills herself with a dagger. (This is where Puccini's own music wraps up, by the way.)

Calaf takes this moment of confusion to kiss Turandot hard. The ice queen melts in his mouth. She falls into his arms, sobbing. Confident that her personality makeover is complete, Calaf reveals his name. Princess Turandot, a softie now and forevermore, tells the assembled crowd: "I now know the stranger's secret. His name is *Love*."

*Twilight of the Gods . . . Look under Ring Cycle*

*Un Ballo in Maschera . . . Look under A Masked Ball*

*The Valkyrie . . . Look under Ring Cycle*

*Die Walküre . . . Look under Ring Cycle*

# Chapter 13

# The Best of the Rest

## In This Chapter

▶ The plots of 24 more operas

▶ An introduction to more recent operas

*I*n Chapter 12, you can read about the 50 most frequently performed operas — the ones you're most likely to run across on TV or in the theater. Just to make sure that you're covered, though, here are 24 of the next wave. These operas aren't performed as often, but don't let that fool you; most of them are absolute masterpieces.

You may notice that several of these operas are fairly recent, complete with what people call *modern* classical music. At first, this kind of music strikes most people as — well, let's just say that it strikes most people. But don't forget: Even Beethoven was considered avant garde in his time. This stuff really grows on you, so give it a try.

The following summaries include the vital statistics and just the spine of the plot — enough for you to decide whether or not it's for you.

# *Andrea Chénier*

**Vital stats:** Music by Umberto Giordano, libretto in Italian by Luigi Illica. An 1896 historical tragedy in four acts; based on the story of André Chénier, a poet and a dreamer during the French Revolution.

**The plot:** At a fancy party, special poet guest Chénier shocks the guests (and pretty Madeleine) with a poem that viciously condemns the upper class. As the perfect ending to a ruined evening, hostile servant Gérard lets a handful of grubby beggars into the party. The hostess, horrified, fires him on the spot.

Shortly thereafter, Chénier waits in a café to meet the secret admirer who's been writing him perfumed letters. (**Hint:** It's Madeleine.) At last she arrives. They sing a passionate love duet — until ex-servant Gérard, now a Revolution mob leader, raging with jealousy, uses his power to have Chénier arrested.

Madeleine offers her heart to Gérard in exchange for Chénier's freedom, but the mob is not to be persuaded; they sentence Chénier to death for his radical views. But *wow,* does she love him; she actually bribes the prison guard to let her take the place of a woman scheduled for death in the morning. Now she and her beloved Chénier may be together at last, if only in the grave. (Clearly, Madeleine has seen *Aïda.*) As she and Chénier await the dawn, they sing happily together: "Death comes with the morning. Happy is my lot!"

# Arabella

**Vital stats:** Music by Richard Strauss, German libretto by Hugo von Hofmannsthal. A 1933 romantic drama in three acts.

**The plot:** Count Waldner, a gambler, is broke. His only hope is to marry off his gorgeous soprano daughter, Arabella, to somebody rich. It doesn't occur to him that Zdenka, his *other* soprano daughter, may be useful — because, having wanted a boy, Mr. Waldner *raised* Zdenka as a male (named Zdenko), therapy costs be damned. Besides, Arabella doesn't *care* about being rich; she just wants to meet Mr. Right, singing *"Aber der Richtige"* (which is on Track 11 of the CD in this book).

Poor officer-tenor Matteo is madly in love with Arabella, no thanks to Zdenka, who's been fueling his ardor with phony letters from "Arabella." Arabella soon has a dream suitor: Mandryka, who's rich *and* good-looking *and* adores her. In the second act, Arabella's the belle of the ball, dancing with lucky Mandryka. Sister Zdenka's up to her usual tricks, however, giving poor Matteo another phony letter "from Arabella" — this one includes the key to her hotel room.

Mandryka, having learned about the seductive letter "from Arabella," is horrified that she's making moves on another man. The next morning, Mandryka calls off the romance and challenges Matteo to a duel. Fortunately, Zdenka reveals that *she* wrote the letter to Matteo and included the key to her *own* room. Matteo, having taken advantage of "Arabella's" key, unwittingly slept with *Zdenka!* Now, of course, he has to marry her, while Arabella gets the rich hunk she's always wanted.

# The Bartered Bride

**Vital stats:** Music by Bedřich Smetana, libretto in Czech by Karel Sabina. An 1866 comedy in three acts.

**The plot:** Pretty soprano Marenka is madly in love with handsome tenor Jenik — a bummer, because the marriage broker has arranged for her to marry fatuous drunk Vasek, son of rich Micha. But hero Jenik has a plan. In exchange for 300 crowns from the marriage broker — a lot of money in those days — Jenik agrees to back off and allow the arranged match to proceed. He signs a contract saying that Marenka shall marry Micha's son, and nobody else.

Following much hilarity involving fatuous Vasek wearing a bear costume at a traveling circus — and falling for the woman tightrope walker — Marenka's parents call everyone to the moment of truth. But surprise! Hero Jenik *is* Micha's son, by a previous marriage. Who knew? The parents give their blessing, and everyone's happy except the marriage broker, who's out 300 crowns.

# Billy Budd

**Vital stats:** Music by Benjamin Britten, libretto in English by E.M. Forster and Eric Crozier, based on Herman Melville's short story. A 1951 psychological sea drama, with an all-male cast, in four acts. Talk about No Soprano Zones!

**The plot:** Old Captain Vere has an opera-long flashback, remembering the days when he captained a ship in the 1797 war against the French. We watch his flashback now: His sailors, singing sea chantey after sea chantey, board another ship, the *Rights o' Man,* and "enlist" (by force) some new recruits. Among them: our hero, Billy Budd.

Billy bids farewell to his old ship by singing, "Farewell, *Rights o' Man,*" which the other sailors, unable to perceive the italics, take as a political statement. The officers tell ultravillain ship's cop John Claggart to keep an eye on the Budd boy.

Jealous of Budd's youth and good looks, Claggart vows to destroy him. He orders another sailor to plant money in Budd's knapsack; Budd catches the would-be planter and beats him up. Claggart's next effort: to bribe the popular Budd into leading a mutiny. Budd doesn't fall for it.

Finally, in front of Captain Vere, Claggart formally accuses Billy of planning a mutiny. Billy's stammer gets the best of him and, because he's unable to speak, he responds by killing Claggart with a single punch.

Captain Vere orders his officers to chain Billy and hang him. The men offer to rescue him, but Billy, aware of how tragic operas must end, says that he'd prefer no intervention. Billy sings "Starry Vere, God bless you!," and then gets dragged up the mast to be hanged.

And now we're back to Captain Vere as an old man, remembering, and trying to explain himself. He sings, "I was lost on the infinite sea, but I've sighted a sail in the storm . . . and I'm content."

# La Cenerentola

**Vital stats:** Title translation: *Cinderella*. Music by Gioachino Rossini. Libretto in Italian by Jacopo Ferretti. An 1817 opera version of the Cinderella fairy tale in three acts. There's no glass slipper, fairy godmother, pumpkin coach, or wicked stepmother; otherwise, this version is very faithful to the original.

**The plot:** Cenerentola ("chen-a-REN-to-lah"), alias Cinderella, makes a fire in the fireplace, while her two evil stepsisters admire themselves. The door bursts open; the prince's staff has come to announce a party at the palace, where the prince will pick a bride. The Prince himself appears, but he and his valet, Dandini, are disguised as each other. In disguise, the prince thinks that he'll be better able to scope out the wife candidates' true natures. He and Cenerentola sing a love-at-first-sight duet. Alidoro, court philosopher, offers to smuggle her into the party wearing — naturally — a disguise.

At the party, Dandini, still pretending to be the prince, proposes to Cenerentola — but she turns him down, saying that she's in love with his *valet*. Now the *actual* prince proposes. But Cenerentola, not wanting too much happiness all at once, gives him the bracelet from her arm, challenges him to find her again, and disappears.

Just as in the fairy tale, it all gets worked out in the end. The prince reveals himself, finds her again, and joins her before the altar. The crowd sings to the happy couple about how the wheel of destiny has finally stopped on a winning number *("Della Fortuna instabile")*. And in an incredibly fancy final aria, kind Cenerentola forgives her dysfunctional family.

# The Coronation of Poppea

**Vital stats:** Music by Claudio Monteverdi, libretto in Italian *(L'Incoronazione di Poppea)* by Giovanni Francesco Busenello. A 1642 mythological epic in a prologue and three acts — the earliest still-famous opera.

**The plot:** Two goddesses, Fortune and Virtue, bicker about which one of them dominates earthlings more. Verone, Goddess of Love, claims that *she* does, and here's the proof.

Big hero Ottone (a baritone) comes home from the wars looking forward to some quality time with his main squeeze, Poppea (a soprano). But while he was away, Emperor Nerone (aka Nero; tenor or soprano) has taken a fancy to her. Nero wants to divorce his current wife and take Poppea for his empress. Unfortunately, his wife finds out, and prays to the gods to do damage to the lovers. When old philosopher Seneca (a bass) warns Poppea not to proceed with her power-grubbing plan, Nero orders the old philosopher to kill himself.

Rejected by ex-girlfriend Poppea, hero Ottone drowns his tears with another old girlfriend, Drusilla (a soprano). With Mrs. Nero's encouragement, he decides to kill Poppea, wearing Drusilla's dress by way of disguise — but he's stopped by the Goddess of Love. Naturally, everyone thinks that *Drusilla* tried to chop up Poppea (hey, it was her outfit). Just as Nero and his soldiers are about to execute the real Drusilla, Ottone confesses. Nero pardons them but sends them both into exile. He also banishes his own wife for her part in the plot (thereby also divorcing her). Nero and Poppea are married, and Poppea gets her coronation.

# Dialogues of the Carmelites

**Vital stats:** Music by Francis Poulenc, French libretto by Ernest Lavery. A 1957 historical-based tragedy in three acts, with martyrs.

**The plot:** During the French Revolution, slightly disturbed, easily flustered soprano Blanche enrolls in the Carmelite convent, renaming herself Sister Blanche of the Agony of Christ. Young Sister Constance befriends Blanche, despite having had a dream that they'll die together.

Soon their world is rocked, however, as the Mother Superior dies after having horrible visions. Soon enough they come true, as new revolutionary laws forbid nuns. Mother Marie proposes that the nuns kill themselves rather than abandon their faith. When the nuns vote for martyrdom, Blanche freaks out and runs away.

Now we're in the Place de la Revolution, where the decapitations take place. A crowd sings "oh" and "ah." The nuns start up the steps to the guillotine. As each loses her head, the sound of the nuns' chorus grows weaker and weaker. Eventually, only Constance is left. Alone on the scaffold, she spots Blanche in the crowd. As Constance goes off to be beheaded, Blanche, probably feeling a bit guilty, takes up the song and walks toward the guillotine so that she, too, may join her sisters in their vow of death.

# Dido and Aeneas

**Vital stats:** Music by Henry Purcell, libretto in English by Nahum Tate. An epic tragedy in three acts, which premiered at Josias Priest's School for Young Gentlewomen in 1690.

**The plot:** The queen of Carthage, Dido (a soprano), falls in love with the heroic Aeneas, prince of Troy. Much celebration ensues.

But in a dismal cave, a Dido-hating witch plots to upset her and wreck Carthage. She and her cronies conjure up a storm that wreaks havoc on the royal couple's hunting trip and drives them back to the palace. They also send an elf, disguised as Mercury, to intercept Aeneas. The elf tells him that Jupiter, king of the Gods, wants him to return to Italy and restore the city of Troy. Aeneas is reluctant, knowing that this sudden trip will look fishy to Queen Dido.

As Aeneas's sailors prepare to sail off to Italy, the witches gloat. But Aeneas tells Dido that he loves her so much, he'll ignore the commands of the gods. But she tells him that it's too late; she can't trust him anymore. He leaves; she dies of a broken heart ( but not before singing the famous "Dido's Lament"); and the chorus asks cupids to drop rose petals on her body.

# Don Carlo

**Vital stats:** Music by Giuseppe Verdi, French libretto by François Joseph Méry and Camille du Locle. An 1867 politically tinged love story in five acts. Unless the production you're going to see has made cuts, be prepared for a long evening.

**The plot:** As part of a peace treaty, Prince Carlo of Spain is supposed to marry the king of France's daughter, Elisabeth. The music swells, and they're head over heels for each other. Unfortunately, there's been a clerical error: Princess Elisabeth is supposed to marry Carlo's *father,* not Carlo. She glumly agrees.

To get Carlo's mind off his own stepmother, his best friend Rodrigo encourages him to get involved in Flemish politics. But when Carlo asks his father for a job running Flemish relations, King Dad refuses. Hothead Carlo draws his sword. Carlos is jailed; Rodrigo is eventually shot by the King's men.

King Dad, alone, has learned (from his mistress, the unstable Princess Eboli) of his son's crush on Elisabeth, whom he now confronts. Elisabeth, her marriage and her true love both falling apart, prays at the monastery. She meets Carlo for a last farewell duet before he leaves for Flanders to carry on dead Rodrigo's work. But who should spring out of hiding but Carlo's furious father, *really* annoyed now. Just as Carlo is about to get seriously punished, a voice is heard from inside the tomb of Emperor Charles V. The king assumes that the person now stepping out of the crypt is the ghost of the emperor (it's actually a friendly monk helping Carlo out, but no IDs are requested), and allows this frightening person to lead Carlo into the safety of the monastery. Yes, you read that right: The main characters of this opera are all still alive at the final curtain!

# The Girl of the Golden West

**Vital stats:** Title translation: *La Fanciulla del West.* Music by Giacomo Puccini, libretto in Italian by Guelfo Civinni and Carlo Zangarini, based on David Belasco's play. A 1910 *wild-West opera,* Italian style (!). May this opera forever disabuse you of the notion that operas are about women wearing Viking helmets.

**The plot:** The story takes place in California at a mining camp in 1849. Inside a saloon called The Polka, Ashby, a bass Wells Fargo agent and minor miner, announces that the bandito Ramerrez, whose WANTED poster hangs on the wall, has been seen in the valley. A mysterious stranger enters, calling himself Dick Johnson; nobody notices that he looks *just* like the guy in the WANTED poster. He and Minnie, the pretty dance-hall owner, fall for each other and go for a waltz. She invites him to her cabin later.

Just as they're getting smoochy at Minnie's house, Rance the sheriff bursts in, having learned that Johnson *is* the bandit Ramerrez! Desperate, in love, Minnie proposes a poker game: If she wins, Ramerrez goes free; if the sheriff wins, he gets Ramerrez and Minnie, too! (Did we mention that the sheriff also desires Minnie? Never mind that he's already married. . . .)

Minnie cheats and wins the poker game. The bandit goes free — only to be captured a week later by Sheriff Rance and his men. Minnie rushes in on horseback and begs them not to hang him. The miners, moved by her love, agree to let her go with Johnson. Minnie and her bandito exit arm-in-arm to start their new life together: *"Addio, mia California, addio!"*

# Jenůfa

**Vital stats:** Music and words (in Czech) by Leoš Janáček; the opera took him 27 years to write. A grim, searing 1904 tragedy, although with a semi-happy ending, in three acts.

**The plot:** Jenůfa (soprano), a pretty young Moravian, wonders where tenor Števa is. And well she might: He's her cousin, boyfriend, and the father of her unborn baby all rolled into one. The local mill foreman brings news that Števa wasn't drafted by the army, as had been expected; Jenůfa and her grandmother (also Števa's grandmother) are delighted.

Števa isn't such a great catch, though; he returns home drunk and boasting of his sexual conquests. Jenůfa's foster mother, a church officer, sternly tells Števa that he can't marry Jenůfa until he stays sober for one full year. Števa's half-brother Laca teases Jenůfa — a giveaway that he's in love with her — and then insults her, and finally, in a rage of jealousy, slashes her face with a knife.

In the second act, the baby has been born. Števa intends to pay child support, but he's now engaged to the mayor's daughter. Jenůfa's stepmom is aghast. Knife-slasher Laca hints that *he'll* be happy to marry Jenůfa; her stepmom is thrilled, but worries that he'll lose interest if someone else's baby is in the picture — so she announces that Jenůfa's baby has died. Always one to follow through, Jenůfa's stepmother drowns Jenůfa's baby in the river.

Now Jenůfa and Laca can marry happily — until the townspeople find the baby's body and come to stone Jenůfa to death. Fortunately, Jenůfa's foster mom admits her horrible crime, and she's led away. Jenůfa, shamed and exiled, is touched when Laca asks to spend his life with her anyway.

# Julius Caesar

**Vital stats:** Music by George Frideric Handel, libretto in Italian by Nicolò Francesco Haym. A 1724 adventure in three acts. In Italian, the title is *Giulio Cesare.* The title role is usually played by a woman, because it was originally written for a castrato (see Chapter 5).

**The plot:** There's actually about 189 pages' worth of plot, but here's the thrust: Julius Caesar has just captured his enemy, Pompeo, and returns to a jubilant Egypt. Mrs. Pompeo (Cornelia) and her soprano son (Sesto) beg Caesar to spare Pompeo's life. But its too late: Egyptian Captain Achillas chooses this moment to bring in Pompeo's severed head. Son Sesto vows revenge.

Just about everyone who sees pretty, newly widowed contralto Cornelia falls in love with her; Captain Achillas is no exception. The king of Egypt makes a deal with Achillas: Assassinate Caesar, and he can marry Cornelia. But when Caesar finds out about the plot, he jumps off a balcony into the sea. Assuming that Caesar is dead, Achillas asks the king of Egypt if he can *now* marry Cornelia. Unfortunately, the king now wants her for himself.

The Egyptians fight the Romans, led by the king of Egypt's power-hungry sister Cleopatra (who loves Caesar — long story). The Romans lose. Cornelia's son Sesto, still seeking revenge, comes across the dying Achillas. Regretting his complicity in the plotting, Achillas gives Sesto a signet ring that gives Sesto command of Achillas's troops. (Still with us?) Caesar takes the ring for himself, however, and leads the soldiers to victory. Sesto gets to kill the king, Cleopatra gets to be queen, and Cleopatra and Caesar get each other.

# Lulu

**Vital stats:** Complex music and words (in German) by Alban Berg in 1937, based on plays by Frank Wedekind. A two-thirds completed, disturbing tale of a gold-digging seductress. Sometimes performed with a third act added in 1979 by another composer. (**Caution:** Don't expect to walk out humming the tunes; there aren't any. *Lulu* is a modern, *12-tone* opera, meaning that the composer constrained his writing by a set of mathematical rules, which results in some pretty alien-sounding stuff.)

**The plot:** Lulu, a soprano in the late 1800s, dispatches the men in her life as only a cruel beauty can. When her husband walks in on her while she's having sex with a painter, he dies of a heart attack. She cheats next on the *painter,* who slits his own throat. Her next boyfriend thinks that he'll beat Lulu to the punch by shooting her — but she kills him first.

Her next knight in shining armor sells her to a bordello, where her customers include: a high-baritone professor, a lyric-tenor who kills her stepson (who was yet another of Lulu's lovers), and, of all people, Jack the Ripper. Jack kills both her and the mezzo-soprano lesbian who's been in love with Lulu during the entire opera.

Better leave the kids at home for this one.

# Manon

**Vital stats:** Music by Jules Massenet, libretto in French by Henri Meilhac and Philippe Gille. An 1884 tragedy in five acts.

**The plot:** Manon (a soprano), a flaky young girl, arrives at an inn, where her cousin, Lescaut, will escort her the rest of the way to the convent (she's being forced to become a nun). He leaves her alone for only a moment, but two guys make a pass at her: an icky tenor named Guillot and a handsome tenor named Des Grieux, whom she really likes. Des Grieux steals her away; Guillot vows revenge.

Des Grieux and Manon are now happily ensconced in a Paris apartment. Cousin Lescaut arrives with his friend De Brétigny (a baritone), who wastes no time persuading Manon that *he's* a better bet. Never one for long-term relationships, she now runs off with De Brétigny.

Later, at a street festival, Manon hears that her old beau Des Grieux, distraught over losing her, has become a priest. She finds him at the monastery, where she seduces him anew. (We *told* you that she's flaky.)

Soon enough, however, they run out of cash, so they go to a casino to win some money. Des Grieux has some incredible luck, but rival Guillot accuses him of cheating and has the two lovers arrested. Des Grieux's influential father gets him out of prison, but no one helps Manon. Lescaut and Des Grieux come up with a plan to rescue her as she's being transported. Unfortunately, as she's being rescued, she dies in Des Grieux's arms.

# Manon Lescaut

**Vital stats:** Music by Giacomo Puccini, libretto in Italian by Puccini (and five other guys). An 1893 tragedy in four acts. When asked why he wrote an opera on a subject that Massenet had already used, Puccini replied, "Why not? A woman like Manon should have more than one lover."

**The plot:** Pretty much the same plot as *Manon.* Sergeant Lescaut (a baritone) is escorting his beautiful sister, Manon (a soprano), to the convent. A student, Des Grieux, falls for Manon, and convinces her to run off with him. Another suitor, old Geronte (a bass), tells Lescaut to chase after them; but Lescaut anticipates that Geronte, who's rich, will have no problem winning gold-digger Manon back from a poor student.

Lescaut is right: By the second act, fickle Manon's living in the lap of luxury in old Geronte's home. Manon tells Lescaut that true love would probably be better, although jewels are pretty good. When Des Grieux shows up, however, she falls in love with him again. She and Des Grieux try to escape, stealing Geronte's jewelry in the process, but they get caught, and Geronte has Manon arrested as a prostitute.

Manon is to be deported to New Orleans, USA, where they send all the bad girls. Des Grieux persuades the captain of the ship to let him sneak aboard. In America, the lovers escape, but their trek through the wilderness takes a toll on Manon's health. Des Grieux goes to find help. When he returns, it's too late; she dies.

# A Midsummer Night's Dream

**Vital stats:** Music by Benjamin Britten, libretto in English by Britten and Peter Pears based on Shakespeare's play. A 1960 comic fantasy in three acts.

**The plot:** Lover Pair A, Lysander and Hermia, are eloping to escape an arranged marriage. Lover Pair B, Demetrius and Helena, aren't really lovers; she loves him, but he's not interested. Oberon, king of the fairies, sends assistant fairy (and speaking part) Puck to put a love potion on Boyfriend B. Unfortunately, Puck puts the potion on Boyfriend A by mistake, which makes *him* fall in love with Girlfriend B. King Oberon puts the potion on his fairy wife, Tytania, with whom he's been quarreling.

Meanwhile, some amateur actors are rehearsing a play that they plan to perform. Puck puts a spell on one of them, the buffoonish Bottom, giving him a donkey's head — and Queen Tytania, under the spell of the love potion, falls in love with ass-headed Bottom. Pure comedy!

Trying to fix his previous mistake, Puck puts the love potion on Boyfriend B. Now, at last, Boyfriend B falls in love with his girlfriend — who has always loved him, but now doesn't believe any of this. Everyone fights until they fall asleep, and Puck undoes his damage, getting the couples sorted out while King Oberon removes the spell from Queen Tytania. Ass-headed Bottom gets his real head back and thinks that it was all a dream.

# Nabucco

**Vital stats:** Music by Giuseppe Verdi — his first hit — with libretto in Italian by Temistocle Solera. An 1842 tragedy in four acts.

**The plot:** The Hebrews have been defeated by Nabucco, king of Babylon (not to be confused with Nabisco, king of cookies). Hebrew Prince Ismaele falls in love with Nabucco's daughter, Fenena, who's been taken prisoner by the Hebrews. To the horror of the other Hebrews, Prince Ismaele frees Fenena and returns her to her father, Nabucco — who shows his appreciation by ordering his men to trash the Hebrew temple. Before marching back into battle, he puts daughter Fenena in charge of his kingdom.

Fenena's jealous sister, Abigaille, meanwhile, hears that King Nabucco has been killed in battle, and she seizes power. But Nabucco returns — not dead after all — and grabs the crown back. With a clap of thunder, however, a supernatural force knocks the crown off his head and makes him nutty. Nasty Abigaille winds up with the crown. Her first act is to sentence the Hebrew prisoners (including her sympathizing sister Fenena) to death — and to imprison the raving, pathetic Nabucco.

The enslaved Hebrews cheer themselves with the classic patriotic chorus *"Va, pensiero, sull'ali dorate"* ("Fly, thought, on golden wings"), which you can hear on Track 6 of the CD that came with this book (see Chapter 11 for the lyrics and a complete description). As Fenena is led to be executed by her evil sister, Nabucco wakes from his delirium, escapes from prison, rescues Fenena, and converts her to Judaism. Sister Abigaille, who's awfully sorry, swallows poison and dies.

# Norma

**Vital Stats:** Music by Vincenzo Bellini, libretto in Italian by Felice Romani. An 1831 lyric tragedy in two acts (sometimes performed in four). The action takes place in ancient Gaul in about 50 B.C.

**The plot:** Druid High Priestess Norma has secretly broken her vows of chastity and had two sons by the Roman (enemy) Pollione. Unfortunately, *he* loves a virgin named Adalgisa. Norma protects enemy Pollione, telling her people that the time for war has not yet come.

When Norma hears that Pollione plans to elope with a girlfriend, she goes berserk, interrupting her suicide attempt only when she sees her two kids quietly sleeping. She asks virgin Adalgisa to care for them after her death — until Norma learns that *Adalgisa* is the one who's about to elope with Pollione!

In a rage, Norma bangs the gong signaling war against Pollione's people. Pollione is captured; Norma offers to save his life if he'll give up virgin Adalgisa. He refuses. Fine, Norma says; then I'll kill myself. (Hey, I broke my chastity vow anyway, so I deserve to die.) She gives her kids to her father. Moved by her selflessness, Pollione kindly offers to die with her; and they walk hand-in-hand into the bonfire.

# Orfeo ed Euridice

**Vital stats:** Music by Christoph Willibald von Gluck, libretto in Italian by Ranieri Calzabigi. A 1762 opera in three acts, with lots and lots of dancing — one of the very first opera hits.

**The plot:** At the tomb of his wife Euridice ("ay-oo-ree-DEE-chay"), famous musician Orfeo ("or-FAY-o") bewails the unfairness of her death. Amor, the God of Love (played by a soprano), makes a deal with him: If he goes to the Underworld and sings so beautifully that the rulers of the place give their okay, he can bring his wife back to life. As so often happens in this kind of supernatural contract, however, there's a catch: He's not allowed to *look* at her as he leads her out.

Orfeo sings his way past the evil Furies at the gates of Hell, and he successfully sings his way into getting permission to retrieve his late wife. But on the trip back to earth, Euridice pesters Orfeo with a lot of questions — such as why won't he, for crying out loud, *look* at her? He asks her just to trust him, but she keeps badgering: "Don't you *love* me anymore?" He finally gives in, but when he looks at her, she dies. He sobs piteously. In a shocking reversal of the original Greek myth, Amor, the God of Love, restores Euridice to life, because (a) she's so moved by Orfeo's grief, and (b) she loves his tunes.

# The Pearl Fishers

**Vital stats:** Also known as *Les Pêcheurs de Perles,* music by Georges Bizet, libretto in French by Eugène Cormon and Michel Carré. An 1863 tragedy in three acts.

**The plot:** Long, long ago — no, even before that — in Ceylon, a baritone named Zurga is made big chief of the fishermen. A tenor named Nadir shows up. He's been gone for years because he and Zurga used to fight over the same girl. Now they decide to be friends forever.

A brand new priestess, Leïla (a soprano), goes up the mountain to offer her prayers. She shows the high priest, Nourabad (a bass), a necklace she got from some stranger whose life she once saved. Nadir overhears her — hey, *she's* the girl he and Zurga used to fight over. She and Nadir rekindle their affair — but the high priest Nourabad catches them kissing. That's a no-no for a priestess like Leïla. The high priest turns them over to the newly minted Chief Zurga, who condemns the two lovers to death by bonfire.

The condemned couple is about to step into the pyre. Resigned to dying, Leïla asks Zurga to give her necklace to her mother after she's gone. But Zurga recognizes the necklace as the one he gave to a girl who saved his life years ago! He decides to help the young lovers get away, and he creates a distraction by setting the village on fire. Good news: The lovers get away. Bad news: Zurga gets caught by the high priest, who makes *him* die on the bonfire.

# I Puritani

**Vital stats:** Music by Vincenzo Bellini, libretto in Italian by Count Pepoli. An 1835 historical drama in three acts, whose title means *The Puritans.*

**The plot:** Soprano Elvira is engaged to Sir Arthur, even though he's (a) of the wrong political persuasion, and (b) a tenor. But on the day of their wedding, Sir Arthur gets it into his head to help a political prisoner, Queen Henrietta, escape from prison — by dressing *her* as his bride and marching her right past all the guards.

The plan works, all right, but poor Elvira believes that Arthur's *actually* marrying somebody else. She goes quietly nuts, and all the king's horses and all the king's men set out to kill Arthur for being such a cad. Just as he's about to be executed, a messenger brings news of a peace treaty: All prisoners are forgiven. The good news snaps Elvira out of her insanity, and the lovers live happily ever after.

# Rusalka

**Vital stats:** Music by Antonín Dvořák, libretto in Czech by Jaroslav Kvapil. A 1901 drama in three acts.

**The plot:** The soprano Rusalka, a mermaid, falls helplessly and hopelessly in love with a handsome human tenor prince. She turns to a creepy witch named Ježibaba (a mezzo-soprano) for help. Ježibaba agrees to make Rusalka human so that she can marry the prince. (Sound familiar, Disney fans?) But there's some fine print to the deal: (1) Rusalka becomes mute; and (2) if the prince cheats on her, they're damned for eternity.

The prince falls in love with this silent beauty and sings a one-sided love duet. Rusalka and the prince marry and live happily for a while, but he gets the one-year itch and has an affair with an irritable but glamorous foreign princess. Rusalka turns into a wandering, miserable, white-haired, ice-cold ghost, as per the witch's contract. The prince sees the error of his ways, however, and begs Rusalka the ghost to kiss him, even though it means that he'll die. She does; he does; she spends eternity floating around remembering her one great fling.

# Werther

**Vital stats:** Music by Jules Massenet. Libretto in French by Edouard Blau, Paul Milliet, and Georges Hartmann; based on the partly autobiographical novel by the German philosopher Johann Wolfgang von Goethe. An 1892 tragic tale of forbidden love in three acts. Boy meets girl; girl's already engaged; boy kills himself.

**The plot:** Pretty 20-year-old Charlotte is engaged to the practical, mirthless Albert (thanks to her mother's deathbed request). But because Albert is away, a tenor idealistic dreamer named Werther has been asked to escort Charlotte to this evening's ball. Charlotte and Werther fall deeply in love. But Charlotte doesn't want to rock the boat; she marries boring Albert anyway.

Three months after the wedding, Werther's going crazy: *"Un autre est son époux!"* ("She married someone else!"). He decides to go abroad until he can control his feelings. While on the road, Werther writes Charlotte some absolutely killer love letters. She finally admits to herself that she loves him.

The following Christmas, Werther returns. He and Charlotte happily look at the books they once read and the harpsichord they once played. From one of the books, Werther reads her a tragic love poem: *"Porquoi me réveiller?"* ("Why even wake me up?"), now a famous aria. He tries to kiss her, but she runs from the room. Later, Werther sends a note to Albert: "I'm going on a long trip. Could I borrow your pistols?"

Alone at home, Werther shoots himself; Charlotte runs through a blinding snowstorm to his house. As he dies, Charlotte tells him that she's always loved him. (Some consolation.)

# *Wozzeck*

**Vital stats:** Music and libretto in German by Alban Berg. A 1925 drama in three acts. Read about *Lulu* earlier in this chapter to find out about Berg's complex, alien-sounding music. No wonder the first production of this show required *137 rehearsals!*

**The plot:** Poverty-stricken, slow-witted servant/soldier Wozzeck ("VAW-tseck") is shaving the beard of his captain (a tenor), who criticizes Wozzeck for having had an illegitimate son. Baritone Wozzeck comments that poor people can't afford to be virtuous. Meanwhile, a doctor has been performing weird experiments on poor Wozzeck. When Wozzeck demonstrates symptoms of insanity, the doctor promises him a raise.

Wozzeck's girlfriend, Marie, mother of his son, has an affair with the drum major, and a local idiot suggests that Wozzeck murder her. As the perfect ending to a perfect day, the drum major admits to having the affair, and then beats up Wozzeck.

Wozzeck stabs Marie in the throat, tries to wash the blood off himself, and drowns in a lake. The next morning, heartless children tell Marie's little boy that his mother is dead. The other kids run off to look at the dead body. After a moment, the boy goes after them, not understanding.

Something tells us that *this* one will never be an animated Disney classic.

# Part V
# The Part of Tens

## In this part . . .

If you've dutifully traversed the pages of this book from the beginning, congratulations — you've waded through some truly complicated stuff. And if, by chance, you've also *read* it, you're in great shape to face the world of opera without fear.

This part is truly for those low-attention-span moments, times when you need a break from the rigors of *...For Dummies* text.

Herewith, Dave 'n' Scott's Top Tens.

# Chapter 14

# The Ten Most Common Misconceptions about Opera

● ● ● ● ● ● ● ● ● ● ● ● ● ● ● ● ● ● ● ● ● ● ● ● ● ● ● ● ● ● ● ● ● ● ● ● ● ● ● ● ● ● ● ● ● ● ●

*I*f you've read any of this book, you know that opera is nothing like the boring, antiquated, overwrought fat farm it's sometimes made out to be. Still, just to make sure, here are some of the myths we hope we've debunked.

## Opera is for snobs

If you delve deeply enough into *any* art, you'll meet a few people who consider themselves superior because they *know* more. They come up with their own jargon and use it like a password to an exclusive club.

But ironically, the great opera composers originally wrote their shows as entertainment for the *masses* — operas were movies before there were movies. So saying that opera is just for snobs is just as nutty as saying that good *movies* are just for snobs.

## Opera singers are fat ladies who wear helmets with horns

The stereotype of the fat opera singer is dead. It started dying, actually, the day opera started being shown on TV. Famous roly-poly singer Renata Scotto saw herself in *La Bohème*, was stunned, and promptly lost 40 pounds. The great Jessye Norman lost 100 pounds, and Deborah Voigt lost 70; TV has changed the rules for hiring opera singers. In fact, we can think of only five internationally famous opera stars who qualify as Unusually Large — Jane Eaglen, Sharon Sweet, Alessandra Marc, Ben Heppner, and Luciano Pavarotti — and their talent makes them worth the weight.

Meanwhile, we can name plenty more opera stars who are great-looking: Angela Gheorghiu, Karita Mattila, Waltraud Meier, Roberto Alagna, Dmitri Hvorostovsky, and the chart-topping Cecilia Bartoli, for starters. No question about it: The Era of Girth is over.

As for the horned Viking helmets, they appear prominently in Wagner's *Ring* cycle — in *Die Walküre (The Valkyrie)*, to be exact. The Valkyries are warrior goddesses whose job is to pick up fallen warriors from earthly battlefields and bring them back to Valhalla. They're often pictured wearing breastplates and, yes, helmets with horns. But they don't appear in other operas. And you hardly ever see a Valkyrie nowadays.

And as for all opera singers being ladies: This part is only 50 percent true.

## Operas are long

Here's another Wagner-induced oversimplification. True, several of *his* operas last a full evening — four or even five hours, counting intermissions. But tons of operas get you in and out in under three hours. That's less time than it would take to see *The English Patient, Schindler's List,* or the final episode of *Cheers.*

In fact, some operas are so short that opera companies regularly pair them up in one evening. Pietro Mascagni's opera *Cavalleria Rusticana* and Ruggiero Leoncavallo's *I Pagliacci* usually play together for just that reason — neither one would fill an evening by itself. And Giacomo Puccini, the world's most popular opera composer, wrote three operas (*Il Tabarro, Suor Angelica,* and *Gianni Schicchi*) that are so short, he designed *all three* of them to be performed together.

 By the way: According to *The Guinness Book of World Records,* the shortest opera ever written is *The Deliverance of Theseus,* by Darius Milhaud. It lasts seven minutes and 37 seconds. Actually, one of your present authors has written an opera that beats that record, but Guinness has yet to announce it.

## Opera characters need at least ten minutes to die

Opera cliché: The tenor has been stabbed late in the third act. He's gasping for air. He's choking in his last breaths. And just before he expires, he sings for ten minutes, hitting his famous high C.

Two reasons why that's a misconception:

✔ First, what the tenor sings before he dies is an *aria* — a special kind of song in which he expresses his feelings. What happens during an aria, plot-wise, is *nothing*. For a few moments, there's no action at all. Time stands still. An aria is just an instant of time, telescoped out to display all the emotional weight it contains. So even if the tenor seems to take ten minutes to explain his feelings before he dies, you're really experiencing only a split-second of the story.

You don't complain when the action goes into slo-mo in a movie, do you?

✔ Second, a great number of operas portray events almost as a gritty documentary would. When a character gets stabbed in *these* operas, he doesn't sing *at all* — he screams and collapses. Exhibits A and B: Scarpia in *Tosca* or Carmen in *Carmen.*

## You need to know foreign languages to "get" an opera

Let's face it: Most operas aren't in English. In the old days, if you went to an opera presented in its original language, you had to either memorize the action of the opera in advance (which meant hours of study beforehand) or bring along a translation of the libretto and a little flashlight just to understand what was going on. Neither prospect was much fun.

Today, however, most professional opera houses have *surtitles* — those wonderful English translations that are projected over the stage. (And you get *subtitles* in most TV broadcasts and videocassettes of operas.) Now you can just enjoy the show and glance at the titles whenever you need them.

For more on the opera libretto, translations, and surtitles, see Chapter 2.

## Opera is boring

If you watch an opera and can't understand what the characters are saying, *of course* it's boring. Surtitles (or a reading of the libretto) can put an end to that.

Furthermore, we admit that certain moments in certain operas — just *moments,* mind you — *are* boring. We might make thousands of Wagner fans go instantly bald in horror by saying this, but we think that a few scenes in the *Ring* cycle could stand a little trimming.

But don't let those moments fool you. Overall, opera is one of the most exciting art forms. Listen to the last act of Puccini's opera *Tosca*. (You can hear the last few minutes of it on Track 8 of the CD that accompanies this book.) The music is passionate and powerful; the melodies are gorgeous and hummable; the story is tragic and human; the mood is intense and super-charged. We'll bet that this opera will have an actual, measurable effect on your pulse, mood, and attitude toward opera.

Appendix A contains the names of 20 decidedly unboring operas like *Tosca*. Listen to them, and see what you think. *Then* we'll talk.

## You have to dress up to go to the opera

This is one of the saddest misconceptions, because it actually prevents some potential rip-roaring opera fans from even stepping into an opera house.

You may not believe this, but it's true: You can dress however you like at the opera! (See the section entitled, "Can I Wear a Toga to *Julius Caesar*?" in Chapter 10.) Sure, *some* people dress up to go to an opera. And for many people, dressing up makes the occasion a lot more fun. But then, some people dress up to go to the post office. That doesn't mean that *you* have to.

## Opera plots are far-fetched and creaky

You always hear people say that opera is unrealistic, that it has nothing to do with real life. But the fact is, opera plots are *exactly* what you read about on the front page every day.

The O.J. Simpson story, for example, is *totally* operatic — amazingly, Leoncavallo's tragic clown opera *I Pagliacci* tells the same story. How about the Menendez brothers murder case? Right out of the opera *Elektra* — siblings gang up to murder their parents.

Opera is about love and desire, jealousy and greed, devotion and betrayal, justice and injustice. The plots of the operas you're likely to see these days are as pertinent as the day they were written.

# Opera isn't worth the prices they charge nowadays

A good seat at an opera house can cost $50, $60 — even $100 for a ticket. Yikes! Can the experience possibly be worth the price?

We have two answers to that: yes and no.

An opera ticket is worth the price because of the enormous size of the production — especially a great production. Look at what you're getting: a cast of big-voiced opera singers (each of whom receives several thousand dollars *per night* to sing); beautiful set designs that transform the stage into Paris or Egypt; incredible lighting effects; a parade of elephants, or Valkyries swooping in on flying horses (though usually not both); a huge chorus of serfs, ballroom guests, or Roman soldiers with spears; a world-class orchestra; hundreds of staff people backstage (and over it, and under it, and on either side) who make it all happen; and a building big enough to house all of the above.

On the other hand, no, it's not worth the price if you don't enjoy yourself. But we hope that, armed with this book, you will have gained the understanding, insight and insider information to have a ball every time. Nor do you even *have* to pay exorbitant prices; see Chapter 10 for hints on how to get ticket deals.

# Opera singers have it easy

Show up, work for three hours, collect $12,000, and go home. What a life!

Actually, the showing-up, collecting-the-money, and going-home parts are easy enough. The work — the singing — is a problem.

As you can read in Chapter 4, no performing art is more difficult and taxing than singing opera. Opera singers must sing, sometimes at the top of their lungs, for *hours* on end. Many operas last for three hours, and some Wagner operas last *five*.

Singers have to be almost superhuman to perform this feat. They have to be in the best vocal shape imaginable, which often entails exercises and warm-ups as involved as those of an Olympic decathlete. When it comes to producing sound big enough to fill a concert hall, a singer requires a perfect coordination of lungs, diaphragm, and vocal apparatus. The fact is, opera singing is closer to pig hollering than anything else.

In fact, the job is much harder today than it ever was. First, the stresses of travel are enormous. A performer may have to sing *Aïda* in Milan tonight and rehearse *Tosca* in New York tomorrow. Second, the pressure is on to be perfect. Many people in the audience have heard the CD, which was recorded under ideal circumstances in a studio, with a microphone right by the singer's lips. They expect the performer to project the same effortless sound to a hall of 3,000 people.

The very best opera singers make it *look* easy to sing their roles. That's part of their art. We adore them for that. But don't forget: They're only pretending.

# Chapter 15
# The Ten Best Opera Terms for Cocktail Parties

· · · · · · · · · · · · · · · · · · · · · · · · · · · · · · · · · · · · · · · ·

*I*f you were a fly on the wall in the gentlemen's restroom during intermission at the opera, you might overhear this typical (and extremely realistic) opera conversation. How much can you understand?

*Answer:* None; you're a fly.

**Frank:** Yo, Tony! Howzit shakin'?

**Tony:** Can't complain. Took care of a 72-cubic-foot Freez-O-Matic today with a faulty Freon tube. What a headache.

**Frank:** Ain't they the worst? Gimme a side-by-side Kenmore any day.

**Tony:** Didja get a loada that *prima donna* tonight? Whoa, what pipes.

**Frank:** You got that right. I never heard such a pure *bel canto* sound. Floatin' it right out there. Right out there in her *head voice.*

**Tony:** Yeah. Can't wait 'til she gets a piece o' that soldier guy. Hey, what does he think he is, a *Heldentenor* or what? *Chest voice, chest voice,* nothin' but *chest voice.* Ain't this 18th-century *Italian* opera?

**Frank:** He did okay on his *recitative,* though. Not like that bonehead *basso buffo.* What a louse.

**Tony:** Tell me abowdit. From the way he butchered that Act I *aria,* ya'd think he ain't never even seen the *libretto.*

**Frank:** Well, he probably ain't! *(Laughs and moves to the washbasin.)*

**Tony:** He's prol'ly singin' what he's actually thinkin'!

**Frank:** Now *that's* what I call *verismo!*

**Tony:** *(laughs)* Okay, Frank. You take care now. See you at *Swan Lake* next week?

**Frank:** I'll be there.

This conversation uses all ten of the Best Opera Terms for Cocktail Parties:

- ✔ **Aria:** In most operas, every major character gets to sing at least one *aria* (pronounced "AH-ree-ya"). This common term means "air," or "song." Most of the great opera tunes that you know come from arias. In an aria, the action of the drama stops, and one character comes forward to express her feelings (or explain her predicament) at that instant.

- ✔ **Basso buffo:** Many comic operas have a *basso buffo* ("BAHSS-soe BOO-foe") — literally, a "buffoon bass." This standard role, always sung by a male singer with a low voice, is usually a servant (or at least a member of the service industry). His arias usually contain quickly repeated notes way down low — a really funny effect when it's done right. Two of the greatest basso buffo characters are Leporello in *Don Giovanni* and Don Pasquale in *Don Pasquale*.

- ✔ **Bel canto:** Literally, "beautiful singing," these words refer to a style of opera — and opera performance — in which the splendor of the human voice receives the most importance — more than the words or even the story. Rossini, Bellini, and Donizetti were the greatest composers in the *bel canto* (pronounced "bell CAHN-toe") style, writing gorgeous, brilliant arias to show off the human voice.

- ✔ **Chest voice:** A singer's term, *chest voice* refers to a particular way of producing a tone. Singers imagine that this sound is resonating within the chest cavity. (See Chapter 4 to try your own.)

- ✔ **Head voice:** Another singer's term, this is the opposite of chest voice. Notes produced with *head voice* are higher, rounder, and usually softer. Singers imagine that this sound is resonating in the bones and cavities of the head. (See Chapter 4 for much more.)

- ✔ **Heldentenor:** The male lead of any Wagner opera usually gets sung by a *Heldentenor* ("HELL-din-tay-NOR") — literally, "heroic tenor." This man has an extraordinarily strong singing voice, capable of trumpeting over a huge orchestra. A good Heldentenor is extremely rare.

- ✔ **Libretto:** Every opera has a *libretto* ("lee-BRETT-toe") — literally, "little book." The libretto is the script, the screenplay, the book, and the lyrics of the show (see Chapter 2).

- ✔ **Prima donna:** Means "first lady." The *prima donna* ("PREE-mah DOAN-na") is the singer who plays the heroine, the main female character in an opera. And in real life, a prima donna is anyone who believes that the world revolves around her.

- ✔ **Recitative:** In most operas, you hear sections during which a lot of action takes place quickly. The characters sing almost as if speaking, in a very free and natural rhythm. This is *recitative* ("ress-it-uh-TEEV," meaning a form of recitation). In operas of the Baroque and Classical periods in music, the recitative is usually accompanied by a harpsichord.

✔ **Verismo:** This kind of opera, made popular by such composers as Puccini, Leoncavallo, and Mascagni, exposes the gritty reality of life. The word *verismo* ("vay-REEZ-moe") means "truth-ism" (or realism), and verismo operas look more like docudramas than fantasies.

Now that you understand these terms, see if you can understand the following conversation, overheard backstage, just before an opera:

**Anita:** Just look at you, dear. You look *fabulous!*

**Conchita:** Thank you, darling. The *prima donna* has got to look her best!

**Anita:** The prima donna? I think not. That would be me.

**Conchita:** Nonsense, darling. Obviously, you haven't consulted the *libretto.*

**Anita:** I beg your pardon? Which of us gets to sing one *aria* after another?

**Conchita:** Excuse me, but I'd hardly call it an aria, the way you sing it. It's more like a *recitative* for *basso buffo.*

**Anita:** The nerve! You're simply jealous of my mastery of *chest voice,* which you can only begin to dream of!

**Conchita:** If you had my *head voice,* darling, you wouldn't need to sing that way. It's hardly what I'd call *bel canto.*

**Anita:** It's not supposed to be. It's *drama* — something you'd know nothing about. You're about as dramatic as a rock. A *Heldentenor* couldn't get a rise out of you.

**Conchita:** I beg your pardon. I'm simply responding to the *verismo* style.

**Anita:** *Verismo?* Since when is a statue *verismo?*

**Attendant:** *(from outside the door)* Conchita! Anita! Curtain going up!

**Anita:** Oh! All right. Sing well, Conchita!

**Conchita:** *(giving her a peck on both cheeks)* You too, darling!

# Chapter 16
# Ten Great Opera Jokes

• • • • • • • • • • • • • • • • • • • • • • • • • • • • • • • • • • • • • • • • • • •

Most opera singers have a great sense of humor. Good thing, too, because they're constantly getting ribbed. Here are some of the jokes their colleagues love to tell.

## Sleep tight

Q: Why do opera singers have to be awake by 6:00?

A: Because most stores close for the night at 6:30.

## Knock knock

Q: How do you know when there's a singer at the door?

A: He has the wrong key and has to be told when to come in.

## Sweet disposition

Q: What's the difference between a soprano and a terrorist?

A: You can negotiate with a terrorist.

## That special sparkle

Q: How do you put a sparkle in a soprano's eye?

A: Shine a flashlight in her ear.

## Altitude

Q: How many altos does it take to change a lightbulb?

A: Four — one to climb the ladder and three others to complain how high it is.

## Tenor spotlight

Q: How many tenors does it take to change a lightbulb?

A: One. He just holds the bulb and the world revolves around him.

## Dead giveaway

Q: How do you tell if a tenor is dead?

A: The wine bottle is still full, and the comics haven't been touched.

## Bass instincts

Q: How do you tell if a *bass* is actually dead?

A: Hold out a check (but don't be fooled: A slight, residual spasmodic clutching action may occur even hours after death).

## In the orchestra pit

Two bass players were hired for a series of *Carmen* performances. After a couple of weeks, they each agreed to take an afternoon off in turn to watch the matinee performance from the front of the opera house.

Joe duly took his break. Back in the pit that evening, Moe asked how it was.

"Great," says Joe. "You know that part where the music goes 'BOOM Boom, BOOM Boom?' Well, there are some guys up on stage singing a terrific song about a toreador at the same time!"

# Chapter 17

# Ten Ways to Keep Discovering Opera Forever

. . . . . . . . . . . . . . . . . . . . . . . . . . . . . . . . . . . . . . . . . . . . . .

*T*here's more to enjoying opera than going to the opera house once a year or watching the Three Tenors on TV. We live in an age in which alternate forms of musical contact are plentiful, easy, and fun. Don't just listen to opera — *live* it!

## *Become a super*

In the Intermission at the end of Part III, you can find out all about the extras of the opera world, who play everything from slaves to spear-carriers, from happy villagers to citizens of Thebes. These are *supernumeraries* — affectionately known as *supers*.

You, too, can be a super. If you're a good singer, you may want to audition for a singing part in the opera chorus. But even if you can't sing, you're not out of luck. Some operas call for non-singing crowds who just hang around the stage looking throng-like.

Being a super is a lot of fun. You get to dress up in wild costumes and makeup, several nights a week. You get to work with a great director and experience the fascinating rehearsal process. You get to wander around backstage. You sometimes get free or discounted tickets for your loved ones. You get to meet lots of other supers, who are interesting people like you. Onstage, you rub elbows with great opera stars.

You don't earn a whole lot of money as a super — in many places, you earn nothing at all. And you do have to commit a fair amount of time for the duration of a particular opera production. But those are the only disadvantages we can think of. Being a super is the best way we know to experience opera from the inside out.

Opera companies often need more supers — but they don't always advertise this fact. Call your local opera house and ask.

## Go to a pre-opera talk

More and more opera companies these days offer pre-performance lectures to their audience. (See Chapter 10.) They take place somewhere in the opera-house building (although not in the auditorium itself), anywhere from one hour to two weeks before the performance. These talks are usually free, short (45 minutes to an hour and a half), and incredibly interesting. They give you insights into the opera you're about to see, much more effectively than the notes in the program.

What's especially nice is that the speaker often points out interesting moments in the music and plays recordings of them. Even if you have your own CD or tape at home, you'll leave the talk with a much better feel for the music you're about to hear.

Almost everyone who goes to these talks just loves them. Try one for yourself.

## Join an opera tour

"Join an opera tour?" we can hear you asking. "Like a rock-group tour? Do we travel around the country wearing tie-dyed helmets and breastplates? Do we help haul Valkyrie equipment? Do we drop Valhallium? *Götterdämmerung,* dude — that's so *coooool!*"

No, no, we're talking about touring with *other opera fans,* not opera singers. Every once in a while, groups take tours to some cool place to check out the opera scene there. Some trips are elaborate and expensive — to Europe, for example. But others are much more modest and affordable. You may find a group that's taking a day trip to the next city or somewhere only a couple of hours away.

The advantages of this type of tour are twofold. First, you find out all about the music you're going to hear from people who love to talk about it. And second, you're guaranteed to make friends on an opera tour — friends who will be delighted to join you at the opera again and again.

For information about opera tours, contact one of these organizations:

- **Dailey-Thorp Travel:** 330 W. 58th St., New York, NY 10019, USA; phone 212-307-1555. This group has been organizing tours for over 25 years.
- **Great Performance Tours:** 1 Lincoln Plaza, Suite 32V, New York, NY 10023, USA; phone 212-580-1400. This little outfit organizes tours all over the world.

✔ **International Curtain Call:** 3313 Patricia Ave., Los Angeles, CA 90064, USA; phone 310-204-4934. This organization offers deluxe (read: expensive) tours to the great opera festivals of the world.

✔ **Morgan Tours:** 1090 Ambleside Dr., Suite 110, Ottawa, Ontario, K2B 8G7, Canada; phone 800-667-4268 or 613-820-0221; fax 613-721-9875; e-mail `travel@morgantours.com`; Web site `http://www.morgantours.com/~travel`. This Canadian group organizes departures from any city.

## Subscribe to an opera series

If you live in or near a town that has its own opera house, you're in luck. Most of these offer subscriptions, which give you the chance to enjoy live opera for much less money than you'd pay to hear all the performances individually.

Depending on the size of the opera house or opera series, a subscription can contain anywhere from 2 to 25 operas, spread out between September and May or June. Often you have the choice of how many operas you'd like to hear. Sometimes, you even get to mix and match different operas from various subscription series, creating your own custom series.

Opera houses usually plan their seasons so that subscribers are constantly introduced to a variety of interesting musical styles. They're unlikely to program the same opera two years in a row. These organizations know that by subscribing to a series, you're placing your trust in their ability to help you discover opera afresh, year after year.

## Make opera friends on the Internet

If you have a computer and a modem (or one of those WebTV-type gadgets), you can find about 500 years' worth of information, lists, discussions, and news about opera on that global computer network known as the Internet.

For instructions on getting hooked up to the Net, we gently nudge you in the direction of books such as *Macs For Dummies, America Online For Dummies,* and *The Internet For Dummies* (all published by IDG Books Worldwide) — or your local computer guru.

Once online, you can find opera plot summaries, complete librettos, history, reviews of recordings, lists of upcoming productions, endless discussion on the merits of various singers, productions, and recordings — and much more. As a first stop, use the Yahoo search page (`http://www.yahoo.com`), type in **opera**, and use the resulting list as a launching pad for your cyber-tour of opera.

Or use our handy starter list — keeping in mind that, like anything on the Web, these sites and their addresses are subject to change by the time you finish this sentence. Here are some highlights:

- ✔ **The NYCO OnLine Opera Library** (`www.nycopera.com/libmenu.html`): Opera plot synopses and composer biographies.

- ✔ **OperaWeb** (`www.opera.it/English/OperaWeb.html`): Reviews, pictures, history, world records, funny stories — a blast from Italy, birthplace of opera.

- ✔ **Opera America** (`www.operaam.org/`): News and schedules of upcoming performances.

- ✔ **Phil's Tenor Page** (`http://falcon.jmu.edu/~lawsonpc/index2.html`): Biographies of famous tenors, definitions of tenor types; nothing to write home about — we just liked the name of the page.

- ✔ **The Opera Pronouncing Dictionary** (`http://gray.music.rhodes.edu/operahtmls/works.html`): 100 composer and opera names, spoken from your computer's speaker!

- ✔ **OperaGlass** (`http://rick.stanford.edu/opera/main.html`): Links to individual Web pages for composers, operas, librettos, and more.

- ✔ **The Aria Database** (`www.aria-database.com/`): Over 500 arias: Words, musical ranges, analysis, and even MIDI files that play the music right on your computer. Speed them up, slow them down, even play them backwards when you're *really* punchy.

Finally, for pure discussion, the Internet offers several extremely lively and interesting bulletin boards catering to music lovers. Using a program such as Netscape Navigator, Newswatcher, or even the America Online keyword NEWSGROUPS, you can visit `rec.music.opera` — an electronic bulletin-board where people from around the world carry on opera discussions in gargantuan quantities. Every one of these people is a potential friend. Have fun!

## Listen to opera on your local classical station

Your city or town probably has a classical music radio station. It's almost always a public radio station, often affiliated with a college; you can usually find it between 87 and 92 on the FM dial. This station may very likely play operas nearly every week. On many Saturday afternoons from September to May, the Metropolitan Opera in New York broadcasts its productions live from Lincoln Center.

We highly recommend these broadcasts. The singers are great, the orchestra is fabulous, and the atmosphere is charged with an excitement that only a live performance can provide. The audience, in the background, usually goes wild. You'll really enjoy being a part of this experience.

More recently, the Lyric Opera of Chicago began broadcasting some of its operas as well. And the public radio station in your area may carry performances from other opera houses around the world. Check them out!

## Join a CD/tape club

You know these clubs: "Buy four rock CDs now for 15 cents, and never buy anything else, ever again!"

Well, you can find record clubs for classical music as well — and most of them have a great opera selection. A CD/tape club picks out pieces of music that you're likely to enjoy, often in wonderful performances by world-class artists. The club gradually introduces you to the greatest masterpieces of human expression — one at a time. All you need to do is listen and have fun. (And make the easy monthly payments of $14.95. . . .)

Here are some popular CD/tape clubs that offer opera recordings. Write to them for information, and see if any strike your fancy.

- ✔ **Berkshire Record Outlet, Inc.:** Route 102, Pleasant St., Lee, MA 01238-9804, USA; phone 413-243-4080; fax 413-243-4340; Web site http://www.berkshirerecoutlet.com. This service offers closeouts, deletions, and remaindered items (CDs, tapes, and LPs) from various record companies at very low prices.

- ✔ **H&B Recordings Direct:** 112 South Main St., Stowe, VT 05672, USA; phone 800-222-6872; e-mail address staff@hbdirect.com; Web site http://www.hbdirect.com. A very popular service. For a low yearly fee ($8.00 at this writing), you get a catalog, monthly flyers, a 10 percent discount on each item, a 30-day guarantee, and online advice about recordings.

- ✔ **BMG Classical Music Service:** For a membership application, write to P. O. Box 91117, Indianapolis, IN 46291-0048, USA.

## Borrow free CDs from the library

There's a problem with good opera recordings: They're expensive. Unlike a typical classical or rock CD, which may cost $14.95, an opera usually stretches over three, four, or even more CDs. $44.95 is not an unusual price for a beautiful CD box set of an opera, complete with libretto and pictures of the opera singers.

That's where public libraries come in. They have videos, Internet access, sheet music, computer programs — and *dozens* of opera CDs! This is your chance to immerse yourself in opera under the best of all possible circumstances: in your own room, with expensive recordings, all for free.

## *Watch operas on video — or opera movies*

The best way to experience an opera is live. But short of chartering a plane to the destination of your choice, you can't always find a live performance of every opera you're interested in.

The best alternative is video. With their great visuals, operas are a natural for video — and video stores are full of them.

There are two kinds of operas on video. By far the most common is a live opera performance in a great opera house. The performances are great, but sometimes the visuals are lacking, and you can't always count on getting subtitles.

The other kind of opera video is a *movie* version of the opera, filmed on location, with singers in the main roles. Here the sound is spectacular, but it's not live — it was dubbed in at a different time, which can get distracting, no matter how hard the actors try to lip-sync. The sets and costumes are realistic, of course — but sometimes the realistic setting just points out the implausibility of the whole thing, making it much harder to ignore the fact that everybody's singing when they should be speaking, the teenage heroine is 50 years old, and the plot has holes in it the size of Pavarotti.

The following section offers some of the most interesting videos in each category.

### *Videos of live opera performances*

- ✔ *Aïda* by Giuseppe Verdi. Taped in 1995, this production stars Cheryl Studer as Aïda, with Luciano D'Intino and Dennis O'Neill. Conducted by Edward Downes.

- ✔ *La Bohème* by Giacomo Puccini. This is the famous Met performance staged by the great Italian film director Franco Zeffirelli. Starring Teresa Stratas, Renata Scotto, and José Carreras, and conducted by James Levine. A truly spectacular re-creation of the Latin Quarter of Paris in the wintertime — it even snows onstage!

✔ *Boris Godunov* by Modest Mussorgsky. This 1978 recording from the Bolshoi Opera is a rare chance to see an opera performance from the former Soviet Union. Yevgeny Nestrenko stars in the title role.

✔ *Don Carlo* by Giuseppe Verdi. From the Metropolitan Opera, released in 1983. Plácido Domingo and Mirella Freni sing the lead roles; James Levine conducts.

✔ *Elektra* by Richard Strauss. Look for the version conducted by Karl Böhm — it's one of the best opera videos ever. There's also a 1989 production starring Eva Marton, Brigitte Fassbinder, and Cheryl Studer, and conducted by Claudio Abbado.

✔ *Die Fledermaus* by Johann Strauss, Jr. We recommend the 1983 version from Covent Garden in England. Starring Kiri Te Kanawa and Hemann Prey, and *conducted* by Plácido Domingo.

✔ *Tosca* by Giacomo Puccini. Another amazing Zeffirelli production at the Met, this one offers life-size re-creations of three actual Roman settings. With Plácido Domingo, Cornell MacNeil, and Hildegard Behrens (sounding a bit like a Valkyrie) as Tosca. Conducted by Giuseppe Sinopoli.

✔ *Die Walküre* by Richard Wagner. A 1991 Met production with an all-star cast: Christa Ludwig, James Morris, Hildegard Behrens, and Jessye Norman. Conducted by James Levine.

## Operas on film

✔ *La Traviata* by Giuseppe Verdi. Directed by Franco Zeffirelli, this 1982 film stars Plácido Domingo, Teresa Stratas, and Cornell MacNeil. Conducted by James Levine.

✔ *Tosca* by Giacomo Puccini. Filmed on location in Rome, this 1996 version stars Plácido Domingo and Maria Malfitano. Conducted by Zubin Mehta.

✔ *Carmen* by Georges Bizet. This 1985 Triumph Films production, filmed on location in Andalucia, stars Julia Migenes-Johnson and Plácido Domingo. Conducted by Lorin Maazel.

✔ *Carmen Jones.* A 1954 modern retelling of the *Carmen* story, with much of the same music and new lyrics by Oscar Hammerstein II. Starring Harry Belafonte and Dorothy Danridge.

✔ *The Magic Flute* by Wolfgang Amadeus Mozart. The best of all the opera movies, this is the brilliant 1973 Ingmar Bergman version. Actually, it falls somewhere between a live performance and a film, as the setting switches magically back and forth between the stage and real life. An all-Swedish cast sings in Swedish, with subtitles. Eric Ericson conducts.

And speaking of Mozart . . .

✔ ***Amadeus.*** Based on the play by Peter Shaffer, this movie tells the apocryphal story of Wolfgang Amadeus Mozart's demise at the hands of his vengeance-seeking rival, Antonio Salieri. Probably the best movie about a composer ever made, it includes wonderful (if short) scenes from his operas *The Abduction from the Seraglio, The Marriage of Figaro, Don Giovanni,* and *The Magic Flute,* as well as a few scenes from Salieri's operas.

For information and a free catalog with tons of opera videos and laser discs, you may want to contact:

✔ **Opera World:** P. O. Box 800, Concord, MA 01742, USA; phone 800-99-OPERA (800-996-7372) or 508-263-5006.

✔ **Lyric Distribution, Inc.:** 9 Albertson Ave., Suite 1, Albertson, NY 11507, USA; phone 800-325-9742 or 516-484-5100; fax 516-484-6561; e-mail lyricl@ix.netcom.com; Web site http://www.lyricdist.com.

✔ **The Met by Mail**, the merchandise service of the Metropolitan Opera Guild: 70 Lincoln Center Plaza, New York, NY 10023-6593, USA; phone 800-566-4646 or 212-769-7012 from 9 a.m. to 5 p.m. EST, Monday through Friday; fax 212-769-7007; e-mail f.meaux@metguild.org.

# *Study up*

When you become an opera fan, certain names come up again and again. Take Verdi, for example. We mention his name dozens of times in this book. And in your exploration of the world of opera, you'll hear it mentioned hundreds of times more. The same thing goes for all the great composers — as well as the famous opera stars.

Chapter 4 mentions some of the great singers of the opera world, past and present. And Part II outlines the lives of the most important composers. But there's much more to discover.

Hit your library and check out the biographies of composers or singers you enjoy. Get to know their lives in detail. Finding out about them as people will give you a much better understanding of what they were trying to express in their music. And it will certainly lead you to discover new operas that you never knew existed.

This is exactly how we learned what we know about this beautiful art form: One thing led to another. We wish you a lifetime of true discovery and enrichment through opera.

# Part VI
# Appendixes

The 5th Wave          By Rich Tennant

"For tonight's modern reinterpretation of Carmen, those in the front row are kindly requested to wear raincoats."

# In this part . . .

The final part of this book is for reference, information, or (if you hold the book so that it's visible only to you and recite from it) wowing your friends. You can find the following:

- ✔ A section on how to start familiarizing yourself with this art form — one opera at a time.

- ✔ A detailed timeline of opera history.

- ✔ A glossary of the most important opera terms we mention in the book.

# Appendix A
# Getting Started

. . . . . . . . . . . . . . . . . . . . . . . . . . . . . . . . . . . . . . . . . . . . .

*I*f we've done our job well, we've managed to whet your opera appetite. And we hope that you'll want to become more and more familiar with this exciting world. But with so many great operas to choose from, this task can seem truly daunting.

Not to worry. We'll help you get started.

## One at a time

The trick is to become acquainted with one opera at a time. That way, you can become very familiar with a particular opera — including all the characters, the story, the music, and the composer's style — before moving on to the next.

Whenever you get to know a new opera, try to *really* get to know it. Buy a CD or borrow it from the library. Over the course of a few days or weeks, read through the libretto a few times. Listen to the opera in chunks — say, an act at a time — so that the music really has a chance to sink in. The more you listen, the more you'll enjoy. Then, if at all possible, go to a performance of that opera.

## First things first

Exploring operas in a certain order really helps, too. Some operas are more easy to understand, digest, and appreciate than others. That's where our indispensable Lists 1 and 2 come in.

### List 1

We'd like to suggest that you begin your exploration with the following ten operas, *in any order.*

*Aïda*

*The Barber of Seville*

*La Bohème*

*Carmen*

*Die Fledermaus*

*Lucia di Lammermoor*

*Madame Butterfly*

*The Marriage of Figaro*

*Porgy and Bess*

*Tosca*

### List 2

After you've become familiar with most or all of the operas in List 1, you're ready to move to a new level. List 2 consists of operas that are just slightly more challenging to absorb and understand.

*Don Giovanni*

*Faust*

*The Flying Dutchman*

*The Magic Flute*

*Otello*

*I Pagliacci*

*Rigoletto*

*Tales of Hoffmann*

*Il Trovatore*

*Turandot*

Twenty operas — what a great start! After you're familiar with all of them, something amazing will happen: You will start to discover what you like. And once you know that, you can approach any new opera without fear. You're ready to take charge of your own opera adventures.

# Opera Timeline

. . . . . . . . . . . . . . . . . . . . . . . . . . . . . . . . . . . . . . . . . . . . . .

*C*amerata, Mozart, *La Bohème*. . . . After several hundred pages, you'd be forgiven for getting confused about which operatic events happened when. Here, for your reference pleasure, is a timeline of the major composers, pieces, and events that made opera what it is today.

**about 800–100 B.C.:** The Greeks develop dramatic versions of their religious tales, which include singing and chanting.

**800 A.D.:** Charlemagne is crowned King. Monks begin using primitive versions of opera to illustrate Biblical stories at about this time.

**1066:** The Normans conquer England.

**1215:** King John I of England signs the Magna Carta.

**about 1400:** The Italian Renaissance begins.

**1533:** The first Italian madrigals appear.

**1567:** Claudio Monteverdi is born in Cremona, Italy.

**1590:** The Florentine Camerata, the group responsible for the birth of Italian opera, begins performing at the houses of noble patrons.

**1601:** Shakespeare writes *Hamlet*.

**1607:** Monteverdi writes *The Tale of Orpheus*.

**1628:** Monteverdi writes *Mercury and Mars* for the wedding of the Grand Duke of Parma.

**1637:** In Venice, *Andromeda* becomes the first opera to be performed in public.

**1642:** Monteverdi writes *The Coronation of Poppea,* one of the first operas about real historical figures.

**about 1650:** The Baroque era begins, characterized by florid ornamentation and the stylized expression of emotion.

**1687:** Jean-Baptiste Lully (born in 1632), inventor of the *comédie-ballet*, plunges his conducting staff into his foot during a performance in honor of Louis XIV's recovery from an illness. The wound becomes gangrenous, and Lully dies soon after.

**1689:** Henry Purcell (1659–1695) writes his English opera *Dido and Aeneas*.

**1724:** Handel writes one of his most famous operas, *Julius Caesar*.

**about 1750:** The Classical period begins, typified by balance, symmetry, and restraint in music.

**1756:** Wolfgang Amadeus Mozart is born is Salzburg, Austria.

**1759:** Handel dies in London.

**1762:** Christoph Willibald von Gluck (1714–1787) writes his Italian opera *Orpheus and Eurydice*.

**1770:** Ludwig van Beethoven is born in Bonn, Germany.

**1775:** The American Revolution begins.

**1782:** Mozart writes his comic escape Singspiel, *The Abduction from the Seraglio*.

**1786:** Mozart writes *The Marriage of Figaro*.

**1787:** Mozart writes *Don Giovanni*.

**1789:** The French Revolution begins. George Washington becomes the first President of the United States.

**1790:** Mozart writes *Così fan tutte*.

**1791:** Mozart dies at age 35 in Vienna, less than a year after writing his Singspiel *The Magic Flute*.

**1804:** Napoleon crowns himself Emperor of France.

**1805:** The first version of Beethoven's *Fidelio* (originally called *Leonore*) is produced in Vienna.

**1813:** Giuseppe Verdi is born in Le Roncole, near Busseto, Italy. Richard Wagner is born in Leipzig, Germany.

**1814:** The third and final version of Beethoven's opera *Fidelio* premieres in Vienna.

**1816:** Gioachino Rossini (1792–1868) writes his comic masterpiece, *The Barber of Seville.*

**1817:** Rossini writes *La Cenerentola* (*Cinderella*).

**1821:** Carl Maria von Weber ( born 1786) writes *Der Freischütz* (*The Free-Shooter*), a ground-breaking opera with stunning atmospheric effects.

**about 1825:** The Romantic style begins to take hold in opera and classical music, marked by an increase in the unabashed expression of emotion.

**1826:** Weber dies in London while on tour to conduct his opera *Oberon.*

**1827:** Beethoven dies in Vienna.

**1829:** Rossini writes his last opera, *William Tell* — even though he still has 40 more years to live.

**1832:** Gaetano Donizetti (1797–1848) writes *The Elixir of Love.*

**1835:** Bellini writes *I Puritani* (*The Puritans*). Donizetti writes *Lucia di Lammermoor.*

**1836:** Giacomo Meyerbeer (1791–1864) writes *The Huguenots.* Mikhail Glinka (1804–1857) writes *A Life for the Tsar.*

**1838:** Music is taught in an American public school for the first time, in Boston. Georges Bizet is born.

**1842:** Richard Wagner writes his first successful opera, *Rienzi.* Verdi writes his first successful opera, *Nabucco.* Mikhail Glinka (1804–1857) writes *Ruslan and Lyudmila.* The New York Philharmonic is founded. The Vienna Philharmonic is founded. This is a really good year.

**1843:** Donizetti writes *Don Pasquale.* Wagner's *The Flying Dutchman* becomes his second great success.

**1850:** Wagner completes *Lohengrin.*

**1851:** Verdi writes *Rigoletto.* Herman Melville writes *Moby Dick.*

**1853:** Verdi writes *Il Trovatore* (*The Troubadour*) and *La Traviata* (*The Fallen Woman*).

**1858:** Jacques Offenbach (1819–1880) writes his comic opera *Orpheus in the Underworld,* a parody of previous operatic versions of the Orpheus legend. Hector Berlioz writes *Les Troyens (The Trojans).* Verdi writes *Un Ballo in Maschera (A Masked Ball).* Giacomo Puccini is born in Lucca, Italy. Another really good year.

**1859:** Charles Gounod (1818–1893) writes *Faust.* Wagner writes *Tristan und Isolde.*

**1861:** The American Civil War begins. Wagner's opera *Tannhäuser* receives its disastrous premiere in Paris.

**1866:** Bedřich Smetana writes *The Bartered Bride.*

**1867:** Wagner finishes *Die Meistersinger von Nürnberg (The Master-Singers of Nuremberg).* Verdi writes *Don Carlo.* Gounod writes *Roméo et Juliette.*

**1869:** Verdi revises *La Forza del Destino (The Force of Destiny),* first written in 1862.

**1871:** Verdi's opera *Aïda* — the most popular opera in the world — receives its world premiere in Cairo.

**1874:** Modest Mussorgsky (1839–1881) writes *Boris Godunov.* Johann Strauss, Jr. (1825–1899) writes *Die Fledermaus (The Bat).*

**1875:** Bizet writes *Carmen* and dies believing that it is a failure.

**1876:** The first complete performance of Wagner's *Ring* cycle takes place in a theater built according to Wagner's exact specifications in Bayreuth, Germany.

**1877:** Thomas Edison invents the phonograph.

**1879:** Peter Ilych Tchaikovsky (1840–1893) writes *Eugene Onegin,* based on a tale by Pushkin.

**1881:** Offenbach's only serious opera, *The Tales of Hoffmann,* premieres posthumously.

**1882:** Wagner's "Stage-Consecrating Festival Drama," *Parsifal,* is performed for the first time at Bayreuth.

**1883:** The Metropolitan Opera House opens in New York with a performance of Gounod's *Faust.* Wagner dies.

**1887:** Verdi writes his last dramatic opera, *Otello.*

**1890:** Pietro Mascagni (1863–1945) writes his most famous opera, *Cavalleria Rusticana (Rustic Chivalry).* Tchaikovsky writes *The Queen of Spades.*

**1892:** Ruggiero Leoncavallo (1858–1919) writes his most famous opera, *I Pagliacci* (*The Clowns*). Massenet's opera *Werther* premieres in Vienna.

**1893:** Engelbert Humperdinck (1854–1921) writes *Hansel and Gretel*. Puccini composes his first great success, *Manon Lescaut*. Verdi writes his last opera (and his only comedic work), *Falstaff*.

**1894:** Nicolas II, the last Tsar of Russia, is crowned in Moscow.

**1896:** Puccini writes *La Bohème*. Umberto Giordano (1867–1948) writes *Andrea Chénier*.

**1900:** Puccini writes his first opera about the Orient, *Madame Butterfly; Tosca* premieres in Rome.

**1901:** Verdi dies in Milan. Antonín Dvořák (1841–1904) writes *Rusalka*.

**1904:** *Jenůfa* by Leoš Janáček (1854–1928) premieres in Prague.

**1905:** Richard Strauss (1864–1949) writes his first scandalous opera, *Salome*.

**1907:** Rimsky-Korsakov writes *The Golden Cockerel*. Music is broadcast over the radio for the first time.

**1909:** Strauss writes his second scandalous opera, *Elektra*.

**1910:** Puccini writes his Italian opera about the American frontier, *The Girl of the Golden West*.

**1911:** Scott Joplin (1868–1917) writes a ragtime-folk opera called *Treemonisha*. Béla Bartók (1881–1945) writes *Bluebeard's Castle*. Strauss writes *Der Rosenkavalier* (*The Knight of the Rose*).

**1914:** World War I begins.

**1918:** World War I ends. Puccini writes *Gianni Schicchi* and *Il Tabarro* (*The Cloak*).

**1924:** Puccini writes most of his second opera about the Orient, *Turandot,* before dying. George Gershwin (1898–1937) writes *Rhapsody in Blue.*

**1925:** Alban Berg (1885–1935) writes his first atonal opera, *Wozzeck.*

**1926:** Puccini's *Turandot,* completed by a friend of the composer, premieres in Milan.

**1935:** Alban Berg (born in 1885) writes *Lulu* and dies the same year. Gershwin writes his jazzy opera, *Porgy and Bess.*

**1940:** A performance at the Metropolitan Opera is broadcast on the radio for the first time.

**1945:** World War II ends. Benjamin Britten (1913–1977) writes *Peter Grimes.*

**1951:** Gian Carlo Menotti (born in 1911) writes the first made-for-television opera *Amahl and the Night Visitors.* Britten writes *Billy Budd.*

**1956:** Francis Poulenc (1899–1963) writes *Dialogues of the Carmelites.*

**1958:** Barber's opera *Vanessa* wins the Pulitzer Prize for music.

**1960:** Britten writes *A Midsummer Night's Dream.*

**1969:** Man walks on the moon for the first time.

**1975:** Philip Glass (born in 1937) writes *Einstein on the Beach.*

**1978:** John Paul II is elected to the papacy.

**1981:** Barber dies.

**1987:** John Adams (born in 1947) writes *Nixon in China.*

**1991:** The opera *The Ghosts of Versailles,* by John Corigliano (born in 1938), premieres at the Metropolitan Opera in New York.

**1997:** *Opera For Dummies* is published.

# Appendix C

# Glossary

• • • • • • • • • • • • • • • • • • • • • • • • • • • • • • • • • • • • • • • • • •

**accelerando** (Italian): A sheet-music marking that means "gradually speed up." Abbreviated *accel.*

**accessible:** Music that's easy to listen to and understand.

**aria:** Italian for "air" — a main song; a big number where the singer reveals her feelings and shows off her voice.

**arietta** (Italian): Literally, a little aria. Ariettas are generally short and relatively light-hearted.

**arioso** (Italian): A song that falls halfway between an aria and recitative. It has melody like an aria, but it advances the action of the plot like recitative.

**atonal:** Refers to music that's not in any specific key. Sounds alien to most people.

**baritone:** A male voice of medium range — lower than a tenor, but higher than a bass.

**Baroque** (French): The period of music history from the mid-1600s to the mid-1700s; characterized by emotional, flowery music within strict forms.

**bass:** The lowest of the male voice types. Basses usually play priests or fathers in opera, but they occasionally get star turns as the Devil.

**bass-baritone:** The he-man of the opera world, combining the ringing quality of the baritone with the depths of the bass. Bass-baritone roles avoid the extremes of either range, singing in the most beautiful central part.

**basso buffo** ("BAHSS-so BOO-fo"): Italian for "buffoon bass." A stock character (often a servant), always sung by a bass. His arias usually contain quick repeated notes way down low.

**bel canto** ("bell CAHN-toe"): Italian for "beautiful singing." A style of opera — and opera performance — in which the splendor of the human voice receives the most importance, more than the words or even the story.

**breath control:** The technique — some might say the art — of using your breath efficiently as you sing a long melodic line so that you don't run out of wind before the last note.

**breath mark:** A big, black comma floating in the sheet music, which is the composer's friendly way of suggesting that a singer breathe at that moment.

**cabaletta** (Italian): In bel canto operas, a fast aria (or the second part of an aria), allowing the singer to display her vocal pyrotechnics. It usually has a high note just before the end that the singer sustains, driving the audience into fits of ecstasy.

**cadenza** (Italian): A moment near the end of an aria for the singer alone — a stretch of difficult, fast, high notes, designed for showing off.

**castrato** (Italian): A castrated male of centuries past, prized for his high, powerful singing voice. (The plural is *castrati.*)

**cavatina** (Italian): In bel canto operas, a slow, expressive, melodic aria (or first part of an aria), allowing the singer to show off her beautiful voice.

**chest voice:** A singer's term for a particular sound that resonates within the chest cavity. All low notes are produced by using the chest voice.

**chorus** (also *coro, Chor, choeur*): A group of singers onstage, playing a happy band of villagers, for example, or a bevy of victorious warriors. Also, a big number during which the chorus gets to sing.

**claque** (Italian, "CLAHK"): A group of people hired by composers of Italian opera to cheer their works — or to boo the works of their rivals.

**Classical:** The period of music history from the mid-1700s to the early 1800s; music of this time is sparer and more controlled than music of the Baroque period.

**color:** A word used to describe a voice's sound characteristics. Opera voices come in two basic colors: lyric (sweet) and dramatic (very strong).

**coloratura soprano:** The tweety-bird of the musical aviary. This voice type is light, pure, flutelike, and capable of great agility way up high.

**contralto:** The lowest (and rarest) female voice category; on her lowest notes, she sounds almost like a man.

**counterpoint:** The technique of writing two, three, four, or more melodic lines to be played at the same time.

**countertenor:** A man who trains his falsetto voice rather than his lower range. Countertenors specialize in parts originally written for castrati.

**crescendo** (Italian): Getting progressively louder.

**diminuendo** (Italian, "dee-mee-noo-EN-doe"): Getting progressively softer.

**dissonant** (Italian): Harsh, discordant. Sounds like the notes are wrong.

**diva:** Literally, "goddess" — a female opera star. Sometimes refers to a fussy, demanding opera star.

**dramatic voice:** A voice with a steely edge that helps it cut through a large orchestra more easily than a sweet (lyric) voice could.

**dress rehearsal:** Usually the final rehearsal before the first performance.

**duet** (Italian, also known as *duo* or *duetto*): An aria built for two. Two characters express their feelings, to each other or to the audience (or both).

**dynamics:** The loudness or softness of a musical composition, or the markings in the sheet music that indicate volume.

**Fach** ("FAHkh"): German for "compartment." A voice category (such as soprano, alto, tenor, or bass).

**falsetto** (Italian): The high part of a man's voice, way up high above the "voice-cracking" part, where it sounds like a woman's voice.

**fermata** (Italian, "fair-MAH-ta"): A musical marking that means to stop the music on a certain note for as long as it feels right.

**finale** (Italian, "fee-NAH-lay"): The last song of an act, often involving a large group of singers.

**finale ultimo** (Italian): The final finale, often involving a *really* large group of singers.

**forte** (Italian): Literally, "strong." Usually means loud.

**fortissimo** (Italian): Literally, "very strong." Usually means very loud.

**French grand opera:** A style of opera, invented by Giacomo Meyerbeer, in which the sets are lavish and realistic, the machinery is breathtaking, and the musical forces (choirs and orchestra) are designed to blow the audience away.

**German dramatic soprano:** The horn-and-helmet lady, the heavy hitter of the opera world. Her voice must be able to cut through a huge orchestra; therefore, it must be both metallic in color and immensely powerful. Required in operas by Wagner.

**head voice:** The opposite of *chest voice*. The upper notes in a singer's range, above the "voice-cracking" break.

**Heldentenor** ("HELL-din tay-NOR"): German for "heroic tenor." The male lead of any Wagner opera, a tenor with an extraordinarily strong singing voice, capable of trumpeting above an orchestra.

**intermission:** Twenty-five minutes of high society in between the acts of an opera.

**Leitmotif** (German, "LIGHT-mo-teef"): A musical theme assigned to a main character or idea of an opera; invented by Richard Wagner.

**libretto** ("lee-BRET-toe"): Italian for "little book"; the script of an opera. The guy who writes it is called a *librettist*.

**lyric voice:** A voice type that sounds sweeter and softer than its *dramatic* counterpart.

**mezzo soprano:** A woman whose voice is slightly lower than a soprano's. Mezzos come in two varieties: *dramatic* and *lyric*.

**minimalism:** A type of music composed of very repetitive snippets of music, with subtly shifting rhythms and harmonies.

**motive** or **motif:** A short, repeating melody, often made up of only two or three notes.

**opera buffa** (Italian, "BOOF-a"): Literally, "buffoon opera." Funny opera, especially of the 18th century. The plural is *opere buffe*.

**opera seria** (Italian, "SAY-ree-ya"): Formal, serious opera, especially from the 18th century.

**operetta** (Italian): A light-hearted opera with spoken dialogue; a musical.

**oratorio** (Italian): A musical piece for solo singers, chorus, and orchestra, usually with words from the Bible.

**orchestra pit:** The hollowed-out area beneath the stage, and slightly in front of it, where the orchestra players sit.

**overture:** A piece written to introduce an opera (sometimes called a prelude or an introduction).

**prima donna** ("PREE-mah DOAN-na"): Italian for "first lady." The singer who plays the heroine, the main female character in an opera; or anyone who believes the world revolves around her.

**quartet** (Italian, also *quartetto, quartett, quarttuor*): A piece of music for four singers.

**quintet** (Italian, also *quintetto, quintett, quintette*): A piece of music for five singers.

**rallentando** (Italian, "RAHL-len-TAHN-do"): A marking in sheet music that means to gradually slow down. Abbreviated *rall.*

**recitative** (Italian, "ress-it-uh-TEEV"): Speech-singing, in which the singer semi-chants the words, imitating the free rhythms of speech.

**register:** The highness or lowness of music or singing.

**Renaissance:** French for "rebirth." The period of musical history from the 1500s to the mid-1600s.

**ritardando** (Italian, "ree-tar-DAHN-doe"): A marking in sheet music that means to gradually slow down. Abbreviated *rit.*

**Romantic:** A period of music, art, and literature (mostly the 1800s and early 1900s) characterized by the unabashed expression of emotion.

**sextet** (also *sestetto, Sextett, sextuor*): A piece of music written for six singers.

**Singspiel:** German for "sing-play." A German opera with spoken dialogue (instead of recitative) between arias.

**slur:** A long, curved line above the notes that tells the singer to run the notes together, gliding smoothly from one to the next.

**soprano:** The female voice category with the highest notes and the highest paycheck.

**soubrette:** A special category of soprano, accustomed to playing cutesy-pie or streetwise servant-girl roles.

**spinto** (Italian): Literally, "pushed." A voice with a strong dramatic edge.

**spinto soprano:** A soprano with a spinto voice. She plays the long-suffering, victimized characters in opera — the grand roles, the meat of the operatic repertoire.

**staff:** The five-line horizontal "timeline" that's the underlying grid for sheet music.

**Stehplatz** (German, "SHTAY-plahts"): A "standing room only" area in a German or Austrian opera house.

**surtitles** (or **supertitles**): Slides projected on the wall above the stage with translations of the lines in a foreign-language opera.

**tenor:** A high male voice type.

**tonal:** Refers to music that is in an identifiable key.

**trio** (Italian): A piece of music within an opera, for three characters to sing together.

**trill:** The quick alternation of two adjacent notes.

**trouser role:** A male role played by a woman.

**unison:** Several singers singing the same notes (as opposed to singing in harmony).

**verismo** (Italian): Literally, "truth-ism." A realistic, "documentary" style of opera (and filmmaking) that depicts the gritty, seamy underbelly of life.

# Index

### • C •

*(continued)*

### • T •

# LISTEN OR BOOT UP!

## NEW ENHANCED CD PLAYS ON YOUR STEREO, MAC, OR PC!

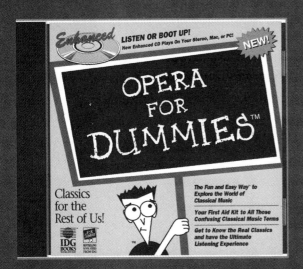

Now that you have learned all about Opera, why not enjoy the music by purchasing a collection of CDs from the brand new "Classical Music For Dummies" series.

The 36 CDs include everything from BACH to RACHMANINOV, PIANO to BAROQUE.

Classical Music For Dummies - the best way to listen and learn about great music!

Collect all 36!

Available at major record stores everywhere!

Simply place this new, Enhanced CD in your stereo or CD ROM drive — it's an uncomplicated reference source which includes great music, a pronunciation guide, a glossary and recommended recordings. It's easy, and it makes listening to — and interacting with — classical music even easier.

| TITLE | CD UPC# | TITLE | CD UPC# |
|---|---|---|---|
| Beethoven For Dummies | 7243 5 66264 0 9 | Rimsky-Korsakov For Dummies | 7243 5 66782 0 5 |
| Debussy For Dummies | 7243 5 66265 0 8 | Sibelius For Dummies | 7243 5 66283 0 4 |
| Mahler For Dummies | 7243 5 66266 0 7 | J. Strauss II For Dummies | 7243 5 66284 0 3 |
| Mozart For Dummies | 7243 5 66267 0 6 | R. Strauss For Dummies | 7243 5 66285 0 2 |
| Tchaikovsky For Dummies | 7243 5 66268 0 5 | Stravinsky For Dummies | 7243 5 66286 0 1 |
| Vivaldi For Dummies | 7243 5 66269 0 4 | Wagner For Dummies | 7243 5 66287 0 0 |
| J.S. Bach For Dummies | 7243 5 66270 0 0 | Baroque For Dummies | 7243 5 66400 0 9 |
| Berlioz For Dummies | 7243 5 66271 0 9 | Gregorian Chant For Dummies | 7243 5 66401 0 8 |
| Brahms For Dummies | 7243 5 66272 0 8 | Opera For Dummies | 7243 5 66402 0 7 |
| Chopin For Dummies | 7243 5 66273 0 7 | Piano For Dummies | 7243 5 66403 0 6 |
| Prokofiev For Dummies | 7243 5 66274 0 6 | Puccini For Dummies | 7243 5 66404 0 5 |
| Verdi For Dummies | 7243 5 66275 0 5 | Violin For Dummies | 7243 5 66405 0 4 |
| Handel For Dummies | 7243 5 66276 0 4 | Classical Music For Dummies | 7243 5 66559 0 4 |
| Dvorak For Dummies | 7243 5 66277 0 3 | Early Music For Dummies | 7243 5 66560 0 0 |
| Grieg For Dummies | 7243 5 66278 0 2 | Romantic Music For Dummies | 7243 5 66561 0 9 |
| Mendelssohn For Dummies | 7243 5 66279 0 1 | Soprano For Dummies | 7243 5 66562 0 8 |
| Rachmaninov For Dummies | 7243 5 66280 0 7 | Tenor For Dummies | 7243 5 66563 0 7 |
| Ravel For Dummies | 7243 5 66281 0 6 | Waltzes For Dummies | 7243 5 66564 0 6 |

The IDG Books Worldwide logo, ----For Dummies, the Dummies Man, and ...For Dummies Bestselling Book Series logo are trademarks under exclusive lic
IDG Books Worldwide, Inc., from International Data Group, Inc. Used with permission. © 1997 EMI CLASSICS

ense to

# Installation Instructions

• • • • • • • • • • • • • • • • • • • • • • • • • • • • • • • • • • • • • • • •

*T*he *Opera For Dummies* CD-ROM includes a demo version of the Angel/
EMI *Classics For Dummies* multimedia interface. To use that demo
software, find the instructions for your type of computer below.

To run the demo software on Windows 95 machines with AutoPlay CD-ROMs:

1. **Insert the CD into your CD-ROM drive and wait. (Be patient; it might take a while for anything to happen.)**

2. **A photo of an opera house eventually appears. When it does, click the button labeled Run Setup in the upper left corner of the screen.**

3. **Read the dialog box that appears and click on Continue if appropriate. The rest is automatic.**

4. **To run the demo, click on the Start button and then on Programs... Classics For Dummies... Opera Enhanced CD.**

To run the software on Windows 3.1 machines and non-AutoPlay CD-ROMs:

1. **Insert the CD into your computer's CD-ROM drive.**

2. **For Windows 3.1: In Program Manager, choose File and then choose Run.**

   **For Windows 95: Click on the Start button and then click on Run.**

3. **In the Run dialog box, enter the following:** `d:\setup.exe`**. (Substitute your actual CD-ROM drive letter if it's something other than D.)**

4. **Click on OK.**

5. **A photo of an opera house eventually appears. When it does, click on the button labeled Run Setup in the upper left corner.**

6. **Read the dialog box that appears and click Continue if appropriate. The rest is automatic.**

7. **To run the demo for Windows 3.1: Open the program group called Classics For Dummies and then double-click on the Opera Enhanced CD icon.**

   **To run the demo for Windows 95: Click on the Start button and then on Programs... Classics For Dummies... Opera Enhanced CD.**

To run the software on a Macintosh:

**1. Insert the CD into your CD-ROM drive.**

**2. Click on the icon created for the CD.**

**3. Double-click on the GoOpera icon. The rest is automatic.**

# IDG BOOKS WORLDWIDE REGISTRATION CARD

Visit our Web site at °http://www.idgbooks.com

**ISBN Number:** 0-7645-5010-1

**Title of this book:** Opera For Dummies ™

**My overall rating of this book:** ❏ Very good [1] ❏ Good [2] ❏ Satisfactory [3] ❏ Fair [4] ❏ Poor [5]

**How I first heard about this book:**

❏ Found in bookstore; name: [6] _____   ❏ Book review: [7] _____

❏ Advertisement: [8] _____   ❏ Catalog: [9] _____

❏ Word of mouth; heard about book from friend, co-worker, etc.: [10]   ❏ Other: [11] _____

**What I liked most about this book:**

_____

_____

**What I would change, add, delete, etc., in future editions of this book:**

_____

_____

**Other comments:**

_____

**Number of computer books I purchase in a year:** ❏ 1 [12] ❏ 2-5 [13] ❏ 6-10 [14] ❏ More than 10 [15]

**I would characterize my computer skills as:** ❏ Beginner [16] ❏ Intermediate [17] ❏ Advanced [18] ❏ Professional [19]

**I use** ❏ DOS [20] ❏ Windows [21] ❏ OS/2 [22] ❏ Unix [23] ❏ Macintosh [24] ❏ Other: [25] _____

(please specify)

**I would be interested in new books on the following subjects:**

(please check all that apply, and use the spaces provided to identify specific software)

❏ Word processing: [26] _____   ❏ Spreadsheets: [27] _____

❏ Data bases: [28] _____   ❏ Desktop publishing: [29] _____

❏ File Utilities: [30] _____   ❏ Money management: [31] _____

❏ Networking: [32] _____   ❏ Programming languages: [33] _____

❏ Other: [34] _____

**I use a PC at** (please check all that apply): ❏ home [35] ❏ work [36] ❏ school [37] ❏ other: [38] _____

**The disks I prefer to use are** ❏ 5.25 [39] ❏ 3.5 [40] ❏ other: [41] _____

**I have a CD ROM:** ❏ yes [42] ❏ no [43]

**I plan to buy or upgrade computer hardware this year:** ❏ yes [44] ❏ no [45]

**I plan to buy or upgrade computer software this year:** ❏ yes [46] ❏ no [47]

Name: _____   Business title: [48] _____   Type of Business: [49] _____

Address ( ❏ home [50] ❏ work [51] /Company name: _____ )

Street/Suite# _____

City [52] /State [53] /Zip code [54]: _____   Country [55] _____

❏ **I liked this book!** You may quote me by name in future
IDG Books Worldwide promotional materials.

My daytime phone number is _____

**IDG BOOKS WORLDWIDE**

THE WORLD OF
COMPUTER
KNOWLEDGE®

# ☐ YES!

Please keep me informed about IDG Books Worldwide's World of Computer Knowledge. Send me your latest catalog.

BESTSELLING
BOOK SERIES
FROM IDG

NO POSTAGE
NECESSARY
IF MAILED
IN THE
UNITED STATES

**BUSINESS REPLY MAIL**
FIRST CLASS MAIL   PERMIT NO. 2605   FOSTER CITY, CALIFORNIA

*IDG Books Worldwide*
*919 E Hillsdale Blvd, Ste 400*
*Foster City, CA 94404-9691*